SOUTH ASIA
SOCIETIES IN POLITICAL AND ECONOMIC TRANSITION

South Asia

Societies in Political and Economic Transition

Edited by

TAN TAI YONG

Institute of South Asian Studies

National University of Singapore

MANOHAR

First published 2010

ISBN 978-81-7304-846-3

Published by
Ajay Kumar Jain *for*
Manohar Publishers & Distributors
4753/23 Ansari Road, Daryaganj
New Delhi 110 002

Typeset by
Kohli Print
Delhi 110 051

Printed at
Salasar Imaging Systems
Delhi 110 035

Contents

Tables

Figures

Preface

At the Institute of South Asian Studies (ISAS), the focus of work is on contemporary issues in South Asia. Within this broad ambit, its scholars work on aspects of emerging regional and strategic issues, economic dimensions and the political economy of the South Asian countries. The Institute has been fortunate to be associated with a group of renowned scholars from the various South Asian countries, experts in their own fields, who contribute regularly to the academic output of the Institute. This volume captures their expertise and looks at contemporary political as well as economic issues in South Asia. In addition, there are contributions from country experts in areas where external expertise was needed.

South Asia is an exciting region. There are common problems of political governance and the role of the state, as well as economic issues of development and poverty. The year 2007 has been significant in that there have been fundamental political and economic transitions in several of the countries. Bangladesh opted for an interim government, followed by the election of a democratic government. Pakistan saw the assassination of a former Prime Minister, followed by peaceful elections and, perhaps, hope for stability. Nepal went through substantial change, with the Maoists initially in power and, subsequently, opting out of the government. In contrast, elections in Bhutan have brought a smooth transition to democracy. The chapters in the first part of the book attempt to capture these changes, and analyze the reasons and the consequences.

On the other hand, India, the largest constituent of South Asia, political transition has not been as important in 2007 as economic change. Economic issues have dominated and these include trade and manufacturing, reforms in the financial sector, response to increasing costs of energy, inflation, and the management of urban transformations.

In an attempt to capture these changes, the publication is divided into two parts. The first part deals with political issues in the countries that have witnessed the most change and turbulence during the year, while the second part deals with economic issues that have been of concern to all the South Asian countries, and to India in particular. Together, this collection of essays attempts to capture and analyse the happenings in South Asia in 2007.

In Chapter 1, 'Bangladesh: 2007–2008', Farooq Sobhan traces the developments that led to the establishment of the caretaker government. He describes the steps taken by that government to introduce a transparent, clean administration and the attempts to clean up the political processes. He argues that the caretaker government would be judged by its ability to put in place strong foundations of good governance. He recognizes that this is possible only with the help of the political parties, which themselves need to reform into more transparent, democratic entities with the ability to aggregate voter interests. The task of the caretaker government has been made even more difficult by the escalation in prices of food and energy in recent months, leading to growing inflationary pressures in the economy.

In Chapter 2, 'Decentralization, Democratization and Development in Bhutan', Caroline Brassard traces the history of development in Bhutan, outlining its unique characteristics that have led to the definition of a gross national happiness index as more relevant than a human development index. She is confident that the recent democratic process and the deepening of decentralization would lead to greater capacity building at the local levels, leading to greater empowerment and legitimacy of decentralized institutions. She traces the rapid developments of the past six years to the recent elections and speaks of the major changes in governance that democracy is likely to bring about in the country.

In Chapter 3, 'The Pakistan Garrison State: Pre- and Post-9/11', Ishtiaq Ahmed provides a deeply analytical and conceptual study of Pakistan as a garrison. He argues that the ruling elite in Pakistan sought power by emphasizing a perceived threat from India, weakness of civilian institutions, and identifying with the strategies of the United States. He concludes that a strong and sustained movement in favour of democracy would be crucial in reducing the influence of the military, and is hopeful of the outcome of the recently concluded elections.

In Chapter 4, 'Pakistan-China Relations in the 21st Century: Retrospect and Prospect', Rajshree Jetly and Iftikhar A. Lodhi analyze Pakistan-China relations from the standpoint of South Asia. The economic liberalization of India and China has pushed the two into a closer trade partnership, dampening Sino-Pakistan relations. The rise of Islamic fundamentalism around the world has also put some strain on Sino-Pakistan relations. However, the two authors argue that these would not weaken Sino-Pakistan relations. Greater economic engagement between the two countries is likely, and Pakistan would be seen as a gateway for China to the oil-rich Gulf States. Jetly and Lodhi conclude that the relationship will be evergreen and strong.

S.D. Muni is an acknowledged expert on Nepal and is currently with ISAS. In Chapter 5, 'Building a New Nepal: Travails of Transition', he traces the transition in Nepal from a monarchy to civilian democratic rule, explaining the origins of the conflicts, the developments, and the role played by India and other neighbors. The transition of the Maoists into a political movement willing to abide by the rules of democratic poll processes is a fascinating tale that reveals the resilience and pragmatism of the Maoists in dealing with the issues of mainstreaming their ideas. Muni concludes that building an inclusive democratic state structure in Nepal is a long and delicate process that would require the treatment of the Maoists with sensitivity and participation as partners, not as adversaries.

In Chapter 6, 'Old Conflicts, New Futures: Understanding Nepal's Political Transformation', Anindita Dasgupta gives a different perspective on Nepal. She stresses the importance of the Madhesi movement that needs to be handled with urgency and sensitivity by the national government. Dasgupta emphasizes the need to bring the Maoists into the mainstream of the democratic process and argues that traditional political parties need to reorient their outlook to include the concerns of the Maoists in their strategies.

Jayadeva Uyangoda looks at Sri Lanka in Chapter 7, 'Politics of

Sri Lanka: 2007–2008'. He states that Sri Lanka had a difficult year in 2007 for it brought the ethnic conflict out into the open once again. Uyangoda is critical of the shifting loyalties of the international communities, and examines the various alternatives to a political solution to the conflict. His thought-provoking analysis offers some insights and clues to solutions that may be relevant to bring this nation to peace.

The second part of the book deals with a set of very different issues. There have been economic changes and pressures on the countries in South Asia that have defined their strategies and responses, both internal as well as external. The second part examines some of these strategies and responses.

In Chapter 8, 'South Asia in Global Trade: Participation and Prospects', K.V. Ramaswamy analyzes South Asia's participation in international trade in goods and services. The performance of South Asia, excluding India, is considered to be rather poor, and Ramaswamy examines structural weaknesses in South Asian exports. The obstacles to growth in trade in the South Asian countries are discussed, and suggestions for governmental policy support for technology and policy upgrading are made.

Jayan Jose Thomas examines the development of manufacturing in India in Chapter 9, 'Indian Manufacturing: The Road Ahead'. He provides a comprehensive analysis of the manufacturing sector, listing strengths and weaknesses, and the periods of growth and stagnation. He examines selected sectors and their geographical dispersion as well as future opportunities. Thomas concludes that, despite rapid growth, the manufacturing sector is considerably behind that in China. He also points to the emerging regional concentration in India's manufacturing growth in the western and southern Indian states, especially Maharashtra, Gujarat, Andhra Pradesh and Tamil Nadu.

Chapter 10, 'Financial Sector Reforms in South Asia: A Perspective', by D.M. Nachane and M. Shahidul Islam on financial sector reforms, is one of the seminal papers in this collection. They analyze the impact of financial liberalization on economic growth and the likely consequences for income distribution and poverty.

The authors examine the reforms in India that have been much more extensive and deep, and compare the reform initiatives in the other South Asian countries. Their chapter is an exhaustive overview of the developments, and offers an opportunity for further deep study of the different country issues raised. Nachane and Islam argue that financial liberalization is easier than liberalization in the real sector because it meets with much less political resistance. South Asia is an example of unbalanced reforms where a highly reformed financial sector co-exists with a largely unreformed real sector.

S. Narayan looks at strategies of the South Asian countries in coping with increases in oil prices in Chapter 11, 'Adjustment Strategies in Energy Pricing: South Asian Experiences'. He points out that there has been reluctance in almost all the constituent countries to pass on the increases to the consumer, and that subsidy regimes have been mostly ad hoc and arbitrary. Narayan argues that the concern over inflation as a consequence of oil price pass-through is real and has been witnessed in some South Asian countries. He defends the subsidies in the context of the development duality and poverty in South Asia, and argues that the consequences of the higher fiscal burden are perhaps a necessary concomitant to achieving inclusiveness in the growth process.

In Chapter 12, 'Urban Growth and Governance in South Asia', Shreekant Gupta and Indu Rayadurgam examine the patterns of urbanization in South Asia. The patterns of governance in South Asian cities are analyzed to point to the inadequacies of the institutions in dealing with contemporary urban problems. They examine alternative measures of revenue and responsibility sharing between the state and local governments. The two authors recommend greater autonomy and financial flexibility for the urban bodies.

In summary, this volume is an eclectic mix that covers a spectrum of current issues in South Asia. This is a melting pot of politics and change, of reforms and stagnation, of growth and disparity. It brings together a varied range of experiences across the South Asian region. Most importantly, the publication reflects the dynamism of the region and the fast pace of change in politics, as well as in economic policy. The book has been titled *South Asia: Societies in Political and Economic Transition* to reflect this dynamism.

I am grateful to the authors who have so diligently worked on their chapters. I am confident that this publication will go down as a definitive study of South Asia in 2007 and 2008.

TAN TAI YONG
Director
Institute of South Asian Studies

PART I

1

Bangladesh: 2007–2008

FAROOQ SOBHAN

THE TENURE of the elected government in Bangladesh that was headed by Begum Khaleda Zia ended on 28 October 2006. Under the Constitution, a caretaker government was required to take over the reins of power for a three-month period, during which time elections would be held. The caretaker government would then, in turn, hand over power to the party securing a majority in the elections. The three previous elections in 1991, 1996 and 2001 had been held under caretaker governments. Most people, both inside and outside Bangladesh, were of the view that these three elections had been, by and large, free and fair, with a voter turnout in excess of 70 per cent. However, in October 2006, the caretaker formula received a big jolt.

The Awami League launched street demonstrations against Justice K.M. Hassan who, as the last retired Chief Justice, was to take over as the Chief Adviser or Head of the caretaker government. No doubt influenced by the violent demonstrations against him, Justice Hassan declined to be sworn in as the Chief Adviser. Although the Constitution provided for the post to be offered to the Chief Justice who retired just before Justice Hassan, Begum Zia and the Bangladesh National Party (BNP) persuaded, some would say maneuvered, the President to assume the additional responsibility of Chief Adviser. Within a very short period of time it became evident that the President was a pawn in the hands of Begum Zia and her party, the BNP, and that the country was heading for a rigged election that would ensure the return of Begum Zia and her party to power.

Sheikh Hasina, the head of the Awami League, was for a while convinced that the BNP, thanks to its government's unprecedented corruption and misgovernance, had become so unpopular that no matter how much it tried to rig the elections, it could not prevent her party from winning the elections. It was only in late December that it finally dawned on Sheikh Hasina that the BNP's comprehensive rigging plans would ensure its return to power notwithstanding its widespread unpopularity. It was then that Sheikh Hasina decided to boycott the elections, a move that was backed by all the other parties, except the Jamaat, which was an alliance partner of the BNP.

Ignoring, some would say welcoming, the decision of most of the parties to boycott the elections, the BNP and the Jamaat decided to go ahead with the elections on 22 January 2007. Bangladesh was heading for a disaster of monumental proportions; if the rigged one-sided elections took place, there would be countrywide disturbances and the country could witness something close to a civil war. As a whole the disturbances had serious repercussions on investments and on the overall economy; they also adversely impacted on security and the daily lives of citizens. Consequently, when the army stepped in on 11 January 2007 and invited Dr Fakhruddin Ahmed, a respected former civil servant who until recently had been the Governor of Bangladesh Bank, to take over as the Chief Adviser and Head of a new caretaker government, the country heaved a sigh of relief.

THE RESPONSE OF DR FAKHRUDDIN'S CARETAKER GOVERNMENT TO VARIOUS CHALLENGES

11 January 2007 was clearly an important milestone in the history of Bangladesh. The people felt that their political leaders had betrayed the country. They felt that all that the politicians were interested in was self-aggrandizement. Dr Fakhruddin and his Council of Advisers were faced with a daunting task. Not only were they required to ensure free, fair, and credible elections but

they would also have to try and repair the extensive damage done by the previous BNP government to virtually every government institution, from the judiciary to the bureaucracy, from the Election Commission to the Anti-Corruption Commission. In each case, a process of politicization had taken place, undermining both the efficiency and independence of these key institutions.

The new caretaker government also had to deal with a sharp escalation in the price of daily necessities and an acute power crisis. Both were legacies of the previous BNP government. The caretaker government during the course of the year did its best to tackle each of these problems. The Election Commission was revamped and preparations for the next elections were undertaken in earnest. There had been progress by the end of the year in the task of preparing a new voters list with photographs and entering all the relevant information in a database. While both the Chief Adviser and the Election Commission had on several occasions reiterated their commitment to holding the general elections before the end of 2008, the Election Commission, having earlier announced that municipal elections in the six major metropolitan areas would be held in March 2008, indicated in December 2007 that the municipal elections would take place in April 2008 instead of March.

THE STATE OF THE ECONOMY

Bangladesh has established a credible record of sustained growth since 1998, when growth averaged around 5 per cent, and has since then remained at over 5 per cent with growth likely to come in around 6 per cent in FY2007.[1] The gross domestic product (GDP) growth rate in FY2006 was 6.6 per cent.[2] The economy remains largely consumption driven (total consumption is 80 per cent of GDP and has remained stable over the years), with private consumption accounting for 74 per cent of GDP in FY2006. An emerging trend has also been the steady improvements in private investment, up 18.5 per cent of GDP during the year from 15.6 per cent in FY2000. Expansion in GDP in 2006–7 was also driven by strong trends in workers' remittances and a strong performance in the export sector.[3]

In US dollar terms, export earnings recorded a growth of 15.8 per cent, while the growth of import payments remained at a sustainable level of 16.6 per cent. At the same time, remittances from non-resident Bangladesh nationals increased substantially by 24.5 per cent (see Table 1.1). The country's external current account balance continued to record a significant surplus with a substantial increase in remittances more than offsetting trade deficit and services deficit.[4]

The growth rate in the agriculture sector achieved a moderate growth of 3.2 per cent in FY2007, resulting mainly from lower growth in the crops and horticulture sub-sector. The industry sector attained a robust growth of 9.5 per cent in FY2007, slightly lower than the 9.7 per cent growth rate in FY2006. Overall, the services sector surged by 6.7 per cent in FY2007, higher than the 6.4 per cent growth recorded in the previous fiscal year.[5]

Exports increased by 15.8 per cent from US$10,412 million in FY2006 to US$12,053 million in FY2007 and remittances from workers abroad recorded 24.5 per cent growth from US$4802 million in FY2006 to US$5,979 million in FY2007 (see Table 1.2), while imports went up by 16.6 per cent from US$13,301 million in FY2006 to US$15,511 million in FY2007. Gross foreign exchange reserves held by the central bank increased by US$1,593 million to US$5,077 million at the end of FY2007 from US$3,484 million at the end of FY2006, about 3.9 months of import cover.[6]

Table 1.1: Trade Balance 2005–7

(*in US$ million*)

Items	2005–6 July–June	2006 –7 July–June	% changes (3 over 2)
Trade balance	–2889	–3458	
Export f.o.b. (including EPZs)	10,412	12,053	15.76
Of which Readymade garments (RMG)	7,901	9,211	16.59
Import f.o.b. (including EPZ)	–13,301	–15,511	16.62

Source: Statistics Department, Bangladesh Bank.

Table 1.2: Wage Earners' Remittance Inflows to Bangladesh (Yearly), 2002–8

Year	Remittances	
	In million US$	In million Taka
2002–3	3,061.97	1,77,288.20
2003–4	3,371.97	1,98,698.00
2004–5	3,848.29	2,36,469.70
2005–6	4,802.41	3,22,756.80
2006–7	5,998.47	4,12,985.29
2007–8*	2,187.78	15,021.93

Source: Foreign Exchange Policy Department, Bangladesh Bank.
Note: *Data up to the month of October of FY2007–8.

Challenge to Sustainable GDP Growth

The current government undertook various measures to revitalize the economy. The government adopted a national budget of Tk87,137 crore (US$12.5 billion approximately) in June 2007 with an estimated GDP growth of 7 per cent for FY2007–8 (1 July 2007 to 30 June 2008), with a target of keeping the inflation rate below 7 per cent. However, many quarters termed the growth target as too ambitious and the International Monetary Fund in September 2007 projected that the GDP growth would not go beyond 5.5 per cent.[7] The Asian Development Bank estimated that the (GDP) growth would be below 6 per cent in FY2008.[8] Bangladesh Bank has projected economic growth between 6.2 and 6.5 per cent in FY2008.[9]

Inflation

In October 2007, on a point-to-point basis, inflation was at a high of 10.06 per cent compared to that of 7.31 per cent in October 2006 (see Table 1.3).

The rise in international commodity prices, domestic food grain shortfall, and the drive against corruption and hoarding exacerbated the pressures on prices.[10] Bangladesh Bank's monetary policy statement, announced in mid-July 2007, set an objective of limiting

Table 1.3: Rate of Inflation in Bangladesh, 2006–7

(*in per cent*)

Rate of Inflation (as measured by Consumer Price Index, base 1995–6)	October 2006	September 2007	October 2007
Point-to-point	7.31	9.60	10.06
Monthly Average (12 months)	6.98	8.01	9.25

Source: Bangladesh Bureau of Statistics.

inflation to a range of 6.5–7 per cent in FY2008. The statement noted that the central bank would review the need for adjusting its policy instruments.[11] Maintaining a cautious monetary policy would be a challenge because the country was first badly hit by floods in July, August and in November by Cyclone Sidr. Consequently, the second half of the year witnessed high monetary expansion and rising inflation. Nevertheless, achieving the upper end of the range appeared feasible, though it represented only a marginal improvement over FY2007.[12] Furthermore, the tension between the IMF-prescribed 'contractionary monetary policy' and an 'accommodative monetary policy' has become a serious policy issue for the current government. The IMF has been asking for a contractionary monetary policy to tackle inflation whilst many Bangladesh economists have argued that at a time when domestic credit demand is depressed, investment is stalled, and the banking sector is flush with excess credit, a rise in the lending rate could further discourage investment. This remains a major policy issue for the government.

Food Production and Prices

Food production in the country was not satisfactory in 2007–8 while food prices have been increasing almost daily on the international market. Food import increased by 269 per cent between July and September compared to the same period in the previous fiscal year. Food-price inflation, at around 11 per cent, is already the biggest grievance of most Bangladeshis.[13] Prices of rice and other staple food of the country have been increasing every month amid low domestic production and high prices on the international market. A look into the current prices of essential food items in the local market revealed that the price of rice increased by 29–37 per cent in 2007. The price of wheat flour increased by 49–63 per cent, while the price of soybean oil increased by 50–62 per cent in November 2007.[14]

Price of Petroleum

Increases in the prices of petroleum products and food imports created some pressure on foreign currency reserves. Bangladesh spent 2 billion dollars to import petroleum products in 2007, which were then sold in the domestic market at heavily subsidized prices. Based on domestic and international prices at the end of October 2007, the subsidy for diesel was $0.25 per liter and for kerosene $0.26 per liter. Bangladesh Petroleum Corporation losses are estimated at US$794 million or 1.1 per cent of GDP in FY 2008.[15] Fuel prices were last adjusted by the government in April 2007 to establish parity with global prices (when the global price of oil was about US$60/barrel). Since then, prices have risen by more than 50 per cent. This puts constant pressure on the budget and the budget deficit. However, it is a major concern for the government that any changes in the fuel price will trigger a price spiral in other sectors.

Energy Sector

With generating capacity short of needs, supply notoriously unreliable and power outages common, access to reliable power is a prime concern for most manufacturing firms in Bangladesh. Table 1.4 reflects the lamentable state of affairs in the power sector.

A report by the World Bank in 2007 confirms the conventional perception that electricity supply, transmission, and distribution are serious problems.[16] What is most alarming is that since 2002, there has been an addition of less than 300 MW to the national grid. Also the prospects of mid-term and long-term solutions

Table 1.4: Summary of daily electricity generation in Bangladesh (as of 22 November 2007)

Forecast maximum demand	Installed generation capacity	Debated generation capacity	Generation at the time of max demand (peak hours)		Probable maximum generation	
			Morning	Evening	Morning	Evening
3,575	5,187	4,604	2,530	3,516	2,946	3,538

Source: Bangladesh Power Development Board, 2007.

appear to be extremely bleak. The demand for electricity is expected to rise from the existing 5,000 MW to 21,000 MW in 2021, if a 7–8 per cent GDP growth is to be sustained. Bangladesh must be at rock bottom when it comes to supply of electricity. The entire blame for this lamentable state of affairs must be attributed to atrocious governance, politicization, and corruption.[17] Therefore, a major challenge facing the government will be to undertake initiatives for bringing in rented power, as an urgent short-term measure, preferably from neighboring countries. Simultaneously, the government needs to speed up the development of the substantial coal resources and also ensure on a priority basis the exploration for oil and gas, both onshore and offshore.

Foreign Direct Investment

A declining trend in foreign direct investment flows into Bangladesh was mentioned in the World Investment Report, 2007 of the United Nations Conference on Trade and Development. Foreign direct investment in Bangladesh declined by 6 per cent against the 2005 level instead of 9.6 per cent as stated in the report.[18]

The rate of investment decreased by 30 per cent in the first nine months of 2007, as a result of the prevailing chaotic political situation. Only firm adherence to the electoral road map accompanied by a steady implementation of the reform agenda can restore confidence in the country's investment climate.[19] On the positive side, Chittagong Port's efficiency has improved and investment in

Table 1.5: Foreign Direct Investment Overview, 1999–2006

(*in US$ million*)

FDI Inflows	1990–2000 (annual average)	2003	2004	2005	2006
Inward	218	350	460	692	625
Outward	4	6	6	2	8

Source: World Investment Report 2007, UNCTAD.

the share market has increased substantially, although according to the Securities and Exchange Commission, the rapid jump in share prices can be partly explained by the shift of funds from government savings instruments and fixed deposits in banks to the stock market, since in the latter case it may be more difficult for tax authorities to establish the net worth of individuals. What remains to be done now is to identify rules and regulations and simplify them in order to cut back on the stages involved in the decision-making process. Lack of investor confidence is an issue that should receive the utmost attention of the Better Business Forum led by the Chief Adviser. It is common knowledge that foreign direct investment flows tend to increase in a place where local investment has thrived. It is especially important that the present government tackles the problem of the low level of annual development program disbursement on a priority basis if investments are to pick up.

Foreign Assistance

Due to lack of donor confidence, foreign assistance and loans decreased. In 2006–7, total foreign assistance amounted to US$1,624 million compared to US$1,703 million in 2005–6, indicating a decrease of 4.6 per cent compared with a 9.4 per cent decline in the previous year. The assistance included US$312 million as grants and US$1,312 million as loans. This indicates a decrease in grants by 15.4 per cent and in loans by 1.7 per cent compared with the decrease in grants by 14.2 per cent and in loans by 7.9 per cent in the previous year. Total net external assistance decreased by 11.3 per cent in 2006–7 compared with 16.6 per cent decrease in 2005–6 after the repayment of foreign loans, which increased by 11 per cent in 2006–7 and by 14.3 per cent in 2005–6.[20] This trend of loan and grant components will have future consequences for debt servicing, although as of now the government has been able to comfortably service foreign debts, which constitute only 5–6 per cent of Bangladesh's total export earnings.

Investment and Savings

The savings-investment gap as a ratio of GDP widened to 4.8 per cent in 2006–7 from 3.0 per cent in 2005–6 and 1.3 per cent in 2004–5 due to an increase in national savings by 1.5 per cent as against a decline of 0.4 per cent in government investment. The higher savings-investment gap in 2006–7 mainly resulted from the negative impact of a prolonged period of high interest rates, as well as the weak performance of the share market and political uncertainty in the first half of the year. The level of gross capital formation declined to 24.3 per cent of GDP in 2006–7 from 24.7 per cent of GDP in 2005–6. The reduction in government investment accounted for 100 per cent of this decline. The total national savings-GDP ratio increased to 29.2 per cent in 2006–7 from 27.7 per cent in 2005–6, mainly due to high inflow of remittances and higher prices of public goods.[21]

Readymade Garment Exports

Despite widespread doubts about the fate of Bangladeshi readymade garment (RMG) exports after the end of the Multi-Fiber Agreement, the country's export performance, especially in the case of the RMG sector, was impressive with 22 per cent growth. Not only knit exports but also garments made from woven fabrics increased significantly. However, the RMG sector, which is the mainstay of the economy and accounts for more than 75 per cent of Bangladesh's exports, is facing some difficulties. There has been a drop in export orders from the United States (US), although exports to the European market remain strong. The efforts to get a

Table 1.6: Comparative Statement on RMG Exports and Total Exports

Year	Export of RMG (US$ million)	Total Export of Bangladesh (US$ million)	% of RMGs to Total Exports
2006–7 (Dec.)*	4,730.36	6,220.61	76.04
2005–6	7,900.80	10,526.16	75.06
2004–5	6,417.67	8,654.52	74.15
2003–4	5,686.09	7,602.99	74.79
2002–3	4,912.09	6,548.44	75.01
2001–2	4,583.75	5,986.09	76.57

Source: Export Promotion Board, Compiled by Bangladesh Garment Manufacturers and Exporters Association, 2007.
Note: * Projected.

Figure 1.1. Decline in RMG Exports

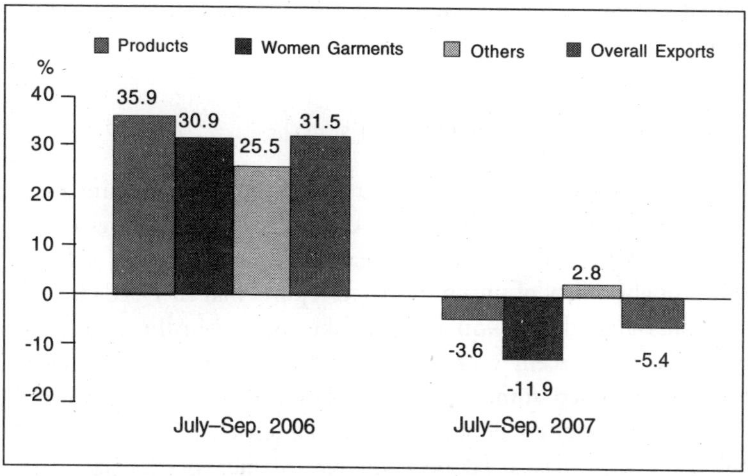

Source: Asian Development Bank, *Bangladesh Quarterly Economic Update*, September 2007.

bill through the US Congress to extend duty-free access to all Least Developed Countries, including those in the Asia-Pacific region, for RMG exports to the US, thus become very important. The competitive pressure from China and erosion of preferences in view of falling tariffs under World Trade Organization negotiations should be considered as reasons for Bangladesh's preferential access in the US, all the more so since the existing restrictions on Chinese garment exports to the US will no longer be there from 1 January 2009.

Revised Income Tax Scenario

Income tax collection posted robust growth of 45.3 per cent during the tax year 2006–7. The drive by the government to increase the number of taxpayers and intensive supervision and monitoring of income tax have increased collection. Ongoing tax reforms, including expanding taxpayer registration, modernizing the National Board of Revenue along functional lines, and strengthening audit functions are also necessary to maintain this performance. Lists of tax exemptions, exclusions, and incentives need to be reviewed to expand the tax base and avoid tax evasion. Tax administration should be more focused on updating and simplifying income tax and value added tax laws. Revenue must increase to mobilize resources for investment and avoid debt burdens.[22]

The Fear of Extremism

Fears have been raised that extremist groups, both mainstream and fringe groups, have become more active. The activities of the Jamaa'tul Mujahidin Bangladesh gave Western countries a fright and brought a slew of unsubstantiated reports that Al-Qaeda leaders were in Bangladesh. Nonetheless, like many Muslim countries, Bangladesh in recent years has, propelled partly by its domestic politics, spawned some extremist Islamic groups. With around 7 to 10 per cent of the popular vote, the Jamaat-e-Islami—an Islamist political party—has so far been unable to increase the size of its vote. But, through shifting alliances, it has increased its influence. It had its first two ministers in the previous government and 18 seats in parliament. Its violent student wing, Islami Chattra Shibir, is relatively strong, controlling the campuses of two of Bangladesh's four biggest universities, in Chittagong and Rajshahi. However, unlike its sister group in Pakistan, both the Jamaat and the more militant groups are interested only in domestic politics. This, of course, could change. The government has yet to enact any anti-terrorism legislation or adopt a comprehensive counter-terrorism strategy.[23]

Strengthening Democracy and Rule of Law

Strengthening democracy and the establishment of rule of law have posed problems for the current government. Any effort to do so would require transparency, accountability, participation, and effectiveness in the governance system and among public functionaries. In order to enable future Parliaments to take the lead role in overseeing the Executive, watchdog institutions such as the Anti-Corruption Commission, National Board of Revenue and the Bangladesh Bank, establishment of the Office of Ombudsman and the National Human Rights Commission should be made independent and autonomous, free from government control. To improve the law and order situation in the domestic sphere, the police and other law enforcement agencies should be revamped and restructured. There is also need for a serious review of the salary and incentive structure of law enforcement agencies. To improve law enforcement agencies and to respond to terrorism and crimes effectively, efficiently and rapidly, Bangladesh should adopt a national counter-terrorism strategy and a detailed action plan.

Natural Disasters

The climate and weather in Bangladesh have been its sources of weakness and strength since time immemorial. Its 145 million people live on a delta twice the size of Ireland, 40 per cent of which is flooded for three months of each year. The country is desperately overcrowded. By 2050, its population is projected to reach 250 million. With almost half the country only inches above, or even below, sea-level, the prospect of climate change and rising sea levels is nightmarish. Around 1 per cent of agricultural land is lost to river erosion each year.

Floods

The recent floods in July–August 2007 and Cyclone Sidr posed another set of challenges to the economy. According to government data, the July–August 2007 floods caused damage of about Tk2,700 crore. During the two phases of the floods, the loss in *aman* rice production was about 1,000,000 metric tons.[24] Besides, floods have damaged (i) 8,891 kilometers of paved rural infrastructure; (ii) municipal infrastructure in 77 municipalities covering urban roads, bridges, culverts, water supply, drainage, and sanitation systems; (iii) 1,420 kilometers of national, regional, and district roads, including 114 bridges and culverts; and (iv) water resource structures such as large- and medium-scale flood control and irrigation schemes. The flooding also damaged education and health services. The combined losses to assets and output from the 2007 flooding are estimated at US$1 billion, or 1.4 per cent of GDP.[25]

Cyclone Sidr

An updated official report from the Ministry of Flood and Disaster Management estimates that the number of deaths caused by Cyclone Sidr has killed 3,295 persons and affected 8.7 million people or 2 million families.[26] The agricultural ministry has a preliminary estimate that Cyclone Sidr has caused a loss of at least 600,000 metric tons of *aman* crops in the coastal areas. Responding to the floods, the government reallocated a food safety net budget of Tk2,100 crore to meet immediate relief requirements while another Tk2,100 crore as maintenance budget was reallocated for post-flood rehabilitation programs. While there was a prompt response from the international community in providing relief in the immediate aftermath of the cyclone, the government's priority now is to tackle the issue of reviving the economy in the devastated coastal belt. A firm commitment from the international community to assist the government in its plans to rehabilitate the millions of people who lost practically everything they had either due to Cyclone Sidr or the floods, will certainly help.

MAJOR REFORM INITIATIVES

Despite the economic challenges, the government was committed to pursuing some critical reforms with a focus on combating corruption, ensuring the effectiveness and independence of the judiciary and depoliticizing the civil service. To materialize these commitments, the government has undertaken the following initiatives:

The Election Roadmap

The Election Commission has proposed a roadmap for holding a credible general election by December 2008. It brings tangible form to the assurance given by the caretaker government to hold a free and fair election by the end of 2008. The roadmap proposes an indicative timeline for the election and looks a bit ambitious on certain points. The plan includes dialogue with the political parties on the electoral reforms, completion of the voter list by mid-October 2008 and holding of elections in December 2008. The roadmap sets about completing some legal and institutional reforms by February 2008, including reforms of the following: Representation of People's Order, 1972; the Electoral Roll Ordinance, 1982; the Election Commission (registration of Political Parties) Rules, 2001; the Conduct of Election Rules, 1972; and the Parliament Election Code of Conduct for the Political Parties and the Contesting Candidates Rules, 1996.[27] The Election Commission plans to complete registration of the political parties by June 2008, which is do-able provided the Election Commission has competent staff on its payroll.

Separation of the Judiciary from the Executive

The separation of the judiciary from the executive should be considered as a fundamental concern to any initiatives of democratic reforms that the current government aims to bring. After long delays during the regimes of the two previous elected governments, the present caretaker government has undertaken tasks to separate the judiciary from the executive. The legal process for separating the judiciary from the executive has been completed. However, the major challenge is ensuring the efficiency and neutrality of the existing human resources within the judiciary. It should be noted that establishing the independence of the judiciary is a long-term and expensive process requiring continual revision and improvement of the system, process, and institutions of the judiciary.

The Electoral Institutions

The Election Commission has been revamped and preparations for the next elections are on in full swing. The task of preparing a new voters list with photographs and entering all the relevant information in a database is a time-consuming process. While the Election Commission has announced that the general elections will take place before the end of 2008, both the Chief Adviser and the Election Commission announced recently that every effort will be made to hold the elections at the earliest possible. The Election Commission has also announced that once the electoral rolls are prepared for the major metropolitan areas, municipal elections will be held in these places.

The Anti-Corruption Commission

To expedite the campaign against corruption, long-pending reforms of the Anti-Corruption Commission have been initiated under this government. The government has reconstituted the Anti-Corruption Commission with new commissioners; framed new laws to tackle corruption; taken tough legal and prosecutorial actions against a number of corrupt politicians, public officials, and others; and ratified the United Nations Convention against Corruption. A former army chief, Lt. Gen. Hasan Mashud Chowdhury, has been appointed as Chairman of the Commission. National and district task forces have been constituted to tackle serious crimes, including corruption. The Asian Development Bank has approved a US$150 million loan for a good-governance programme of the current government. Much of the money will be spent on supporting the Anti-Corruption Commission.[28] The Commission now aims to build a reputation for being competent, efficient and independent. The Anti-Corruption Commission is doing its utmost to proceed with the prosecution of various anti-corruption cases. Since it is equipped with emergency powers to arrest, search, and detain, there is little doubt that it will succeed. However, five special courts are not enough to deal with the flood of cases, and more are being created.

Anti-corruption Drive

To strengthen the anti-corruption drive, a number of initiatives were taken to reform the legal and institutional structures. The enormity of corrupt practices that have surfaced during the ongoing anti-corruption drive must have baffled and surprised most Bangladeshis. The illegal acquisition of wealth by persons occupying high public office, however, was not a well-kept secret. Nobody took any serious note of the malfeasance and misfeasance of the high and mighty until early January 2007. The depth and breadth of corruption in Bangladesh have been pervasive, with losses estimated to be nearly 3 per cent in terms of GDP. According to a recent study by Transparency International Bangladesh, per capita loss of household income to bribery in six selected sectors of public service delivery was estimated to be 7.94 per cent. With the ratio of loss being higher at 9.56 per cent for low-income groups compared to 2.36 per cent for the high-income category, the poorest have been the worst victims.[29] A series of high-profile initiatives have been undertaken by the current government to criminalize corruption by prosecuting the allegedly corrupt individuals, irrespective of their political and other status in society. The anti-corruption drive could turn out to be the strongest-ever signal in Bangladesh's history that corruption is a punishable offence. Several of the politicians have been tried and sentenced to several years in jail. The two former prime ministers, Begum Zia and Sheikh Hasina, were both arrested and are expected to face a variety of charges. One of the major developments during 2006–7 has been the arrest of a large number of politicians and prominent businessmen on corruption charges, as well as charges arising out of incorrect disclosure of their assets. Many of these politicians have been tried and received lengthy jail sentences.

The Public Service Commission

The Public Service Commission, the lone constitutional body responsible for recruitment of government officers in Bangladesh, during the tenure of the two earlier governments, in particular, the last BNP government, was riddled with corruption. Its image and reputation sank to an all-time low. The present government has undertaken comprehensive reform measures, including reconstitution of the Public Service Commission to make it once again an independent and credible institution, as provided for in the Constitution of Bangladesh. It would be worth mentioning that as a result of student movements, the Public Service Commission has formed a committee to review the existing quota system in the appointments made by the Public Service Commission.

Reforms in Political Parties

The Election Commission has also proposed a comprehensive set of reforms for political parties. This includes registration of all political parties, rules and regulations in respect of their accounts, full details of expenditure on elections, a code of conduct and strict criteria in respect of eligibility of candidates for elections. The Election Commission has entered into dialogues with the political parties before finalizing the reforms. The caretaker government and the Election Commission believe that this process of both electoral and political reforms is essential in order to restore the credibility of the democratic process and to ensure that the next elected parliament can fulfill its responsibilities in a meaningful and effective way, unlike the three previous parliaments.

The National Human Rights Commission

The government has enacted the National Human Rights Commission Ordinance, 2007 which had been pending in the government since 1995. Pledges by previous political governments to set up the NHRC were never translated into any concrete action, though much lip service was rendered to the need for setting up such a commission.[30] However, the NHRC needs to be a truly effective body that is capable of doing enough to bring violators of human rights to justice. In other words, its functions should not remain confined to surveys, observations and issuing statements.

Establishment of the Regulatory Reforms Commission

To do away with outdated administrative rules and regulations and either streamline and consolidate regulations that remain relevant or introduce new regulations in place of the outdated ones, the government has formed a 17-member Regulatory Reforms Commission (RRC). The RRC has been mandated to prepare recommendations aiming to modernize the existing rules and regulations after holding consultations with the private sector and other relevant bodies. With a tenure of one year, the commission will be chaired by former Adviser and Finance Secretary, Dr Akbar Ali Khan, and includes former Adviser Manzur-e-Elahi, currently the Administrator Federation of Bangladesh Chamber of Commerce and Industry, the apex chamber in the country, former Adviser and Secretary to the Government, Abdul Muyeed Chowdhury, two prominent economists, private sector representatives, and government secretaries.

The Better Business Forum

To restore a sense of confidence in the business community, which in turn is vital to the efforts to energize the economy and accelerate the rate of growth, the government established the Bangladesh Better Business Forum (BBF) in November 2007. The BBF, chaired by the Chief Adviser, Dr Fakhruddin, has been established with the objective of providing the private sector with a high-level platform to engage the government at the highest level in order to resolve as speedily as possible some of the problems faced by the private sector in doing business in the country. The BBF has been conceived as a public-private joint initiative to improve the business climate in the country and restore the confidence of the business community. The BBF has formed six working committees on business entry and operations, business finance, foreign direct investment and investment promotion, total infrastructure and facilities for private sector development, human skills development, and monetary and fiscal policy. The committees will recommend measures for improving the country's business environment and help the economy grow.

Revamped Chittagong Port Facilities

The government has undertaken extensive measures to upgrade and improve the efficiency of Chittagong Port. The port is a key infrastructure for the economy as 90 per cent of the export- and import-related activities in Bangladesh are executed through it. Before the current government's initiatives, Chittagong Port was trapped in the hands of a vicious circle, which included the port authority, equipment operators, dock laborers, corrupt businessmen and political leaders, and it had turned out to be a very expensive, corrupt, and inefficient port. Port efficiency has increased by 30 per cent and the cost of running business has been reduced by 40 per cent since the proclamation of emergency rule in January this year.[31] In fact, there was no magic working behind the scenes, and the change occurred with the same groups of people who worked inside the port before proclamation of the emergency. Soon after the deployment of army personnel to help the civil administration on 11 January 2007 a taskforce under the joint forces began assisting port officials in running the facilities. The task force reviewed the problems with all the stakeholders and got hold of the corrupt trade union leaders, port officials and other criminals. Private operators, who were not allowed to work by the so-called union leaders, quickly got going with the job as part of the reform measures and, suddenly, the improvements were visible. Recently, a memorandum of understanding has been signed between Chittagong Port and Penang Port for establishing infrastructural and technological cooperation between the two important harbors of Bangladesh and Malaysia.[32]

RESPONSE OF THE INTERNATIONAL COMMUNITY

The caretaker government has accelerated economic and sectoral reforms in several areas where previous governments had difficulty moving forward for political reasons. Although the economy continues to maintain reasonable growth with key macro-economic indicators remaining reasonably healthy, the government had to face a number of challenges from internal or external sources. The international community's response to developments in Bangladesh has been quite supportive. Both the European Union and the US have on several occasions expressed their support for the caretaker government and have offered assistance for the forthcoming elections. The position of the United Nations (UN) has been equally supportive. However, both the European Union and the US have stressed the importance of holding the elections at the earliest possible time. The western countries have also welcomed the reforms initiated by the caretaker government.

The caretaker government has made a special effort to improve relations with its neighbors, both in South Asia and in South-East Asia. Strong support has been given to strengthening regional cooperation in South Asia through the South Asian Association for Regional Cooperation (SAARC). The Chief Adviser, Dr Fakhruddin, attended the SAARC summit in Delhi held in April 2007. During the summit he also had bilateral meetings with the Indian Prime Minister and other heads of government attending the SAARC summit. Relations between Bangladesh and India, which had remained at a virtual standstill during the previous BNP government, have shown some progress in several areas including trade, transportation, and security-related issues. More recently in the wake of Cyclone Sidr, the Indian Minister of External Affairs, Pranab Mukherjee, visited the cyclone-affected areas and met with the Chief Adviser and the Foreign Affairs Adviser. Mr Mukherjee announced during his visit that India, as a very special case, had decided to lift the embargo on rice exports, in order to allow Bangladesh to import 500,000 tons of rice from India to meet the shortfall caused by Cyclone Sidr. This gesture was widely appreciated in Bangladesh and should contribute to improving bilateral relations between the two countries.

Bangladesh, represented by the Foreign Affairs Adviser, Dr Iftekhar Ahmed Chowdhury, for the first time participated as a full member of the Association of Southeast Asian Nations (ASEAN) Regional Forum, held in Manila earlier this year. Apart from the US, with whom there have been regular consultations, close and cordial relations have also been maintained with the other four members of the Security Council. During the course of the year Dr Chowdhury paid official visits to London and Moscow, where he held talks with his respective counterparts. He also paid official visits to Sweden and Norway, and Australia. Relations with the European Union and its member states remain cordial, as also with Canada, Japan, the Republic of Korea and ASEAN countries.

The present government has continued to participate actively in multilateral affairs and Bangladesh remains one of the foremost contributors of troops for UN Peacekeeping operations. The Chief Adviser, partly to demonstrate Bangladesh's strong commitment to the UN, paid a visit to New York in September to attend the General Assembly session. The Chief Adviser, both in his UN speech, as well as in other speeches and interviews during his visit to New York, mentioned that one of the critical elements of a functioning democracy was an independent judiciary. He mentioned his government's initiative to separate the executive from the judicial branches of government. He reaffirmed Bangladesh's 'unflinching commitment to universal and inalienable human rights' and announced on the floor of the General Assembly that his government had taken the decision 'to establish a National Human Rights Commission to ensure that our laws and public institutions reflect international standards and norms of human rights'.

Bangladesh has in recent years attracted a lot of adverse publicity due to several incidents of terrorism. In his UN General Assembly speech, Dr Fakhruddin mentioned that Bangladesh is now a party to all terrorism-related UN conventions and added 'Bangladesh remains resolute in its campaign against international extremism and terrorism'. He mentioned that stern measures had been taken against the Islamic militant groups and stated that 'Bangladesh is steadfast in its commitment to curb religious fundamentalism in all its manifestations'.

The Chief Adviser, Dr Fakhruddin, attended the annual meeting of the World Economic Forum in Davos at the end of January 2008. He pointed out the existing problems in Bangladesh and drew the attention of participants to two major challenges faced by Bangladesh: the adverse impact of climate change and lack of duty-free access to US markets. Tony Blair, co-chairman of the forum, voiced strong support for Bangladesh's efforts to meet these challenges and emphasized that Bangladesh had suffered heavy losses almost every year due to natural disasters. Representatives of foreign companies who have already made investments in the country called for implementation of reforms in the financial sector to attract more overseas investment. Multi-national corporations said they wanted to see the actual implementation of reforms so far undertaken by the government in the financial sector. Dr Fakhruddin and the Chief Executive Officers of seven leading companies had discussions at Davos on the ongoing reforms in Bangladesh.[33]

The Foreign Adviser, Dr Chowdhury, attended the Kampala Commonwealth Summit Conference and discussed the current reforms in Bangladesh. He spoke of Bangladesh's position on several international issues, including climate change and peacekeeping, and agreed to keep working with the international community. During his participation in the Islamic Conference of Foreign Ministers meeting in Islamabad, the Foreign Adviser stressed Bangladesh's stand on the Organization of Islamic Conference (OIC) by asserting that 'the OIC is confined to platitudes in the political arena', adding that the organization has become 'moribund' and unable to respond to changes and present-day requirements. He stressed the need for the OIC to undergo effective reforms to make it operational and more relevant for the member states.[34]

Bangladesh participated in the Bali Climate Conference in December 2007 with a specific set of proposals, aligned to the position of the G-77 and the Least Developed Countries. The proposals were: (i) drastic emission reductions to prevent global warming; (ii) legally binding emission reduction targets for all responsible countries; (iii) equitable reduction targets; (iv) access to carbon-neutral technology and funds for technology transfer to help secure energy requirement; (v) matching adaptation needs and elements of framework in future commitments; (vi) developing countries' need for defense in depth, including infrastructure to address risks and impact; (vii) climate refugees to be granted legal rights to provide for their rehabilitation and recovery; (viii) innovative financial mechanisms; (ix) fast-tracking of funds for climate change; and (x) equity principles to apply as a denominator.

Bangladesh has a very energetic private sector, which has done remarkably well notwithstanding the many constraints to doing business in the country. It also has both human and natural resources; what is required is an effective strategy to develop these resources. Perhaps one of Bangladesh's biggest advantages is its strategic location. Bangladesh is surrounded by India, China, and the ASEAN countries, all doing remarkably well. If Bangladesh can successfully integrate its economy and infrastructure with these countries, and develop Chittagong Port into a regional hub, there is no reason why Bangladesh should not be able to share, as well as contribute significantly to, the prosperity and growth of the region as well as realize its full potential.

CONCLUDING REMARKS

Bangladesh today stands at a crossroads. The key to Bangladesh's success will be determined by not simply free and fair elections but the elections putting in place a government committed to good governance which can build on the many reforms initiated by the present caretaker government. During this transition period if the efforts of the caretaker government to put in place a solid foundation of reforms are successful, Bangladesh can look forward to a prosperous future.

The international community should keep its focus on the electoral process and broader systemic institutional problems mentioned in this chapter. The focus on the political parties and push for internal reforms and political party laws should remain a priority. Reform initiatives undertaken by the present government can happen only with the involvement of the political parties. Any efforts towards reform that exclude the parties will be reversed as soon as the political parties regain power. Given the practices in Bangladesh, we should remember that the parties themselves are not democratic. Party leaders are not elected by party members and both the Awami League and BNP operate as *de facto* dynasties under their strong and entrenched leadership structures with little will or ability to aggregate interests.

Bangladesh is in dire need of politicians who can build on the agenda of good governance and who can work closely with the private sector and the people of the country in creating a stable, peaceful and prosperous Bangladesh—a Bangladesh that can join hands with its neighbors in the region as an equal partner in the tremendous growth and success of Asia.

The performance of the Bangladesh economy will remain of critical importance, in particular the food situation. Much will depend on the *boro* harvest and, prior to that, the ability of the government to distribute fertilizers to farmers at affordable prices. Equally important will be the ability of the government to import and distribute an adequate quantity of food grain during the critical months of March and April 2007. The quantum jump in global food prices, as well as the problem of availability of food grains, has added to the problems of Bangladesh.

Thus, both the political and economic outlook pose serious challenges for the existing caretaker government. It is essential that the government mobilizes as much support as possible from both within the government and from non-government actors to face this dual challenge. The student demonstrations in August 2007 should serve as a reminder that if the government fails to meet the expectations of the people there could be more demonstrations. The government would like to forge a national consensus to face both the political and economic challenges facing the country. Above all, it would like to ensure that the reforms initiated by the government are sustained after the elections. As such, ensuring political reforms and the fielding of candidates who enjoy a good reputation in the parliamentary elections become a matter of vital importance. There is also talk of a national government to ensure political stability and the continuation of the reform process. What are not clear is what form and shape such a national government might take and whether all the political parties will be willing to support such a government after the elections.

NOTES

1. Asian Development Bank (2007). *Bangladesh Quarterly Economic Update*, September. http://www.adb.org/Documents/News/BRM/brm-200705.asp.
2. Asian Development Bank (2007). *Bangladesh Quarterly Economic Update*, June. http://www.adb.org/Documents/News/BRM/brm-200702.asp.
3. Mamun Rashid (2007). 'Economic and business challenges for Bangladesh', March 2007. http://www.thedailystar.net/forum/2007/march/economic.htm,
4. Bangladesh Bank (2007). *Annual Report 2006–7*. www.bangladesh-bank.org.
5. Ibid.
6. Ibid.
7. International Monetary Fund (2007). http://www.imf.org/external/country/BGD/index.htm.
8. Asian Development Bank (2007). *Bangladesh Quarterly Economic Update*, September.
9. *The Financial Express* (2007). *Inflation Stabilization a Key Challenge for Policy Makers*, 27 December.
10. Ibid.
11. Bangladesh Bank (2007). *Monetary Policy Statement*, http://www.bangladesh-bank.org/, July 12.
12. Asian Development Bank (2007). *Asian Development Outlook 2007 Update*, http://www.adb.org/Documents/Books/ADO/2007/update/default.asp.
13. *The Economist* (2007). 'Bangladesh's cyclone: yet another calamity', 19 November. www.economist.com,
14. *The Daily Star* (2007). 'Economy Sidr-struck', 22 November. http://www.thedailystar.net/story.php?nid=12556,
15. Asian Development Bank (2007). *Bangladesh Quarterly Economic Update*, September.

16. World Bank (2007). *Doing Business 2008 Bangladesh,* Washington, D.C.
17. K.Z. Islam (2007). 'Foreign Direct Investment in Bangladesh'. Paper presented at the ICAB Seminar *Foreign Direct Investment in Bangladesh.*
18. UNCTAD (2007). *World Investment Report.*
19. *The Daily Star* (2007). 'Downtrend in foreign direct investment flow'. http://www.thedailystar.net/story.php?nid=7803, 18 October.
20. 'Bangladesh economy during 2006–7', Metropolitan Chamber of Commerce and Industry, Dhaka, Bangladesh. http://www.mccibd.org/bdecon.html.
21. Ibid.
22. Asian Development Bank (2007). *Bangladesh Quarterly Economic Update,* September.
23. *The Economist* (2007). 'Everybody but the politician is happy', 8 February. http://www.economist.com/world/asia/displaystory. cfm?story_id=8670354
24. Ministry of Flood and Disaster Management (2007). *Situation Report,* 8 December. http://www.cdmp.org.bdH, www.dmb.gov.bd
25. Asian Development Bank (2007). *Bangladesh Quarterly Economic Update,* September.
26. Ministry of Flood and Disaster Management (2007). Situation Report, 8 December. http://www.cdmp.org.bdH, www.dmb.gov.bd
27. *The Daily Star* (2007). 'Election roadmap', Editorial, 16 July. http://www.thedailystar.net/2007/07/16/d70716020130.htm
28. *The Economist* (2007). 'The clean up', 8 November. http://www.economist.com/world/asia/displaystory.cfm? story_id=10113855
29. Iftekharuzzaman (2007). 'Corruption in Bangladesh: upside down?', *New Age.* http://www.newagebd.com/store/anni07/15.html.
30. *The Daily Star* (2007). 'A milestone decision', 11 December. http://www.thedailystar.net/story.php?nid=14978.
31. The turnaround time of vessels at Chittagong Port dropped and container handling rose substantially in recent times. Regular monitoring by the joint forces and the introduction of private operations contributed to the remarkable improvement in activities at the port. The vessel stay-time at jetties in August 2007 averaged 3.10 days against 3.26 days in July 2007, but it was only 48 hours at the modern Chittagong Container Terminal (CCT) of the port during August 2007. The CCT is equipped with sophisticated rail-mounted quay gantry cranes and other modern facilities. Container handling rose by 8.8 per cent in August over that of July 2007. The port handled a total of 85,116 containers of twenty-foot equivalent Units (TEU) in August against 78,540 containers in July 2007. The

number of container vessels that called at the port also rose in August in comparison with the month of July 2007. See *The Financial Express* (2007). 'Reforms add new dimension to Chittagong Port', 30 September. http://www.thefinancialexpress-bd.com/search_index. php?page= detail_news&news_id=12789.

32. *The Financial Express* (2007). 'Building quality infrastructure for competitiveness', 14 December. http://www.thefinancialexpress-bd.com/search_index.php? page=detail_news&news_id=19885.
33. *The Daily Star* (2008). 'Davos Economic Forum promises creative capitalism', 9 February.
34. *The Daily Star* (2007). 'OIC needs reforms to meet challenges', 21 May.

2

Decentralization, Democratization and Development in Bhutan

CAROLINE BRASSARD

THIS CHAPTER analyzes the recent developments in Bhutan on the political and economic fronts, from 1980 onwards. It examines the impacts of the administrative and political reforms as well as the policy implications on socio-economic development and good governance in the country. The chapter is organized as follows.

The first section of the chapter focuses on the decentralization and democratization processes that have taken place since the early 1980s. It provides an overview of the historical developments leading up to the first parliamentary elections, and discusses the likely implications of devolution on social, economic, and political development in Bhutan. The second section discusses the rationale for the transfer of power within the monarchy and examines the implications of the new constitution of 2008. The third section introduces the concept of Gross National Happiness (GNH) based on economic growth and development, the preservation and promotion of cultural heritage, the preservation and sustainable use of the environment, and good governance. The fourth section analyzes the macroeconomic and human development contexts, including an analysis of the results of recent surveys such as the Labor Force Survey of 2006 and the Population and Housing Census of 2005.

The final few sections conclude on the impact of these economic and political reforms on capacity-building requirements for good governance in Bhutan, and identify some of the key challenges ahead to ensure sustainable development in the country. In the fifth section, the GNH framework for development is analyzed in terms of the implications in the areas of policy planning and formulation, decentralization, and the institutionalization of good governance. Finally, the sixth section focuses on the implications for capacity-building at the individual and institutional levels. A brief historical background follows, putting these recent reforms into context and providing a deeper understanding of the significance and speed of the economic, administrative, and political reform processes.

DECENTRALIZATION AND PUBLIC ADMINISTRATION REFORMS

Bhutan is a small landlocked country between India and China in the eastern Himalayan region. It recently celebrated the 100th year of the establishment of the Wangchuck Dynasty, which had first unified the country. Bhutan entered a new era when King Ugyen Wangchuck was chosen as the hereditary King of Bhutan on 17 December 1907 by an assembly of higher civil and religious officials. The National Assembly was established in 1953 under King Jigme Dorji Wangchuck and comprised 130 members, followed by the foundation of the Council of Cabinet Ministers 15 years later. The king assumed the role of head of government and state, and was at the center of the country's governance.

Development planning officially began with the First Five-Year Plan (FYP) (1961–6). At that time, the local economy, mainly based on self-subsistence, was rural and insular. Many of Bhutan's monarchs initiated processes towards democratization of the country through various political and legal changes, but the turning point came in the early 1980s at the end of the Fourth FYP (1976–81). The king, Jigme Singye Wangchuck, introduced a program of decentralization at the political and administrative levels, further enhancing the democratization process through the empowerment of the citizenry at the local levels. Since then, many improvements in the social sectors occurred. For example, a comprehensive non-monastic education system was established and modern medical facilities were built, mainly concentrated in urban centers.

The country is divided into 20 administrative districts (*dzongkhags*) and 205 development blocks (*geogs*, or village clusters), with a central administration based in Thimphu. In Bhutan, the three aspects of decentralization—political, financial, and administrative—are strongly interlinked and self-reinforcing, and occur simultaneously. To be successful, the process of decentralization must involve devolution of functions as well as financial decentralization, and ensure greater autonomy to the regions. Consequently, participation of the local population in the decision-making, planning, implementation, and evaluation processes is at the heart of ensuring good local governance and requires capacity building at the individual and institutional levels. Moreover, legal support necessary to strengthen the mandate of the participating local individuals was strengthened recently with the new Constitution of 2008.

The modernization of governance in Bhutan began with economic and political decentralization during the Fourth FYP, which further involved local bodies as administrative and financial powers were increasingly given to the districts and village clusters. By the Fifth FYP (1981–6), new levels of administration replaced the centralized administration. *Dzongkhag Yargay Tshogdus* or District Development Committees were established, followed by the *Geog Yargay Tshogchungs* (GYT) or Block Development Committees in the 1990s.[1] From then onwards, these committees formed an integral part of the decentralized system of economic planning, ensuring direct participation of the local communities in the development process through the division and dispersal of power.

By the late 1980s, with better infrastructure in place, the country was able to take better advantage of its natural resources. Hence, the focus of the Sixth FYP (1987–92) was to foster economic growth primarily through the exploitation of hydro-electric power on the basis that it was deemed less harmful to the environment than the promotion of heavy industry. Only 1.71 per cent of the total hydroelectric 'theoretical' potential of 20,000 MW had been estimated to have been captured by then.[2]

Economic development in Bhutan is constrained by limited domestic demand, a shortage of skilled labor, and a small and scattered population, as well as other geophysical characteristics (that is, mountainous regions). Indeed, financial aid requirements remained above 60 per cent of the total budget until the Eighth FYP (1997–02). There are two types of assistance: the general process of decentralization, including supporting devolution of power, delegation, and fiscal decentralization; and development activities directly implemented by the GYTs or community groups. However, questions remain about the role of donors, how integrated their assistance is, and in what way they support the decentralization process.

Up to the late 1990s, the development plans had been designed primarily by the central government, but for the Ninth FYP (2002–7), local planning contributed to its preparation. The priority sectors were infrastructure and the social sectors, especially the health sector. Within the total resource allocation of Nu 70,000 million, according to the plan, over 75 per cent would be allocated to the central level of government, just above 21 per cent to the districts and about 3 per cent to the GYTs. The long-term goal 'is to arrive at an integrated national planning process that is both bottom-up and top-down' (UNDP 2002: 20).

More recently, following the mid-term review report of the Ninth FYP (Planning Commission 2005), several issues were identified as priorities for the Tenth FYP (2007–12) such as:

(a) Lack of streamlining between the various development programs, the national goals within the GNH framework, and the objectives of the Millennium Development Goals (MDGs), where sectoral goals and long-term vision may not be in tandem;
(b) Lack of coordination between the various levels of government and among sectors;
(c) Lack of a systematic, transparent, and participatory policy formulation process and lack of systematic macro-economic analysis and evaluation of effectiveness of the adopted policies;
(d) Lack of rational resource allocation criteria, where allocations are based on proposals from ministries and agencies leading to unbalanced regional development; and
(e) Inadequate capacity, especially for community leaders, at the district and sub-district levels, in terms of results-based planning skills and tools, and lack of trained people in macroeconomic

analysis (for example, MDG costing and gender budgeting) and policy analysis and evaluation.

The details of the Tenth FYP (2007–12) have recently been made available online at the GNH Commission website.[3] Its focus is on poverty reduction and the institution of new bloc grants as a means for resource distribution between districts. The key question will be how to compensate for those that cannot use their natural resources due to regulations on environmental protection.

Overall, the experience of Bhutan shows that the extent and level of success of implementation of decentralization varies between and within regions, due to varying levels of economic development, lack of qualified people, and non-availability of funds. Communication problems and lack of a clear understanding of the new regulations have also emerged, leading to a lower degree of decentralization in some districts, where administrators are still implementers as opposed to facilitators in the development process. Nevertheless, as a result of this process, local priorities are increasingly set by the relevant localities and economic plans are implemented within the development framework of Bhutan.

There is perhaps insufficient discussion on the concept of civil society and its relevance and role in the decentralization process. There are various types of community-based development institutions, each specific to the geographical contexts. These are central to the 'retaining' of cultural values, yet their role in the decentralization process may be at risk of being undervalued. These need be an integral part of the institutional framework and not simply 'integrated in' the framework.

This process also requires a bottom-up approach where community-based institutions are also given a chance to grow within this new framework as opposed to being 'integrated'. For example, the government's decision to centralize natural resource management led to the degeneration of age-old institutions of community resource management. Recognizing this problem, the government is now trying to decentralize natural resource management back to the community, creating a significant level of confusion among the local people.

MONARCHY, POWER AND DEMOCRATIZATION

In parallel with the reforms towards decentralization, a process of democratization has also been taking place. A major political turning point came when the fourth king transferred most of his administrative duties to the Cabinet of Ministers. Following the 76th session of the National Assembly in 1998, devolution of power occurred as a Royal Edict that led to the election of members of the Council of Ministers via a secret ballot at the National Assembly. One year later, the introduction of television, followed shortly by the Internet, further reinforced the commitment of the government towards modernization of the country.

Following a royal decree commanding the draft of a new constitution in 2001, representatives from the monk body, the people, the judiciary, and the government formed a 39-member drafting committee.[4] The Ninth FYP (2001) includes a quote from His Majesty Jigme Singye Wangchuck:

> The basic purpose of the Constitution is to ensure sovereignty and security of the nation and the well-being of the Bhutanese people for all times to come. The Political system of the country must evolve so that the people would continue to enjoy peace, prosperity, justice, and the fundamental rights which have always been enshrined in the Bhutanese system.

The separation between the legislature and the executive came in mid-2002 and, in 2005, the first universal franchise election for GYTs was held in order to elect the head of the Geog for a period of three years. The National Council of Bhutan, the upper house of Parliament, was created in late December 2007 in the first national poll, with the election of 15 youthful members from a turnout of 55 per cent of eligible voters.[5]

The first parliamentary elections were held on 24 March 2008 when nearly 80 per cent of eligible voters cast their vote. The Druk Phuensum Tshogpa (Bhutan Peace and Prosperity Party) took 44 of the 47 seats in the National Assembly, marking the end of more than a century of absolute monarchy. However, the 28-year-old King Jigme Keshar Namgyal Wangchuck remains head of the State and Jigmi Y. Thinley, who has already served twice as prime minister, will be sworn in as the first democratically elected prime minister of Bhutan. The remaining three seats went to the rival People's Democratic Party, whose leader, Sangay Ngedup, lost his own constituency.[6] With such a weak result for the opposition party, questions remain as to the functioning of the new democracy.

At the end of March 2005, a draft constitution had been distributed to the Bhutanese population for discussion, which included a proposal to adopt a parliamentary democracy. The Constitution paves the way for a two-party democratic system and replaces the 1953 Royal Decree that gave the king absolute power. Notable articles in the Constitution include Article 2 on the Institution of Monarchy, which gives parliament the authority to impeach the king by a two-third vote, Article 9 on the principles of party policies, and Article 18 on the Opposition party, as well as Article 27 on the anti-corruption commission.

Irrespective of the existing polity, decentralization is a requirement for rural development with equity and a focus on pro-poor issues within good governance. A democratic framework is best suited to facilitate the decentralization process and outputs. Moreover, the participation of the people in the development and governance processes constitutes a fundamental human right. Decentralized institutions should have the necessary legal support to ensure that their mandate can be achieved, and models for good governance in rural development are context-specific. Among the necessary legal modalities to facilitate good governance with equity by local governments and the citizenry is that the elected representation should include proportional representation of different groups (for example, females, poor farmers, elderly, and youth), or at least a minimum representation in the local electorate.[7] This would ensure that their voice is taken into consideration in the planning, design, and implementation of development activities.

A constitutional mandate provides the framework for decentralized institutions at the local level to be recognized as the third tier of government. This ensures that a change of government would not affect the continuation and stability of the decentralized institutions. The Bhutanese government could also consider enacting a

Citizens' Right to access information from any level of government bodies or any organization as part of its effort towards increased good governance. For example, the Right to Information Act in India paves the way towards greater transparency and accountability.

HUMAN DEVELOPMENT AND GROSS NATIONAL HAPPINESS

Next, we turn to the development framework promoted in Bhutan, GNH, and contrast it with the Human Development framework. While quantitative measurements of development have rested primarily on gross domestic product (GDP) and gross national product figures, in recent decades there has emerged a flourishing literature on alternatives to GDP as a measure of economic development that use more wide-ranging indicators. Efforts to find alternative indicators of GDP as an indicator of well-being were stepped up following the development of the Human Development Index (HDI) by the United Nations Development Program (UNDP) in 1990.

HDI is a summary measure of the average achievements in a country along three basic dimensions: life expectancy, adult literacy, and adjusted GDP per capita, using equal weights for each component. These are essential to people's well-being but fall short of providing a comprehensive policy framework for human-centered development. Also, it is well known that although wealth is a factor of well-being, it is also subject to diminishing returns. As a recent debate over economics and happiness suggests, *economic* well-being may not be the ideal proxy for one's overall well-being level. Although a trend analysis of HDI in Bhutan is unavailable, compared to other countries in the region, HDI in Bhutan in the past few years ranked better than HDI in Bangladesh, Nepal, and Pakistan, but worse than in India, Maldives, and Sri Lanka (Table 2.1). An interesting contrast with overall governance indicators in South Asia is presented later in this chapter.

At a disaggretated level, the latest available data on life expectancy, education, and GDP show a clearer picture, as seen in Table 2.2.

Table 2.1: Human Development Index in South Asia, 1975–2005

FDI	1975	1980	1985	1990	1995	2000	2004*	2005	Rank in 2005
Bangladesh	0.347	0.365	0.392	0.422	0.453	0.511	0.530	0.547	140
Bhutan	–	–	–	–	–	–	0.538	0.579	133
India	0.419	0.450	0.487	0.521	0.551	0.578	0.611	0.619	128
Maldives	–	–	–	–	–	–	0.739	0.741	100
Nepal	0.301	0.338	0.380	0.427	0.469	0.502	0.527	0.534	142
Pakistan	0.367	0.394	0.427	0.467	0.497	0.516	0.539	0.551	136
Sri Lanka	0.619	0.656	0.683	0.702	0.721	0.731	0.755	0.743	99

Source: UNDP, Human Development Report 2007–8, Table 1.
Notes: *UNDP, Human Development Report 2006.
–Not available.

Table 2.2: Disaggregated Human Development Index for South Asia, 2005

Human Development Index (HDI) Rank 2005		Human Development Index	Life Expectancy Index	Education Index	GDP Index
140	Bangladesh	0.547	0.64	0.50	0.50
133	Bhutan	0.579	0.66	0.49	0.59
128	India	0.619	0.65	0.62	0.59
100	Maldives	0.741	0.70	0.86	0.66
142	Nepal	0.534	0.63	0.52	0.46
136	Pakistan	0.551	0.66	0.47	0.53
99	Sri Lanka	0.743	0.78	0.81	0.64

Source: UNDP, Human Development Report 2007–8, Table 1.

First, we note that although the overall HDI is higher in Bhutan than in Nepal, its education index falls short of expectations. On the other hand, the life expectancy index is higher than in India despite the lower overall HDI in Bhutan.

Of course, this only represents a small part of the story. Many commonly used indicators, such as the HDI, fall short of considering the role of values and culture, as highlighted by Sen's (1999) capability approach. Hence, policy makers require more systematic information on these less tangible aspects of the development process. The debate has taken off on the required supporting public policies for increasing well-being entrenched in these cultural values, but the operationalization of the various frameworks is an even greater challenge.

For example, improving on UNDP's HDI, the Fraser Institute developed an Index of Human Progress (IHP) that uses unadjusted (actual) GDP per capita and includes additional indicators (notably on technology), each deemed as desirable outcomes of development.[8] The advantage of the IHP over the HDI is that the greater number of sub-indicators allows for better differentiation among countries, and reduces potential bias of the overall index due to unreliable data. On the other hand, the unavailability of these sub-indicators implies that a smaller number of countries may be included.

Many other spin-offs from the HDI have since emerged, for example, the Gender-Related Development Index and the MDGs. However, there is increasing dissatisfaction with the framework provided by the MDGs, due to its emphasis on quantitative indicators over qualitative ones. The focus on increasing enrolment rates in primary schools, for instance, ignores issues related to the poor quality of educational systems. Finally, from an environmental perspective, indicators, such as the Green Development Index and the Pollution-Sensitive Human Development Index (HDPI),[9] are seen as indicators aiming at a better representation of social welfare as they integrate environmental performance.

All these indicators provide an alternative to the practice of equating progress and development with economic growth alone, as they include natural capital, social capital, and socio-economic variables. Evidence-based public policy towards better quality development processes can be enhanced by the development of well-being indicators that are entrenched in the political, economic, and social context, and studies on the determinants of well-being are flourishing in the four corners of the world.

Inevitably, the diverse roles of policy instruments in ensuring well-being vary across different schools of thought and from country to country, for example, pro-poor strategies using educational subsidies, or rights-based strategies that ensure adequate land property rights. A few frameworks also include policies to promote and conserve cultural heritage as part of ensuring well-being, which is one of the innovations of the GNH framework, as described next.

The term GNH was first coined by Bhutan's King Jigme Singye Wangchuk in 1972. It came as a result of dissatisfaction with conventional economic development theories focusing on economic growth to achieve general well-being. GNH is an attempt at defining standards of living in more holistic terms, based on the development philosophy of the Bhutanese, strongly influenced by Buddhist and non-material values.

The GNH framework is based on four main components: (i) the achievement of self-sufficiency in economic terms; (ii) the protection of the environment; (iii) good governance; and (iv) the promotion of local culture. The origin of the efforts to build an indigenous political, social, and cultural identity, it has been argued, comes from the historical background of Bhutan and its need for indigenous nation-building and absence of foreign domination.[10] Although the first three components have often played a major role in the development of indicators, this last component has been the least studied and the most contentious, especially on the adequacy of measurement of cultural factors. Each of these components is briefly introduced below, highlighting some of the challenges in translating these objectives into measurable indicators for public policy purposes.

Ensuring self-reliance through economic growth and development is perhaps the least controversial aspect of the framework. Yet, the geopolitical realities as well as the national security concerns in Bhutan may pose further challenges. In terms of indicators, the large size of the informal sector may make traditional per capita indicators somewhat biased. Official data on the total population seem to vary according to different organizations present in Bhutan. There have been reports on difficulties in obtaining registration of citizens that will need to be addressed.

In terms of environmental protection, some observers have pointed out inherent contradictions that have yet to be addressed, such as forest protection at the expense of agricultural development. One area of analysis for policy research is to examine how the selection of 60 per cent forest protection was achieved. In the name of GNH, forests need to be protected (72 per cent of land is covered by forests),[11] but this means less land available for cultivation and rural development. Indeed, 87 per cent of the population depends on 7.7 per cent arable land.[12]

On the issues facing environmental sustainability, Bhutan's environmental legacy encounters many favorable factors. First, the country is endowed with enormous hydro-electricity potential, due to its mountainous topography. Second, there exists an indigenous institutional system to manage common property resources such as irrigation water, wood lots, and grazing land. Third, between 1969 and 1981, important legislation was enacted and enforced in order to protect the environment. Finally, there is a strong culture of conservation and Buddhist ethics with respect to the environment.[13]

Many of the institutional and legislative structures necessary to ensure good governance in Bhutan have been in place for less than 10 years. A major initiative on the government's restructuring and democratic reforms occurred in 1998–9 and the administrative decentralization process a few years later. With the first local elections occurring in 2002 and the first election of a new National Assembly in the first quarter of 2008, it is relatively early to evaluate the efficiency of these newly established procedures and institutions. These decentralization and democratization processes also add significant pressures and needs for capacity building towards good governance, as will be discussed later.

Turning to cultural promotion, the GNH framework includes promotion of a strong sense of identity with the Bhutanese culture, for example, dress code, language, and religion. It is important to distinguish between the social and personal dimensions when studying the relationship between cultural heritage and 'happiness'. While indicators of cultural preservation would most likely address the social dimension at the country-level indicator, personal well-being may be showing different trends. Its measurement may require specific market research and surveys on life satisfaction, which would inevitably be subjective. It is not necessarily desirable to design indicators which avoid this subjectivity at the personal level. However, the challenge is to develop the indicator at the national level, which minimizes subjectivity in order to be comparable over time and across countries.

These four main components of the GNH framework were originally conceived as a guiding framework, but international pressure has gradually been put on making GNH internationally applicable and comparable, through the design of a GNH index. In order to capture the complexity of national development processes, many questioned whether it is wise to require that the indicator be internationally comparable. Others argue that the interesting challenge for academics and practitioners alike is to maximize the usefulness of GNH as an alternative framework for measuring well-being and how to design an indicator of GNH that can ultimately be 'maximized'.

A recurrent criticism of the GNH framework has been that 30 years after it was first introduced, the concept has yet to be 'operationalized' into a set of indicators, so as to measure progress towards its sets of objectives. A second concern is to develop a useful indicator to serve as a policy tool towards increased well-being for the Bhutanese. But should GNH be kept as a 'governing principle' as opposed to being represented as an indicator or a list of indicators? If it remains a set of governing principles, how useful is it for policy makers? This chapter looks into the extent to which, based on the GNH framework, a GNH index can provide the bridge between qualitative economics and measures of well-being and become a powerful policy tool.

The question remains how GNH is to be defined and used as an indicator that is helpful for policy makers. For example, how much weight to give to each component, whether GNH could be an improvement over the HDI indicator (which gives equal weight to health, education, and income as part of human development) and whether there is any possibility that the use of GNH may involve some conflicting policies. Some of the potential areas for further discussion would be to address the possibility of any missing components in the framework. Finally, another challenge may be posed if there are any inconsistencies between national and international indexes.

Despite the international hype about operationalizing GNH, there does not appear to be a real sense of urgency on the implementation of indicators and their implications on local policy makers. However, this situation is about to change with the recent formation of the GNH Commission, which demonstrates a new level of commitment on the part of the government.[14] The other influencing factors come from the socio-economic context in the country, as discussed next.

SOCIO-ECONOMIC DEVELOPMENT

This section analyzes the main socio-economic developments over the past 10–20 years. Starting with an analysis of Bhutan's sectoral growth and trade relations in the region and trends in Foreign Direct Investment (FDI), we then discuss key development issues based on poverty-related indicators and the MDGs.

Compared to other South Asian countries, annual GDP growth has been relatively stable, especially since 2003 (Table 2.3). During this period, the agricultural sector has been growing slower than any other sector, except in 1997 when the industrial sector suffered -1 per cent growth. In 2005 (the latest year available), the average growth rates for industry and services were 6.7 and 9.1 per cent, respectively. Relative to its neighboring countries, these sectors have been growing very well in Bhutan.

In addition, the sectoral composition of GDP indicates a structural change since 1996, where agriculture contributed 32.8 per cent of GDP in 1996 and only 22.4 per cent by the year 2006, whereas industry and services each contributed approximately 36 per cent in 2006 (see Table 2.4).

Bhutan is a founding member of the South Asian Association for Regional Cooperation (SAARC). The SAARC was established when its Charter was formally adopted on 8 December 1985 by the Heads of State or Government of Bangladesh, Bhutan, India, Maldives, Nepal, Pakistan, and Sri Lanka. Bhutan signed a Free Trade Agreement with India and a Preferential Trade Arrangement with Bangladesh and there are some initiatives to develop closer trading relations with Nepal and Thailand. In addition, Bhutan has also been a member of the Bay of Bengal Initiative for Multi-Sectoral Technical and Economic Cooperation (BIMSTEC) since 2003.[15] The seven member nations are planning for a free trade pact by 2017.

Since the early 1980s, Bhutan's exports in South Asia as a proportion of GDP have more than doubled, reaching nearly 26 per cent in 2005 (Table 2.5). In the past five years, India accounted for about 95 per cent of exports and Bangladesh has accounted for about 4 per cent of total exports, leaving less than 1 per cent for all other countries.. The major exports are electricity, timber, cement, fruits, precious stones, and spices. Its total export trade is just above US$500 million per year whereas imports totaled nearly US$1 billion in the early years of this century.

On the imports side, Bhutan imports principally from India, Japan, Germany, the United Kingdom, Singapore, South Korea and the United States. Its major imports are fuels, grain, machinery,

Table 2.3: GDP Annual and Sectoral Growth in South Asia, 1996–2006 (per cent)

Country	Per cent annual growth	1996	1997	1998	1999	2000	2001	2002	2003	2004	2005	2006
Bangladesh	GDP	4.6	5.4	5.2	4.9	5.9	5.3	4.4	5.3	6.3	6.0	6.7
	Agriculture	3.1	6.0	3.2	4.7	7.4	3.1	0.0	3.1	4.1	2.2	4.5
	Industry	7.0	5.8	8.3	4.9	6.2	7.4	6.5	7.3	7.6	8.3	9.6
	Services	4.0	4.5	5.0	5.2	5.5	5.5	5.4	5.4	5.7	6.4	6.5
Bhutan	GDP	6.2	5.3	5.6	7.9	5.5	7.2	10.0	7.6	6.8	6.5	7.8
	Agriculture	2.0	3.9	2.3	1.5	4.6	5.0	3.1	2.7	2.5	2.2	–
	Industry	5.2	-1.0	4.2	15.4	5.2	13.4	16.0	4.0	7.3	6.7	–
	Services	13.5	11.4	10.9	6.7	9.5	2.7	8.2	11.7	7.2	9.1	–
India	GDP	7.4	4.5	6.0	7.1	4.0	5.2	3.7	8.4	8.3	9.2	9.2
	Agriculture	9.6	-2.4	6.2	0.3	-0.2	6.3	-7.2	10.0	0.0	6.0	2.7
	Industry	7.1	4.3	3.7	4.8	6.4	2.7	7.1	7.6	9.6	9.4	10.1
	Services	7.2	9.8	8.4	10.1	5.7	7.2	7.4	8.4	9.6	9.9	11.1
Maldives	GDP	8.8	11.5	9.3	7.8	4.4	3.3	6.1	9.2	11.3	-4.1	18.7
	Agriculture	2.2	1.3	6.4	3.3	-0.2	5.0	17.0	1.6	2.7	4.0	4.3
	Industry	3.4	23.1	11.0	12.1	1.2	8.0	9.9	8.2	12.8	3.0	11.7
	Services	10.6	11.0	9.4	7.5	5.5	2.3	4.2	10.3	12.0	-6.2	21.7
Nepal	GDP	5.3	5.3	2.9	4.5	6.1	5.6	-0.6	3.4	3.7	2.7	1.9
	Agriculture	3.8	4.4	0.9	2.9	4.9	5.5	2.2	2.5	3.9	3.0	1.7
	Industry	8.8	6.5	2.3	6.0	8.7	3.2	-2.9	3.6	0.8	1.5	3.5
	Services	5.9	4.8	6.7	5.4	5.7	5.3	-1.3	3.4	4.8	2.4	-5.9

Pakistan	GDP	4.8	1.0	2.6	3.7	4.3	2.0	3.2	4.9	7.4	7.3	6.2
	Agriculture	11.7	0.1	4.5	1.9	6.1	-2.2	0.1	4.3	2.3	6.7	2.5
	Industry	4.7	-0.3	6.1	4.9	1.3	4.1	2.7	4.2	16.3	11.4	5.9
	Services	5.0	3.6	1.6	5.0	4.2	3.1	4.8	5.2	5.9	8.0	8.8
Sri Lanka	GDP	3.8	6.4	4.7	4.3	6.0	-1.5	4.0	6.0	5.4	6.0	7.4
	Agriculture	-4.6	3.0	2.5	4.5	1.8	-3.4	2.5	1.6	-0.7	2.5	2.5
	Industry	5.4	7.6	5.9	4.8	7.5	-2.1	1.0	5.5	5.2	6.0	6.0
	Services	6.0	7.1	5.1	4.0	7.0	-0.5	6.1	7.9	7.6	5.1	4.4

Source: WDI Online, World Bank, 2007a.
Note: –Not available.

Table 2.4: Sectoral Contribution to GDP, South Asia, 1996–2006 (per cent of GDP)

Country	Per cent GDP	1996	1997	1998	1999	2000	2001	2002	2003	2004	2005	2006
Bangladesh	Agriculture	25.7	25.8	25.4	26.2	25.5	24.1	22.7	21.8	21.0	20.1	19.5
	Industry	24.9	25.1	25.8	25.2	25.3	25.9	26.4	26.3	26.6	27.2	28.1
	Services	49.5	49.1	48.7	48.7	49.2	50.0	50.9	52.0	52.4	52.6	52.4
Bhutan	Agriculture#	32.8	33.0	31.5	29.2	28.5	27.1	27.7	26.7	26.6	25.2	22.4
	Industry#	34.2	34.5	33.6	36.3	35.2	37.9	38.6	38.3	39.0	38.1	35.9
	Services#	33.0	32.5	35.0	34.5	36.3	35.0	33.7	35.0	34.4	36.7	37.2
India	Agriculture	29.2	27.8	27.7	25.0	23.4	23.2	20.9	20.9	18.8	18.3	17.5
	Industry	27.4	27.2	26.5	25.3	26.2	25.3	26.4	26.2	27.5	27.3	27.7
	Services	43.4	44.9	45.8	49.7	50.5	51.5	52.7	52.9	53.7	54.4	54.7
Maldives	Agriculture*	–	–	–	–	8.8	–	–	–	–	–	8.4
	Industry*	–	–	–	–	15.0	–	–	–	–	–	16.7
	Services*	–	–	–	–	80.1	–	–	–	–	–	78.8
Nepal	Agriculture	40.5	40.4	38.8	40.1	39.6	38.3	39.4	39.1	38.6	38.2	39.5
	Industry	22.3	22.3	21.9	21.2	21.5	21.3	21.1	21.1	20.9	21.0	21.1
	Services	37.2	37.4	39.3	38.7	38.9	40.3	39.4	39.8	40.5	40.8	39.5
Pakistan	Agriculture	25.5	26.7	27.3	27.0	26.2	24.4	23.6	23.6	22.2	22.2	-
	Industry	24.2	23.5	23.8	23.7	22.6	23.1	22.9	23.0	27.0	26.5	20.5
	Services	50.4	49.8	48.9	49.2	51.2	52.5	53.4	53.4	50.8	51.3	26.7
Sri Lanka	Agriculture	22.4	21.9	21.1	20.7	19.9	20.1	20.5	19.0	17.8	16.8	-
	Industry	26.4	26.9	27.5	27.3	27.3	26.9	26.3	26.4	26.8	26.1	16.4
	Services	51.1	51.2	51.4	52.1	52.8	53.1	53.2	54.6	55.4	57.1	26.5

Source: World Bank (2007a).

Notes: # Data for 2006 from ADB, *Key Indicators 2007* and based on GDP at constant purchasers' prices.

*Data from ADB, *Key Indicators 2007.*

Table 2.5: Exports in South Asia as per cent of GDP, 1981–2005

	1981	1985	1990	1995	2000	2005
Bangladesh	3,7	4.4	5.1	9.5	12.7	14.7
Bhutan	13.3	11.6	27.0	34.8	23.6	25.8[r]
India	6,2	4.3	7.3	8.5	14.0	11.3
Maldives	–	8.8	16.3	13.7	14.1	17.0
Nepal	–	10.7[c]	–	19.0[k]	–	17.5[s]
Pakistan	10.5	8.0	12.4	13.5	11.7	12.8[s]
Sri Lanka	23.9	22.2	24.1	29.5	32.9	27.7

Source: SAARC, 2005.
Note: c: 1984; k: 1994; r: 2003; s: 2004.

vehicles, fabric, and rice. Within the South Asian region, Bhutan is hugely dependent on imports (Table 2.6). Moreover, about 80 per cent of it comes from India alone.

At the international level, Bhutan was granted observer status to the World Trade Organization (WTO) 10 years ago. Bhutan is now nearing conclusion of its accession process; however, most official works are temporarily on hold and will only resume upon the formation of the new government. However, the Ministry of Trade and Industry recently conducted a National Awareness Workshop and discussion forum with private sector participants organized with assistance from UNESCAP in June 2007.

Table 2.6: Imports in South Asia as per cent of GDP, 1981–2005

	1981	1985	1990	1995	2000	2005
Bangladesh	13.1	12.5	12.7	16.0	18.4	20.4
Bhutan	-45.4	-39.4	-31.5	-39.6	-46.6	-40.2[r]
India	9.8	6.5	9.9	11.5	16.6	15.7
Maldives	–	18.3	42.7	73.8	72.1	121.4
Nepal	–	19.4[c]	–	31.4[k]	–	31.3[s]
Pakistan	19.3	19.0	17.4	17.2	14.1	16.2[s]
Sri Lanka	41.7	31.1	33.2	36.9	38.1	38.7

Source: SAARC, 2005.
Note: c: 1984; k: 1994; r: 2003; s: 2004.

In terms of progress on bilateral and multilateral negotiations, the negotiation on the Offer in Goods is nearly resolved.[16] However, there are a few major areas that remain to be concluded related to the Offers in Services. Notably, Bhutan is currently TRIMS (Agreement on Trade-Related Investment Measures)[17] non-compliant due to foreign exchange restrictions on access to foreign exchange by FDI-related companies. All FDI-related companies are expected to meet foreign exchange requirements from their net foreign exchange earnings.[18] On the services offer, inclusion and greater commitments in key service sectors including construction, financial services, and distribution services are still in progress.

At present, the Bhutanese economy is heavily reliant on hydropower. Exports from that sector account for 45 per cent of total government revenues. This is especially important given the current process of decentralization of development expenditure to the districts and village clusters. Hence, Bhutan needs to expand the economic base and have export diversification which constrains foreign currency earnings and causes an over-reliance on external assistance, as discussed later.

Many internal barriers restrict private sector developments, such as the problem of high transportation costs, requiring higher levels of investments in basic infrastructure. Also, the high cost of banking transactions (and requirement of 300 per cent collateral by commercial banks) has been identified as a major constraint. Finally, there is a need to lower and rationalize the domestic interest rate to allow it to be more market-driven. They are still administratively determined, with borrowing rates as high as 15 per cent in the late 1990s. This will greatly help open up the private sector and allow for increased competition. As seen in Table 2.7, the net inflow of FDI has picked up since 2002, but its low level is a clear sign of the internal barriers the country needs to address.

Table 2.8 shows that the reliance on foreign development assistance has deepened especially in the past five years. This is not only due to the underdeveloped infrastructure, but also as a result of the geophysical characteristics of the country, where the sparse population in mountainous and difficult terrains hampers communication and access to basic services.

Table 2.7: Foreign Direct Investment in South Asia, 1995–2005

	Foreign Direct Investment, net inflows (US$ million)										
	1995	1996	1997	1998	1999	2000	2001	2002	2003	2004	2005
Bangladesh	1.9	13.5	139.4	190.1	179.7	280.4	78.5	52.3	268.3	448.9	802.5
Bhutan	0.1	1.4	-0.7	–	9.0	-0.1	0.3	0.3	1.1	1.0	0.8
India	2,143.63	2,426.1	3,577.3	2,634.7	2,168.6	3,584.2	5,471.9	5,626.0	4,584.5	5,474.0	6,598.0
Maldives	7.2	9.3	11.4	11.5	12.3	13.0	11.7	12.4	13.5	14.7	9.5
Nepal	–	19.2	23.1	12.0	4.4	-0.5	20.9	-6.0	14.8	-0.4	2.5
Pakistan	722.6	922.0	716.3	506.0	532.0	308.0	383.0	823.0	534.0	1,118.0	2,183.0
Sri Lanka	56.0	119.9	430.1	193.4	176.4	172.9	171.8	196.5	228.7	232.8	272.4

Source: ADB, *Key Indicators, 2007.*
Note: –Not available.

Table 2.8: Development Assistance/Official Aid in South Asia, 1981–2005

	1981	1985	1990	1995	2000	2005
Bangladesh	1,146	1,269	1,810.0	1,739	1,588	1,033[s]
Bhutan	76.1	94.1	59.3.0	52.2	18.1	108.9[r]
India	2,192	–	1,407.0	–	1,485	1705[r]
Maldives	21.4[a]	–	21.2	–	30.7	–
Nepal	180.6	234.0	426.0	432.6	389.6	427.3
Pakistan	–	–	1,129.0	–	732	1242
Sri Lanka	–	–	–	–	–	–

Source: SAARC, 2005.
Notes: a: 1980; r: 2003; s: 2004.
All figures in US$ million.

In terms of reaching the targets set within the MDG framework, the proportion of people suffering from hunger is still twice as much as the target of 1.9 per cent (Table 2.9). In the education sector, the achievement of universal primary education may be attainable, though there are questions about the quality of these services in more remote areas. Another challenge will be to increase the ratio of females to males in tertiary institutes. With regard to the health sector, although there has been considerable progress in immunization programs, the number of births attended by skilled health personnel is nowhere near the target, and contributes significantly to maternal deaths in the country. Finally, the proportion of people without sustainable access to safe drinking water and sanitation is also far below target.

Table 2.10 presents a snapshot of poverty and inequality in the region, for the latest year available. Based on the national poverty line, Bhutan is the second poorest country in South Asia. Moreover, the difference between rural and urban poverty rates is the highest in Bhutan, where urban poverty is about 4 per cent.

The Population and Housing Census of Bhutan 2005 reveals a clear pattern of urbanization where the districts of Thimphu and Chhukha have seen the highest rate of in-migration, with respectively 14.53 per cent and 15.71 per cent. In absolute numbers, the

Table 2.9: Status of Millennium Development Goals for Selected Indicators in Bhutan

Goals	Targets	Indicators	2004	2015
Eradicate Extreme Poverty and Hunger	Halve by 2015 the proportion of people living below the poverty line	Proportion of population living below national poverty line (per cent)	31.7	20
	Halve by 2015 the proportion of people who suffer from hunger	Percentage of population below minimum level of dietary energy consumption (2,124 (Kcal)	3.8	1.9
Achieve Universal Primary Education	Ensure by 2015 children everywhere, boys and girls alike, will be able to complete a full course of primary schooling	Gross Primary Enrolment Ratios (per cent)	84	100
		Proportion of pupils starting grade 1 who reach grade 5 (per cent)	94	100
		Proportion of pupils starting grade 1 who reach grade 7 (per cent)	86	100
Promote Gender Equality and Empower Women	Eliminate gender disparity in primary and secondary education preferably by 2005, and to all level of education by 2015	Ratio of girls to boys in primary school (per cent)	95	100
		Ratio of girls to boys in secondary school (per cent)	96	100
		Ratio of females to males in tertiary Institutes (per cent)	53	100
Reduce Child Mortality	Reduce by two-thirds, between 1900 and 2015, the under-five mortality rate	Proportion of children covered under immunization programme	90	95
Improve Maternal Health	Reduce by three-quarters, between 1990 and 2015, the maternal mortality ratio	Births attended by skilled health personnel	32	100
Ensure Environmental Sustainability	Halve by 2015, the proportion of people without sustainable access to safe drinking water and sanitation	Proportion of population without sustainable access to an improved water source	16	27.5
		Proportion of population without access to improved sanitation	7.4	17.5

Source: Millennium Development Goals, Bhutan, Progress Report 2005.

Table 2.10: Poverty and Inequality in South Asia (latest available year)

Country	Population in poverty (per cent) (National poverty line)[a]				Income[b] ratio of highest 20 per cent to lowest 20 per cent	Year	Gini coefficient[c]
	Total	Urban	Rural	Year			
Bangladesh	40.0	28.4	43.8	(2005)	5.0	(2005)	0.341
Bhutan	31.7	4.2	38.3	(2003)	7.4	(2000)	0.341
India	27.5	25.7	28.3	(2004)	5.5	(2004)	0.362
Maldives	21.0	–	–	(2004)	–	(2005)*	0.410
Nepal	30.9	10.0	35.0	(2004)	9.5	(2003)	0.473
Pakistan	23.9	14.9	28.1	(2004)	4.5	(2004)	0.312
Sri Lanka	22.7	7.9	24.7	(2002)	6.8	(2002)	0.402

Source: ADB, Key Indicators 2007; * Data from ADB report on Maldives: Country partnership strategy, September 2007.

Notes: – Not available.

a When available, official poverty lines are used. In some countries, no official poverty line is available, and data may have been computed by non-governmental agencies.

b Refers to income or expenditure.

c Derived from per capita expenditures from household surveys except for Fiji, Korea, Chinese Taipei, and Tuvalu, which are based on per capita, and Federated States of Micronesia and Tonga, which are based on per household income. However, the basis for computing Gini coefficients is unknown for Hong Kong (China) and Singapore. The reference year is the same as that for the income ratio.

lowest and highest figures on net-migration were respectively from the district of Trashigang with 8,407 fewer people and Thimphu with 20,629 more people.[19] Moreover, there seems to be a trend towards out-migration especially from the west, from the districts of Pemagatshel (-15.2 per cent) and Trashiyangtse (-14.89 per cent). This may be partly explained by the over-reliance on the public sector as the primary sector of employment for graduates.

Another implication of the rural-urban migration is that, according to the latest Labor Force Survey of 2006, the unemployment rate in urban areas peaked in 2006 at 4.9 per cent, bringing the national average to an all-time high of 3.2 per cent. Women are particularly affected, with an unemployment rate of 3.8 per cent compared to 2.6 per cent for men. The unemployment rate in the rural sector has reached 2.5 per cent, which may not reflect the presence of underemployment in the agricultural sector (see Table 2.11).

The economic development challenges described above highlight the need to streamline policies within and between the ministries and development programs. In particular, there needs to be better alignment between sectoral goals and the longer-term objectives contained in the GNH framework. As a consequence of the decentralization process and to avoid unbalanced regional development, tighter coordination between the various levels of government and among sectors should be prioritized. Other aspects of good governance requiring special attention are discussed in the next section.

Table 2.11: Unemployment Rate in Bhutan, 2001–6

	2001	2003	2004	2006
Unemployment Rate (per cent)	1.9	1.8	2.5	3.2
Rural	0.6	1.5	2.6	2.5
Urban	4.1	2.9	2.0	4.9
Male	1.3	1.6	2.1	2.6
Female	3.2	2.0	3.3	3.8

Source: Bhutan Labour Force Survey 2006.

GOOD GOVERNANCE

As defined by the Royal Civil Service Commission, good governance is guided by the principles of efficiency, accountability, transparency, justice, equality, and empowerment in order to meet the goals of peace, progress, security, and sovereignty; people's welfare, well-being, and happiness; and equal opportunities and rights.[20] As shown in Table 2.12, compared with other countries in the region, Bhutan's ranking on perceptions of governance is the highest in the region on four out of six indicators. On two indicators, voice and accountability and regulatory quality, Bhutan is ranked higher than Nepal and Pakistan but lower than India and Sri Lanka.

The trend of individual indicators for Bhutan in the period 1996–2006 is shown in Table 2.13. During this period, significant improvement is seen in the perception-based indicator of governance related to political stability made since the year 2000, from just above 60 per cent to the top 95 per cent of the participating countries. However, the government's ranking with respect to its effectiveness declined during that period, from a high of 78 per cent down to 66 per cent. Regulatory quality and voice and accountability are the weakest components relative to other indicators. Interestingly, despite the decentralization trend, the latter indicator has not progressed according to expectations. In terms of control of corruption, there has been a sharp improvement in ranking with a turning point in the year 2003. Finally, perceptions on the rule of law situation in Bhutan have steadily improved since 2003.

Good governance is strongly perceived as a prerequisite for the success of GNH and its impact should be felt in all five sectors: social, economic, environment, culture, and political. However, some critical issues need to be addressed. In the social sector, at the minimum, good governance implies free access to education and health for all. However, there are some problems with registration which hamper the promise of equal opportunity to all. Also, the quality and financial sustainability of these services in the more remote regions need further attention.

In the economic sector, given the overall goal of self-reliance, private sector development is a prerequisite, yet it remains under-

Table 2.12: Governance Indicators in South Asia, 2006 (percentile ranks)

Indicator	Bangladesh	Bhutan	India	Maldives	Nepal	Pakistan	Sri Lanka
Voice and accountability	30.8	22.6	58.2	20.2	13.0	12.5	36.1
Political stability	8.7	95.2	22.21	72.1	1.9	4.8	8.2
Government effectiveness	23.7	65.9	54.0	56.9	19.0	34.1	42.2
Regulatory quality	20.0	47.3	48.3	59.5	28.8	38.5	50.2
Rule of law	22.9	68.1	57.1	58.1	29.0	24.3	54.3
Control of corruption	4.9	80.6	52.9	39.3	25.2	18.0	36.1

Source: Kaufmann et al. (2007).

Table 2.13: Governance Indicators for Bhutan, 1996–2006 (percentile ranks)

Indicator	1996	1998	2000	2002	2003	2004	2005	2006
Voice and accountability	9.6	18.8	18.8	14.9	14.9	20.7	18.8	22.6
Political stability	74.5	61.5	61.5	64.4	70.2	74.5	87.0	95.2
Government effectiveness	64.5	73.0	78.7	69.2	69.7	64.0	64.9	65.9
Regulatory quality	47.8	42.0	37.6	37.6	56.6	23.4	49.8	47.3
Rule of law	7.6	61.4	59.0	57.6	63.3	63.8	66.2	68.1
Control of corruption	N/A	72.8	70.4	71.8	81.1	79.6	80.1	80.6

Source: World Bank (2007b).

developed. Also good governance implies sustainable economic development through renewable natural resources and infrastructure development. Yet, in the environmental sector, one of the main challenges is to maintain local institutions' autonomy in natural resource regulation and community-based management of these resources, including conflict resolution.

This will require balancing cooperation, competition, and control in the environmental sector in a relatively 'new' context of democratic community. Furthermore, this will in turn have a direct impact on the cultural sector, especially with respect to the preservation of traditions, social values, and the promotion of national identity and security. Finally, the guiding principle of good governance in the political sector is decentralization and community empowerment. The decentralization program initiated by the fourth and fifth kings needs to be a continuous process. They had personally visited and met with citizens in all twenty *dzongkhags* in an intensive consultation process with the people. Efforts to raise awareness of rights and responsibilities regarding the new Constitution, aimed at stimulating local institutions of decision-making, require a long-term and continuous effort from all levels of government.

Whether the GNH framework has the potential to become an international standard for good governance and an overarching goal for both developed and developing countries remains to be seen. But as GNH becomes a measurable objective, some policy changes may be needed in Bhutan. One of the biggest challenges in using GNH as a goal is to ensure that policies and priorities are compatible with the good governance framework. However, there may be sets of policies that conflict with it. There may even be a potential mismatch between public policy and the overall objective of GNH. This mismatch can take various forms if policy makers in Bhutan do not address these challenges promptly and appropriately.

For example, the GNH framework may affect or shape bureaucratic behavior creating a new type of competition within and between various ministries, as they try to tie in their activities with the GNH framework. This can give rise to conflicting policies that are made 'in the name of GNH'. Hence, although it is meant to streamline the development strategy, it may lead to an uncoordinated approach to development between stakeholders and between sectors. The dangers of indicator-led as opposed to strategy-led development must constantly be monitored.

There may also be an imbalance between efficiency and equity within the GNH framework. Several dichotomies can be highlighted given the socio-economic profile of the country, for example, land use versus environment conservation. Currently, about 87 per cent of the population depends on less than 8 per cent cultivable land. Policies need to be put in place so as to avoid the high social costs due to rural development pressures and the need to ensure food self-sufficiency. Ultimately, employment pressures in urban centers may put further stress on the government's meager financial resources.

Exogenous factors may also significantly affect Bhutan's success in implementing GNH as an overarching goal, despite the country's advantages of being relatively small and of having one of the most stable political situations in the world. First and foremost, Bhutan is highly dependent on foreign aid and investment. Second, it is extremely vulnerable to India's shifts in policies. Indeed, the high dependency on India, as Bhutan's major trading partner, means that a sudden weakening of the Indian Rupee would immediately hurt the trade balance and spark spiraling inflation in Bhutan. Third, whether the GNH framework can transcend regional economic destabilization remains to be seen.

Despite the challenges ahead, the Bhutanese expect to achieve sustainable development and ensure high levels of well-being for their people in a framework that goes beyond social, economic, and environmental aspects. This brings forth the need to address the implications on capacity-building for local leaders directly involved in the development process as well as enhancing institutional capabilities, as discussed below.

IMPLICATIONS ON CAPACITY-BUILDING REQUIREMENTS

The recent democratic process and the deepening of decentralization put much pressure on capacity-building both at the individual level (especially for community leaders at the district and sub-district levels) and institutional level. Adequate skillsets, access to relevant information, and appropriate mindsets are necessary for the empowerment and legitimacy of all participants in the decentralization process. This will ensure that qualified staff and institutions can efficiently perform their tasks and provide quality services.

Capacity-building efforts need to differentiate between three groups: those with executive powers, elected members, and those belonging to marginalized groups. Indeed, the economically disadvantaged group should receive a relevant type of capacity building, adapted to their basic knowledge and skillsets. This can be imparted via various actors and tools, including the media, educational institutions, government and non-government institutions, and also through cultural activities such as the use of drama and folk songs. Efforts towards capacity-building should be done in the residing areas of elected and mandated members and should not hamper their day-to-day life or affect their livelihood. An overarching goal is to address the vertical and horizontal integration of institutions.[21]

The use of information technology tools, for example, e-governance education, can help provide capacity-building to more remote areas.

Given the decentralization process and the participatory framework in which development plans are designed, basic skills related to budgeting, accounting, and computer literacy are essential. In addition, some communication skills in terms of facilitating focus group discussions and group meetings are also needed. In order to ensure a collaborative mindset, a continuous and sustained interface between the elected representatives and the local bureaucracy is required. This continuous process of discussion is an integral part of capacity building in terms of shaping appropriate attitudes when working within a consultative process. Finally, the elected local representatives need to be aware of their roles and responsibilities, and know how and where to obtain the relevant information. The representatives should be fully aware and understand the principles of good governance, the new decentralized mechanisms, the Constitution, and basic law.

At a broader level, educational institutions in Bhutan should incorporate the study of decentralization into their curricula. For example, students of public administration should be able to compare and contrast different models of decentralization and understand the various types of supporting mechanisms in decentralization. A strong element of ethics and values should be at the center of the curriculum. For this purpose, setting up schools of Local Governance catering to the population, civil society, and elected and mandated representatives is one way to provide an adequate academic set-up.

As for institutional capacity-building, the important aspects are being able to identify the right people to do the right task, including an understanding of staff requirements and how to enlarge the pool of eligible people. Also, local institutions must ensure that the recurring budget meets their functional requirements. Finally, there is a need for ongoing training of the establishment of that institution, including legal requirements and their functions so that it is executed efficiently.

The emerging democracy requires strong leadership and unity as well as stability on the economic and political fronts. But as the country opens up further to international trade, influences of increasing flow and extent of information will have a significant impact on its cultural values and national identity. The final section of this chapter highlights some of the major events that may shape the success of the decentralization, democratization, and development processes in the coming year.

CONCLUDING REMARKS

The economic and the political development of Bhutan have picked up incredible speed in the past few years. The government and the citizenry must have a full understanding of the distribution mechanisms that would ensure that every Bhutanese benefits from economic growth and development. This requires ensuring a clearly enunciated and realistic type of development, equitable and sustainable economic development goals, the identification of potentially conflicting policies with their goals, an understanding of the types of costs and risks involved in the policy choices, and a balance between development, security and human rights.

For this, the Bhutanese will not only need to ensure that the country makes use of its comparative advantage in its development strategy, but also to look back and see whether they have achieved their target and learn from past mistakes. For example, information gaps will need to be filled to generate relevant information for the development plans. Ultimately, this will require major efforts in addressing capacity-building needs so that all leaders are ready for change.

Finally, in the coming years, a few internal and international events will significantly affect the future economic and political developments in Bhutan. Internally, the National Assembly election in March 2008 had already raised security concerns in late January and early February 2008. For example, reports from the National Newspaper, *Kuensel*, mentioned some attempts at hampering the process as bombs exploded in five districts.[22] On the international scene, along with fostering economic growth, Bhutan's expected accession to the WTO will hopefully help improve business regulation and private sector development.[23]

NOTES

1. UNDP (2004:19).
2. Planning Commission (1987), Sixth Five-Year Plan, p. 2.
3. See www.pc.gov.bt .
4. Source: http://www.cmseducation.org/wconsts/bhutan.html accessed January 15, 2008.
5. According to the *International Herald Tribune*, 2 January 2008, 11 out of 15 were aged below 40.
6. *International Herald Tribune*, 25 March 2008.
7. The government of Bhutan has strict directives that political representation will not be based on socio-economic groups but based on the overall population in a district so as to avoid communal feelings and problems due to politics based on socio-economic groups.

8. The indicators included in the Index of Human Progress, with each sub-indicator weighted equally are: health (life expectancy, infant mortality, mortality of children under five and adult mortality rate); education (literacy, combined enrolment ratio); technology (television, radios, and telephones per 1,000 persons); and actual GDP per capita in US dollars. See Emes and Hahn (2001: 14–15).
9. HDPI defines an environmental factor measured in terms of CO^2 emissions from industrial processes per capita. The income variable in the HDI is then reduced by the environmental factor, penalizing those countries that have obtained growth in income at the expense of increasing CO^2 emissions. See Lasso de la Vega and Urrutia (2001).
10. Priesner (1999).
11. Dey (2003).
12. Ibid.
13. Dasho Bap Kesang (2004a: 6).
14. *Kuensel*, 'GNH takes centre stage', 19 January 2008.
15. Formed in 1997, the current member nations of BIMSTEC are Bangladesh, Bhutan, India, Nepal, Myanmar, Sri Lanka, and Thailand.
16. The revised offer for agriculture products stands at 57.5 per cent, whereas for non-agricultural products the revised offer stands at 35.7 per cent. Market access in goods now works out to an average of 37.9 per cent.
17. Trade Related Investment Measures.
18. Bhutan is currently under Article XIV Status with the IMF due to its unique reserves position, and thus requires remaining under transition until there are corresponding improvements in the sustainability of its scarce hard currency reserves.
19. Population and Housing Census of Bhutan (2005). Tables 4.1 and 4.2.
20. Dasho Bap Kesang (2004b), who is the Secretary of the Royal Civil Service Commission.
21. For example, in Pakistan, the setting up of a 'Devolution for Community Empowerment Trust' to facilitate the understanding of the new powers is a useful and easily replicable intervention that helped to build capacity of the community.
22. *Kuensel*, 4 February 2008. According to the *International Herald Tribune*, 21 January 2008, these bombings may be linked to the Communist Party of Bhutan based in Nepal.
23. Recently, the World Bank (2007c) ranked Bhutan's business regulatory framework 138th out of 175 countries reviewed.

REFERENCES

Asian Development Bank (ADB)(2007). *Key Indicators 2007*. Asian Development Bank, Manila.

Dey, Dipayan (2003). 'Community Forestry in Bhutan Himalayas: Sustaining Life and Environment through Participation'. Paper presented at the XII World Forestry Congress, Quebec City, Canada.

Emes, Joel and Tony Hahn (2001). 'Measuring Development: An Index of Human Progress', *Public Policy Sources*, No. 36. Fraser Institute Occasional Paper, Vancouver.

Kaufmann, D., A. Kraay and M. Mastruzzi (2007). *Governance Matters VI: Aggregate and Individual Governance Indicators 1996–2006*. World Bank Policy Research Working Paper 4280, Washington, D.C.

Lasso de la Vega, M.C. and A.M. Urrutia (2001). 'HDPI: A Framework for Pollution-sensitive Human Development Indicators', *Environment, Development and Sustainability*, 3, 199–215.

Planning Commission (1987). *Sixth Five Year Plan (1987–1992)*. Royal Government of Bhutan, Thimphu.

——— (2005). *Ninth Five Year Plan (2002–7): Mid Term Review Report*. Royal Government of Bhutan, Thimphu.

Priesner, Stefan (1999). 'Gross National Happiness—Bhutan's Vision of Development and its Challenges'. In S. Kinga et al. (eds.), *Gross National Happiness: Discussion Papers* (pp. 24–52). Centre for Bhutan Studies, Thimphu.

Dasho Bap Kesang (2004a). 'Gross National Happiness'. Presentation at the Institute of Public Studies, Singapore, 7 September.

——— (2004b). 'Good Governance in Bhutan'. Presentation at the Lee Kuan Yew School of Public Policy, Singapore, 10 September.

Royal Monetary Authority (2008). *Royal Monetary Authority Report 2006–7*. Thimphu, Bhutan.

Royal Government of Bhutan (2005). *Millennium Development Goals Progress Report 2005 Bhutan*. Department of Planning, Ministry of Finance, Thimphu, Bhutan.

——— (2006). *Population and Housing Census Bhutan 2005*. Thimphu, Bhutan.

——— (2007). *Bhutan Labour Force Survey 2006*. Thimphu, Bhutan.

SAARC (2005). *Poverty Reduction in South Asia through Productive Employment*. South Asian Association for Regional Cooperation.

Sen, Amartya (1999). *Development as Freedom*. New York: Alfred Knopf.

Sinha, C. A. (2001). *Himalayan Kingdom Bhutan: Tradition, Transitions and Transformation.* New Delhi: Indus Publishing Company.

UNDP (2002). *Millennium Development Goals Progress Report Bhutan 2002.* United Nations Development Programme, Thimphu, Bhutan.

——— (2004). *Joint Donor Database Report 2002.* United Nations Development Programme, Thimphu, Bhutan.

——— (various years). *Human Development Reports.* United Nations Development Programme, New York.

World Bank (2007a). *World Development Indicators.* accessible online.

——— (2007b). *Worldwide Governance Indicators by Country 1996–2006.* accessible online.

——— (2007c). *Doing Business in South Asia.* Washington, D.C.

3

The Pakistan Garrison State: Pre- and Post-9/11

ISHTIAQ AHMED

INTRODUCTION

PAKISTAN'S CHEQUERED 61-year history is replete with recurring military takeovers. In early spring 2008, however, after nearly nine years of rule under General Pervez Musharraf a transition to civilian, democratic government took place. Will the military desist from interfering in politics and staging another coup? Some clues to this question will be sought in this chapter.

THE PAKISTAN MILITARY AND THE GARRISON STATE

The Pakistan military is a voluntary service. It has a total active fighting force of nearly 650,000 and a reserve of more than half a million. The army is the largest service with 550,000 personnel; the air force has a workforce of 45,000; and the navy has 25,000 personnel (Siddiqa 2007: 59). Its defense expenditure claims nearly one-fourth of government spending. Besides conventional weapons, the military now has nuclear weapons at its disposal. Its professional readiness is not a matter of doubt. What is equally true, but politically problematic, is its domination over political institutions and civil society. This aspect of the military's pervasive influence has retarded Pakistan's evolution as a civilian polity and, therefore, calls for closer inspection. Several studies attest to the overwhelming power it wields in Pakistan (Alavi 1972; Aziz 2008; Faruqui 2003; Jalal 1991; Rizvi 2000; Siddiqa 2007; Siddiqi 1996).

The military (primarily the army but also the navy and air force) conventionally does not deny such a role, but asserts that Pakistan's integrity and survival is gravely threatened by its next-door neighbor, India (Khan 1967; Khan 1973: 1–4; Khan 1988: 8–17 and 135–40). The former Head of the Inter-Services Intelligence (ISI), Lt. General Asad Durrani described Pakistan as a 'Security State'.[2]

The same assessment was made by former Chief of Army Staff, General Mirza Aslam Beg, and Brigadier (Retd) Yasub Ali Dogar, the ISI Director on Afghan Affairs during 1991–2. Stating that Pakistan has to ensure its survival in the face of a constant threat posed to its security by India, all three pointed out that the latter country is much bigger in terms of population and territory; it initiated the nuclear weapons program in 1974, spends enormous amounts of money on buying arms, possesses one of the largest militaries in the world, and has been to war with Pakistan on several occasions, with the 1971 war resulting in the break-up of Pakistan. Consequently, Pakistan must maintain a credible defense against Indian designs. Emphasis was also laid on the additional burden on Pakistan caused by domestic incompetence and the corruption of the civilian government, as well as on threats posed by regional nationalists allegedly engaged in conspiracies to secede from Pakistan.

Stephen Cohen, who has written extensively on both the Indian and Pakistani militaries and security issues in South Asia, confirmed that for a long time the Indian leadership did not reconcile to the partition of the subcontinent.[3] Consequently, security and national survival became the top priority of all governments in Pakistan and, by virtue of that, placed the Pakistan military in the pivotal role to build up a credible defense. Such developments resulted in national security and survival becoming over time the *lietmotif* of Pakistan's official nationalism. This was exploited by the generals to establish a power structure that subordinated civilian institutions to the military's paternalism.

Considered in the light of such circumstances we can argue that Pakistan's development as a garrison state was facilitated considerably by American economic and military aid that started pouring in from 1954 onwards. The United States (US) began to provide military assistance to Pakistan because the latter committed itself to partake in the former's worldwide policy of containing Soviet Communism (Lohalekar 1991). After the fall of the Soviet Union, the alliance to contain Soviet influence has become redundant. On the other hand, after the terrorist attacks of 11 September 2001 by Al-Qaeda on several targets in the US, Pakistan has begun to be seen by its former benefactor as the fountainhead of global Islamic radicalism and militancy. Below we probe how these developments have affected Pakistan and the implications they carry for the garrison state.

The Concept of a Garrison State

The Merriam-Webster Dictionary proffers the following definition of a garrison state: 'a state organized to serve primarily its own need for military security; *also*, a state maintained by military power'. Most typically, a garrison state seeks its justification around the perception that an external enemy is gravely threatening the security of the nation. Harold Lasswell first proposed the concept of a garrison state in 1937, in the context of the Sino-Japanese war. In 1941, he elaborated his 'developmental construct' of the garrison state. It was a projection about the future course of world politics, which he believed could result in totalitarian societies even if democratic institutions continued to exist formally. The fact of war or the constant threat of it would result in the military elite acquiring greater importance and centrality in the provision of security and management of society. The distinctive characteristic of the garrison state in comparison to states ruled by the military in the past will be the close connection between modern technology and the military elite; only in advanced industrial societies could the garrison state consolidate because of the technical instruments at hand to control society in a totalitarian manner. He asserted:

> The military men who dominate a modern technical society will be very different from the officers of history and tradition. It is probable that the specialists on violence will include in their training a large degree of expertness in many of the skills that we have traditionally accepted as part of modern civilian management. (Lasswell 1997: 59)

Further, he argued, an officer corps recruited from a broad social base rather than the traditional narrow social base of ruling or aristocratic families would dominate the garrison state. The aim would be to create a large and competent military force dominated by a corps of officers that can provide a broad range of societal services besides security. The garrison state will strive to manage the economy and production so as to provide employment and other services but the aim will not be to create an active citizenry but rather its opposite: an obedient and docile population indoctrinated to believe in the inevitability of war and the need to maintain the garrison state. To carry out concerted propaganda and indoctrination in the 'socialization of danger', technology would be put to full use (Lasswell 1997: 64–6). As the garrison states grows stronger and more firmly entrenched:

> Decisions will be more dictatorial than democratic, and institutional practices long connected with modern democracy will disappear. This means that instrumental democracy will be in abeyance, although the symbols of mystic 'democracy' will doubtless continue. Instrumental democracy is found wherever authority and control are widely dispersed among the members of a state. Mystic 'democracy' is not, strictly speaking, democracy at all, because it may be found where authority and control are highly concentrated yet where part of the established practice is to speak in the name of the people as a whole. Thus, any dictatorship may celebrate its 'democracy' and speak with contempt of such 'mechanical' devices such as majority rule at elections or in legislatures. (Ibid.: 66–7)

Lasswell's fear that the garrison state could supplant civilian democracy did not transpire in the US. Democratic institutions survived notwithstanding the scourge of witch-hunting of suspected leftist intellectuals and public figures during the McCarthy era that lasted from the end of the 1940s to the end of the 1950s. In 1962, he re-examined the garrison state hypothesis in light of the fact that total war through nuclear weapons was a distinct possibility. He recognized that while the world was not 'moving soon into a world relatively free of the chronic threat of serious coercion, a policy that favored enhancing human dignity and thus "civilianism" in opposition to "militarism" could help in maintaining effective institutions of free society' (ibid.: 106–7). In other words, he wanted public policy to strengthen civilian hold over the state to obviate the garrison state emerging in the US.

In this regard, the contrasting attitudes of President Dwight D. Eisenhower towards, on the one hand, the rise of the military-industrial complex in the US and, on the other, his firm conviction that military alliances with other nations had to be built to contain Soviet influence in the world (Kux 2001: 51) are quite interesting. He warned that the obsession in the US with a nuclear attack by the Soviet Union and the spread of communism would 'turn the US into a garrison state, with an economy dominated by military spending and civil liberties eroded' (Schwartz 2005). On 17 January 1961, Eisenhower observed succinctly:

> This conjunction of an immense military establishment and a large arms industry is new in the American experience. The total influence, economic, political and even spiritual, is felt in every city, every State house, every office of the Federal government. . . In the councils of government, we must guard against the acquisition of unwarranted influence, whether sought or unsought, by the military-industrial complex. The potential for the disastrous rise of misplaced power exists and will persist.
>
> We must never let the weight of this combination endanger our liberties or democratic processes. We should take nothing for granted. Only an alert and knowledgeable citizenry can compel the proper meshing of the huge industrial and military machinery of defense with our peaceful methods and goals, so that security and liberty may prosper together.

Thus, while his government did not succumb to the growing power of the military-industrial complex, it simultaneously followed an active policy of garrison building all over the world. At present, the US has 860 military bases in 130 countries (Fuchs 2006). It also maintains alliances with authoritarian regimes headed by military strongmen. Moreover, it has constantly been engaged in armed conflicts and wars in many regions of the world, and its involvement in destabilizing governments that the US perceives inimical to its interests is also well known. The classic case is indeed Chile under Allende in 1973. After the terrorist attacks of 9/11, notes Lowell H. Schwartz, the garrison-state mindset has again revived in the US (Schwartz 2005).

The British Indian Empire: A Garrison State

Tan Tai Yong argues that British rule in India was mediated through a garrison state. The British were fully aware of the fact that they ruled India by the force of arms and could hold on to it for the same reason (Tan 2005: 23). Therefore, they needed to maintain a strong and formidable British Indian Army. Recruited locally but mainly under the command of British officers, the British Indian Army comprised select castes belonging to specific regions (ibid.: 57–97).

Moreover, from the second half of the nineteenth century, the fear of a Russian advance into India began to haunt British strategic planning. Because of its geographical location, the Punjab in north-western India became the natural frontline province from where the British partook in the Great Game against perceived Russian threats (ibid.: 69). Consequently, a strong, but dependent army with a large Punjabi component was raised. It was sent to serve in foreign lands and took part in both the First and Second World Wars.

The political linchpins of British rule in the Punjab were the Punjabi landlords, the vast majority of whom were Muslims. They were staunch supporters of the Raj. Pakistan inherited a large portion of that army and indeed the powerful Muslim landlord class of Punjab that had been loyal to British rule till almost the end of the colonial era (ibid.: 240-80). Consequently, Pakistan, asserts Tan, inherited the garrison state legacy in South Asia (ibid.: 296–309).

Post-colonial Garrison States

Now, Lasswell's observation that the garrison state could emerge in advanced industrial societies because of technical experts gaining control over government, economy, and other significant sectors of the polity and, thus establishing totalitarian regimes needs to be put into perspective. In developing societies, the technical elite is likely to be in the military while much of society may still be dependent on an agrarian basis for producing its livelihood.

The military elite can acquire control over the rest of society because of precisely the same reasons, namely, that it represents the most educated, well-informed, educated, and competent section of society. The theoretical literature of the period of military rule even suggested that the military was the agent of modernity and progress in poor, resource-deficient societies lacking a strong middle class and entrepreneurial skills (Huntington 1996). In such societies, the military branch of the state can emerge as the most powerful organization while democracy, if it exists, is brittle and precarious. Many garrison states emerged in Asia and Africa in the 1950s and 1960s (LaPorte 1969: 842).

Robert LaPorte, Jr. emphasized in his article entitled 'Succession in Pakistan, Continuity and Change in a Garrison State' that the chief attributes of Lasswell's garrison state, the specialists in violence dominating society and military dictatorships overthrowing elected governments, were salient in many Asian and African states (ibid.: 842). He examined the process of political succession that had developed in Pakistan, where the military had come to power twice, in 1958 and again in 1969. He observed that the military strongman, Field Marshal Mohammad Ayub Khan, candidly expressed disdain for civilian rule (ibid.: 843–5). With regard to the importance of a popular movement in bringing about the fall of the government of Field Marshal General Mohammad Ayub Khan in 1969, LaPorte was rather dismissive. He believed disgruntled military officers brought down the Ayub government, because of a number of economic and other grievances. Hence, his conclusion was that the military would play a decisive role in future political successions in Pakistan (ibid.: 851–61).

In the preface to his book, *The Military in Pakistan: Image and Reality*, Brigadier (Retd) A.R. Siddiqi gives a description of the Pakistan garrison state in terms that are very similar to Lasswell's description of that general concept. He writes:

> Since there is no other institution to rival the military in organization and discipline, above all, in its control of the instruments of violence, its image grows apace, and presently reaches a point of predominance and power where it becomes an object of mass reverence or fear. A sort of prussianism is born to produce an army with a nation in place of a nation with an army. The national

identity and interest is progressively subordinated to the growing power of the military image. (Siddiqi 1996: ii)

In several chapters of his book, Siddiqi provides empirical evidence to establish that through a range of inputs the military contrived to project the image of guardian of national interests but it bore the main responsibility for the political crises that hit Pakistan. The period covered is from 1947–71, but focus is on the processes that resulted in the break-up of Pakistan in 1971.

Mazhar Aziz (2008) adopts a similar position, deriving from institutional theory and the concomitant path-dependency it entails. The argument is that if civil institutions are not firmly anchored in the polity, the state apparatus represented by the military and the civil bureaucracy comes to dominate the political system. He argues further that the military has prioritized its own institutional interests over the interests of the nation. Ayesha Siddiqa (2007) has described such institutional interests as control over vast economic and financial sources through ownership of land, businesses, and industrial enterprises.

In a seminal essay 'The Post-colonial State in Pakistan and Bangladesh', Hamza Alavi (1972) suggested that the state in Pakistan was a continuation of the colonial imbalance between state and society, the former being more developed than the latter. As a result, the civil service and military constituted an oligarchy that dominated both politics and economics. International capitalism exploited the wealth or surplus produced by the Pakistani working class and peasantry through the oligarchy, which in turn received a share from that surplus. Alavi argued that the oligarchy enjoyed relative autonomy *vis-à-vis* the social classes and segments of society, which enabled it to mediate between their competing interests.

Alavi theorized within the influential dependency paradigm that informed leftist scholarship during the 1960s and 1970s. Such a disposition provided little room for the relative autonomy of the periphery from the center as the center was considered all-powerful and overwhelming. Consequently, Alavi too did not probe the possibility of the Pakistani state or rather the oligarchy being autonomous *vis-à-vis* the center of world capitalism, the US. However, a study of the political and military relations between Pakistan and the US calls for a more flexible and interdependent perspective, because the evidence below is indicative of greater leeway for Pakistan to maneuver its position in the international system in spite of an unequal relationship with the US (Cohen 1992: 9; Kux 2001).

It is important to note that where colonial empires were split, the leaderships of the nascent nation states sometimes claimed the same territory. Inevitably, disputes and conflicts ensued over territory, borders, and colonial assets between the successor states as happened between India and Pakistan; or, as in the case of the Israel-Palestine conflict, between a successor state and a rival nation denied full statehood. Notwithstanding regular elections, Israel has behaved like a garrison state, especially since 1967 when it went to war with the Arabs and occupied the West Bank and Gaza (Stanley 1997: 35; Stanley and Segal 1997: 132).

At the same time, all states can sometimes perceive a threat to their existence from external and internal sources. Historically, tension and conflicts have marred relations between states. States almost invariably maintain armies and weapons to defend themselves against aggression or to launch offensive actions on enemies. It is in the very nature of the beast, so to say, because the interests of states or rather their governments and power elites clash and that can end up in armed conflict (Morgenthau 1948; Waltz 1979).

Now, scholars draw a distinction between the terms 'threat' and 'threat perception' (Walt 1987). Whereas the former simply means the possibility of trouble or danger, the latter refers to how trouble or danger is sensed or felt. Pervaiz Iqbal Cheema writes, 'Perceptions can deviate from reality as a result of incorrect information or misinformation or factual distortion or because of the incumbent force of preconceived ideas and the professional bias of the perceiver' (Cheema 1990: 68). One can develop this argument further and say that the threat perception can be exaggerated or underplayed because those authoritatively defining and describing it can use their vantage position to manipulate the facts to serve their vested interests. Thus, for example, an exaggeration of the threat to national security can be used to justify heavier spending on defense or on the maintenance of a very large fighting force. At the bottom of all descriptions of threats to national security and survival is the claim by the military on the scarce resources the state has at its disposal. Security, it may be noted, is an effect of the threat perception (Walt 1987).

What sharply distinguishes the garrison state from ordinary security states is the diminution of civilian and democratic government in favor of military rule or at least military domination over civil institutions. Historically, the military in Pakistan has constantly increased its claim on national resources by maintaining the fear of aggression from India. This has translated not only into vast spendings on defense but because of lack of democracy and autonomous control over its activities, the military has acquired ownership of many businesses, thus becoming the most powerful corporate entrepreneur (Siddiqa 2007). Simultaneously, it has extended its influence and power to civil administration and politics.

However, given the underdeveloped nature of the overall economy and technological infrastructure, the post-colonial garrison state is unable to produce the weapons it wants or generate enough economic wealth to buy them. Therefore, in order to maintain a credible defense capability such states must at least initially enter into cooperation and alliances with powerful states to stimulate economic development and acquire military capability to thwart perceived or real threats to their security. We shall call them the donor and recipient states, respectively.

The donor state, driven by its own national interests, calculates that providing such help and assistance will furnish it advantage over the recipient state. A donor enjoying the status of a great power or superpower intends to use its advantage over the recipient state to realize its global and geopolitical interests. It provides weapons and training to the recipient state but not such that can be used to threaten its own interests and security.

In the process, connections between the defense establishments of the two countries are established. The ramifications of such connections are that they share and exchange information and intelligence. The routine contacts, common training in the same institutions, and training together for battle bring the officer corps from both the military establishments into close relations of both a professional and personal nature.[4] In this multifaceted networking, the connections between the elite forces on both sides especially acquire central importance. Nevertheless, the relationship remains ambiguous as both sides only share as much intelligence as they deem lies in their national interests.

Such a relationship, it should be reiterated, is unequal but not one-sided. In the international system, anarchy rather than order prevails because there is no authoritative center of authority from which a unified chain of commands emanates to which all states comply unflinchingly (Jackson and Sorenson 2007: 74–9). In addition, under international law states are in principle sovereign and this property helps them assert their autonomy. Consequently, even weak recipient states enjoy a degree of autonomy, because even when there are strong donor states (great states or superstates) that can impose their will on them, their ability to do so is oftentimes limited by circumstances. Moreover, dependent states can try to decrease their dependence on only one strong state; they may instead seek to diversify their sources of military and economic aid to enhance their autonomy.

Equally, the donor state may not enter into military cooperation or a proper alliance with only one recipient state. In order to increase its influence in a specific region it may try to develop friendly relations, a tacit understanding or even alliances with several states. These can include two rival states. Thus, while with Pakistan the US entered into a formal agreement to provide weapons, it also cultivated friendly relations with India, presumably to discourage too much reliance on the Soviet Union and to assure it of help against the People's Republic of China that India feared posed both a military and ideological threat to its security.

One can even say that the stronger the recipient state in relative terms, the greater its ability to act autonomously in relation to the donor state. Thus, middle-range powers are able to assert their autonomy more successfully *vis-à-vis* a stronger patron state than a weak one (Cohen 1992: 12–18). Additionally, if such a state has acquired nuclear technology and weapon capability, despite the opposition of the donor state, it can flex its muscle more defiantly.

This autonomy expands or contracts depending on the overall geopolitical context. The relationship being unequal, the patron state can ordinarily continue to exercise power and influence on the recipient state to alter the behavior of the client state according to its wishes.

However, even when their interests clash severely relations between the two states do not sever completely. The accumulated social capital that exists between them helps maintain communications, and efforts are soon afoot to restore good relations. Notwithstanding the ambiguities and uncertainties inherent in interstate defense alliances, if both sides calculate that they stand to gain more from it than without it, they are likely to maintain the relationship. Overall, of course, the great (or super) power in the role of the donor consistently enjoys far greater advantage over the dependent, recipient state.

MILITARY DOMINATION OF CIVILIAN GOVERNMENT (1947–99)

Pakistan emerged as an independent Muslim-majority state on the world map on 14 August 1947. The founding of Pakistan was a very different, if not unique, occurrence in modern history. It was not the usual type of territorial state with consolidated territory and an integrated population; West Pakistan and East Pakistan were separated from each other by more than 1,000 kilometers of Indian territory. Moreover, Pakistan inherited territorial and border disputes with its two immediate neighbors—India on its eastern border and Afghanistan on its western border—which have remained unresolved.

The internal power structure that devolved upon Pakistan in 1947 and was later consolidated contained asymmetries that considerably complicated its politics. Thus, whereas East Pakistan alone formed the majority of the total Pakistan population the locus of state power was firmly located in Western Pakistan especially in the Punjab. Within West Pakistan Punjabi domination of the civil bureaucracy and military generated resentment among its Pushtun, Sindhi and Baloch populations. Over the years, the Pushtun share in the state services increased but not that of the Sindhis or Balochis. Meanwhile a significant minority of the population of Sindh, the Urdu-speaking settlers known as Mohajirs, were always well represented in the civil bureaucracy and military (Ahmed 1998: 1735).

Given these peculiarities, not only nation building but also state building required extraordinary effort and skill. The political system was poorly developed to take upon itself such huge tasks. Moreover, neither in the West Pakistani provinces (Balochistan, North-West Frontier Province, Punjab, and Sindh) nor in East Pakistan was any industry worth the name to be found. The level of education was extremely low and overall social development poor. Pakistani society comprised rich landlords, a small intelligentsia, and vast millions of peasants, artisans, and other poor. On the other hand, a substantial middle-class was conspicuous by its absence. This difficulty was further compounded by the fact that the party that led the struggle for Pakistan, the Muslim League, became a victim of factionalism and intrigues. It split and dissipated soon after Pakistan became independent (Ahmed 1998: 173–4). Moreover, the death of the founder of Pakistan, Mohammad Ali Jinnah, on 11 September 1948 deprived Pakistan of its ablest leader at a very early stage of its formation.

Military in Politics

The military initially kept away from politics. Most of its senior officers, besides the top British chiefs, were trained in the liberal Sandhurst tradition (Cloughley 2000). In March 1951, Pakistan intelligence agencies claimed to have uncovered a plot hatched by some nationalist military officers in connivance with leaders of the Pakistan Communist Party to overthrow the government of Prime Minister Liaqat Ali Khan and establish a pro-Soviet regime. In ideological terms, the failed conspiracy was an aberration in that the general tenor of the Pakistan military was strongly anti-communist. Only a handful of officers were party to the conspiracy and the Communist Party had withdrawn its support in advance of it being carried out.

The news of the foiled plot was exaggerated out of proportion to impress the US. General Ayub Khan played the leading role in exposing the conspiracy (Cloughley 2000: 28–9; Venkataramani 1984: 151–4). On 16 October 1951, Prime Minister Liaqat was assassinated during a public meeting in Rawalpindi. The powerful civil bureaucracy, in an understanding with the military, subsequently began to assume a more authoritative role in Pakistani politics.

The first direct intervention of the military in politics took place in 1953 to restore law and order in the Punjab when mainstream Muslims attacked the controversial Ahmadiyya community. Despite putting up resistance in some places, the Ahmadis were largely victims of mob attacks. These attacks resulted in loss of life and property, mostly of the Ahmadis. A Court of Inquiry later established that the Muslim League government in the Punjab had been involved in fomenting the disturbances. Some of the leading trouble-makers were tried under court martial, found guilty, and sentenced severely, including the use of the death penalty, but were later pardoned (Court of Inquiry 1954).

Military Takeovers: The Evolution of the Garrison State

From 1947 to 1958, Pakistan had seven prime ministers and eight cabinets (Siddiqa 2007: 69). General (later Field Marshal) Ayub Khan was brought into the federal cabinet as Defence Minister in 1954. Constant political wrangling and palace intrigues had become endemic in the political system. General elections were never held and governments had become largely unrepresentative and were largely lacking legitimacy. On 27 October 1958, Ayub carried out a military coup. He abrogated the Constitution adopted in 1956 (but never promulgated) and became the chief martial law administrator and president of Pakistan. Many politicians were barred from politics and a promise was made to provide Pakistan with clean and efficient government. It was the beginning of a process of posting military officers to civilian positions in the administrations. In subsequent military takeovers, that trend continued to grow. Consequently, a convoluted paternalistic authoritarian type of government got entrenched in Pakistan.

During Ayub's early years (1958–9) the first armed conflict between regional forces and the central government broke out in Balochistan. The Baloch were opposed to allotment of agricultural land to military officers in the Pat Feeder area (Ahmed 1998: 186). In any event, Ayub introduced a presidential type of government under a new Constitution in 1962. The argument was that Pakistan needed a strong leader and the parliamentary system did not provide one. Moreover, it was argued that the presidential type of government was more in line with the pristine Islamic tradition of a caliph (Khan 1967: 205). He won the presidential election based on an indirect system of voting in 1964–5. However, his authoritarian policies and a stalemate war with India in 1965 set in motion a process that saw his popularity plummeting rapidly. A popular student agitation broke out in 1968 and soon engulfed the larger society. In March 1969, Ayub fell from power when the countrywide agitations would not abate despite considerable repression. Even the military considered it expedient to abandon him (LaPorte 1969). Ayub handed over power to General Yahya Khan.

General Yahya became the new president and martial law administrator of a caretaker government that would hand over power to the elected representatives of the people after general elections at the end of 1970. The first general elections in Pakistan's history were held in both wings of the country in December 1970. In East Pakistan, the Awami League led by Sheikh Mujibur Rahman won 160 out of the 162 seats in the 300-member National Assembly. The Bengalis of East Pakistan had developed, over the years, a deep sense of deprivation and exploitation at the hands of the Punjabi-dominated central government. The Awami League's election manifesto was patently anti-centrist and its implementation would have resulted in Pakistan becoming a weak federation (Ahmed 1998: 220–3).

Consequently, Yahya Khan refused to hand over power to the Awami League. Negotiations between the government, West Pakistani leaders, and the Awami League ended in deadlock. On the evening of 25 March 1971, the army launched a military operation against perceived targets of a growing insurgence. The Awami League was denounced as a secessionist party that was aided and abetted by India. The civil war that ensued for several months resulted in the deaths of hundreds of thousands of people, the majority being the Bengalis of East Pakistan. On 3 December 1971, the Indian army intervened and defeated the Pakistani army. East Pakistan broke away to become Bangladesh (ibid.; Arif 2001: 94–137; Niazi 1998; Qureshi 2004: 9–16).

The main victor of the 1970 election in West Pakistan, Zulfikar Ali Bhutto of the Pakistan People's Party (PPP), came to power in the truncated Pakistan, briefly as the president but then as prime minister. Bhutto had won elections on a leftist manifesto that included promises of food, clothing, and shelter. In 1973, the third Constitution was adopted by the Pakistan National Assembly. Article 3 stated the state's aim as 'the elimination of all forms of exploitation and the gradual fulfillment of the fundamental principle, from each according to his ability to each according to his work'. Such a commitment, along with land and industrial reforms that were also undertaken, greatly perturbed his ideological opponents, mostly with a conservative Islamist persuasion, the propertied classes, and the military. It set in motion a process that culminated in all major opponent groups closing ranks (Ahmed 1999: 230). In July 1977, Bhutto was overthrown after a prolonged nationwide campaign against him by the combined opposition who accused him of authoritarian and vindictive government. General Muhammad Zia-ul-Haq, a committed fundamentalist, staged the third coup (Arif 2001: 168–70).

Consolidation of the Garrison State

When Zia-ul-Haq captured the reins of power in 1977, a long tradition of relying on Islam to define national identity and the rights of citizens was already in place, although the fundamental rights of Pakistani citizens continued to be defined in general liberal terms. Under him, a dramatic expansion in the role of dogmatic Islam in the polity took place. He visualized a social order in which all sectors of life, including administration, judiciary, banking, trade, education, agriculture, industry, and foreign affairs, were regulated in accordance with Islamic precepts (Noman 1988: 141). In 1979, Zia announced the imposition of the Hudud Ordinance, that is, punishments believed to be laid down in the Quran for the offences of adultery (death by stoning), fornication (100 lashes), false accusation of adultery (80 lashes), drinking alcohol (80 lashes), theft (cutting off the right hand), highway robbery (when the offence is only robbery, cutting off hands and feet; for robbery with murder, death either by the sword or crucifixion) (Ahmed 1999: 231–7).

In 1980, the Islamic welfare tax, *zakat,* began to be collected from Muslim citizens. However, the Shias refused to pay *zakat* to what they alleged was a Sunni government. The government initially dismissed the Shia protest. It resulted in widespread agitation and finally, they were exempted from paying *zakat* (Ahmed 1999: 231-7). In 1984, a new Law of Evidence was adopted that reduced the worth of the evidence give by a female witness in a court of law to half in value of a male witness. The same year many restrictions were imposed on the Ahmadiyya group (already declared non-Muslims in 1974 by the National Assembly). They were prohibited from using Islamic nomenclature in their religious and social activities. In 1985, separate electorates were reintroduced (they had been abolished in 1956), whereby non-Muslims were to constitute a separate body of voters and thus entitled only to elect non-Muslim legislators to the various assemblies. Their right to take part in ordinary law-making was severely restricted.

In 1982 and 1986, so-called blasphemy laws were enforced which made any derogatory remark about Islam and Prophet Muhammad a crime that carried severe punishments, including capital punishment. Such measures helped to create a social and political environment that was patently oppressive of women, non-Muslims and other sects. Later, during the 1990s, Sunni-Shia sectarian clashes began to take place, resulting in hundreds of deaths (Ahmed 2005: 203–11).

During the same period, the military helped set up the Mohajir Quomi Movement (MQM) in the Sindh province as a counterweight to the PPP of the executed prime minister of Pakistan, Zulfikar Ali Bhutto. The Mohajirs constituted a compact minority of Urdu-speaking settlers who had migrated to Pakistan from northern India, mainly in 1947. Over the years, they came to dominate the urban areas of Sindh and especially Pakistan's main industrial base and port city of Karachi. During the late 1980s and well into the 1990s, ethnic terrorism by the MQM and PPP and other Sindhi nationalists claimed the lives of hundreds of innocent people (Ahmed 1998: 200–9).

General Zia was killed in a mysterious plane crash on 18 August 1988. The death of Zia created an opportunity for new elections, but the democratically elected governments that came to power could not complete their terms. Benazir Bhutto was dismissed twice as prime minister on corruption charges. In 1990, President Ghulam Ishaq Khan and, in 1996, President Farooq Leghari used the extraordinary powers acquired by the president through the Eighth Amendment enacted by General Zia. Similarly, her rival, Nawaz Sharif, was also dismissed twice. In the first instance, he was ousted on corruption charges by Ghulam Ishaq Khan in 1993. On the second occasion, the Chief of Army Staff, General Pervez Musharraf, overthrew him on 12 October 1999 to pre-empt the latter's bid to dismiss him the same day, and replace him with another general. Musharraf's period in power is examined later in this chapter.

PAKISTAN–INDIA RELATIONS (1947–99)

The roots of the bitter India–Pakistan rivalry can be traced to their painful and bloody birth through partitioning of British India into two separate states. Grievances about the distribution of the assets of the British Indian Army further compounded their bad relations. Pakistan received assets from the British Indian Army in the proportion of 64:36, India receiving the greater share since it was bigger in terms of territory and population in roughly the same proportion. Pakistan received 6 armored divisions while India received 14, 8 artillery regiments to India's 40, and 8 infantry regiments to India's 21. There was an acute dearth of officers and technically trained personnel (Cohen 1992: 17). Moreover, Pakistan claimed that it received outdated material, hundreds of tanks were never delivered and all the ordnance factories were left in areas given to India (Cheema 2003: 18; Khan 1993: 118).

THE FIRST WAR

In mid-August 1947, British colonial rule in the Indian subcontinent ended. The ruler of the princely state of Jammu & Kashmir (hereafter referred to only as Kashmir), Maharaja Hari Singh Dogra, a Hindu, had to decide whether to accede to India or Pakistan or remain independent. Some 80 per cent of his subjects were Muslim. All three options were technically possible, because unlike those territories that formed part of the British colonial state, the princely state could choose to remain independent (Ahmed 1998: 137–8). However, the general understanding was that the rulers should seek union with either of the two states. The main party in Kashmir, the National Conference, headed by secular-minded Muslim leaders, preferred closer ties with India, but pro-Pakistan forces in one of the regions, the Poonch Valley, mounted a revolt that was crushed ruthlessly by the Kashmir army (ibid.: 141–3).

In these circumstances, tribal forces backed by Pakistani regulars entered Kashmir on the night of 21–22 October 1947 with a view to liberating it and making it join Pakistan. The Maharaja decided to sign the bill of accession with India. The two sides fought a small-scale though protracted war in Kashmir. On 1 January 1949, a ceasefire brokered by the United Nations (UN) came into effect with both sides maintaining control over the territory they had acquired during the various battles—approximately two-thirds stayed within India and the rest went to Pakistan. Subsequent Security Council resolutions called for a plebiscite, but were never implemented because India claimed that they had become redundant after 1954 when the Kashmir Assembly voted in favor of permanent merger with India (Subrahmanyam 1990: 170–80). Pakistan did not accept the elections to the Kashmir Assembly as valid and representative (Ahmed 1998: 137). The Kashmir problem became a lasting source of ill will between the two countries.

The Second War

In 1951, the Indian military carried out military exercises close to the Pakistan border, which the latter considered threatening (Cloughley 2000: 28–32). However, a few years later, some peace overtures were also made. Thus, for example, Ayub proposed joint defense in 1959 but it was spurned by Nehru. In 1964, however, Nehru, badly shaken by a defeat in the border war with China, sent the Kashmiri leader, Sheikh Abdullah of the National Conference to Pakistan to find out if some agreement on Kashmir could be reached. While Abdullah was in Pakistan, Nehru died. The peace initiative was put on hold.

In March 1965, India and Pakistan were drawn into a border skirmish in the remote marshy region known as the Rann of Kutch near the Sindh border. Apparently, the Pakistanis outclassed their Indian counterparts in the battles that took place (Khan 1993: 163–6). In the summer of 1965, Pakistan launched Operation Gibraltar, a major military adventure that ended in a full-fledged war with India. It was masterminded by the then foreign minister of Pakistan, Zulfikar Ali Bhutto, the foreign secretary Aziz Ahmed and Maj. General Akhtar Hussain Malik (Arif 2001: 46–9). It began with Pakistan dispatching agents into Indian-administered Kashmir to instigate a popular uprising. However, the Kashmiris showed little enthusiasm for the Pakistani initiative. Pakistani regular forces crossed the Line of Control at Chamb; in retaliation, Indian troops crossed the international border near Lahore on 6 September 1965 and the conflict escalated into a full-scale war which raged for more than a fortnight. A ceasefire ordered by the UN Security Council brought hostilities to an end on 23 September.

The 17-day war greatly accentuated anti-India feelings in Pakistan. Government propaganda portrayed India as the aggressor, ignoring the fact that it had sent infiltrators into Indian Kashmir. Much to the chagrin of Pakistan, which had allied itself with the US, the latter imposed an arms embargo on both India and Pakistan. The Soviet Union and the US invited President Ayub Khan and Prime Minister Lal Bahadur Shastri to meet and discuss their problems. The two met in Tashkent in 1966. However, no progress was made on the Kashmir question.

The Third War

The third war between India and Pakistan took place on 3 December 1971 when the Indian army intervened in the ongoing civil war in East Pakistan. The Pakistan army was quickly defeated as its links with West Pakistan were completed severed. On 17 December the Pakistan army surrendered and 93,000 of its troops were taken prisoners of war (POWs) by India. In the summer of 1972, President Bhutto and Prime Minister Indira Gandhi met at the Indian hill station, Shimla. The discussions resulted in the Shimla Agreement. Besides the POWs, some 12,893 square kilometers of Pakistani territory on the western border was also returned to Pakistan. Both sides agreed to settle their differences by peaceful means through bilateral negotiations.

Article 4 (ii) stated,

> In Jammu and Kashmir, the line of control resulting from the ceasefire of 17 December 1971 shall be respected by both sides without prejudice to the recognized position of either side. Neither side shall seek to alter it unilaterally, irrespective of mutual differences and legal interpretations. Both sides further undertake to refrain from the threat or the use of force in violation of this Line.

Article 6 stated,

> . . . the representatives of the two sides will meet to discuss further the modalities and arrangements for the establishment of durable peace and normalisation of relation, including . . . a final settlement of Jammu and Kashmir. . .
>
> However, soon afterwards, both sides returned to their intransigent positions and put conflicting interpretations on the Shimla Agreement. (Ahmed 1998: 148–9)

Nuclear Test Explosions

An arms race between India and Pakistan in conventional terms had been going on for a long time but, after India exploded a nuclear device in 1974, Pakistan resolved to produce its own nuclear weapon at all costs. In 1998, the Hindu nationalist party, the Bharatiya Janata Party (BJP), won the elections and formed the government. On 11 and 13 May 1998, India detonated altogether five nuclear devices. On 28 and 30 May, Pakistan conducted six nuclear test explosions. However, Prime Minister Atal Behari Vajpayee made friendly overtures to Nawaz Sharif who invited him to visit Lahore, the capital of the Pakistani Punjab. Both signed the Lahore Declaration on 21 February 2001. The Lahore Declaration obliged both sides to seek a peaceful solution to their disputes (Lahore Declaration 1999).

The Kargil Showdown

In May 1999, General Pervez Musharraf and some of his colleagues masterminded a maneuver that resulted in some unoccupied posts at Kargil on the Indian side of the Line of Control in Kashmir being taken by men sent by Pakistan. It precipitated a bloody showdown between them and Indian troops (Mazari 2003). Direct and indirect threats of using nuclear weapons were issued at least 13 times by Indian and Pakistani officials (Ramana 2006: 1). According to Indian sources, the Kargil conflict claimed nearly 1,300 Indian and Pakistani lives while Pakistani estimates put the figure at over 1,750 (Bidwai 2006: 52). Prime Minister Sharif complained that Musharraf kept him in the dark about the Kargil operation. Sharif went to the US to seek the intervention of President Clinton to end the conflict. Clinton put him under great pressure to order a withdrawal of the men who had occupied the Indian posts, which he did forthwith. Musharraf was later to write in his autobiography, *In the Line of Fire* (2006: 87–98), that Sharif was in the know about the whole operation, and that he should not have given in to American pressure without exacting some concessions on Kashmir because Pakistan had gained the upper hand at Kargil.

In any event, a rift between Sharif and Musharraf took place, which culminated in the military coup of 12 October 1999. Sharif was exiled to Saudi Arabia for ten years.

US–PAKISTAN RELATIONS 1947–1979

There is evidence to suggest that before transferring power to India and Pakistan, the British military wanted to co-opt Pakistan into their strategy of retaining a foothold in the Indian subcontinent (Sarila 2005). In a meeting held on 12 May in London, the chiefs of staff of various branches of the armed forces, with the Royal Air Force's Marshal Lord Tedder in the chair, and in the presence of Field Marshal Montgomery and Lord Ismay, it was observed:

> From the strategic point of view there were overwhelming arguments in favour of Western Pakistan remaining within the Commonwealth, namely, that we should obtain important strategic facilities, the port of Karachi, air bases and the support of the Moslem manpower in the future. . . A refusal of an application to this end would amount to ejecting loyal people from the British Commonwealth, and would probably lose us all chances of ever getting strategic facilities anywhere in India. . . From a military point of view, such a result would be catastrophic. (Mansergh and Moon 1981: 791–2)

However, Britain's role as a great power in South Asia diminished quickly after the transfer of power to India and Pakistan. The new leader of the Western world, the US, had taken a keen interest in the Indian freedom struggle. It was not in favor of the partitioning of India, but once India and Pakistan emerged as separate states, it exchanged messages of goodwill with both (Kux 2001: 7–16).

The Pakistan government began at an early date to make overtures to the Americans to consider it as an ally against communism and the Soviet Union. The founder of Pakistan, Mohammad Ali Jinnah, made this known on 7 September 1947 in a cabinet meeting: 'Pakistan [is] a democracy and communism [does] not flourish in the soil of Islam. It [is] clear therefore that our interests [lie] more with the two great democratic countries, namely the United Kingdom and the US, rather than with Russia' (ibid.: 20). Pakistan requested military aid to the tune of US$510 million but it was rejected.

At that time, South Asia did not figure as an important region for the US. When India and Pakistan fought in Kashmir, the US imposed an arms embargo on both. President Truman urged the two governments to work together in the interest of peace and to move forward with their social and political progress (ibid.: 30). In mid-1949, Truman invited Indian Prime Minister Jawaharlal Nehru to visit the US but a similar invitation was not extended to his Pakistani counterpart, Liaqat Ali Khan. Pakistan countered it by getting itself invited by the Soviet Union, even when the two countries had not established embassies in each other's capital and their relations lacked warmth.

Adroit diplomatic maneuvering by Pakistan resulted in an American invitation. Liaqat visited the US in May 1950. In response to a question from a reporter about how large a standing army Pakistan wanted to have, he said it depended on Washington's intentions: 'If your country will guarantee our territorial integrity, I will not keep any army at all' (ibid.: 35). During the same trip, Pakistan supported the US position on Korea, but when a tangible request to send troops as part of the UN contingent was made, Liaqat found a way out by saying that 'as long as Pakistan felt threatened by India, he could not commit his country's limited security resources for other causes' (ibid.: 38).

It was the army chief, General Mohammad Ayub Khan, who took the initiative to woo the US to co-opt Pakistan in its strategy to contain Soviet influence (Cheema 1990: 146–8). In the autumn of 1951, a Pakistan mission arrived in Washington to seek arms, but since Pakistan had not sent troops to Korea, the Americans were not forthcoming with any major commitment. The foiling of a pro-Soviet military coup in Pakistan in March 1951 by General Ayub Khan had gained him admirers in the US administration. In late 1951, Henry Byroade became the US regional assistant secretary. He was more sympathetic to Pakistani overtures. He began to think that a 'defense arrangement extending from Turkey to Pakistan—a geographical arch of Muslim, but mainly non-Arab, states—bolstered by small amounts of military assistance from the US, would help stabilize the region and make it less vulnerable to Soviet inroads' (Kux 2001: 47).

However, it was only after January 1953 when Eisenhower was elected president of the United States that Pakistan began to receive significant attention in US strategic thinking. Eisenhower advocated building collective security pacts to contain the Soviet bloc (Cheema 1990: 145). His secretary of state, John Foster Dulles, was also convinced about the need to contain 'Godless Communism'. Both found Pakistan amenable to their worldview. In May 1953, Dulles visited India and Pakistan. In their meeting with him, the Pakistani leaders 'stressed their allegiance to the anticommunist cause and emphasized Pakistan's desire to join the free world's defense team' (Kux 2001: 55). General Ayub gave a strategic assessment of Pakistan's situation to the US secretary of state fashioned on the classic Great Game doctrine, and highlighted 'the possibility of a massive Soviet invasion through the warm waters of the Arabian Sea. The proposed reform was an expanded Pakistani army properly equipped for the task of blocking the Soviets' (ibid.: 55). He spoke enthusiastically of the Pakistan government's willingness to cooperate with the supply of manpower and bases (ibid.: 55). In order to allay US concerns about the impact on India, Ayub argued, 'If Pakistan were strengthened by US economic and military aid, it would result in India dropping its intransigent position attitude [on Kashmir]' (ibid.: 55).

Upon his return to Washington, Dulles gave a very favorable impression of Pakistan. He claimed to have been impressed by the 'martial and religious qualities of the Pakistanis' (ibid.: 56). In contrast he found India's Prime Minister Nehru to be an 'utterly impractical statesman' (ibid.: 56). Thereafter a process was set in motion which culminated in Pakistan being described as the United States' 'most allied ally in Asia' (ibid.: 70).

Defense Agreement and Military Pacts

The cumulative effect of such interactions and overtures was that a US–Pakistan Mutual Defense Agreement was eventually signed on 19 May 1954. It was laid down that the US would provide Pakistan with 'equipment, materials and services or other assistance' that would be consistent with the Charter of the United Nations.

In this regard, Clause 2 of Article 1 is particularly interesting. It reads:

> The Government of Pakistan will use this assistance exclusively to maintain its internal security, its legitimate self-defence, or to permit it to participate in the defence of the area, or in United Nations collective security arrangements and measures, and Pakistan will not undertake any act of aggression against any other nation. The Government of Pakistan will not, without prior agreement of the Government of the US, devote such assistance to purposes other than those for which it was furnished. (Jain 2007: 303)

In this bilateral agreement there was explicit mention neither of the defense agreement being a part of the overall anti-communist military strategy of the US nor that the material and equipment Pakistan would receive should not be used in a war against India. Meanwhile, some Republicans, such as Nixon, were of the view that arming Pakistan should be used to marginalize Nehru (Kux 2001: 62). The Indian prime minister's active participation in the Non-Alignment Movement clearly irked the conservative sections of the US power elite. On the other hand, the US wanted to keep military aid at a modest level, somewhere between US$29 million and US$30 million, because South Asia continued to be considered peripheral to the containment of the Soviet Union. This was very different from the expectations of the Pakistanis, who expressed deep disappointment. Robert McMahon notes:

> A gaping chasm existed between the free-flowing dollars that Pakistani military officers and bureaucrats conjured up as their just reward for open alignment with the West and the modest dollar figures contemplated by Washington planners. (Kux 2001: 67)

Constant lobbying by Pakistan that it was willing to play an important role in containing Soviet influence in the Middle East as well as in South-East Asia impressed Eisenhower and Dulles. Finally, besides a steep increase in economic aid, a total defense program costing US$171 million was offered in a secret *aide-memoire.* It was to equip 4 army infantry and 1.5 armored divisions; provide aircraft for 6 air force squadrons; and supply 12 vessels for the navy (ibid.: 69).

Pakistan joined the Baghdad Pact in 1955 and its successor, the Central Treaty Organization, in 1959. It had joined SEATO in 1955. These military pacts were sponsored by the US but Washington only became a formal member of the Southeast Asia Treaty Organization (SEATO). From the Pakistani point of view, membership in such pacts was to be seen as indicative of a willingness to play the role of a frontline state in the campaign against the Soviet Union in case of aggression by the latter. As a result, Pakistan was indeed increasingly treated as relevant to the Eisenhower-Dulles Doctrine propounded in 1957 to contain Soviet influence in the Middle East. There is some evidence that the first military coup of 1958 by Ayub Khan was endorsed by the Eisenhower administration, although the US apparently expected that this support would help pave the way for the development of democracy (Aziz 2008: 43).

United States–Pakistan Agreement of Cooperation

The US–Pakistan agreement of 5 March 1959 obliged the US to take appropriate action, including military action, in case of aggression against Pakistan. The agreement had been negotiated within the framework of the US' overall commitment to promote peace and stability specifically in the Middle East. A few weeks later, on 6 May, Secretary of Defense, Neil H. McElroy, in a hearing before the Senate Committee for Foreign Relations, made it clear that such an agreement should not be construed to include military aid or intervention in case of an India–Pakistan war. He stated:

> So the Pakistan military assistance program is geared to preparing Pakistan to defend against aggression from the north and is not in relationship to any possibility of conflict with India. . . . This defense, of course, is not against India. This is allocated to Pakistan for defense against Russia and China. (Jain 2007: 35)

On 1 May 1960, the Soviet Union shot down an American U-2 reconnaissance aircraft that had taken off from the Badaber Airbase near Peshawar in northern Pakistan. The pilot, Gary Powers, was captured. The Soviet Union threatened to punish Pakistan severely if it allowed further such flights from its territory. Notwithstanding such close cooperation with Pakistan, a tilt towards India in US policy became noticeable when John F. Kennedy of the Democratic Party defeated the Republican candidate, Richard Nixon, vice-president under Eisenhower. A border war between China and India in 1962 served as the occasion for India and the US to come closer. The Indians were badly defeated in that conflict. Nehru pleaded not only for military aid but also for direct US intervention in the conflict to halt the advancing Chinese army. The Chinese advanced some distance beyond the disputed border but then withdrew. This way, a major conflagration was avoided. On the other hand, thenceforth, the US began to offer economic and military aid to India on a significant scale (Kux 2001: 136).

On the other hand, during the 1965 India-Pakistan war, the US under another Democratic president, Lyndon B. Johnson, imposed an arms embargo on both India and Pakistan. The latter protested as its fighting machine was almost entirely dependent on American supplies. In his autobiography, *Friends Not Masters* (1967), Ayub expressed disappointment that India, a neutral state, was given greater attention by the US while Pakistan, an ally, was not. He expressed this succinctly: 'By this time it was becoming clear to us that, in the event of India attacking us, it was most unlikely that the US would honor its commitment to come to our assistance' (ibid.: 153).

It is, however, important to point out that during the 1971 India–Pakistan war, President Nixon warned Indian Prime Minister Indira Gandhi not to invade West Pakistan. Thus, while East Pakistan separated and became Bangladesh, West Pakistan survived as a truncated Pakistan. Earlier, in July 1971, Pakistan had helped facilitate a secret visit by Secretary of State Henry Kissinger to China, which set in motion a process that later helped normalize relations between the US and Communist China (Khan 2006).

Pakistan Diversifies its Military Strategy

While remaining an ally of the US, Pakistan had since the mid-1950s been trying to improve relations with China. The former had seen such developments with some reservations but since

Pakistan played a central role in brokering contacts between it and China, and a split between the Soviet Union and China was emerging, the US did not strongly oppose the liaison between Pakistan and China. The Sino–Indian war of 1962 brought China and Pakistan even closer. They reached an agreement in 1963 on the demarcation of their international border. Pakistan conceded some territory to the Chinese from areas of Kashmir under its control. Both agreed on building a road connecting China's Muslim-majority Xingjian Province with Pakistan's northern region. A trade agreement was also signed. Pakistan Foreign Minister, Zulfikar Ali Bhutto, was the main architect of this policy of developing a closer understanding with China (Bhutto 1969).

But, more significantly, after the 1965 war Pakistan began to acquire, in increasing measure, Chinese arms, including aircraft. China is also believed to have rendered considerable assistance to Pakistan in its nuclear program (Burr 2004). Moreover, Pakistan started buying arms from other Western nations such as France, and, by allying itself with Saudi Arabia in the 1970s, it managed to procure much-needed economic aid and other assistance. The close relations with Saudi Arabia facilitated the migration of an increasing number of Pakistani workers to that country and the Gulf States. More importantly, the Pakistan military also became involved in providing security to these states. Consequently a large number of Pakistani troops were stationed in Saudi Arabia and elsewhere in the Gulf region (Ahmed 1998: 177). There can be little doubt that such close connections with the Saudis resulted in the spread of the extremist Wahabi ideology in Pakistan and influenced the Pakistani state institutions, particularly the large body of military personnel that served in that country. As in the case of close collaboration with the US a similar relationship with Saudi Arabia established networks between the Saudi and Pakistani military establishments.

The Soviet intervention in Afghanistan in 1979 saw Pakistan's erstwhile role as a frontline state in the US strategy to contain the spread of communism come back to life with unprecedented zeal. The governments of the two countries and that of Saudi Arabia closed ranks together into a grand alliance to repulse the Red Army.

THE AFGHAN JIHAD

An interesting feature of the ethnic structure of the Pakistan military machine is that 75 per cent of the army continued to be recruited from the Punjab and North-West Frontier Province (NWFP), as was the case during the colonial period. The recruitment continues to be restricted largely to the districts of Rawalpindi, Jhelum, and Attock (earlier called Campbellpur) in the Punjab, and Kohat and Mardan in the NWFP. Together, they represent only 9 per cent of the male population of Pakistan and, therefore, the army is not representative of the total ethnic and linguistic diversity of Pakistan (Cohen 1992: 44).

One can add that officers from Urdu-speaking backgrounds, popularly known as Mohajirs (refugees from India), such as General Pervez Musharraf, are also found in small numbers. In any event, after the 1965 war Pakistan embarked on rapid expansion and upgrading of its armed forces. Less elitist criteria were introduced for the officer ranks. Consequently, people from traditional backgrounds with a strong Islamic orientation began to find their way into the officer grade. The defeat of 1971 and the loss of East Pakistan traumatized not only the West Pakistanis but also played a major role in the radicalization of the military along ultranationalist and Islamic lines. Nothing confirmed better the self-fulfilling prophesy that India was an enemy hell-bent on destroying Pakistan.

Although a symbolic connection to Islamic identity of the military had started with the creation of Pakistan, it was not until General Zia came to power in 1977 that a patently fundamentalist environment in the military began to be cultivated (ibid.: 86–104). In this regard, Brigadier S.K. Malik's *The Quranic Concept of War* (1979), which includes a foreword by Zia, is an interesting work in which the author argues that jihad (holy war) is obligatory upon Muslims so as to spread the Word of God, but that peace temporarily can be established by treaty with pagans. He emphasizes the need to 'strike terror in the hearts' of the enemy but not to attack the old, women, and children. Verses from the Quran supporting such a thesis are quoted at length. It is a typical amalgam of extreme dogmatism tempered by concerns to present the Islamic theory of war as just and righteous.

Another book elaborating on the Islamic principles of war is *Pakistan Army Green Book: . . . Year of the Commanding Officer 1991*. It is replete with verses from the Quran and examples from the life of Prophet Muhammad and his pious successors in their role as ideal military leaders and administrators. The book comprises a large number of short essays by officers from the rank of Major-General to Lieut. Colonel on various aspects of modern warfare. Most of them profusely cite Islamic sources to argue their position. In the literature used in the syllabus at Quetta Staff College for officers, Islamic writings figure prominently and wars with India are referred to as the basis for constant vigilance and preparation for war.

It is estimated that at the beginning of the twenty-first century some 30 per cent of the officer corps comprised hardcore Islamists (Nordland 2002). In particular, the intelligence agencies were dominated by Islamists. In 1995, Major-General Zaheer Abbasi plotted a coup against Prime Minister Benazir Bhutto. The plan was to establish an Islamic state. The plot was foiled and Abbasi received 14 years in prison (Nordland 2002). In this regard it is important to bear in mind that in the 1980s, when Sikh separatists launched a secessionist movement to break out of India, they were covertly provided safe haven in Pakistan. It was also a period when bomb blasts began to take place in Indian and Pakistan towns. It was widely understood as the doing of the secret services of the two countries.

When the Soviet Union intervened in Afghanistan in 1979 on behalf of the Communists who had captured power a year earlier, Pakistan became a sanctuary for a huge influx of Afghan refugees. Its generous humanitarian help and the provision of facilities to establish an Afghan resistance against Soviet occupation received sympathy and support from many Western and Islamic countries. The US, under President Jimmy Carter, offered US$400 million in aid, which Zia rejected as 'peanuts'. Later, under President Ronald Reagan, negotiations started in real earnest on Pakistan's participation in a jihad against the Soviet occupation of Afghanistan.

It resulted in an aid package of US$3.2 billion for the period 1982–7. It was divided equally between economic aid and military sales. Pakistan began to be praised as a 'pivotal state', a 'frontline state', and so on (Arif 2001: 184–5). In reward for such services, Gen. Zia demanded a free hand in organizing the resistance and a right to dispose of the funds, which was readily conceded by the US. Although some concerns about Pakistan's nuclear program were expressed by prominent members of the American Congress, the US government looked the other way (Haqqani 2005: 216). Pakistan continued clandestinely to pursue its nuclear program (ibid.: 185–6).

Inter-Services Intelligence

The ISI is one of the most powerful intelligence-gathering agencies in the Pakistani military establishment representing all the three branches of the armed forces, viz., the army, navy and air force. The ISI gained a political role during the time of Z.A. Bhutto, but it was Gen. Zia who greatly enhanced its role in politics—a role that continued later on. The ISI was assigned the primary responsibility for masterminding actions against the Soviets and the Afghan communists. General K.M. Arif observes that foreign military assistance was funneled to the Afghan Mujahedeen through Pakistan, and an elaborate network was established to collect military and economic intelligence from the Soviet Union and its troops in Afghanistan. The Central Intelligence Agency and the ISI Directorate worked in concert with each other in providing tools and know-how to the different Afghan groups fighting in their respective operational areas within Afghanistan (ibid.: 186). While the role of the ISI in both the Afghan jihad and in Pakistani domestic politics has been the subject of considerable discussion and debate, little has been written on the Special Services Group (SSG), an elite fighting force in the Pakistan military. A brief sketch is provided below.

The Special Services Group

In a major work written by an insider, Lt. Colonel Ghulam Jilani Khan presents an exhaustive account of the history, evolution, composition and tasks undertaken by the SSG. The 479-page *SSG:*

Tarikh key Ayeney Mein (2004) [The SSG in the Mirror of History] is written with great passion but the author had to rely essentially on interviews with people who had served in it because its charter remains classified. The foreword has been written by General Pervez Musharraf who himself was a member of the SSG. Its official strength currently is estimated at 2,500 officers and additional men who volunteer to join it. Although based on top-class fighting men of the army, it has representation both in the Pakistan navy and air force.

The SSG was initiated as an elite group in 1953–4 with the support of the US military, but became fully operational in 1956 with its headquarters at Cherat, near Peshawar, and another facility at Attock. It had come into being essentially to facilitate the US war strategy against the Soviet Union. In case of a Soviet advance into Pakistan or neighboring Afghanistan and other territories the SSG was to assist in launching a guerilla resistance. However, this brief, according to Brigadier Dogar, was not adhered to by Pakistan. Rather it was prepared secretly by Pakistan to take on active commando operations in enemy territory. Thus, the SSG was deployed during the 1965 war when its commandos entered Indian Kashmir to foment an uprising against Indian rule.

In any case, some 100 officers and men were also air-dropped into India near air bases during the war in what was generally considered an ill-planned operation. The SSG was also involved during the 1971 war in the then East Pakistan, where they managed to perform daring attacks on the Indian army more successfully. During the Soviet invasion of Afghanistan, the SSG played a very prominent role in covert actions against the Soviet Union, inflicting heavy casualties on the Red Army. At both Siachen and Kargil the SSG played an important role. The SSG has had both American and British instructors. The training is rigorous and the emphasis is on training soldiers as individual commandos capable of taking independent initiative. The SSG has been involved in counter-insurgency operations within Pakistan too (Khan 2004).

General Mirza Aslam Beg expressed the view that it was not in Pakistan's interest to ally so closely with the US. He particularly did not consider it right that the SSG was used in the Afghan jihad since the Soviet Union was not occupying any Pakistani territory.

United States–British–Arab Involvement

While US leadership and military aid was essential to sustain the Afghan jihad, British army veterans who had served on the Afghan border during the colonial period were also consulted, and much of the overall economic costs were borne by Saudi Arabia with help from some rich Arab emirates. A call to jihad (holy war) was heralded all over the world and Muslim zealots from different parts of the world began to arrive in the Pakistani city of Peshawar. The CIA and British advisers and experts were at hand to advise Pakistani officers who in turn trained the Islamic warriors to use modern weapons and explosives. These Islamic warriors known as Mujahideens included Egyptians, Algerians, Saudis, Chechens, and many other nationalities (Ahmed 2002: 24). Religious schools proliferated from a few hundred in the 1970s to 15,000, where some 1.5 to 1.7 million pupils (Taliban) were indoctrinated in an extremist and violent ideology of jihad (Ahmed 2005).

In this regard, the role played by the US in promoting the jihad ideology is noteworthy. According to Joe Stephens and David B. Ottaway who wrote an article entitled 'The ABC of jihad in Afghanistan' (*Washington Post*, 23 March 2002), special pictorial textbooks, designed by the Centre for Afghanistan Studies at the University of Nebraska-Omaha under a USAID $51 million grant, were published with a view to promoting the idea of jihad among the Mujahideen. The books were printed mostly in Pakistan and, during 1984–94, over 13 million were distributed at Afghan refugee camps and Pakistani madrasa 'where students learnt basic math by counting dead Russians and Kalashnikov rifles' (Jan: 2002).

The Taliban Regime

After the Soviets withdrew in 1989 from Afghanistan, a conflict over power erupted between various Afghan ethnic and sectarian factions. Pakistan initially threw its weight behind the Pushtun leader Gulbadan Hikmetyar in his opposition to the government of the Tadjik Burhanuddin Rabbani and his Uzbek ally Shah Ahmed Masud, who were supported by India. Later, a Pakistan-loyal group known as the Taliban, comprising the Pushtun tribes in the south and center of Afghanistan, was promoted (Rashid 2000). It comprised mainly Afghan and Pakistani students who were indoctrinated in extremism and terrorism in the madrasa. A bitter and bloody 'Great Game' began to be fought in which India and Russia sided with the so-called Northern Alliance of non-Pushtuns while Pakistan and the US threw their weight behind the Taliban. The Taliban came to power finally in 1996. The Talibani jihad ideology was now generalized to include all non-Muslims as legitimate targets (Ghazali and Ansari 2000; Stern 2000). Not only India, but the US, Israel, and in fact the whole non-Muslim world were declared enemies of Islam (Wright 2000).

While expanding its role in Afghanistan the Pakistan Army had begun to redefine its stature in the region. Pakistani defense strategists had always worried about Pakistan's lack of 'strategic depth' *vis-à-vis* India (Cheema 2003: 3). Many major cities and towns in the Pakistani Punjab were too close to the international border with India. In case of war, that gave Indians considerable advantage because, whereas the latter could retreat in the face of military setbacks to various major cities and industrial and military complexes, Pakistan could rather quickly be paralyzed if its major cities and roads were cut off in the face of an Indian advance. Consequently, ambitions to overcome such a disadvantage, combined with optimism that Islamic ideology and belief had created a strong fighting force which defeated the Soviet Union (and precipitated its collapse), led to the evolution of a project aiming at the creation of an Islamic state initially comprising Pakistan, Afghanistan, and Kashmir that they hoped to win through jihad.

More ambitious plans hoped to bring in the various central Asian Muslim republics, Iran, and Turkey into a confederation of Islamic states. In an interview Selig Harrison, a leading American South-Asia expert, claimed that General Zia's involvement in Afghanistan was meant to promote a pan-Islamic superstate in the region.

He also alleged that such a scheme had powerful backers in the Pakistani military establishment (Harrison 2001). Frederic Grare has argued that the military has used the Islamic militants to establish firm control over the Pakistani state and society (Grare 2006).

Jihad Turns to Indian-Administered Kashmir

The end of the Afghan jihad left scores of Islamic warriors looking for other similar opportunities to fight non-Muslims perceived to be oppressing Muslims. At that time a popular insurgency had emerged among Kashmiri Muslims against Indian rule in India-administered Kashmir. Many Mujahideen shifted their activity to Indian-administered Kashmir where popular protests were going on at that time against Indian rule (Hussain 2000). Several Pakistani fundamentalist organizations became active in recruiting volunteers to fight in Indian Kashmir. It became standard practice that, after the weekly Friday prayers, donations were collected from the worshippers to carry on jihad in Indian Kashmir. The three most important organizations that took part in that grand mission were the Lashkar-e-Tayyaba, Harkatul Mujahideen and Jaish-i-Muhammad. Anthony Davis noted the following about the annual meeting of the Lashkar-e-Tayyaba held on 3–5 November 1999 at Muridke, a town some 25 kilometers from Punjab's capital Lahore:

> This 200,000-strong gathering in the annual congregation of the Lashkar-e-Tayyaba (Army of the Pious), arguably Pakistan's largest organization committed to the defense of Islam through jihad (holy war). . . . Lashkar is the militant wing of the Markaz al-Dawa wall Irshad (Center for Preaching and Guidance), which runs a local Islamic university. Though the Army, Lashkar-e-Tayyaba has been recruiting since the late 1980s, its rise to prominence has been more recent with funds and donations from Saudi Arabia and local donations. Lashkar has 2200 units across Pakistan, military training camps in Pakistani-administered Kashmir, and thousands of active members and many more sympathizers. It also enjoys shadowy but close links with Pakistan's ruling military establishment. Lashkar fighters are at the forefront of the Islamabad-backed conflict in Kashmir against India. (Davis, 15 November 1999)

The Indian government alleged many times that these organizations received support from the Pakistan government, and that training camps for the militants existed in Pakistani Kashmir as well as in parts of Pakistan. The Pakistan government denied their existence; instead it described the militants as freedom fighters (Rana 2004).

Pakistan in the Aftermath of 9/11 Terrorist Attacks

On 11 September 2001, a group of terrorists believed to be members of the Al-Qaeda movement led by a veteran of the Afghan jihad, Osama bin Laden, hijacked civilian aircraft in various US cities. Two planes were forced to dash into the World Trade Center, the third into the Pentagon, and the fourth crashed in the fields in a rural county of Pennsylvania. An estimated 2,749 US and foreign citizens were killed, thus constituting the most massive terrorist attack on US soil. It traumatized the American nation deeply and put Pakistan under great pressure to join the US-led war on terror.

Impact on Relations with the United States

President George W. Bush began forthwith to establish a worldwide anti-terrorist coalition, which included several Western nations among whom the United Kingdom was the most prominent. On 12 September Secretary of State Colin Powell called President Musharraf who was in Karachi at that time. The latter narrates:

> The next morning I was chairing an important meeting at the Governor's House when my military secretary told me that the US secretary of state, Colin Powell, was on the phone. I said I would call back later, but he insisted that I come out of the meeting and take the call. Powell was quite candid, 'You are either with us or against us.' I took this as a blatant ultimatum. . . When I was back in Islamabad the next day, our director-general of Inter Services Intelligence, who happened to be in Washington, told me on the phone about his meeting with the US deputy secretary of state, Richard Armitage.

In what has to be the most undiplomatic statement ever made, Armitage added to what Colin Powell had said to me and told the director-general not only that we had to decide whether we were with America or with the terrorists, but that if we chose the terrorists, then we should be prepared to be bombed back to the Stone Age. This was a shocking barefaced threat, but it was obvious that the US had decided to hit back, and hit back hard. (Musharraf 2006: 201)

Armitage was later to confirm that the conversation had taken place but denied using the threat of military action. At any rate, Musharraf asserted that he made a dispassionate, 'military-style' analysis and concluded that Pakistan stood no chance—militarily, economically, or otherwise—to survive an all-out attack by the US. The next day the US Ambassador to Pakistan, Wendy Chamberlain, brought a set of seven demands. According to Musharraf (2006: 200–5) these were:

1. Stop Al-Qaeda operatives at the Pakistan border and prevent all supply of weapons and logistical support to Bin Laden.
2. Provide the US with access to Pakistani airspace to conduct military and intelligence operations.
3. Provide to the US territorial access to all allied military intelligence against the perpetrators of terrorism, including access to Pakistan's naval ports, air bases, and strategic locations on borders.
4. Provide the US immediately with intelligence, immigration information, and databases, and internal security information to prevent the terrorists from committing further such crimes.
5. Continue to publicly condemn the terrorists and curb all domestic expressions of support [for terrorism] against the US, its friends, or its allies.
6. Cut off all supply of fuels to the Taliban and prevent recruitment from Pakistan.
7. Should the evidence strongly implicate Osama bin Laden and the Al-Qaeda network in Afghanistan and the Taliban continue to harbor him and his network, Pakistan should break off diplomatic relations with the Taliban government and assist in the destruction of Osama Bin Laden and his network.

Musharraf claims he rejected the second and third demands since they jeopardized Pakistani security. What was offered was a narrow flight corridor that was far away from sensitive areas. Moreover, limited access to only two bases, Shamsi in Balochistan and Jacobabad in Sindh, for logistics and aircraft recovery was granted. These could not be used to launch attacks. Therefore no 'blanket permission' was given for anything. 'The rest of the demands we could live with. I am happy that the US government accepted our counter-proposals without any fuss,' the general concluded (Musharraf 2006: 206).

After a meeting with his top generals the next day on 13 September Musharraf issued a statement, in which he said, among other things:

> I wish to assure President Bush and the US government of our unstinted cooperation in the fight against terrorism. . . We regard terrorism as an evil that threatens the world community. . . Concerted international effort is needed to fight terrorism in all forms and manifestations. . . Pakistan has been extending cooperation to international efforts to combat terrorism in the past and will continue to do so. (Jain 2007: 167)

On 19 September Musharraf addressed the Pakistani nation. Beginning with a condemnation of the terrorist attacks and condolences for the bereaved he informed the people that the Americans were greatly angered by those attacks and were going to retaliate. Their first and foremost targets were Osama bin Laden and the Al-Qaeda as well as the Taliban for giving them refuge. He also mentioned that for a long time the US had been demanding extradition of Osama bin Laden and his associates for earlier attacks on US embassies and personnel in other parts of the world. The war on terror was going to be a protracted one. However, the Americans were not calling it a war on Islam or the people of Afghanistan. It was a war on terrorists (Musharraf, 19 September 2001).

He further stated that Pakistan had been contacted to help the campaign in three ways—with intelligence and information, permission to use Pakistani airspace, and general logistical support. The US was going to launch the concerted campaign with the help of a UN Security Council resolution and it enjoyed the support of the UN General Assembly as well, he stated, adding that many Islamic countries had supported the resolution. He then went on to describe the internal situation in Pakistan as critical and the worst since 1971 when the eastern wing seceded, further stating that the most serious threat was posed to Pakistan's strategic nuclear assets and the cause of Kashmir (Musharraf, 19 September 2001).

Musharraf then referred to Indian designs:

> They [Indians] offered all their military facilities to the US. They have offered without hesitation all their facilities, all their bases and full logistic support. They want to enter into an alliance with the US and get Pakistan declared a terrorist state. They want to harm our strategic assets and the Kashmir cause. (ibid.)

The speech also reflected populist rhetoric. Musharraf referred to pristine Islamic history and examples of the Prophet Muhammad making pragmatic compromises in the larger interest of Islam, thereby suggesting that working with the US did not constitute an act of cowardice but rather the best way to safeguard the security of the country from external threats, preservation of the strategic nuclear and missile assets, and the Kashmir cause.

Pakistan's Nuclear Program

US administrations had been expressing concerns for Pakistan's (and India's) nuclear ambitions at least since the late 1970s. It was widely suspected that Pakistan was developing nuclear weapons capability with the help of the Chinese. Some specific legal instruments were also devised to discourage Pakistan from successfully producing a nuclear device. Among them were the Symington Amendment of 1977 on uranium enrichment; the Pressler Amendment of 1985 on possession of a nuclear device (which effectively prevented the sale of F-16 fighter aircraft to Pakistan, although payment had been made for them); and the Glenn Amendment of 1994 on nuclear testing. However, as already noted, since Pakistan had become a frontline state during the Afghan jihad, the US had not come down with too much pressure or threats to prevent Pakistan from continuing secretly with its nuclear program. In Pakistan, the defense experts and the security establishment reached a consensus on developing nuclear weapon capability as the best deterrent for Pakistan's security (Cheema 1996: 103–30; Jan 1995).

In May 1998, when both India and Pakistan carried out nuclear test explosions, the US responded with heavy sanctions. Neither India nor Pakistan caved in to the pressure. However, since Pakistan again became an ally in the war on terror in the aftermath of 9/11, the sanctions were progressively eased and largely removed. Nevertheless, the Americans kept questioning Pakistan about the proliferation of nuclear technology to Iran, North Korea, Libya, and other states (Jain 2007: 445). The announcement by Libya in December 2003 that it was abandoning its nuclear weapons program undermined the Pakistani government's blanket denials as evidence mounted of illicit nuclear weapons technology transfers. Consequently, President Musharraf ordered an investigation into the activities of the man in charge of the nuclear weapons program, Dr Abdul Qadeer Khan. Musharraf asserted that even if there had been wrongdoing, it had occurred without the government of Pakistan's knowledge or approval (ibid.: 447–50). However, critics noted that virtually all of Abdul Qadeer Khan's overseas travels, to Iran, Libya, North Korea, Niger, Mali, and the Middle East, were on official Pakistan government aircraft. Often, senior members of the Pakistan nuclear establishment accompanied him.

In January 2004, Abdul Qadeer Khan was interrogated by Pakistani investigators. On 25 January 2004, the authorities reported that Abdul Qadeer Khan and another high-ranking officer had provided unauthorized technical assistance to Iran's nuclear weapons program in the late 1980s and early 1990s, allegedly in exchange for tens of millions of dollars. It was also reported that General Mirza Aslam Beg, a former Chief of Army Staff at the time, was implicated in the nuclear trade with Iran (John 2007: 174). On 31 January, Abdul Qadeer Khan was dismissed from his post as the Science Adviser to the President of Pakistan. On 4 February, furthermore, Qadeer Khan appeared on national television and confessed to running a proliferation ring. The next day

Musharraf pardoned him (Musharraf 2006: 289–94). He has since then been held under house arrest, but US pleas to permit its experts to interrogate him have been rejected.

In any case, the Pakistan government has been facing extreme pressure from the US to keep its nuclear arsenal under a reliable chain of command; some reports suggest that the Americans have gained control over the Pakistani nuclear weapons (*Times of India*, 20 November 2007), but this is strongly denied by the Pakistani government.

United States Appreciation of Pakistan

Along with the proverbial 'stick' wielded by the US, the 'carrot' offered to Pakistan was also significant. At a press conference given jointly at Islamabad on 16 October by Musharraf and Secretary of State Colin Powell, Musharraf emphasized the need to help the Afghans establish durable peace and to provide assistance to Pakistan with the repatriation of the millions of Afghan refugees from Pakistan. For his part, Powell observed, 'President Bush has lifted a number of sanctions to allow us to resume cooperation with Pakistan. We have also helped reschedule $479 million in Pakistan's bilateral debt and voted for new IMF loans' (Jain 2007: 169).

Further major concessions followed in a statement by Richard Boucher, Spokesman for the State Department, on 31 October 2001:

> President Bush signed into law a bill that authorizes him to waive sanctions against Pakistan through fiscal year 2003. It is the final stage in easing sanctions imposed on Islamabad after the 1999 military coup led by General Pervez Musharraf. President Bush has already exercised his authority to end prohibitions imposed under the Glenn Amendment (nuclear testing), the Pressler Amendment (possession of a nuclear device) and the Symington Amendment (uranium enrichment). (Ibid.: 170–1)

Boucher further elaborated that economic assistance was going to increase dramatically. The US would provide US$1 billion. Several more billions would follow from international aid organizations. Pakistan was also going to receive help in boosting its exports.

More such statements followed when Musharraf and Bush met in New York on 10 November 2001.

Unlinking with Extremist Islam and Kashmir Jihad

While Pakistan had joined the war against terrorism and allied itself even more closely to the US, it continued to maintain that militancy in Indian-administered Kashmir was not to be linked to the Al-Qaeda terrorism and that those who took part in it were freedom fighters. This was, however, going to change too. On 1 October Muslim militants carried out a terrorist attack on the Kashmir Assembly in Srinagar, the capital of Indian-administered Kashmir, which resulted in several deaths. The US, the European Union (EU) and many other states condemned the attack. A few weeks later on 13 December, militants tried to break into the Indian Parliament with the intention of taking some of the members hostages (Hoodbhoy 2006: 160). The whole operation was seen on television screens and was thus flashed across the world. India accused Pakistan of being behind the attacks but the Pakistan government strongly denied any hand in that operation and strongly condemned the attack.

Suddenly South Asia seemed headed for another major armed conflict between the two rivals. India dispatched hundreds of thousands of troops to the 2,900-kilometer India–Pakistan border, including the Line of Control in Kashmir. Pakistan followed suit. More than a million soldiers were amassed on both sides of that border (Yusuf 2006: 18). Once again, the possibility of a nuclear exchange taking place loomed large in case the conflict escalated. As a result, international pressure increased enormously on the two states to withdraw from their standoff. India, however, refused to do that as long as Pakistan supported what it describes as cross-border terrorism. The standoff was eventually defused through pressure from the US, which dispatched several high officials to Delhi and Islamabad (Bidwai 2006: 54). Moreover, the US exerted intense pressure on Pakistan to forgo its support to militant groups (Cohen 2006: 91).

Musharraf gave in, and in an address to the Pakistani nation on 12 January 2002, he made a complete break with the Kashmir militancy and unlinked Pakistan from the global fundamentalist Islam. He stated:

> The Kashmir problem needs to be resolved by dialogue and peaceful means in accordance with the wishes of the Kashmiri people and the UN resolutions. We have to find the solution of this dispute. No organization will be allowed to indulge in terrorism in the name of Kashmir. We condemn the terrorist acts of 11 September, 1 October and 13 December. Anyone found involved in any terrorist act would be dealt with sternly.
>
> Strict action will be taken against any Pakistani individual, group or organization found involved in terrorism within or outside the country. Our behavior must always be in accordance with inter-national norms. (Jain 2007: 174)

He announced that extremist organizations involved in terrorism and sectarianism would be crushed. Besides announcing curbs on the Sunni and Shia militias that had been carrying out terrorist attacks, he declared a ban on the two main militant organizations active in Indian-administered Kashmir and India, the Jaish-e-Mohammad and the Lashkar-e-Tayyaba (ibid.: 174–5).

Musharraf went on to describe Pakistan as a modern Muslim state, which should be based on a moderate, tolerant interpretation of Islam. Later, in an address to Muslim clerics on 18 January, he spelt out a tolerant, non-divisive approach to Islam. He urged them to help him in disseminating such an approach among the people (Musharraf, 18 January 2002).

Such pronouncements were indeed significant. However, according to Cohen, the Taliban and the militants, active in the Indian Kashmir, continued to receive support from rogue elements in the Pakistan military establishment. He believes that the Americans began to exert immense pressure on Musharraf to curb the resurgent Taliban menace much later, sometime from 2005 onwards when the Taliban began to mount frequent attacks on US troops in Afghanistan. It also resulted in significant decrease in support to the militant organizations active in the Indian Kashmir. On the other hand, Musharraf has given details of his government tracing, capturing, and handing over Al-Qaeda operatives in its own territories to the US. Hundreds of suspected Al-Qaeda operatives from different parts of Pakistan were handed over. Musharraf devoted several chapters in his autobiography to highlight the leading role played by his government in smashing Al-Qaeda networks, especially in the borders along Afghanistan (Musharraf 2006: 208–73). Top US officials, however, made contradictory statements. While Bush himself backed Musharraf and his government for their contributions to the war on terror, the American press expressed doubt about Pakistan's firm commitment to the war on terror. Some suggested that more than US$5 billion given to Pakistan to destroy terrorist networks had been wasted (*New York Times*, 24 December 2007). According to Grare (2006), Musharraf fostered the myth of an Islamist takeover in case of his regime falling. In Grare's estimation, the Islamists are not in a position to capture power on their own.

Pakistan–India Relations

Although General Musharraf was the architect of the Kargil operation that greatly undermined the peace initiatives of the 1990s taken by the Indian and Pakistani governments, he changed his stance dramatically when he met Prime Minister Atal Behari Vajpayee at Agra in July 2001 to discuss peace. Although a peace accord could not be agreed on that occasion, it definitely signified a change in approach by the Pakistani military. Presumably Musharraf and his top brass realized that Pakistan's role as a frontline state against communism—already assigned by the US in 1947 and fully exploited during the Afghan jihad—had become redundant and further that the Americans were mainly interested in a restricted role for Pakistan, as a compliant ally in their war on terrorism. Therefore, Pakistan could not afford regional confrontations the same way it could in the past. Consequently, some voices from within the Pakistan military establishment began to be raised in favor of normalization through greater trade and cooperation in the South Asian Association of Regional Cooperation (SAARC) (Durrani 2002).

Moreover, Musharraf announced that Pakistan would be willing to adopt a more flexible attitude on the Line of Control in Kashmir, signaling a major break with orthodox Pakistani foreign policy. On the other hand, the Indians were slow in responding in equal measure to the Pakistani peace overtures. However, in 2006, Prime Minister Manmohan Singh expressed a desire to sign a 'treaty of peace, security and friendship' with Pakistan (Ahmed, 6 January 2007). During much of 2007, progress on the peace question remained suspended as political turmoil within Pakistan demanded the attention of the Pakistan government; India decided to remain aloof. Some significant improvement in the trade and communications between the two countries has taken place in the post-9/11 period. A weekly bus service between Delhi and Lahore and between Amritsar and the Sikh holy place of Nankana Sahib has been launched. Bilateral trade in 2006–7 between India and Pakistan recorded an increase of 88 per cent and stood at US$1.6 billion. It was envisaged to grow to $2.7 billion in 2007 but suffered a decline because of the political turmoil in Pakistan (*India eNews*, 29 November 2007). On the other hand, both sides have continued to modernize and develop their missile programs, thus acquiring greater range and accuracy in their killing power in case of war.

Changes in the Overall External Arena

India and the US had begun to draw towards one another soon after the fall of the Soviet Union, but the terrorist attacks of 9/11 proved to be a catalyst and added great urgency to that process. The centerpiece of their new relationship was a series of negotiations between them purported to close a deal on nuclear cooperation that would privilege India as a nuclear power even without entry into the club of the five recognized nuclear powers, while the US gained access to the expanding Indian market. It resulted in an agreement on a text between the two governments on such a deal. However, it ran into trouble because of opposition from the rival BJP as well as the left allies of the Congress-led government of Prime Minister Manmohan Singh (Nayyar 2007). Even in the US, there was some opposition to it. At any rate, after considerable wrangling in India, it was passed by the Indian Parliament and later ratified by the US Congress. It was passed by the Nuclear Suppliers group on 6 September 2008. The US and India consider each other as strategic partners (Muni 2008: 142).

On the other hand, relations between India and China have been steadily improving, and trade has increased sevenfold (to more than US$20 billion) from the level it was at in 2001 (ibid.: 142). Moreover, Islamic radicalism and extremism in neighboring Pakistan has even affected China, which has a large Muslim population in its Xinjiang Province. The result has been that 'mutual confidence in security field has also been strengthened with joint counter-terrorism exercise between the Indian and Chinese armies in Yunnan in December 2007' (ibid.: 142–3). However, such changes are not to be understood as a major shift in the close relationship between Pakistan and China as long as the rapprochement between India and China is limited to formal gestures of goodwill (Siddiqa 2006: 214).

Internal Fallout of Unlinking with Militant Islam

Not surprisingly, Pakistan's unlinking with Islamic radicalism and the Kashmir jihad generated considerable anger within some sections of Pakistani society. In the tribal areas near the Afghan border, Taliban and Al-Qaeda enclaves survived military action and even hit back against the government. Musharraf and some of his top officers became objects of assassination attempts by the Islamic extremists and ultra-nationalists. Thus on 14 December 2003 a powerful bomb went off minutes after Musharraf's convoy crossed a bridge in Rawalpindi. He was apparently saved by a jamming device in his vehicle that prevented the remote-controlled explosives from blowing up the bridge as his convoy passed over it (*Daily Times*, 15 December 2003). Another attempt to kill him took place 11 days later when on 25 December two suicide bombers unsuccessfully tried to assassinate him. It was found that some junior personnel of the SSG of commandos, to which Musharraf himself belonged, were involved in the conspiracy to assassinate him (Musharraf

2006: 252). One of the militants, Amjad Faruqi, was suspected of masterminding that attack. He was killed by Pakistani forces in 2004 after a long and extensive manhunt (ibid.: 2547).

Terrorism by extremist groups and sectarian militias continued to menace Pakistani society during 2004–5. However, more threatening was the resurgence of Baloch nationalism directed against the central government's alleged denial of a fair share of the wealth produced in their province. It resulted in government troops and the tribesmen of the Baloch leader, Akbar Bugti, being involved in several skirmishes against each other. Bugti was killed on 26 August 2006 by government forces. It raised fears once again about separatism gaining ground in the centrifugal provinces of Pakistan (John 2007: 118–21).

Meanwhile, the Musharraf regime intensified its military operations against Taliban and Al-Qaeda enclaves in the tribal areas. During 2004–6, there were recurrent clashes between Pakistani troops and the Taliban and Al-Qaeda forces. A truce was reached in September 2006 but clashes broke out again when Pakistan ordered air strikes at Chenagai on a madrasa on 30 October 2006 in which 80 people were killed. Some reports suggested that the Americans directly hit those targets. In retaliation on 8 November 2006 a suicide bomber killed 42 soldiers and injured another 20 in Dargai (Raman 2006). It was the beginning of a more focused campaign against military personnel that, in 2007, reached alarming proportions.

Terrorism in 2007

In 2007, in addition to bomb blasts taking place in several places, there were 56 suicide bombings in Pakistan. In the suicide bombings alone, 419 security officials and 217 civilians were killed. The significance of such escalation can be grasped from the fact that, in the previous year alone, 6 suicide bombing had been directed at the military. Despite this tenfold increase in suicide bombings, the regime failed to track down a single culprit (Rashid 2008: 379).

From the beginning of 2007, almost daily reports of attacks on the police and security personnel began to pour in from the tribal areas along the Afghanistan border in Waziristan. On 26 January two persons—the suicide bomber and a security guard—were killed in a blast at the prestigious Marriott Hotel in Islamabad. A meeting to celebrate the Indian Republic Day was scheduled in the hotel and Indian diplomats were scheduled to attend it. The blast was undoubtedly planned for that reception but went off earlier (*Daily Times*, 27 January 2007). The garrison-type security arrangements in the Islamabad–Rawalpindi area were further challenged when an insurgency headed by hardcore fundamentalists began to surface in the Pakistani capital in March 2007.

On 28 March niqab-wearing armed women of the Jamia Hafsa at Lal Masjid in Islamabad, very aptly described by someone as the Lal Brigade, raided the premises of a madam who allegedly ran a brothel, arrested her and her family and forced a confession from her that she was guilty of running the sex trade (*News*, 29 March 2007). The same day, several bomb blasts and rocket and mortar attacks on the security forces and government installations by tribal militants took place in Tank district of Waziristan, NWFP. Twenty-five people, including a soldier of the paramilitary Frontier Constabulary, were killed (ibid.). On 6 April, the Islamists set up a Sharia Court inside the mosque. The most senior cleric, Maulana Abdul Aziz, vowed to launch thousands of suicide attacks if the government interfered in the activities of the court. On 9 April, the Sharia Court handed down a fatwa (edict) against the Punjab Tourism Minister, Nilofer Bakhtiar, accusing her of committing a sin when she was shown in newspaper photographs embracing a parachuting instructor following a charity jump in France (Ahmed, 16 July 2007).

The situation deteriorated further when, on 28 April, an assassination attempt on the then Interior Minister Aftab Ahmad Khan Sherpao took place in Charsadda, NWFP. He survived but 28 people were killed (*News*, 29 April 2007). On 23 June the Lal Brigade cadres raided a Chinese massage parlor in Islamabad and abducted seven Chinese and two Pakistanis from its premises. They released the Chinese couple who owned the parlor and five Chinese girls who worked there.

In a rare display of concern about events in Pakistan, the Chinese Minister for Public Security Zhou Yongang told the visiting Pakistani Interior Minister Sherpao, 'We hope Pakistan will look into the terrorist attacks aiming at Chinese people and organizations as soon as possible and severely punish the criminals' (*Shanghai Daily*, 27 June 2007). Things came to a head when, on 8 July, unidentified gunmen killed three Chinese workers and wounded another near Peshawar in what Pakistani officials said was a reprisal attack linked to the ongoing siege of militants in the Lal Masjid (*News*, 9 July 2007). The same day in Islamabad a senior military officer, Lt. Colonel Haroon Islam, stationed outside the Lal Masjid, was gunned down by the militants inside (ibid.).

With the nationals of Pakistan's closest ally killed and its own writ flouted openly, the Musharraf government felt compelled to act firmly and ruthlessly. The security forces were ordered to carry out Operation Sunrise in full blast. Initially, it had been named Operation Silence (*Dawn*, 12 July 2007). Perhaps the government was hoping to carry out a relatively small-scale assault but the resistance inside the mosque made that impossible. Thus, when Operation Sunrise was launched, it bore the hallmarks of a major military action. While many inside the mosque panicked and surrendered or tried to escape, several hundred diehards decided to go down fighting. The major assault was launched on 10 July. A total of 150 people were reported killed, of which 10 were army personnel, including an officer. However, some people challenge government figures and claim that many more inside the mosque lost their lives.

The attack on the Lal Masjid was supported by the US while Al-Qaeda's second in command, Ayman al-Zawahiri, issued a videotape calling for Pakistanis to join the jihad against Musharraf to avenge the deaths of the Islamists (ibid.). Retaliation followed soon when, on July 15, there was a suicide attack and car bombs exploded in many parts of the NWFP. At least 49 people were killed and hundreds wounded. Among them were 11 security personnel (*News*, 16 July 2007). Further attacks followed on 19 July in Hub, Hangu, and Kohat, in the NWFP. Another 52 persons lost their lives and 127 were injured. Chinese engineers working in that area were the intended targets but, instead of them, security personnel and other ordinary people including women and children suffered (*News*, 20 July 2007).

On 2 August, the police in Sargodha shot dead a suspected suicide bomber after the man failed to detonate the explosives he was wearing. The man, who entered a police training centre, killed a policeman before being gunned down. On 4 September, at least 25 people were killed and 66 injured in two suicide bomb attacks in Rawalpindi cantonment. Among the dead were uniformed officials as well as civilians in a bus carrying them to their workplace (*News*, 5 September 2007). On 13 September, at least 20 off-duty commandos were killed and 11 injured in an apparent suicide blast at an army officers' mess, near the Tarbela Dam, NWFP. Among the targeted men were commandos from the SSG Karar Company, apparently because they were believed to have taken part in the assault on the Lal Masjid (*News*, 14 September 2007).

The arena of terrorism shifted to Karachi when, on 18 October, Benazir Bhutto returned to Pakistan. Shortly after midnight, utter savagery and mayhem was let loose by possibly suicide bombers on the convoy carrying her and other PPP leaders from Karachi Airport towards the mausoleum of Quaid-e-Azam Mohammad Ali Jinnah. Initial reports suggested that 125 people died and more than 500 were injured. Ms Bhutto and the other leaders who were in a bomb-proof truck were saved, however (*News*, October 2007). Benazir Bhutto put the number of dead at 179, including 50 youths from her party who had volunteered to protect her life (Bhutto 2008: 12). It was the single most deadly act of terrorism in Pakistani history.

On 30 October, a suicide bomber struck a police checkpoint in a high-security zone of Rawalpindi, less than a kilometer from General Musharraf's camp office (*News*, 31 October 2007). On 1 November, another suicide bomber blew himself up and seven officers of the Pakistan Air Force and three civilians at Sargodha, where the Pakistan Air Force has its headquarters (*News*, 2 November 2007). There was no let up in the attacks on armed forces personnel.

On 24 November, two separate attacks targeting military personnel and installations in Rawalpindi resulted in 32 deaths. This time it was personnel of the ISI that were particularly targeted (*News*, 25 November 2007). Further attacks followed on 9 December, when 10 people, including three policemen and seven civilians, including two children, perished in a car bombing near Matta, Swat district. The next day, a suicide attack on a school bus carrying children of Air Force employees took place during the morning rush hour in Sargodha (*News*, 11 December 2007). On 13 December suicide bombings near an army check-post in Quetta killed seven people, including three personnel of the Pakistan Army (*News*, 14 December 2007).

At Nowshera, NWFP, on 15 December, a suicide bomber rammed his explosives-laden bicycle into a military check-post, killing five people and injuring 11 others (*News*, 16 December 2007). On 17 December, 12 security personnel were killed and five wounded in a suicide attack in Kohat, NWFP; the victims were members of the army's local football team (*News*, 18 December 2007). On 21 December, a suicide bomb blast again targeted Aftab Ahmad Khan Sherpao, killing at least 57 and injuring over 100 at Jamia Masjid in Charsadda district. Sherpao survived the blast, but his younger son Mustafa Khan Sherpao was injured (*News*, 22 December 2007). On 23 December, at least 13 people, including four security personnel, were killed and another 23 wounded as a suicide bomber targeted an army convoy near Mingora, Swat district (*News*, 24 December 2007).

The Assassination of Benazir Bhutto

While attacks on the security and military personnel continued, Benazir Bhutto was assassinated on 27 December after she had addressed a mammoth public meeting to solicit votes for the general elections announced for 8 January 2008 (*News*, 28 December 2007). Some 20 other people, among them five PPP volunteers, were also killed in the bomb blast that took place. A bitter controversy laced with conspiracy theories broke out with regard to her killers and whether she had died of gunshots fired by the assassin(s) or the bomb blast that accompanied that crime.

The government claimed to have intercepted a telephone conversation between an Al-Qaeda leader, Baitullah Mahsud, and some cleric in which both congratulate each other over her death and praise the men who took part in it (Ahmed, 31 December 2007). Ms Bhutto had committed herself to working closely with the US in the war on terror and even to let the Americans interrogate Abdul Qadeer Khan, a national hero who is fondly referred to as the father of the Islamic or Pakistani atomic bomb. An Al-Qaeda statement describes her death as the end of 'America's most precious asset in Pakistan'. However, a spokesperson for Mahsud denied that the Al-Qaeda leader had anything to do with the murder (Ahmed, 31 December 2007).

Terrorism Continued in Spring 2008

Terrorist attacks by suicide bombers against mainly government personnel and premises continued to take place in 2008. On 10 January, a suicide attack outside the Lahore High Court before a lawyer's protest march was scheduled to begin resulted in 24 deaths and injury to 73 people; the police were the main targets of the attack (*News*, 11 January 2008). On 4 February, students and officials of the Army Medical College near the Military Headquarters in Rawalpindi were the victims of another attack when a suicide bomber crashed his bike into a bus carrying them; 10 people died and 27 were injured (*News*, 5 February 2008). In the NWFP, bomb blasts took place at the election rallies of the PPP and the Awami National Party (ANP) as did attacks on the police and military during February. On 25 February, the head of the medical corps, Lt. General Mushtaq Beg, was killed along with his driver and security guard when a suicide bomber attacked their vehicle. Again the terrorists launched an attack in Lahore when two suicide bombers blew themselves up at the Pakistan Navy War College. Eight people were killed and 24 others injured (*News*, 26 February 2008).

Another gory attack in Lahore took place on 11 March when two suicide bombers carried out separate missions. In the first attack, the Federal Investigation Agency (FIA) Office on Temple

Road in the center of the city was ripped apart and 30 people were killed, including 16 policemen. The target was the office of the personnel being trained by the Americans for counter-terrorism operations. The second attack was on the office of an advertising agency in the posh area of Model Town near Bilawal House, associated with the PPP leaders, the late Benazir Bhutto and her husband Asif Ali Zardari. Three people lost their lives in that assault (*News*, 12 March 2008).

Democratic Protests and General Elections

While the Islamists intensified their attacks on the Musharraf regime, especially on the military as it was involved in ongoing operations against the Taliban and Al-Qaeda, a popular, peaceful movement for the restoration of civilian, democratic rule also gained momentum in March 2007. According to the largely suspended and heavily amended Pakistan Constitution of 1973, general elections had to be held every five years. After overthrowing Nawaz Sharif in October 1999, Musharraf had assumed the position of 'Chief Executive'. On 20 June 2001, he appointed himself as President of Pakistan. To validate his election he took a number of other steps too but the most important was the general election held in October 2002. All tactics, including rigging of elections, gerrymandering, and intimidation were employed to ensure that the majority of the seats in Parliament was won by the pro-Musharraf Pakistan Muslim League-Quaid-e-Azam (PML-Q). EU election observers described the election process as flawed (*Daily Times*, 13 October 2002). The PML-Q formed a majority coalition with the help of some right-wing parties and independents.

Over the years, Musharraf tried to establish for himself the reputation of a moderate and progressive Muslim leader. With regard to Pakistan's economic development, it was noted by several reputable international economic and financial agencies that Pakistan's financial standing improved substantially but inflation, unemployment, and abject poverty continued to ravage the lives of nearly one-fourth of the Pakistan population officially categorized as living below the poverty line (Ahmed, 1 December 2007).

In any case, new elections were due in 2007 and from the beginning of the year voices began to be raised for free and fair elections. Many liberals and secularists, who with some reservations had been backing Musharraf as a counterweight to the Islamists, turned against him in the spring of 2007 when he declared Chief Justice Iftikhar Mohammad Chaudhry of the Pakistan Supreme Court non-functional (a novel term meaning 'practically removed from his office') on allegations of misuse of office. It was widely believed that Justice Chaudhry had told Musharraf that the latter could not contest elections while remaining in uniform, and that the election of president had to be carried out before the end of 2007. Moreover, Justice Chaudhry took up several *habeas corpus* cases of Pakistani citizens, mainly journalists critical of the Musharraf regime and political activists abducted by the security forces, ordering that the detained individuals should be produced in court (*News*, 17 March 2007).

Justice Chaudhry's removal resulted in protest marches and demonstrations, mainly by lawyers and political cadres (Ahmed et al. 2007; Zaidi 2008). The demonstrations and protest actions continued in the premises of the courts despite violent assaults by the police and security agencies. In the absence of political leadership, civil society took the lead in protesting against dictatorship. International support and messages of solidarity also helped the struggle to continue. Subsequently Chaudhry was re-instated on 10 July by a Supreme Court bench. However, that did not mean that the standoff between him and Musharraf had ended; rather, Chaudhry embarked upon judicial activism that clearly sought confrontation with Musharraf. Meanwhile, calls for Musharraf to step down and for a caretaker government to hold free and fair elections began to be given by civil society actors as well as the opposition. In a bid to pre-empt any move that would threaten his presidency Musharraf had himself elected president on 6 October by outgoing members of the national and provincial assemblies who were mostly his supporters. In any event, the Pakistan Election Commission announced 8 January 2008 as the date for the general elections.

The crisis deepened dramatically when the two exiled prime

ministers, Benazir Bhutto and Nawaz Sharif, were allowed to return to Pakistan on 18 October and 27 November, respectively, under intense pressure from the US and Saudi Arabia. Their arrival in Pakistan set in motion popular rallies but also bomb blasts. Meanwhile Musharraf resigned as Chief of Army Staff on 28 November and General Ashfaq Pervez Kayani became the new military chief. Such measures, however, did nothing to stem the rising tide of democratic opposition or terrorist attacks. Musharraf imposed a state of emergency on 3 November 2007 and dismissed many judges of the Supreme Court believed by him to be planning to unseat him as president, and filled the benches with men handpicked by him (*News*, 4 November 2007). The US and the EU came out in support of demands for an end to the emergency and holding of free and fair elections that were now being made in Pakistan. On 16 December 2007, the emergency was lifted and most of the arrested people were released. The Americans had secretly brokered a power-sharing deal between Musharraf and Benazir. Ms Bhutto's death resulted in the general elections being re-scheduled for 18 February 2008 (Ahmed, 22 February 2008: 1–2).

On 22 January 2008, some 100 ex-servicemen, including the highest-level officers from the army, navy, and air force issued a statement demanding that Musharraf should step down and democracy be restored in Pakistan (*News*, 23 January 2008). It was clear that Musharraf's popularity had plummeted drastically and his support base was fast eroding, yet he persisted in remaining president.

Transition to Civilian Rule and Democracy

In any event, the 18 February 2008 general elections proved to be a massive protest vote against authoritarianism. The PPP and the Pakistan Muslim League-Nawaz (PML-N) emerged as the main winners, securing 120 and 90 seats, respectively, in the National Assembly which comprised 342 members altogether. In the provincial assemblies too they did very well in places where their influence was known to exist. In the strategic NWFP on the

Afghan border, where the Taliban and Al-Qaeda extremists had their strongholds, the Islamist parties were wiped out. The main winner was the ANP, a secular-nationalist party that historically always enjoyed significant support in that province. The main pro-Musharraf party, the PML-Q suffered a major loss, winning only 51 seats in the National Assembly. Its support in the provincial assemblies plummeted sharply as well except in Balochistan where it gained a majority because the regional nationalists boycotted the election (Ahmed, 22 February 2008: 2).

The PPP and PML-N, both bitter rivals in the past, decided to form a broad-based coalition government, which also includes the ANP as well as the pro-Musharraf Muttahida Qaumi Movement (MQM) and the Jamiyat Ulema-e-Islam. After several weeks of intense political maneuvering, on 22 March Yousaf Raza Gilani was nominated as the PPP candidate. He was elected on 24 March securing 264 votes while the pro-Musharraf PML-Q candidate, Chaudhry Pervaiz Elahi, received only 42 votes. Gilani was sworn in by Musharraf on 25 March but Zardari, Sharif, and several other leaders did not attend the ceremony, presumably to protest against Musharraf's continuation as president (*News*, 26 March 2008).

Among the first orders Gilani issued after getting elected as prime minister was the removal of all hindrances on the movement of the deposed Chief Justice of Pakistan, Iftikhar Mohammad Chaudhry, and other such judges of the Pakistan Supreme Court. For several months earlier, they had been kept in detention. One can expect Gilani's government to act determinedly to curtail the extraordinary powers acquired by the president through different constitutional and legal subterfuges, especially the Eight Amendment enacted during the rule of General Zia to dismiss an elected government and parliament. In his maiden speech as prime minister, Gilani announced that his government would continue to combat terrorism but the conflict could not be solved only through military means. Efforts would be made to find a political solution that could establish peace and order in Pakistan (*News*, 30 March 2008).

With regard to the military's responses to the restoration of civilian rule, it is to be noted that for the first time it identified the jihadis as threat number one to Pakistan's security and India was relegated to the second position. The new Chief of the Army Staff, Gen. Ashfaq Pervez Kayani, also issued orders to his men not to interact with politicians without proper authorization. More importantly, in a major reversal of the policies of Musharraf, he ordered the withdrawal of more than 300 military personnel posted in various civil departments (*News*, 12 February 2008).

CONCLUDING REMARKS

This chapter demonstrates that the garrison state consolidated in Pakistan through a combination of internal and external factors. While the perceived threat from India and the general incompetence of the politicians initially helped the military obtain a leading role in Pakistan politics, it was its skillful exploitation, with the help of civilians, of the US' worldwide anti-Soviet strategy to get itself co-opted into that strategy that helped to obtain the weaponry and training needed to assert itself *vis-à-vis* India, though it must be emphasized that the US did not encourage such a role.

The garrison state—typified by the domination of society and polity by specialists in violence who claim to be guardians of national security and survival—reached its apotheosis under General Zia-ul-Haq when he captured power in July 1977. He began to promote a totalitarian version of the Islamic state and patronized a culture that demeaned democracy and equal rights of citizens. The convoluted paternalism of the military assumed a moderate and modernistic form when General Pervez Musharraf came to power in 1999. However, both remained convinced that the military should remain at the helm of affairs, and undertook measures to strengthen their position as presidents.

The garrison state was able to expand its power and hold over Pakistan also through external measures. Thus, by joining the Afghan jihad and receiving arms and economic aid on a massive scale from the US and Saudi Arabia, Gen. Zia was able to greatly expand the military's role in South-West Asia and South Asia as well. The military's crowning glory was its success in bringing the

Taliban into power in Afghanistan. However, such a sense of power was short-lived and the garrison state began to receive severe jolts in the aftermath of the 9/11 terrorist attacks on the US. As a middle-range power dependent on external donors, Pakistan's ability to function as a self-contained garrison state was always circumscribed and even after becoming a nuclear power that weakness may have decreased but it has not been surmounted altogether as powerful external actors, especially a superpower such as the US, continue to have leverage on dependent allies. This became quite clear when General Musharraf, who captured power in October 1999, was compelled by overwhelming US pressure to dissociate his regime from the Taliban within Pakistan and to climb down from external jihad in Indian-administered Kashmir.

After the 9/11 terrorists attacks, the US began to see Pakistan as a threat to its interests and world peace, especially if Pakistan's nuclear arsenal were to fall in the hands of Islamists. The US seems no longer interested in bracing Pakistan as a garrison state though it wants it to continue fighting the Taliban and Al-Qaeda, and give it arms as well as economic aid to encourage Pakistan to continue to do so. Not surprisingly the Pakistan and Afghanistan Taliban and Al-Qaeda reacted fiercely by mounting terrorist attacks against Pakistani state employees, particularly those serving in the armed forces. On the whole, events from 2007 suggest that the liaison between the military and the Islamists is precarious and tenuous, and the latter probably receive support from rogue elements from lower rungs in the Pakistan military establishment; they are able to act independently of the generals but are not in a position to capture power. In other words, Grare's thesis (2008) that the Islamists are merely a protégé of the military is not borne out entirely by facts. He is, however, right in his estimation that they are not in a position to capture power in Pakistan on their own.

While the perceived threat from India is the *raison d'être* of building a strong military force and provides the justification as well as legitimacy for building Pakistan into a garrison state, its translation into military strategy and policy is multifaceted and is not simply about maintaining a strong deterrence; rather, it followed a policy of pre-emptive military activism against India. Thus, Pakistan initiated the wars of 1947–8 and 1965 with India. The same is true of the Kargil confrontation of 1999. On the other hand, India intervened in the civil war in Bangladesh in 1971, defeated the Pakistan Army, and brought about the break-up of Pakistan. Moreover, Pakistan always felt vulnerable because of lack of strategic depth and the concomitant weakness that entailed a war with India fought with conventional weapons. It resulted in clandestine activities to acquire nuclear weapons capability as India had already demonstrated its ability to explode a nuclear device in 1974. Currently, both India and Pakistan are nuclear powers capable of unleashing enough destructive material in a nuclear exchange that mutual annihilation or at least destruction of life on a gigantic scale is possible. Therefore, while the perceived threat from India remains constant, Pakistan's ability to hit back is now almost on par. Under the circumstances, the threat of war may have receded but that does not mean that peace is secured as a consequence.

Whether a possible US-India nuclear deal will set in motion another arms race between India and Pakistan is moot. Would Pakistan then seek to enter into a comparable deal with another power with a view to re-establishing the balance of power? From a realist point of view, this seems to be the natural response for Pakistan. However, one can wonder if there is a nuclear power willing to enter into such an alliance. Often China is mentioned as the counterweight that Pakistan will try to cultivate. There is a long history of close relations between both countries and that relationship remains stable. However, the Chinese are not known for entering into military alliances with external powers. Some informal understanding between the two countries, however, exists to counter the perceived Indian hegemony in South Asia.

Yet, the fact that Pakistan is a nuclear power means that the US will have to continue to work with it in the war on terror but at the same time to seek to restrict the nuclear weapons ambitions of Pakistan. Moreover, Pakistan will continue to be important for monitoring the volatile tribal areas on the western border with Afghanistan. However, in the longer run, it is less likely that the US would bolster Pakistan's military as it once did.

It is possible that if a deal on Kashmir that accommodates the interests of the two states and the Kashmiri people is reached, the situation in South Asia can change in favor of peace and economic development. Both sides have been under pressure from the US to change their attitudes towards each other. In particular, Pakistan has been pressed hard by the US to climb down from its covert backing for the Kashmir jihad. Moreover, Pakistan and India have toned down their differences and they seem committed to a peaceful resolution of their conflicts. It is generally believed that Indian and Pakistani officials, especially those of their foreign affairs ministries, have made considerable progress on the Kashmir dispute but preparing their populations for a solution that is acceptable to all sides, including the Kashmiris, will take some time.

The US is not likely to abandon Pakistan altogether, in spite of the strategic understanding it is fast developing with India. Pakistan is actively engaged in the war on terror. It has greatly angered the Islamists and the result has been violent conflict between the military and the extremists. Within Pakistan, it seems that the prestige of the military has suffered considerably in the wake of the democratic movement that emerged after the Chief Justice was declared non-functional. The elections of 18 February were clearly a protest vote against the authoritarianism of the Musharraf regime. LaPorte (1969) argued that in Pakistan military strongmen lose grip on power when the military establishment withdraws its support to them; he did not believe that the mass upsurge of ordinary citizens had much role to play when Ayub Khan was forced to resign.

In the present situation, it seems that the mass upsurge which emanated after the Chief Justice of the Pakistan Supreme Court was declared non-functional played a crucial role in starting a process that culminated in the elections of February 2008 and transition to civilian rule. Indeed, 100 ex-servicemen did issue an appeal to Musharraf to step down, but it was largely a symbolic gesture from people out of power. It is however possible that the military establishment did secretly tell him to let democracy be restored. Also, pressure from the US, the EU, and the British Commonwealth played an important role in free and fair elections being held.

LaPorte's thesis that the transfer of power in Pakistan into civilian hands was not likely to consolidate into democracy as another coup would be in the offing at some stage should not be discounted, however. Aziz (2008) also affirms a similar outcome based on his theory of path-dependency. There can be no denying that when civilian institutions are not firmly grounded in a polity and the military dominates, the probability of military takeovers increases, but this need not be seen as something mechanical and immutable.

The present study seems to suggest that Pakistan has reached a point where cyclical shifts in power from civilian to military hands cannot go on and on forever without the system developing new capabilities or breaking down and disintegrating at some point. Military rule has increasingly proved ineffective in establishing law and order and peace. Therefore, its claims to providing effective government have lost considerable credibility. The proliferation of Islamic extremism laced with suicide bombers and other forms of terrorist mindset has wreaked havoc in all sectors and regions of Pakistan. Unless determined and firm measures are taken to establish a normal political milieu the state can disintegrate as a result of civil war, sectarian killings, and regional separatisms.

Under the circumstances Pakistan may now be on the threshold of democracy. If a sustained movement in favor of democracy and civilian rule develops, the military can be convinced to drastically re-define its role. As mentioned earlier its role as a frontline state against communism is over and its role as an ally in the US-led war on terror has alienated it from significant sections of Pakistani society. Its duty to maintain a credible defense against external aggression will always be there, but its political role should be open to critical review and correction. It is time for the stakeholders in the Pakistan enterprise to agree to supplant the garrison state with a democratic state representative of the wishes of the Pakistani people.

NOTES

1. The author would like to thank General (Retd) Mirza Aslam Beg, Lt. General (Retd) Asad Durrani, Brigadier (Retd) Yasub Ali Dogar, and Professor Stephen Cohen for granting interviews. Thanks are also due to Professor Pervaiz Iqbal Cheema, Professor S.D. Muni, and Associate Professor Kjell Engelbrekt for their valuable comments on earlier drafts of this paper. Dr Engelbrekt went out of his way to share his vast theoretical knowledge of international relations with the author. The author is responsible for the views and analysis presented in this study.
2. Interviews with Lt. General Asad Durraini, 31 November 2007.
3. Interview with Professor Stephen Cohen, 2 April 2008.
4. Ibid.

REFERENCES

Ahmed, Ishtiaq (1987). *The Concept of an Islamic State: An Analysis of the Ideological Controversy in Pakistan.* London: Frances Pinter; New York: St. Martin's Press.

——— (1998). *State, Nation and Ethnicity in Contemporary South Asia.* London and New York: Pinter Publishers.

——— (1999). 'South Asia'. In David Westerlund and Ingvar Svanberg (eds.), *Islam Outside the Arab World.* Richmond: Curzon.

——— (2002). 'The 1947 Partition of India: A paradigm for pathological politics in India and Pakistan'. *Asian Ethnicity,* 3, 1, March.

——— (28 December 2003). 'General Musharraf must make the right decisions', *The Daily Times.*

——— (26 July 2005). 'The madrassa industry'. *The Daily Times.*

——— (2005). 'The politics of group rights in India and Pakistan'. In Ishtiaq Ahmed (ed.), *The Politics of Group Rights: The State and Multiculturalism.* Langham University Press of America.

——— (6 January 2007). 'A year for South Asian peace', *The News International.* Karachi.

——— (6 January 2007). 'Undermining institutions', *The News International.* Karachi.

——— (16 July 2007). 'Biased moralities', *The News International.* Karachi.

——— (2007). 'Election Prospects in Pakistan'. ISAS Insights No. 22, 19 July. Singapore: Institute of South Asian Studies.

——— (1 December 2007). 'All the glitter and the gold', *The News International*. Karachi.

——— (2008). 'The Pakistan elections—A political analysis'. ISAS Brief No. 55, 22 February. Singapore: Institute of South Asian Studies.

Ahmed, Ishtiaq, Rajshree Jetly, and Iftikhar Ahmad Lodhi (2007). 'Pakistan, the road ahead'. ISAS Insights No. 24. Singapore: Institute of South Asian Studies.

Alavi, Hamza (1972). 'The state in post-colonial societies, Pakistan and Bangladesh', *New Left Review*, 1, 74, July–August.

Arif, General K.M. (2001). *Khaki Shadows: Pakistan 1947–97*. Karachi: Oxford University Press.

Aziz, Mazhar (2008). *Military Control in Pakistan*. London and New York: Routledge.

Beg, General Mirza Aslam (2001, 24 March). 'Dialogue for peace and the myth of terrorism', *The Nation*. Lahore.

Bhutto, Zulfikar Ali (1969). *The Myth of Independence*. Oxford: Oxford University Press.

Bhutto, Benazir (2008). *Reconciliation, Islam, Democracy and the West*. London: Simon and Schuster.

Bidwai, Praful (2006). 'Chasing the mirage of nuclear stabilisation'. In Imtiaz Alam (ed.), *Sapana, South Asian Studies*, vol. VII. Lahore: South Asia Policy Analysis Network.

Burr, William (ed.) (2004). 'China, Pakistan and the Bomb: The Declassified File on US. Policy, 1977–97'. National Security Archive Electronic Briefing Book No. 114, 5 March, http//www.gwu.edu/~nsarchiv/NSAEBB/NSAEBB114/index.htm).

Cheema, Pervaiz Iqbal (1990). *Pakistan's Defence Policy, 1947–8*. London: Macmillan Press.

——— (2003). *The Armed Forces of Pakistan*. Karachi: Oxford University Press.

Cheema, Zafar Iqbal (1996). 'Pakistan's nuclear policies, attitudes and postures'. In P. R. Chari, Pervaiz Iqbal Cheema, and Iftekharuzzaman (eds.), *Nuclear Non-Proliferation in India and Pakistan*. Lahore: Vanguard Books.

Cloughley, Brian (2000). *A History of the Pakistan Army, Wars and Insurrections*. Karachi: Oxford University Press.

Cohen, Stephen (1992). *The Pakistan Army*. Oxford: Oxford University Press.

——— (2006). *The Idea of Pakistan*. New Delhi: Oxford University Press.

Davis, Anthony (1999). 'Inside jihad international', *Asiaweek*, Hong Kong, November. www.asiaweek.com/asiaweek/magazine/99/1119/nat.pakistan.jihad.html.

Durrani, Mahmud Ali (Maj. General, Retd) (2002). *India and Pakistan: The Cost of Conflict and the Benefit of Peace.* Oxford: Oxford University Press.

Eisenhower, Dwight E. (1961). *Eisenhower's Farewell Address to the Nation.* 17 January. http//mcadams.posc.mu.edu/ike.htm.

Faruqui, Ahmad (2003). *Rethinking the National Security of Pakistan: The Price of Strategic Myopia.* Hampshire: Ashgate.

Fuchs, Cynthia (23 February 2006). 'A garrison state: An interview with Eugene Jarecki, Why we fight', *Pop Matter.* http//www.popmatters.com/film/interviews/jarecki-eugene-060223.s html

Ghazali, Naziha and Massoud Ansari (2002). 'School of salvation?', *Newsline,* Karachi, June.

Grare, Frederic (2006). *Pakistan: The Myth of an Islamist Peril.* Washington DC: Carnegie Endowment for International Peace.

Haqqani, Husain (2005). *Pakistan: Between Mosque and Military.* Washington DC: Carnegie Endowment for International Peace.

Harrison, Selig (8 March 2001). 'CIA worked in tandem with Pak to create Taliban', *Times of India,* Mumbai.

Hoodhboy, Pervez (2006). 'Nuclear flashpoint, quest for safety'. In Imtiaz Alam (ed.), *Sapana, South Asian Studies,* vol. VII. Lahore: South Asia Policy Analysis Network.

Huntington, Samuel P. (1996). *Political Order in Changing Societies.* New Haven, Conn.: Yale University Press.

Hussain, Zahid (2000). 'In the shadow of terrorism', *Newsline,* Karachi, February.

India eNews (2007). http,//www.indiaenews.com/business/20071129/83435.htm, 29 November. (Accessed on 8 February 2008.)

Jackson, Robert and Georg Sorenson (2007). *Introduction to International Relations: Theories and Approaches.* Oxford: Oxford University Press.

Jain, Rashmi (2007). *The United States and Pakistan 1947–2006: A Documentary Study.* New Delhi: Radiant Publishers.

Jalal, Ayesha (1991). *State of Martial Law.* Lahore: Vanguard Books.

Jan, Abid Ullah (2002). 'Target: Jihad, madrassa or Islam?', *Muslim Uzbekistan,* 9 September 2002. http,//archive.muslimuzbekistan.com/eng/islam/2002/09/ a09092002.html.

Jan, Tarik (ed.) (1995). *Pakistan's Security and the Nuclear Option.* Islamabad: Institute of Policy Studies.

John, Wilson (2007). *The General and Jihad.* New Delhi: Pentagon Press.

Khan, Fazal Muqeem (1973). *Pakistan's Crisis in Leadership.* Islamabad: National Book Foundation.

Khan, Ghulam Jilani (2004). *SSG: Tarikh key Ayeney Mein* (The SSG in the Mirror of History). Cheerat: Headquarters SSG.

Khan, Gul Hassan (1993). *Memoirs of Lt. Gen. Gul Hassan Khan*. Karachi: Oxford University Press.

Khan, Mohammad Ayub (1967). *Friends not Masters*. London: Oxford University Press.

Khan, Sultan Muhammad (2006). *The Second Edition of a Memories and Reflections of a Pakistani Diplomat*. Karachi: Paramount Books.

Khan, Zulfikar Ali (1988). *Pakistan's Security: The Challenge and the Response*. Lahore: Progressive Publishers.

Kux, Dennis (2001). *The United States and Pakistan 1947–2000: Disenchanted Allies*. Oxford: Oxford University Press.

Lahore Declaration, 21 February 1999. http,//cns.miis.edu/pubs/inven/pdfs/lahore.pdf. (Accessed on 24 April 2008.)

LaPorte, Jr., Robert (11 November 1969). 'Succession in Pakistan, continuity and change in a garrison state', *Asian Survey*, 9.

Lasswell, Harold (1997). *Essays on the Garrison State*. New Brunswick, New Jersey: Transaction Publishers.

Lohalekar, Devidas B. (1991). *U.S. Arms to Pakistan: A Study in Alliance Relationship*. New Delhi: Ashish Publishing House.

Malik, S. K. (1979). *The Quranic Concept of War*. Lahore: Wajidalis.

Mansergh, N. and P. Moon (eds.) (1981). *The Transfer of Power 1942–47*, vol. 10, 22 March to 30 May, 1947. London: Her Majesty's Stationery Office.

Mazari, Shireen M. (2003). *The Kargil Conflict 1999*. Islamabad: The Institute of Strategic Studies.

Morgenthau, Hans J. (1948). *Politics among Nations: The Struggle for Power and Peace*. New York: Alfred Knopf.

Muni, S.D. (2008). 'India 2007: Achievements and anxieties', *South Asian Journal*, January–March 2008.

Musharraf, Pervez (2001). Address to People of Pakistan, 19 September. http//www.americanrhetoric.com/speeches/pakistanpresident.htm. (Accessed on 24 April 2008)

——— (2002). Address to the Nation, 12 January. http//www.pak.gov.pk/public/President_address.htm. (Accessed on 9 February 2002.)

——— (2002). Address to the Ulema and Mashaikh, 18 January. http//www.pak.gov.pk/public/President_address.htm . (Accessed on 9 February 2002.)

——— (2006). *In the Line of Fire*. London: Simon and Schuster.

Nayyar, Dhiraj (2007). 'Clearly troubled: The Indian government and a nuclear deal'. ISAS Brief No. 22, 31 August. Singapore: Institute of South Asian Studies.

Niazi, A.A.K. (1998). *The Betrayal of Pakistan.* Oxford: Oxford University Press.

Noman, Omar (1988). *The Political Economy of Pakistan.* London: Kegan Paul International.

Nordland, Rod (11 February 2002). 'A Dictator's Dilemma', *Newsweek*, Hong Kong.

Pakistan Army Green Book: Year of the Commanding Officer 1991 (1991). Rawalpindi: General Headquarters.

Qureshi, Hakeem Arshad (2004). *The 1971 Indo-Pakistan War: A Soldier's Narrative.* Oxford: Oxford University Press.

Raman. B. (2006). 'Dargai and Chenagai, waiting to hear Zawahiri's version'. International Terrorism Monitor, Paper No. 152 (also designated as Paper 2022), 13 November. South Asia Analysis Group. http,//www.south asiaanalysis.org/%5Cpapers21%5Cpaper2022.html (02-04-2008).

Ramana, M. V. (2006). 'Eliminating the nuclear danger'. In Imtiaz Alam (ed.), *Sapana, South Asian Studies*, vol. VII. Lahore: South Asia Policy Analysis Network.

Rana, Muhammad Amir (2004). *A to Z of Jehadi Organizations in Pakistan* (tr. into English by Saba Ansari). Lahore: Marshal Books.

Rashid, Ahmed (2000). *Taliban, Militant Islam, Oil and Fundamentalism in Central Asia.* New Haven: Yale University Press.

——— (2008). *Descent into Chaos.* London: Allen Lane.

Report of the Court of Inquiry constituted under Punjab Act II of 1954 to enquire into the Punjab Disturbances of 1953 (also known as Munir Report) (1954). Lahore: Government Printing Press.

Rizvi, Hasan Askari (2000). *Military, State and Society in Pakistan.* Basingstoke: Macmillan.

Sarila, Narendra Singh (2005). *The Shadow of the Great Game: The Untold Story of India's Partition.* New Delhi: Harper Collins.

Schwartz, Howell H. (2005). *Fear and the Garrison State. United Press International,* 26 April. http//www.rand.org/commentary/042605UPI.html.

Siddiqa, Ayesha (2006). 'Pakistan's security perspective'. In Imtiaz Alam (ed.), *Sapana, South Asian Studies*, vol. VII. Lahore: South Asia Policy Analysis Network.

——— (2007) *Military Inc.: Inside Pakistan's Military Economy.* Karachi: Oxford University Press.

Siddiqi, A.R. (1996). *The Military in Pakistan: Image and Reality.* Lahore: Vanguard.

Stanley, Jay (1997). 'Introduction: An invitation to revisit Lasswell's garrison state'. In Harold Lasswell, *Essays on the Garrison State.* New Brunswick, New Jersey: Transaction Publishers.

Stanley, Jay and David R. Segal (1997). 'Conclusion: Landmarks in defense literature'. In Harold Lasswell, *Essays on the Garrison State.* New Brunswick, New Jersey: Transaction Publishers.

Stephens, Joe and David B. Ottaway (23 March 2002). 'The ABC's of jihad in Afghanistan', *The Washington Post,* Washington.

Stern, Jessica (2000). 'Pakistan's jihad culture', *Foreign Affairs,* 79, 6.

Subrahmanyam, K. (1990). 'Kashmir', *Strategic Analysis,* 23, 11 May.

Tan, Tai Yong (2005). *The Garrison State, the Military, Government and Society in Colonial Punjab, 1849–1947.* New Delhi: Sage Publications.

Venkataramani, M.S. (1984). *The American Role in Pakistan, 1947–58.* Lahore: Vanguard Books.

Walt, Stephen M. (1987). *The Origins of Alliances.* Ithaca: Cornell University Press.

Waltz, Kenneth N. (1979). *Theory of International Politics,* New York: McGraw Hill.

Wright, Robin (28 December 2000). 'The chilling goal of Islam's new warriors religion, in Pakistan, today's militant faithful see the entire world as the battlefield for their holy war', *Los Angeles Times,* Los Angeles.

Yusuf, Moeed (2006). 'Persevering towards nuclear stability'. In Imtiaz Alam (ed.), *Sapana, South Asian Studies,* vol. VII. Lahore: South Asia Policy Analysis Network.

Zaidi, S. Akbar (2008). 'The political economy of military rule in Pakistan: The Musharraf regime'. ISAS Working Paper No. 31, 9 January. Singapore: Institute of South Asian Studies.

INTERVIEWS

General Mirza Aslam Beg, 31 November 2007, Islamabad

Lt. General Asad Durrani, 31 November 2007, Islamabad

Brigadier Yasub Ali Dogar, 25 January 2008, Singapore

Professor Stephen Cohen, 2 April 2008, Singapore

NEWSPAPERS

Shanghai Daily
The Daily Times, Lahore
The News International, Karachi-Islamabad-Lahore
The New York Times
The Washington Post
Times of India

4

Pakistan–China Relations in the 21st Century: Retrospect and Prospect

RAJSHREE JETLY AND IFTIKHAR A. LODHI

INTRODUCTION

PAKISTAN AND CHINA have shared an enduring relationship for over half a century. This paper explores some of the historical reasons for the strong Sino–Pak relationship and analyzes the challenges raised by recent geopolitical developments. The platform on which Sino–Pak relations was built in the post-World War II era was based largely on Cold War politics and Sino–Indian rivalry. The post-Cold War era has seen a fundamental shift in strategic thinking, which has affected Pakistan's relationship with China and the United States (US). The rapprochement between India and China reduced Pakistan's strategic importance as a counterweight to India for China. The recent developments in Indo–US relations, bringing the two countries closer as allies, had further affected Pakistan's significance as the US' strategic gateway to South Asia. However, the events of 9/11 have put Pakistan back in the forefront of the US' strategic calculations and foreign policy. Apart from geopolitical factors, new dynamics in the form of increased economic integration and energy security have played important roles in shaping Sino-Pak relations. As the geopolitical context of the Cold War era gives way to twenty-first century globalization, China and Pakistan relations are at an all-time high. Despite increasing Sino–Indian and Sino–American ties, both Pakistan and China are forging new bonds propelled by economic interests and the emerging strategic landscape with respect to the increasing roles of the US and India in the region.

The first part of the chapter explores some of the historical reasons for the strong Sino–Pak relationship in order to provide the background for the analysis of contemporary Sino–Pak relations. The second part examines the key aspect of this partnership, namely, cooperation in the field of defense, particularly in terms of the supply of arms and China's support of Pakistan's nuclear program. The third part of the chapter locates Sino–Pak relations in the international relations matrix made up of China, India, Pakistan and the US and analyzes the shifting strategic interests as the fundamentals shifted from the Cold War to economic liberalization to Islamic fundamentalism. Finally, the chapter examines the emerging economic aspects of the relationship as well as the all-important energy factor; China is one of the most voracious consumers of energy and Pakistan is a gateway to the energy-rich regions of the world.

HISTORY OF SINO–PAK RELATIONS

Pakistan was one of the first countries to establish diplomatic relations with the People's Republic of China following the Communist takeover in 1949. Prior to the Bandung Conference of 1955, the two countries were not especially close, and indeed viewed each other with some suspicion. Paradoxically, during this early period, India and China enjoyed closer relations than Pakistan and China. Pakistan was seen as being close to the US through its membership of the Central Treaty Organization (CENTO) and Southeast Asia Treaty Organization (SEATO). The Bandung Conference of 1955 brought China and Pakistan closer, as China used this as an opportunity to increase its engagement with the region. Chinese Premier Zhou Enlai was quick to recognize Pakistan's strategic significance in Cold War politics and saw that it was in China's interests to reach out to Pakistan (Cheema 2002: 303). The new mood was quite discernible after Bandung when Pakistani Prime Minister H.S. Suhrawardy reciprocated China's offer of friendship and made a declaration in Parliament that 'when the crucial time comes China will come to our rescue' (Burke 1974: 151).

Pakistan and China also found that they shared a common concern about the strategic risks of a potentially powerful and hegemonic India. Indeed, the India factor was arguably the single biggest factor that brought together these two nations, which culturally and ideologically have little in common. The post-Bandung period also coincided with a deterioration in Sino–Indian relations as border disputes became contentious. Nehru's vision of India and China working together as partners, captured in the slogan '*Hindi Chini Bhai Bhai*' (India and China are brothers), was rapidly being confined to history. The 'brothers' ended up going to a border war in 1962 over disputed territory.

From 1963 onwards, Sino–Pak relations started to acquire more substantive content with the Sino–Pakistan Frontier Agreement, ceding the Trans-Karakoram Tract of approximately 1050 sq. miles to China (Ganguly 2004: 118). A slew of agreements were signed on trade, border disputes, and air services, as well as cultural and technological cooperation (Chaudhri 2001: 320–1). Pakistan supported China's permanent representation in the United Nations Security Council in 1961, and in 1964, Premier Zhou visited Pakistan, and a year later, supported Pakistan in its war against India.

In 1965, India and Pakistan went to war. China gave moral support to Pakistan, condemned Indian aggression, and even applied military pressure on India to stop the war (Amin 2000: 160). One consequence of this war was that the US, which had been supporting Pakistan, ceased its military assistance. Starved of armaments, Pakistan turned to China for arms procurements and this marked the beginning of the close defense cooperation between China and Pakistan. Another outcome of the 1965 war was the Soviet factor. As part of Cold War politics, the Soviets chose to support India in that war, which widened the already growing rift between the Soviets and China. The Sino–Soviet rift brought the US into the play, as they saw the potential for *rapprochement* with China. Pakistan, which had already established close relations with the US, capitalized on this by facilitating the clandestine visit by then US Secretary of State, Henry Kissinger, who visited Beijing secretly in 1971 via Pakistan. This gesture brought Pakistan and China even closer.

Pakistan's close relationship with the US early on in its history was strengthened under General Ayub Khan who seized power in 1958 and immediately courted the US (ibid.: 159). General Khan guessed correctly that the US would be prepared to bankroll Pakistan as a frontline state in its Cold War against the Soviet Union. The Soviet invasion of Afghanistan drew Pakistan support from both the US and China, as both these powers had a vested interest in containing Soviet expansion. Thus, in a similar way to India, the Soviet Union was another factor in the cementing of Sino–Pak relations.

Building on their mutual interests in strategic and defense matters, China and Pakistan continued to strengthen their relations. Following Bangladesh's separation from Pakistan after the 1971 war, China again proved its friendship to Pakistan by using its veto power to block Bangladesh's application for membership to the United Nations.

SINO–PAK RELATIONS AND THE EVOLVING REGIONAL DYNAMICS

Sino–Pak relations have withstood the test of time, and this is reinforced by the exchange of numerous high-level visits by both countries over the years. In the past few years, Chinese Prime Minister Wen Jiabao visited Pakistan in 2005, followed by President Musharraf's visit to Beijing in February 2006. Chinese President Hu Jintao then visited Islamabad in November 2006 and, in April 2007, Pakistani Prime Minister Shaukat Aziz visited China to endorse the good relations and strong ties the countries share with each other.

Taking the strategic relationship forward was the landmark 'Treaty of Friendship, Cooperation and Good-neighborly relations' signed between China and Pakistan in January 2005. In this important agreement, both countries committed that 'neither party will join any alliance or bloc which infringes upon the sovereignty, security, and territorial integrity of the other side'. The treaty also binds both countries to 'not conclude treaties of this nature with any third party' (*Peoples Daily Online*, 6 April 2005). In essence, the treaty ensures continued cooperation between the two countries with a legal aspect to it.

There are four broad themes that may influence Sino–Pak relations in the immediate future. First is the issue of nuclear cooperation and proliferation, which remains under the international spotlight. Regionally, the controversial Indo–US nuclear deal may have created some imbalance that may recalibrate Sino–Pak relations, as discussed above. Second, Sino–Pak relations are cradled within a tense, dynamic matrix of bilateral relations involving India and the US. Third, the rise of Islamist fundamentalism in Pakistan, within the Central Asian states that broke away from the former Soviet block, and within the autonomous region of Xinjiang in China is putting some pressure on Sino–Pak relations. Fourth, the liberalization and integration of the giant economies of India and China have made trade and commerce key drivers of foreign policy. Related to this is energy security: India and China require huge amounts of energy and Pakistan is the gateway to the energy-rich Middle East and Central Asian regions.

THE STRATEGIC MATRIX

Sino-Pak relations cannot just be seen in a strictly bilateral framework and one would have to take into consideration the dynamics at the broader regional and global level. There is no denying that one aspect of Sino-Pak relations is strategic in terms of maintaining the balance of power in the region with the two other major players—India and the US. Sino–Indian and Indo–US relations have historically never been rosy, but recently there has been some warming in both these relations. This part of the chapter briefly examines these dynamics to understand whether Sino–Pak relations are contingent on these related strategic interests or whether China and Pakistan have genuinely forged an independent relationship of 'evergreen friendship'.

We begin by looking at the US relationship with Pakistan and how it has been a factor in terms of driving Sino–Pak relations forward. China's relationship with Pakistan may be contrasted with the US' relationship with Pakistan. Both countries have viewed Pakistan as a strategically significant state and helped Pakistan, especially during periods of regional instability. The difference between China and the US is that China has by and large remained a steady friend to Pakistan throughout the past half century, whereas the US has shown itself to be less consistent. During the early days of the Cold War, the US and Pakistan signed a mutual defense assistance agreement in 1954 followed by its membership in SEATO and CENTO, and Pakistan received over US$900 million worth of military equipment under these agreements (Rizvi 2001: 207).

However, from the mid-1960s, during and following the two Indo–Pak wars, the US stopped supporting Pakistan militarily. Pakistan's attempts in the 1970s to develop a nuclear weapon further distanced the US until the Soviet invasion of Afghanistan brought the US back to support Pakistan with arms and finance. After the Afghan war, the US again cut its support for Pakistan under the Pressler Amendment in 1990 for overstepping the nuclear threshold set by US laws (Schaffer 2003: 172) and refused to deliver military equipment that had already been purchased by Pakistan. Most significant was the failure to deliver F-16 fighter jets for which Pakistan had paid in advance.

China benefited from the US' approach to Pakistan in two ways. First, China picked up Pakistan's demand for defense supplies and cemented its ties with Pakistan in a tangible way. Second, by remaining a friend of Pakistan regardless of the external circumstances, China has gained credibility in the eyes of not just the Pakistani administration but also the Pakistani people. Thus, while the US has returned to pouring endless amounts of money and arms into Pakistan following the events of 9/11, it is not viewed as a friend but as a self-interested opportunist.

However, is China an altruistic friend, or are its strategic interests simply different from those of the US? Arguably, the US' interest in Pakistan has less to do with ongoing regional security and balance of power issues, and has more to do with global issues that wax and wane. During the Cold War, the US needed Pakistan to contain the Soviets. During the post-Cold War period, the US had less use for Pakistan, but in the post-9/11 period, Pakistan has once again become critical to US security interests in the war against terrorism. Pakistan remains a 'frontline ally' in the US war against terrorism since 9/11 and has received massive aid worth US$3 billion as a pivotal ally in US-led counter-terrorism efforts. Beijing remains concerned over Pak–US military cooperation and its wider implications, particularly in the context of continuing interest in Afghanistan. But as long as there is no marked sliding down in Sino–US relations, there is not much likelihood of this creating undue strain in the Sino–Pak strategic alliance.

More recently, the US has again given more impetus to Sino–Pak relations by engaging more closely with India. The end of the Cold War has allowed India and the US to pursue a bilateral strategic relationship on their own terms (Ganguly and Scobell 2005; Schaffer 2002). From the US perspective, India is a natural ally, being a proven democracy that is also emerging as a major economic power. There is enormous potential for trade opportunities, with bilateral trade tipped to swell beyond US$75 billion and US$225 billion by 2010 and 2015 respectively (Gupta 2008). Importantly, just as China sees Pakistan as its ally in the containment of India, the US sees India as a strategic ally in its containment of China, a rising global power, militarily and economically, which could threaten US supremacy in the Asia-Pacific region. In 2005, President Bush called India a natural partner and assured it of US support in its rise as a major power in the new century, and in 2006 the controversial Indo–US nuclear deal was signed.

Both China and Pakistan reacted coldly to the Indo-US nuclear deal. Pakistan, not surprisingly, was unhappy that the US was giving preferential treatment to India in terms of developing its civilian nuclear capability. It wanted the US to treat Pakistan equally and take account of Pakistan's legitimate nuclear ambitions to meet its energy needs. It also expressed concerns that the exception for India would undermine the 'shared objectives of stability in South Asia and a strong global non-proliferation regime' and 'encourage India to continue its weapons programme without any constraint or inhibition' (Pakistan Foreign office responses to Nuclear Deal since March 2006).

The US was clearly making a stand in de-linking India and Pakistan on this issue. China's initial reaction was cautious and insisted that India should first sign the Nuclear Non-Proliferation Treaty (NPT) and the Comprehensive Test Ban Treaty (CTBT) before the international community sanctioned the deal. More recently, China toned down its pronouncements and spoke of possible cooperation by both countries on the peaceful use of nuclear energy, as long as both abided by their respective international obligations (Cherian 2007). During Prime Minister Manmohan Singh's January 2008 visit to China, China remained non-committal on whether it would support India's request to the Nuclear Suppliers Group (NSG) with respect to the Indo–US nuclear deal, but indicated that it would cooperate with India in the field of civil nuclear energy (Ministry of Foreign Affairs, China 2008).

China naturally views the warming Indo–US relations with some concern as it potentially threatens China's position in the region. India is fully aware of Chinese unease with India's *rapprochement* with the US and is conscious that a strong Indo–US relationship is likely to push China closer to Pakistan. While a stable Pakistan is in India's interests, a Pakistan on the receiving end of more arms and nuclear technology is not. At the same time, for its own strategic reasons, India would not want to tie itself too closely to the US' global objectives and end up losing autonomy over its foreign policy (Hathaway 2002: 26). Thus, India has worked towards building good relations with China over the past two decades, and there is evidence that China is also keen on strengthening Sino-Indian ties.

India's first major step came with Prime Minister Rajiv Gandhi's visit to China in 1988. This set in motion a series of high-level exchanges, with Chinese Prime Minister Li Peng visiting India in 1991, followed by the Indian President's visit in 1992 and then Chinese President Jiang Zemin's visit in 1996. A notable consequence of these diplomatic efforts was a shift in China's position on Kashmir. From the 1990s, Beijing adopted a more neutral stand on Kashmir; instead of supporting the Pakistani line on holding a plebiscite, it called for a peaceful settlement of issues. In 1996, Chinese President Jiang Zemin made an official statement urging Pakistan to settle its dispute over Kashmir in a peaceful manner (Faruqui 2003: 89). This is a far cry from the 1960s when the Chinese supported Pakistan's call for self-determination in Kashmir and referred to Pakistanis fighting for Kashmir as 'comrades in arms' (Faruqui 2003: 89). China adopted a similar conciliatory approach to the Kargil crisis (1999) and the December 2001 stand-off between Pakistan and India when it urged both countries to exercise restraint (BBC News, 15 June 1999; 26 December 2001).

The recent visit of Indian Prime Minister, Manmohan Singh to China in January 2008 built upon the November 2006 visit of Chinese President Hu Jintao to India, and sent a positive signal for carrying forward the process of Sino–Indian cooperation. Economic cooperation remains a key objective of both countries, with bilateral trade estimated to reach US$75 billion by 2010. China is also keen to sign a Free Trade Agreement (FTA) with India, which could create the biggest free trade region in the world and provide an enormous boost to economic relations between the two countries.

India sees Pakistan as a major sticking point in Sino–Indian relations and it is sparing no effort in strengthening its ties with China. However, China will continue to have a clear strategic interest in Pakistan, as a counter to India's growing strength and improving relationship with the US. It is for this reason that despite its declared intention of following a balanced policy in South Asia, China has shown no inclination yet to scale down its military and political ties with Pakistan and there is not much likelihood of China seeking better relations with India at the expense of its friendship with Pakistan in the near future. While there are synergistic forces that are capable of propelling Sino–Indian relations to a new level, there are significant geopolitical, economic, and strategic hurdles along the way. It has been argued by many that, at one level, China and India are rivals and competing with each other for economic and political influence, as well as for energy resources. There are also challenges in terms of unresolved border disputes and latent distrust of each other (Yuan 2007: 137–9).[1] Hence, despite China's visible dilution of support in recent years for Pakistan's stand on Kashmir, there is no real weakening of relations between the two countries. According to Mohan Malik (1995: 147):

> China is not going to become less friendly to Pakistan following normalisation with India because the combined strategic and political advantages that China

receives from its relationship with Pakistan (and through Pakistan, other Islamic countries) easily outweigh any advantages that China might accrue from a closer relationship with India. Above all, Pakistan is the only country that stands up to India and thereby prevents Indian hegemony in the region. This fulfils a key strategic objective of China's South Asian policy.

Pakistan continues to receive advanced military and nuclear technology from China, and President Hu Jintao reiterated its strategic commitment to Pakistan during his visit to Pakistan in November 2006 by quoting an evocative Chinese proverb: 'China can leave gold but not friendship with Pakistan' (*Dawn*, 26 November 2006). Pakistan in turn has proved its loyalty to China by continuing to support its core interests in Taiwan, Tibet, human rights and the East Turkestan issue which the Chinese President Hu Jintao duly acknowledged as 'something we in China will never forget' (Ministry of Foreign Affairs, Pakistan 2006).

However, the events of 9/11 and the radicalization of Islamist militants in South and Central Asia may have some impact on Sino–Pak relations. Even before 9/11, China had distanced itself from Pakistan's Afghan policy of supporting the Taliban. It was concerned by the rise of terrorism in its own backyard in Xinjiang carried out by separatist 'East Turkestan' militants. Xinjiang is an autonomous region of China, which is home to over 40 ethnic groups, the largest of which is the Uyghur. The Uyghurs are followers of Islam and have, since the 1980s, been seeking a separate state. In the 1990s, the group began to use violence and terrorist tactics as part of its separatist movement, which caused China considerable concern.

China is clearly worried about the potential spill-over effects of the jihadi mindset of Kashmiri separatists, which could stir up similar sentiments in Xinjiang. It has been speculated that China's recent, more moderate stance on Kashmir was a reflection of its concerns about potential jihadi violence within its own territory. China was already suspicious that the Muslim Uyghur separatists were being supported by external forces (Shirk 2004: 93; Sinha 2004: 224). At first, China did not internationalize the Xinjiang problem, but in the wake of the 'war on terror', it jumped on the bandwagon to counter religious extremism and used the Xinjiang crisis to seek the support of Western powers.

Islamist terrorism is a double-edged sword in Sino–Pak relations. On the one hand, it draws China closer to President Musharraf in Pakistan, which is trying to contain the rise of Islamist fundamentalism and waging war against terrorists. China has its own shared interest in this issue and will be more than willing to do what it can to support the Pakistani administration. According to Yuan, 'Beijing's support of Musharraf arguably lies partly in a desire to maintain stability in that country against the backdrop of rising Islamic fundamentalism' (Yuan 2007: 139). On the other hand, this issue gives China an opportunity to engage with the US, India, and Russia, which are all major powers that have been affected by Islamist terrorism. China's coming together with these powers could be a dampener to Sino–Pak relations, as Pakistan has to walk a tightrope on this, given the nature of its domestic constituencies.

However, Pakistan is fully aware of the potential impact of Islamic terrorism and separatist violence on its relationship with China and has done everything possible to allay the fears of the Chinese. President Musharraf, in his 2001 visit to China, expressed support for the Chinese campaign against the Uyghur separatists in Xinjiang and declared that Pakistan would extend full support to China in its fight against the separatists. Pakistani authorities have also targeted Uyghur settlements in Pakistan, expelled Uyghurs from their madrasas and even killed a few Uyghur extremists, including Hasan Mahsum, the leader of the East Turkestan Islamic Movement (Haider 2004). On 6 August 2004, both countries conducted their first anti-terrorism military exercise named 'Friendship 2004' in Xinjiang (Rahman 2007: 216). Some analysts believe that the storming of the Lal Masjid in July 2007 was partly to appease China which remains concerned about the rising attacks against its nationals on Pakistani soil.[2] This is further evidence of the importance of Sino–Pak relations in Islamabad's calculations. Pakistan would like to keep China firmly engaged on this issue to forestall the possibility of any downward slide in their relations.

DEFENSE COOPERATION

Pakistan and China forged a close strategic bond with each other and this was reflected, in particular, in the defense and nuclear cooperation between the two countries. Following the 1965 Indo-Pak war and the temporary cessation of US arms supplies to Pakistan, China stepped up to become Pakistan's main supplier. Although the US resumed arming Pakistan and Mujaheedin fighters during the Soviet invasion of Afghanistan, China remained a major arms supplier for all the armed forces of Pakistan, including the army, navy, and air force. Though the Chinese weapons were qualitatively not of the same standard as the Western arms, the procurement of arms from an alternative source was welcomed by Pakistan. According to one source, in the 1970s, China supplied 500 T-59 battle tanks, 25 naval vessels, and 300 F-6 fighter jets in a US$600 million deal (Deepak 2006: 136). China was instrumental in rebuilding and modernizing Pakistan's armed forces. By the early 1980s, Pakistan's air force was flying Chinese-made A5 and F-6 aircraft belonging to the MIG-19 family (ibid.: 136).

In the 1990s, China cooperated with Pakistan to develop FC-1 fighter planes which were the equivalent of the F-16 with a Russian engine (ibid.). China also supplied missiles to Pakistan, including portable surface-to-air missiles (Anza-2) and Red Arrow anti-tank missiles (Baktar Shikan) (SIPRI 2002: 235). Recently, there has been a significant increase in naval cooperation between the two countries. A major agreement was signed in 2006 whereby China would supply four frigate ships for the Pakistan navy to be delivered between now and 2013. The deal also included upgrading the Karachi dockyard and assistance in the modernization of Pakistan's surface fleet, including transfer of technology (Aneja 2006: 5; *The Tribune*, 24 May 2006). The defense cooperation was also part of broader investment in the military industrial segment, with the Chinese supporting defense industries, aeronautical complexes, ordinance factories, shipyards, power plants, and communications infrastructure. The first heavy mechanical industrial complex of heavy foundry and forge was established near Taxila with Chinese assistance in 1979, followed by a MIG-19/F-6 repair factory in Kamra.

China's bolstering of Pakistan's defense capabilities were clearly also for its own strategic interests. In particular, China needed to strengthen Pakistan's military capability in the 1980s to contain Soviet incursions into Afghanistan. In the 1990s, China's strategy was targeted at containing India, especially after India's 1998 nuclear tests, when India publicly stated that its nuclear arsenal was necessary as it viewed China as a potential threat.[3] China responded strongly and registered its protest at this insinuation. For Pakistan, China remains its principal supplier of arms and ammunition to contain India, its main adversary. Its relationship with China would also ensure that Pakistan would not be left high and dry and diplomatically isolated when its relations with the US hit a rough patch. The benefits for both China and US were mutual.

This defense cooperation has continued and recently, during President Hu Jintao's visit to Pakistan in 2006, the two countries reaffirmed their commitment for closer cooperation in defense matters, mutual consultation, and reciprocal visits by military delegations (Ministry of Foreign Affairs, Pakistan 2006). The Pakistani Air Force, which is already collaborating with a Chinese aviation company on developing fighter jets (the JF-17 Thunder fighters), signed a memorandum with another Chinese aviation company for long-term collaboration and aircraft manufacturing including Airborne Warning and Control Systems (AWACS). The two countries have also held several joint military exercises, including the Joint Anti-terrorism Friendship Exercise 2004 and the Friendship 2006 China–Pakistan Joint Anti-Terrorism Exercise (Ministry of Foreign Affairs, Pakistan 2006).

Another significant aspect of cooperation between China and Pakistan is China's alleged assistance to Pakistan's nuclear program. This remains a nebulous area, and there is little evidence to verify the extent of nuclear cooperation between the two countries. It is also difficult to ascertain whether there was any nuclear cooperation between China and Pakistan in the early period. According to one source, Zulfikar Ali Bhutto had requested Chinese assistance in the development of nuclear weapons as early as the mid-1960s but the Chinese did not oblige (Perkovich 2004: 200). However, the situation changed as a result of China's strategic calculations *vis-à-vis* India and the Soviet Union. India first tested its nuclear capability in 1974. This caused the Chinese to rethink their nuclear strategy with respect to Pakistan. There was a strategic reason to help Pakistan, as it could provide a counter to India's potential dominance in South Asia, which would be a threat to China. Nevertheless, China refrained from assisting Pakistan with its nuclear program, partly because of concerns of international, especially that of the US, reaction to such assistance.

In 1979, the Soviets invaded Afghanistan. Pakistan's security resources were already stretched in its tensions with India, and having to contend with another threat was a formidable challenge. From China's perspective, if Pakistan were to come under Soviet control, China itself would become vulnerable. To offset this possibility, China began to provide nuclear assistance to Pakistan, knowing full well that at this point the US was unlikely to object too strenuously as the US was very worried about the possibility of the Soviets penetrating through to the Persian Gulf and onwards. US criticism was somewhat muted for a period in the 1980s, during the early period of which China gave considerable nuclear assistance to Pakistan. In 1992, China signed the NPT. It also signed the CTBT in 1996 and issued a statement that it would only make safeguarded nuclear transfers.

However, despite international criticism and restrictions, there is widespread speculation that China has reportedly continued to assist Pakistan, even at the risk of violating its treaty obligations. It has been reported that in 1994 China sold unsafeguarded ring magnets to Pakistan in violation of the NPT. These ring magnets were used in gas centrifuges to enrich uranium (Kan 2007: 3). There were other similar transfers of equipment and technology. Pakistan's nuclear bomb is widely believed to be based on Chinese blueprints. This suspicion was reinforced by the scandal involving A.Q. Khan, the top man in Pakistan's nuclear program who was accused of masterminding a nuclear proliferation program involving Iran, Libya, and North Korea. Although Khan was given clemency by President Musharraf, the evidence from the investigation showed that some of the designs for nuclear weapons obtained by Libya from Pakistan were of Chinese origin (Deepak 2006: 138).

While China reportedly stopped direct assistance to Pakistan's nuclear weapons program in 1994 following its signing of the NPT in 1992, it has contributed to missile technology and supplies as well as to the development of nuclear power plants. In 1993, the Clinton administration imposed sanctions on China for transferring some of the M-11 missile equipment to Pakistan, the technology for which was supposedly transferred in 1988 (Garver 2002: 404–5; Kan 2008: 7). Although China was not a member of the Missile Technology Control Regime (MTCR), it had agreed to abide by the rules of the MTCR but allegedly flouted them, although Chinese officials argued that their action abided strictly by the letter of the law (ibid.: 405).[4] The Pakistani government also agreed and strongly reinforced this message. In 1994, Pakistani President Farooq Ahmed Khan Leghari stated that all missile and missile technology transfer from China was within the MTCR ambit (ibid.: 405). There is also a view that Western and Indian scholars tend to exaggerate allegations of a Sino-Pakistan nuclear nexus which are, in any case, not based on concrete evidence (Cheema 2002: 305).

Another major contribution by the Chinese was the development of nuclear power plants which, although for civilian nuclear energy use, raised concerns that some of the civilian use could easily be diverted to military use. The 300-megawatt (MW) plant at Chashma, developed and built in the 1990s, became operational in 2000 and there are fears that it could be used to covertly produce weapons-grade plutonium. In May 2004, just before it joined the NSG, China signed an agreement to build a second nuclear power plant (Chashma 2). There are reports that China also provided equipment to enable an unsafeguarded reactor at Khushab to generate weapons-grade plutonium (Garver 2002: 404; Kan 2007: 5) but the allegations are speculative and not backed by sufficient proof. Similarly there is a widely held view that China and North Korea provided assistance in the development of Pakistan's ballistic missiles program including the Short and Medium Range Ballistic Missiles, Shaheen 1 and Shaheen 2, and Ghauri 1 and Ghauri 2, respectively (Kan 2007: 9; Rajain 2005: 159). Pakistan and China deny these charges on grounds of inadequate evidence.

In the wake of the Indo–US nuclear deal, Pakistan demanded similar treatment by the US, which was not forthcoming. During Musharraf's visit to China in February 2006, both countries agreed to enhance cooperation in the peaceful application of nuclear energy (Chinese Embassy in Islamabad 2006). The defense and nuclear cooperation between China and Pakistan, despite being mired in some controversies, shows how close the two countries are strategically and in terms of sticking with each other through thick and thin. It suggests that the repeated assurance by China that it will not just be a fair-weather friend to Pakistan is not mere rhetoric, but something that has been proven by its actions.

ECONOMIC COOPERATION: THE NEW DIMENSION

The changing geopolitical landscape has raised questions about the strength of the Sino–Pak *bonhomie* that has been cultivated for so long. Nonetheless, all evidence and rhetoric from both sides suggest that Pakistan and China are committed to their long-term relationship. In fact, there are now two more dimensions that will serve to strengthen the ties. One is the growing economic partnership between Pakistan and China, and the other is the strategic issue of energy security. As Tanvir Ahmed Khan, a former Foreign Secretary and Ambassador of Pakistan, said, 'a new bilateral alliance has emerged and at its heart lies the promise of Pakistan as a conduit of energy and strategic commodities' (Khan 2007). This part of the chapter looks at the burgeoning economic ties between the two countries and the role of energy security in the future of Sino–Pak relations.

Despite their good friendship, economic ties between the two countries remained on the fringes until the 1990s. In the early 1990s, Pakistan embarked on economic liberalization and made structural changes in response to the sweeping wave of globalization. There was greater freedom in trade, enhanced market capitalism, and more investment in infrastructure and communications. China too had embraced the market economy in 1978, although still highly controlled, and it had started yielding economic gains during the 1990s. China had a real incentive to nurture a peaceful and profitable neighborhood in search of markets for its products. The end of the Cold War had ushered in a new era in the regional and international orders by shifting the focus from military power politics to economic competition. India was also affected by these tectonic changes and responded by embracing globalization and emphasizing economic ties with its neighbors, leading to its *rapprochement* with China and Pakistan.

From the Chinese perspective, Pakistan offers great opportunities for Chinese exports and investments. It is a fast growing consumption-led economy and, with a population of 160 million, is a large market for manufactured goods (sixth largest). Chinese business interest in Pakistan has been increasing steadily in recent years. Bilateral trade between the two countries has grown by almost 50 per cent annually from a few hundred millions in the early 1990s to US$1.5 billion in 2001 and to US$5 billion in 2006 (see Figure 4.1). Both countries have set targets to increase trade to US$5 billion by 2011. However, these figures are part of a general trend and should be seen in the context of China's trade volume with other countries in the region, especially India. For example, trade with India has increased threefold in the past five years from US$ 13 billion in 2002 to US$38 billion in 2007, with both countries targeting US$60 billion by 2011.

Islamabad took a bold step when it concluded an FTA with China in 2006, at a time when even advanced and developing economies continue to feel threatened by a flood of cheap Chinese imports affecting local economies. In 2003, both countries signed an Early Harvest Program, which led to the FTA, which came into effect in January 2008. The FTA not surprisingly resulted in Pakistan's trade deficit with China rising sharply, as most of the increase in the trade volume was in terms of Chinese exports to Pakistan, with Pakistani exports recording only modest growth (Figure 4.1). That Pakistan took such a bold step is testament to the high trust between the two countries nurtured over decades. It was also clearly a strategic move by Pakistan.

Policy makers in Islamabad realized that it was important to

Figure 4.1: Pakistan's Trade with China, 1994–2006

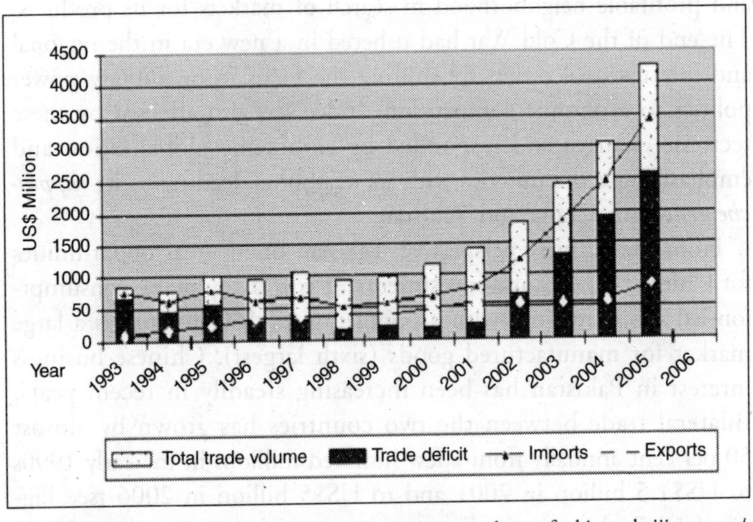

Sources: Embassy of Pakistan in Beijing, http://www.embassyofpakistan-beijing.rg.cn/website/PCTS.htm, and Ministry of Commerce, Pakistan, http://www.commerce.gov.pk/index.asp

engage China in a long-term win-win relationship and were prepared to bear the cost of some trade imbalance and negative impact to the domestic industry in the short term.[5] Outweighing the costs are the benefits of this engagement, which are manifold for both countries, ranging from increased investment flows to Pakistan to long-term geopolitical gains.

To promote Pakistani exports, overcome trade imbalance, and increase overall trade volume, both countries have taken several initiatives including Special Economic Zones exclusively for Chinese investment, special buying arrangements by China, dry ports on both sides of the border, and increased exhibitions, business forums, and conferences. Pakistan also opened new consulates in Shanghai and Chengdu in 2005 and 2007, respectively. Part of the long-term benefit for Pakistan is increased Chinese investment, particularly in infrastructure and developmental projects, which are crucial to Pakistan.

The extent of Chinese economic engagement is reflected in the growing number of public and private projects and joint ventures. Chinese investment in Pakistan has been growing steadily and reached US$6 billion in 2007. More than 60 Chinese firms are operating in Pakistan, undertaking over 100 projects in different sectors, including oil and gas, information technology, telecommunications, power generation, engineering, automobile manufacturing, infrastructure, and mining. Both governments are encouraging their business leaders to take part in the consumer and financial sectors in Pakistan, which have been growing rapidly. The total overall foreign investment in Pakistan has risen by over 600 per cent in the past five years (Rahman 2006a). However, the share of private Chinese investment in the overall Foreign Direct Investment has remained low *vis-à-vis* the US, European Union and the Middle East and, as such, there are huge opportunities for increased Chinese investments.

The reason behind low levels of private Chinese investment in Pakistan can be traced to the capital flows to and from China. Chinese investment abroad grew nominally until 2000 and has taken a gradual upward trend only after that. However, Chinese accumulated outward investment of US$35 billion in 2003 is only equivalent to that of Korea and one-fifth that of Japan (UNCTAD 2003).[6] Nevertheless, encouragement from both governments has started yielding results and Chinese investment in Pakistan has been growing rapidly. The Pakistan-China Investment Forum in 2006 witnessed US$500 million worth of joint venture undertakings in various sectors such as real estate development, the Karachi mass transit communication network, and chemical, fertilizer, automobile, and agro-based industries (Rahman 2006a).

Economic cooperation reached new heights when, during the 2006 high-level visits, both countries agreed to bring the National Development and Reform Commission of China and the Planning Commission of Pakistan together for regular consultations in 2006 and signed a five-year (2007–11) Plan for Trade and Economic Cooperation. The plan is expected to play an important role in the areas of agriculture, manufacturing, infrastructure, energy, information and communication technology and education cooperation by undertaking major development projects. The first major step under the Plan is the establishment of the China Pakistan Investment Company in 2007 with an initial capital of US$200 million which will finance development projects/joint ventures on a commercial basis (Syed 2007).

Many of the projects undertaken or supported by China are major infrastructural projects with long-term strategic and economic implications. These include the Chashma Nuclear Power Plant, Heavy Mechanical Complex, Saindak Copper Mining, Thar Coal Power Plant, Karakoram Highway, Coastal Highway, and Gwadar port. A number of hydropower plants, refineries, railways, exploration, and mining projects are also expected in the near future (Rahman 2006a). These joint ventures not only help Pakistan in its overall development efforts but also reduce its dependency on international financial institutions, whose financial assistance comes attached with many onerous conditions. These projects also have the effect of indirectly increasing Chinese stake in Pakistan's economy, stability, and ultimately politics. Of these, the most significant is the Gwadar port, which will be discussed further below.

ENERGY SECURITY AND GEOPOLITICS

In the past decade, energy has emerged as a key factor in the foreign policy-making of many countries, especially with respect to the energy-rich regions of Asia. Energy is especially critical to China and India, whose rates of growth and consumption are enormous. Each of these two countries has populations of over one billion and their economies are growing at the rate of 7 to 9 per cent, which implies a 5 to 6 per cent growth in their energy demand (International Energy Agency 2007). Within ten years, China has gone from being a net oil exporting country in 1993 to becoming the world's second largest importer of oil, importing 47 per cent of its total 7 million barrel per day consumption. India currently imports 80 per cent of its total oil consumption of 2.7 million barrels per day. The dependency on oil leaves countries vulnerable to external shocks ranging from price hikes, to diplomatic hurdles in acquiring resources, to potential blockade of their cargos in case of hostility with enemies. Given these strategic considerations, and bearing in mind the sheer size of India and China, whose combined populations represent about a third of the global population, it is clear that the foreign policy calculations of these two countries with respect to energy have truly global implications. Many analysts fear that energy would be the primary cause for conflicts and wars in the future (Klare 2001).

Pakistan is well poised at the crossroads of the three important Asian regions and offers connectivity through what has been termed the 'trade and energy corridor'. The corridor includes oil and gas pipelines, railways and road links with Iran, Afghanistan, China, and the Central Asian states (Rahman 2006b). China is not the only country buying into this corridor by providing financial and technical assistance to Pakistan. For example, the Asian Development Bank (ADB) is providing US$500 million for Pakistan's highway infrastructure and is actively supporting the Turkmenistan–Afghanistan–Pakistan gas pipeline, which can be extended to India. The World Bank and many countries have shown interest in financing the Iran–Pakistan–India gas pipeline, large dams, and electricity imports from Tajikistan and Kyrghyzstan. All these endeavors will not only effectively meet Pakistan's development plans and growing energy needs but will certainly accelerate regional interdependency and economic development through these various cross-border projects.

Pakistan is a beneficiary of all of this. It is already playing a leading role in regional cooperation organizations such as the Economic Cooperation Organization[7] and Organization of Islamic Cooperation (OIC). It also has observer status in the Shanghai Cooperation Organization (SCO)[8] and aspires for full membership. The SCO, since 1996, has evolved as a major Asian grouping dealing with security issues, terrorism, and economic and energy cooperation. The organization has been discussed extensively in Western security circles due to its 'potential' in challenging American interests in the region. However, more than security what the SCO can accomplish is to become an 'energy club' feared in Western circles as 'an OPEC [Organization of Petroleum Exporting

Countries] with bomb'. Pakistan hopes to join the club by becoming an 'energy corridor' (Douglass et al. 2006: 10).

Pakistan had plans, even before the SCO came into existence, to exploit the opportunity of a corridor by pursuing a friendly and stable regime in Afghanistan through a 'strategic depth' policy with the Taliban. However, the regional and international powers were wary of the Islamist hardcore Taliban regime and their links with the growing international jihadi movement. The 9/11 incidents and Pakistan's decision to step back from supporting the Taliban has raised new challenges for Pakistan to fully exploit its 'corridor' potential. Pakistan does not enjoy warm relations with the current US-backed Karzai government mired in resistance from the Taliban. Until there is a peaceful and stable environment in Afghanistan, China is the only way for Pakistan to connect with Central Asia.

For China, the acquisition of oil and gas assets abroad and securing their transportation to China is top priority to ensure that its economic growth stays on track. The strong US military presence controlling the sea lanes of communication, through which Chinese oil and gas are imported, is a matter of concern for China, especially given the fact that it already feels encircled by the US (International Institute for Strategic Studies 2002). In addition, these sea lanes are highly congested and prone to piracy attacks. Two such choke points, from where 60 per cent and 80 per cent of the total Chinese oil imports pass through, are the Straits of Hormuz and Malacca, respectively.

Having no blue water navy of its own, China has been pursuing a multi-pronged strategy. It has searched for alternative routes such as: the Kra canal in Thailand; an oil pipeline across Malaysia; onshore oil and gas pipelines from Myanmar, Central Asia, and Russia; strategic oil reserves; modernization of its navy; and building/ assisting commercial and naval ports in friendly countries along the shipping routes. This last strategy is termed the 'String of Pearls' (Pehrson 2006). One supposed 'pearl' in this string is Pakistan's third deep-sea port, Gwadar, 240 nautical miles away from the Straits of Hormuz and 533 kilometers west of Karachi, in the south-west province of Baluchistan.

THE GWADAR PORT

In March 2007, President Musharraf inaugurated Pakistan's third deep-sea port, Gwadar. The vision is to make the port a trade and energy hub for the region, which could potentially turn the desolate fishing town of Gwadar into a world-class commercial port city. The Gwadar port is a flagship of the strong economic and strategic ties between Pakistan and China. The latter has built the port with substantial financial assistance. It continues to assist Pakistan, technically and financially, in mega projects linking the Gwadar port with the existing infrastructure.[9]

Pakistan's economy has been growing at the rate of 6 to 8 per cent in recent years leading to a substantial increase in trade volumes. Pakistan's growing economic needs and its plans to exploit its potential as trade and energy corridor for the landlocked Central Asian states makes it imperative to build another port. The Karachi and Qasim ports have been running at full capacity despite major upgrading. Moreover, strategically both ports remain vulnerable to an Indian blockade in case of any hostile situation. Since the 1971 blockade of the Karachi port by the Indian navy, strategists in Pakistan have been looking westward to avoid such an eventuality. Gwadar had been earmarked as a potential port as far back as the 1960s, but the lack of means and necessary infrastructure impeded its development. In the early 1980s, the US proposed to develop the Gwadar port, but US strategic interest in Pakistan waned when the Soviets decided to leave Afghanistan. In the 1993–8 Five-Year Plan, the development of the Gwadar port was a high priority. Pakistan sought Dubai, US and Chinese firms for assistance, but in the end it was China that came forward (Ramachandaran 2005). The ADB's Central Asian Regional Economic Cooperation initiative also favors the Gwadar port over Karachi, given that it is the shortest distance to Central Asia. The government has declared Gwadar a free economic zone and land has been earmarked for industrial, oil, and gas ventures. The port is being linked to the country's existing rail and road network, which are being linked to Iran, Central Asia, and China.

For Pakistan, the Gwadar port is part of its greater long-term development plans to exploit its geographical location at the crossroads of the energy-rich Middle East, the highly populated energy demand centers of South and East Asia, and the landlocked geostrategically important Central Asia that could potentially emerge as the second largest centre of energy and mineral resources. Pakistan could play a key role in the development and interlocking of this region by providing transit facilities, which can potentially earn Pakistan huge revenues in transit fees. The collapse of the Soviet Union and emergence of the five landlocked independent states[10] had provided a further opportunity for Pakistan to offer its ports as gateways for these states to connect with the outer world. These five states with overwhelming Muslim majority populations and historical links with the territories which today constitute Pakistan provide an underlying synergy for Pakistan to capitalize.

From China's perspective, the commercial importance of the port stems from its potential to eventually become an alternative energy supply route from the Middle East to western China. There have been discussions to build an oil and/or gas pipeline (Trans-Karakoram pipeline) from Gwadar to China. China has been involved in the Iranian and Saudi energy sectors in recent years. Both countries have shown an interest in supplying oil/gas through a pipeline via Pakistan. However, the costs of transportation via sea are economical *vis-à-vis* the cost of transportation overland pipeline at the moment. Nevertheless, such an option in the near future cannot be ruled out.[11] The recent bilateral contracts to upgrade the Karakoram Highway and to build a railway link from Almaty (Kazakhstan) to Gwadar via Kashgar points to a greater engagement between the two countries in coming years.

Moreover, China has recently devised a policy for a concentrated effort for the development of its western regions. China's western regions remain backward *vis-à-vis* its coastal regions. The western autonomous Xinjiang province is closer to the Gwadar port (2,500 kilometers) than to the Chinese ports (3,500 kilometers). Its economy has been growing fast and trade volume has increased from US$1 billion in 1998 to US$18 billion in 2007. The Gwadar port offers great opportunities for the region.

However, Chinese involvement in the project has raised fears amongst other key players in the already geopolitically complex situation in the region. Indian and US strategists are concerned about Chinese engagement and fear that it is part of a 'grand' Chinese strategy that can provide China a foothold in the Indian Ocean. Indian officials have publicly raised concerns over the possibility of Chinese and Pakistani navies being capable of harming Indian interests, and strategists in India are referring to China's 'arc of influence' and 'Indian encirclement' (*Daily Times*, 23 January 2008). Indian strategists are also concerned, not just about Chinese influence in the region, but Pakistan's potential to play a larger role in Central Asia through the Gwadar port.

Central Asia takes priority in Indian foreign policy. This entails resistance to the dominance of any single power in the region; securing energy resources and routes (Sikri 2007); and countering Pakistan's moves to seek strategic depth or relative gains *vis-à-vis* India. These goals are in congruence with the US' goals and there is increasing cooperation between the two in Afghanistan and Central Asia (Cohen 2006; Sachdeva 2006). India, unable to secure transit facilities to Afghanistan from Pakistan, has built a competing port at Chahbahar, Iran, just 200 kilometers west of Gwadar and a road linking it to Afghanistan. It has initiated a North-South corridor along with Iran and Russia to link with Central Asia (and Russia), bypassing Pakistan. India has also secured its first-ever airbase abroad in Tajikistan (120 kilometers away from the greater Kashmir) and is operating a number of consulates in Afghanistan. Pakistan has alleged that the growing Indian involvement in Afghanistan is unjustifiable and is only to stir trouble in Baluchistan province. General Mirza Aslam Beg, former Army Chief, openly accused the US and India of conspiring in Baluchistan (Beg 2006).

The Baluchi secessionist groups have been waging an armed struggle against the federal government. The Gwadar port, along with other mega projects, has invoked internal conflict in Baluchistan, whose secessionist groups believe that they are not being provided their due share of these developments. There have been attacks in Baluchistan on the government and business installations since work on the port started. Chinese engineers have been killed and kidnapped by Baluch as well as Islamic militants. Yet, China and Pakistan remain committed to the project and have condemned the attacks in the strongest possible terms, describing the militants as enemies of 'Pakistan–China friendship' and 'economic development'. The close cooperation and mutual support despite the challenges surrounding the Gwadar port further underscore the close ties between Pakistan and China.

CONCLUDING REMARKS

Sino–Pak relations have come a long way from the immediate post-World War II era, when Sino–Indian relations were relatively better than Sino–Pak relations. From the mid-1950s onwards, in the wake of differences between India and China as well as China's deteriorating relations with the Soviet Union, China began to reach out to Pakistan. There were two major turning points in the 1960s that helped foster the relationship between these two countries, namely, the 1962 Sino–Indian border war and the 1965 Indo–Pak war. The Sino–Indian border war brought China and Pakistan closer as they found they had a common concern over possible Indian hegemony. The Indo–Pak war resulted in suspension of US military support for Pakistan, which created a gap in arms supplies to Pakistan that China gladly filled. Sino–Pak ties, building on these common strategic and military interests, grew in strength over the 1970s and 1980s, during which the two countries even cooperated in the nuclear field. These historic factors provided a very strong foundation for Sino–Pak relations.

The end of the Cold War brought about changes in the geopolitical scene. These included a shift in US policy in the region, as the US strengthened its ties with India. India's nuclear test of 1998 as well as the Indo–US nuclear deal gave further impetus for Sino–Pak strategic cooperation. At the same time, the events of 9/11 heightened US presence in Pakistan and the region; this was obviously a worry for China. Even though the Cold War was over, the balance of power equation remained critical to international relations in the region. India and the US, especially an India and US that are cooperating, will always be viewed with suspicion by Pakistan and China.

Whilst a closer Indo–US alliance could push Pakistan and China towards a tighter embrace, there have also been two important developments in recent years that threaten to dampen Sino–Pak relations. First, the economic liberalization of India and China and a new global order encouraging free trade has created incentives for these two giants to strengthen bilateral trade relations. This has raised fears that the Sino–Indian *rapprochement* could come at the cost of Sino–Pak relations. Second, the rise of Islamic fundamentalism around the world with the heart of the radicalized movement in Pakistan and Afghanistan is putting some strain on Sino-Pak relations, as China fears that its own territories with Muslim majority populations may seek terrorist means to achieve independence or better conditions.

However, it is argued in this chapter that these factors will not result in the dilution of Sino–Pak relations. Despite the recent Sino–Indian *rapprochement* one cannot escape the reality that there will always remain an undercurrent of rivalry in terms of economic development and strategic influence between India and China. The overriding concern for China and Pakistan is maintaining the balance of power in the region *vis-à-vis* India. Pakistan has historic problems with India and needs the defense links with China. From China's perspective, it needs the strategic location of Pakistan to extend its influence in the South and Central Asian region and ensure that India does not become a regional hegemon. As regards Islamic fundamentalism, it is in China's interests to stay involved with Pakistan in order to keep a close eye on the situation rather than to be disengaged. The Pakistani government has in any case given assurances to China that it will not allow radicalism within its borders to affect China.

As we move into the twenty-first century we see new dynamics in the form of greater economic engagement and mutual interest in energy security. Sino–Pak trade and commerce has risen sharply in recent years and both countries have entered into various agreements to boost their economic ties. The most significant area of investment, which has both economic and strategic implications, is Pakistan's energy sector. Pakistan is a gateway for China to the energy-rich Gulf States and its passport to the Muslim West and Central Asia. China is investing heavily in Pakistan's infrastructure and especially in the strategically important Gwadar port, as well as many other areas. These huge commitments can only strengthen Sino–Pak relations.

In the final analysis, Sino–Pak relations have all the necessary ingredients for an evergreen relationship. They are physical neighbors, but unlike India, China and Pakistan have no historical baggage to strain their relations as neighbors. The two countries also have common strategic interests and increasingly are finding common ground in terms of energy security as well as trade and investment. China and Pakistan have a natural symbiotic relationship with the former having the military and economic might and the latter having the critical geo-strategic advantage. Despite some waxing and waning in Sino–Pak relations, the two countries have shown maturity in their relationship by adopting a pragmatic approach to the changing political, economic and strategic landscape of today. This bodes well for their future, making Pakistan–China relations stronger and deeper.

NOTES

1. An in-depth analysis of India and China relations is outside the scope of this paper. However, for a good discussion of the underlying rivalry between India and China despite the improvement in relations, see Malik (1995: 131–60). For understanding different aspects of the Sino–Indian relations, see Harding and Frankel (2004).
2. The Chinese Ambassador to Pakistan, Luo Zhaohui, however, refuted such speculations and said that China did not pressurize Pakistan to undertake the operation against the Lal Mosque/ Jamia Hafsa. He also added that China did not ask for any specific action to be taken on this account as China had a policy of not interfering in the domestic affairs of any country. (Interview with Iftikhar A. Lodhi.)
3. In a letter to US President Bill Clinton, Indian Prime Minister Vajpayee justified the nuclear tests while referring to China as 'an overt nuclear weapon state on our borders, a state which committed armed aggression against India in 1962. Although our relations with that country have improved in the last decade or so, an atmosphere of distrust persists mainly due to the unresolved border problem.' He also referred to the material help this state

had rendered to 'another neighbor of ours to become a covert nuclear weapon state' (*Frontline*, 1998).

4. There is also a view that China's actions may have been in response to the US sale of F-16 military aircraft to Taiwan. This would have clearly displeased China and given it a reason to defy the US by continuing its missile cooperation with Pakistan. Both Perkovich (2004: 185) and Deepak (2006: 138) refer to this in their work.
5. Besides, Chinese high-end value-added exports to Pakistan mainly compete with imports from other countries and do not pose a threat to the domestic industry. It is the agriculture, footwear, and to some extent textile sectors that face problems in competing with Chinese exports not only within Pakistan but in European and American markets as well.
6. Statistics on Chinese inward and outward investments are widely disputed.
7. Afghanistan, Azerbaijan, Iran, Kazakhstan, Kyrgyzstan, Pakistan, Tajikistan, Turkey, Turkmenistan and Uzbekistan.
8. Members: China, Kazakhstan, Kyrgyzstan, Russia, Tajikistan, and Uzbekistan. Observers aspiring for membership: India, Iran, Mongolia, Pakistan.
9. Phase I of the port with financial assistance of US$198 million, out of which US$ 49 million was a grant and the rest was made up of loans and buyer's credit. Pakistan contributed US$50 million. China has also agreed to participate in Phase II of the Gwadar port project, which will be completed at a cost of US$600 million in 2012. China has also provided US$200 million for the construction of the Coastal Highway linking Gwadar with Karachi in addition to the financial and technical assistance for upgrading the Karakoram highway and Pakistan railways.
10. Kazakhstan, Kyrgyzstan, Pakistan, Tajikistan, Turkey, Turkmenistan, and Uzbekistan.
11. Interviews with Chinese, Pakistani and Iranian officials by Iftikhar A. Lodhi.

REFERENCES

Ali, Ghulam (2003). *Sino-Pakistan Relations: The Indian Factor.* Islamabad Policy Research Institute, Summer. http://ipripak.org/journal/summer2003/sinopakistan.shtml, accessed 10 February 2008.

Amin, M. Shahid (2000). *Pakistan's Foreign Policy: A Reappraisal.* Karachi: Oxford University Press.

Aneja, Urvashi (2006). *Pakistan China Relations: Recent Developments.* Institute of Peace and Conflict Studies, New Delhi. http://www.ipcs.org/IPCS-Special-Report-26.pdf, accessed 10 February 2008.

BBC News (1999, 15 June). 'Clinton urges restraint in Kashmir'. http:// news.bbc.co.uk/1/hi/world/south_asia/369320.stm#map, accessed 10 February 2008.

——— (2001, 26 December). 'China urges border restraint'. http://news.bbc. co.uk/2/ hi/south_asia/1728687.stm, accessed 10 February 2008.

Beg, Mirza Aslam (4 January 2006). 'India, US hatching conspiracies in Baluchistan'. http://paktribune.com/news/index.shtml?130345, accessed 10 February 2008.

Burke, S.M. (1974). *Mainsprings of Indian and Pakistani Foreign Policies.* Minneapolis: University of Minnesota Press.

Chaudhri, Mohammad Ahsen (2001). 'Strategic and military dimensions in Pakistan China relations'. In Mehrunnisa Ali (ed.), *Readings in Pakistan Foreign Policy 1971–98* (pp. 317–29). Karachi: Oxford University Press.

Cheema, Pervaiz Iqbal (2002). 'The China threat: A view from Pakistan'. In Herbert Yee and Ian Storey (eds.), *The China Threat: Perceptions, Myths and Reality* (pp. 302–11). New York: Routledge Curzon.

Cherian, John (2007, 16 August). 'Concerned neighbours', *Frontline*, 24. http://www.frontlineonnet.com/fl2416/stories/20070824502402200.htm, accessed 10 February 2008.

Chinese Embassy in Islamabad (2006). 'Pakistan China joint statement', 21 February. http://pk.chinaembassy.org/eng/zbgx/t236947.htm, accessed on 10 February 2008.

——— (2007). 'Ambassador Zhao's interview with the news', http://pk.chinaembassy.org/eng/zbgx/t340650.htm, accessed 10 February 2008.

Cohen, Ariel (2006). 'US interests and Central Asia energy security', The Heritage Foundation, Backgrounder No. 1984. http://www.heritage.org/Research/RussiaandEurasia/bg1984.cfm, accessed 10 February 2008.

Daily Times (23 January 2008). 'Gwadar Port has strategic implications for India'. http://www.dailytimes.com.pk/default.asp?page=2008 percent 5C01 percent5C23 percent5 Cstory_23-1-2008_pg7_53, accessed 10 February 2008.

Deepak, B.R. (2006). 'Sino-Pak "entente cordiale" and India: A look into the past and future', *China Report*, 42, 2, 129–51.

Douglas, K. John, Mathew Nelson, and Kevin Schwartz (2006). 'Fueling the dragon's flame: How China's energy demands affect its relationship in the Middle East', US-China Economic and Security Review Commission.

http://www.uscc.gov/researchpapers/2006/China_ME_FINAL.pdf, accessed 10 February 2008.

Faruqui, Ahmad (2003). *Rethinking the National Security of Pakistan: The Price of Strategic Myopia.* Burlington: Ashgate Publishing Limited.

Ganguly, Sumit (2004). 'India and China: Border issues, domestic integration, and international security'. In Francine R. Frankel and Harry Harding (eds.), *The India-China Relationship: Rivalry and Engagement* (pp. 103–33). New Delhi: Oxford University Press.

Ganguly, Sumit and Andrew Scobell (2005). 'India and the US: Forging a security partnership?' *World Policy Journal*, 22, 2, 37–43.

Garver, W. John (2002). 'The future of the Sino-Pakistani entente cordiale'. In Michael Chambers (ed.), *South Asia in 2020: Future Strategic Balances and Alliances* (pp. 385–448). Strategic Studies Institute, US.

Gupta, K. Anil (2008, January 14). 'The future of India China trade', *The Economic Times.* http://economictimes.indiatimes.com/View_Point/The_future_of_India-China_trade/articleshow/2697720.cms, accessed 15 September 2008.

Haider, Ziad (2004). 'Clearing clouds over the Karakoram Pass', *Yale Global Online.* http://yaleglobal.yale.edu/display.article?id=3603&page=2, accessed 10 February 2008.

Harding, Harry and Francine R. Frankel (2004). *The India-China Relationship: Rivalry and Engagement.* New Delhi: Oxford University Press.

Hathaway, M. Robert (2002). 'The US-India courtship: From Clinton to Bush', *Journal of Strategic Studies*, 25, 4, 6–30.

International Energy Agency (IEA) (2007). 'World energy outlook: China and India insights'. http://www.climateactionprogramme.org/features/article/world_energy_outlook_2007_china_and_india_insights/, accessed 10 February 2008.

International Institute for Strategic Studies (IISS) (2002). 'China feels encircled', http://www.iiss.org/conferences/the-shangri-la-dialogue/press-coverage/press-coverage-2002/the-economist—china-feels-encircled/, accessed 10 February 2008.

Kan, A. Shirley (2007). 'China and proliferation of weapons of mass destruction and missiles: Policy issues', CRS Report for Congress RL 31555, updated 13 December. http://fas.org/sgp/crs/nuke/RL31555.pdf, accessed 10 February 2008.

Kapur, S. Paul, (2007). *Dangerous Deterrent: Nuclear Weapons Proliferation and Conflict in South Asia.* East-West Centre, Palo Alto: Stanford University Press.

Kerr, Paul and Mary B. Nikitin (2007). 'Pakistan's nuclear weapons: Proliferation and security issues', CRS Report for Congress RL 34248, updated 14 November. *http://www.fas.org/sgp/crs/nuke/RL34248.pdf*, accessed 10 February 2008.

Khan, A. Tanvir (2007, 20 April). 'New developments in Pakistan China relations', *Arab News*. http://www.arabnews.com/?page=7&section=0 & article=95216 & d=20 & m=4 & y=2007, accessed 10 February 2008.

Klare, T. Michael (2001). 'The new geography of conflict', *Foreign Affairs*, May/June.

Lowell, Dittmer (2005). *South Asia's Nuclear Security Dilemma, India, Pakistan, and China*. London: East Gate Books.

Ministry of Foreign Affairs, Pakistan (2006). 'The US Administration has sought a waiver from the US Congress for the implementation of US-India Agreement on Civilian Nuclear Cooperation', P.R. No.107/2006, 17/03/2006. http://mofa.gov.pk/Press_Releases/2006/March/PR_108_06.htm, accessed 10 February 2008.

——— (2006). 'Address of President Hu Jintao', 25 November. http://www.mofa.gov.pk/Press_Releases/2006/Nov/Address_China_Pre.htm accessed 10 February 2008.

——— (2006). 'Text of the Joint Statement between the Islamic Republic of Pakistan and People's Republic of China', 25 November. http://www.mofa.gov.pk/Press_Releases/2006/Nov/Joint_Statement.htm, accessed on 10 February 2008.

Ministry of Foreign Affairs, People's Republic of China (2008). 'A Shared Vision for the 21st Century of the People's Republic of China and the Republic of India', 15 January. http://xn—tlq87w5j9b.cn/eng/zxxx/t399545.htm, accessed 10 February 2008.

Mohan, Malik (1995). 'India's Relations with China post-Soviet Union: Less cooperation, more Competition'. In Stuart Harris and Gary Klintworth (eds.), *China as a Great Power, Myths, Realities and Challenges in the Asia-Pacific Region*. New York: St Martin's Press.

Muralidharan, Sukumar and John Cherian (1998). 'The BJP's bombs', *Frontline*, 15 May, 11 and 23–25 June. http://www.frontlineonnet.com/fl1511/ 15110040.htm, accessed 3 October 2008.

Pehrson, J. Christopher (2006). 'String of pearls: Meeting the challenge of China's rising power across the Asian littoral', Strategic Studies Institute, USA. http://www.strategicstudiesinstitute.army.mil/pubs/display.cfm?pubID=721, accessed 10 February 2008.

Perkovich, George (2004). 'The nuclear and security balance'. In Francine R. Frankel and Harry Harding (eds.), *The India-China Relationship:*

Rivalry and Engagement (pp. 178–218). New Delhi: Oxford University Press.

People's Daily Online (6 April 2005). 'China, Pakistan signs treaty of friendship, cooperation, and good neighbourly relations'. http://english.peopledaily.com.cn/200504/06/archive.html, accessed 10 February 2008.

Rajain, Arpit (2005). *Nuclear Deterrence in Southern Asia: China, India and Pakistan.* New Delhi: Sage Publications.

Rahman, Fazalur (2006a). 'Pakistan China economic relations: Opportunities and challenges', *Strategic Studies*, 26, 2. http://www.issi.org.pk/ journal/ 2006_files/no_2/article/a3.htm, accessed 10 February 2008.

——— (2006b). 'Prospects of Pakistan becoming a trade and energy corridor', *Strategic Studies*, 27, 2. http://www.issi.org.pk/journal/ 2006_files/no_2/ article/a3.htm, accessed 10 February 2008.

——— (2007). 'Pakistan's evolving relations with China, Russia and Central Asia'. In Akihiro Iwashita (ed.), *Russia and its Neighbours in Crisis* (pp. 211–29). Slavic Research Centre, Hokkaido University, Sapporo. http://srch.slav.hokudai.ac.jp/coe21/publish/no16_1_ses/11_rahman.pdf, accessed 10 February 2008.

Ramachandran, Sudha (4 March 2005). 'China's pearl in Pakistan's waters', *Asia Times Online.* http://www.atimes.com/atimes/South_Asia/GC 04Df06.html, accessed 10 February 2008.

Rizvi, Hasan Askari (2001). 'Pakistan's defence policy'. In Mehrunnisa Ali (ed.), *Readings in Pakistan Foreign Policy 1971–98* (pp. 199–226). Karachi: Oxford University Press.

Sachdeva, Gulshan (2006). 'India's attitude towards China's growing influence in Central Asia', *China and Eurasia Forum Quarterly*, 4, 3, 23–34.

Schaffer, C. Teresita (2002). 'Building a new partnership with India', *The Washington Quarterly*, 25, 2, 31–44.

——— (2003). 'US influence on Pakistan: Can partners have divergent priorities?' *The Washington Quarterly*, 26, 1, 169–83.

Shirk, L. Susan (2004). 'One-sided Rivalry: China's perceptions and policies toward India'. In Francine R. Frankel and Harry Harding (eds.), *The India-China Relationship, Rivalry and Engagement* (pp. 75–100). New Delhi: Oxford University Press.

Sikri, Rajiv (2007). 'Behind Oil and Gas: India's interest in Central Asia', *Opinion Asia*, 29 June. http://www.opinionasia.org IndiasInterestsin Central Asia, accessed 10 February 2008.

Sinha, Satyabrat (2004). 'The strategic triangle: India-China-Pakistan', *China Report*, 40, 2, 221–6.

Stockholm International Peace Research Institute (SIPRI) (2002). *World Armament and Disarmament: SIPRI Yearbook 1986–2002.* London: Oxford University Press.

Syed, Anwar (1974). *China and Pakistan: Diplomacy of an Entente Cordiale.* Amherst: The University of Massachusetts Press.

Syed, Fazl-e-Haider (2007). 'China deepens business ties with Pakistan', *Asia Times Online,* 19 December. http://www.atimes.com/atimes/South_Asia/IL19Df01.html, accessed 10 February 2008.

The Tribune (24 May 2006). 'Pakistan, China finalise nuclear deal'. http://www.tribuneindia.com/2006/20060524/world.htm#2, accessed 10 February 2008.

UNCTAD (2003). *China: An Emerging Outward FDI Investor.* http:// www.unctad.org/sections/dite_fdistat/docs/china_ebrief_en.pdf, accessed 10 February 2008.

Wu, Xinbo (2004). 'The promise and limitations of a Sino-US partnership', *The Washington Quarterly,* 27, 4, 115–26.

Yuan, Jing-dong (2007). 'The dragon and the elephant: Chinese Indian Relations in the 21st century', *The Washington Quarterly,* 30, 3, 131–44.

5

Building a New Nepal: Travails of Transition

S.D. MUNI

INTRODUCTION

IT IS EASY to destroy and deconstruct; but comparatively far more difficult and exerting to create and reconstruct. This applies to almost every aspect of life, and the state is no exception. The history of political evolution has witnessed umpteen examples of the destruction of the state but its reconstruction has proved to be complex, challenging and a long-drawn process, often left inadequately accomplished at the end.

Nepal experienced a phenomenal and unprecedented rise of peoples' power in April 2006 to deconstruct a feudal state and reconstruct in its place, an inclusive, democratic and secular state. The deconstruction of Nepal's feudal state has in fact been undergoing since 1950, when the Ranacracy was first overthrown for a more representative political order. This was the result of significant geopolitical transformations around Nepal marked by India's independence and the victory of the Communist revolution led by Mao Zedong in China. But the process of constructing a new and democratic Nepalese state initiated after the end of the Ranacracy was thwarted by an ambitious and assertive monarchy under King Mahendra who, in December 1960, overthrew a democratically elected government and assumed direct power to concoct a subservient *Panchayat* system. The protests of the Nepalese Congress and the resulting political turbulence of 1979–80 which led to the national referendum (on the continuation of the Panchayat system or its replacement by a multi-party democracy), managed only to tinker with the concocted feudal order by making the Panchayat system a bit more open. However, it was the popular uprising (*Jan Andolan-I)* during 1989–90 that brought democratization back with force to the political agenda. Even this popular reassertion failed to construct a viable democratic polity in the face of a persisting monarchy and a gullible political leadership, driven more by their narrow vested interests than the ideals of the popular uprising. The frustrations arising out of such failures in building a viable democratic order, in a way, erupted first in the form of a violent and destructive Maoists insurgency that took nearly 14,000 lives and then in the reinforced popular uprising, the *Jan Andolan-II* of 6–24 April 2006.

This paper attempts to look at the nature of the popular uprising of April 2006, the success of which threw up the agenda of restructuring of the Nepalese state. There were two specific aspects of this restructuring, one related to the mainstreaming of the 10-year-old Maoist insurgency through a peace process. The second was of building a democratic polity which is republican and inclusive, based on the integrations of the hitherto neglected and marginalized sections of society, such as those belonging to the Madhesh (the people living in the southern Tarai), Jan Jatis (tribal groups) and Dalits (untouchables and low-caste people). The task of transition from a feudal order to an inclusive democracy which is genuinely participatory, peaceful and stable is a challenging and long-drawn one. The accomplishment of this task would depend not only on the Nepalese leadership but also on the people at large, who made the *Jan Andolan-II* successful, as well as on the international community.

PEOPLE'S UPRISING OF APRIL 2006

The peoples' uprising of April 2006 has been a unique landmark in Nepal's political evolution. It had the elements of the 1989–90 uprising to the extent that all shades of political persuasions joined hands, dissolving their rivalries and political differences in search of a democratic political order. *Jan Andolan-II* was also, to some extent, patterned on the lines of the peoples' uprising in Bangladesh in 1990 when all the political parties had united to throw out the military regime and usher in a democratic political order.[1] And yet *Jan Andolan-II* has been a unique political event, not only in the case of Nepal, but the whole of South Asia. The manifestation of peoples' power was unprecedented when an estimated 12 to 15 million unarmed people marched in the streets throughout the kingdom over a period of nineteen days to end monarchy and establish an inclusive democracy.

In no small way, the *Jan Andolan-II* was made possible by the Maoists who had waged an armed struggle for creating a 'republic' for the past ten years. But then they suddenly decided to change tack, from insurgency and 'peoples' war', to join mainstream democratic politics and create a new state in collaboration with other political parties. People argue that the change has been more tactical than strategic. Only future events will show. However, the shift in the Maoists' position started taking place from 2003, when in their party's Third Plenum they came to a grudging realization that capturing the Nepalese state through armed struggle was not possible. Even if they succeeded in taking over the state, they would not be able to hold onto it in the face of international isolation and pressures. The task of facilitating their shift and the process of uniting not only the disparate mainstream political parties among themselves, but also these parties with the Maoists in a United Front to rise against the autocratic monarchy was greatly encouraged by King Gyanendra himself. In the midst of the Nepalese state's failure to deal with the Maoist challenge, the King decided in February 2005 to assume direct charge of the state and govern ruthlessly in the name of meeting the challenge of 'terrorism'. This alienated the Monarch from the people. While the army remained loyal to the King, it failed to make any dent in the military challenge posed by the Maoists. In *Jan Andolan-II*, even the wives and family members of ordinary soldiers came on the streets to show their disapproval of the way the King was exercising power.

The King's moves also alienated him from the international community which wanted him to work with the political parties and withdraw from direct rule in order to resolutely face the Maoist rebellion. But the polite suggestions of the international community, the United States (US) and India in particular, were consistently ignored by the King. Twice during 2005 King Gyanendra flouted the promises he had made to the Indian Prime Minister, Dr Manmohan Singh, to soften his hold over power. Instead, the King sought the cooperation of countries like China, Russia and Pakistan to hold on to power. This alienation of the King from the international community and his stout refusal to accommodate the mainstream political parties further pushed his antagonists, the mainstream political parties and the Maoists, closer to each other. The first agreement (of Twelve Points) between the political parties and the Maoists was signed in November 2005 in India.[1] Under this agreement, the two sides committed themselves to end 'autocratic monarchy' and establish 'absolute democracy . . . with the force of agitation, forming an all party government with complete authority, holding elections to a Constituent Assembly.'[2] It was this understanding that led to the precipitation of *Jan Andolan-II*.

The agitation came to an end on 21 April 2005 with a Proclamation of the King. In the Proclamation, the King, justifying his takeover by invoking the prerogatives of the Shah Dynasty and the Constitution of 1990 (Art. 35), asked the Seven Party Alliance (SPA) to recommend a name for the appointment of Prime Minister. India had actively worked to secure this proclamation by sending Dr Karan Singh, former princely ruler (Maharaja) of Jammu and Kashmir along with a leading member of the ruling Congress party, as a Special Envoy. While the international community endorsed the Proclamation, the agitating people and the parties refused to accept it. India came in for strong criticism for allegedly trying to subvert the *Jan Andolan-II* by protecting the institution and interests of the monarchy. India's foreign secretary, Shyam Saran, who had accompanied the Special Envoy, had to counter these allegations by saying:

> . . . right from 1 February 2005, India has taken a very clear cut stand with regards to the restoration of democracy. How can there be any question about India's stand? We were the first to stop the supply of arms to Nepal. We persuaded our other international partners to join us in the same action. So it is we who have in fact gathered together the international community also to

work together with us for the restoration of democracy in Nepal. How there can be any doubts about India's credentials in this regard?[3]

India then worked quietly behind the scenes to undo the embarrassment. Accordingly, the King was forced to issue another Proclamation on 24 April under which Nepal's House of Representatives, dissolved arbitrarily by the King in May 2002, was reinstated and executive power was handed over to the SPA, accepting their road map to peace, stability and democracy. The King also expressed condolences 'to all those who lost their lives during the peoples' movement'.[4] There was no excuse in this Proclamation for the King's takeover, nor any reference to the Shah Dynasty and the 1990 Constitution. The agitating parties accepted and the international community endorsed this Proclamation.

TASK OF RESTRUCTING THE NEPALESE STATE

The end of the peoples' uprising set the stage for the reconstruction of a new Nepalese state. The spirit of *Jan Andolan-II* had clearly marked out the agenda of restructuring the state. Nepal's peace process in effect is the manifestation of this agenda which broadly has two dimensions, namely: (i) mainstreaming of the Maoists, and (ii) laying down the parameters of an inclusive 'complete'/'absolute' democracy. These dimensions were inherent in the 12-point agreement concluded between the SPA and the Maoists which also formed the basis for mobilizing people for *Jan Andolan-II*. The mainstreaming of the Maoists involved the questions of (i) giving up of violence by the Maoists for peaceful competitive politics, (ii) security sector reforms to integrate the Maoist armed cadres into the Nepalese national army, and (iii) peace and reconciliation at the social level involving all those who suffered during the 10 years of insurgency and the 14 days of peoples' uprising. The challenge inherent in resolving all these questions has been formidable.

No less challenging has been the task of laying down the parameters of an 'absolute' and 'inclusive' democracy. The very first question in this respect was regarding the fate of the monarchy.

After considerable anxiety and tension, this question has been resolved by declaring Nepal a Republic and ensuring the peaceful eviction of King Gyanendra and his family from *Narayanhiti*, the erstwhile Royal palace. The decision to declare Nepal a Republic was, in principle, taken by the interim parliament that came into existence after the success of *Jan Andolan-II*, and has been endorsed by the elected Constituent Assembly following the elections of 2008. The question of defining an inclusive democracy having proper representation of all sections of society, particularly the hitherto marginalized Madhesis (the Tarai people), the Janjatis (ethnic and tribal groups), Dalits (downtrodden) and women, perhaps seems to be most intricate task before the victors of *Jan Andolan-II*. An inclusive democratic state must also ensure equal and non-discriminatory treatment to all its citizens irrespective of their cast, creed, religion, region or status. These tasks have to be addressed through the new Constitution to be framed by the elected Constituent Assembly.

The two dimensions of Nepal's peace process to restructure the state are closely linked with each other and require to be pursued simultaneously. It is not possible to mainstream the Maoists without carrying forward the task of building an inclusive and democratic state. This newly envisaged state has also to be inclusive, not only socially and culturally but also politically in its power structure, where it is able to find a reasonable share for the Maoists as well as the marginalized. As it unfolds, even after resolving political questions, the agenda of an 'inclusive state' would require due and sustained attention as well as sincere efforts. Let us look at the progress in Nepal's peace process in view of the above identified dimensions of restructuring a new state.

THE MAINSTREAMING OF THE MAOISTS

Ending the Maoist insurgency and mainstreaming the Maoist movement were core concerns even during *Jan Andolan-II* which otherwise focused on removal of autocratic monarchy. One of the considerations that brought the people to the streets was that the King had assumed direct power in the name of ending the Maoist insurgency but had utterly failed in doing so, even after resorting to the worst repressive methods. As we noted earlier, the shift in the Maoists' own position on the question of violence for systemic change and alliance with the political parties, had started getting crystallized since 2003 when the Maoists moved from the goal of 'new democracy' and 'dictatorship of the proletariat' to 'the development of democracy in the twenty first century', recognizing the importance of political competition.[5] There is no doubt that the Maoists had taken into account the post-9/11 developments where their movement was treated only as a 'terrorist' enterprise to be confronted by the entire international community in the context of the 'global war on terrorism'. Subsequently, in their 12-point agreement with the SPA, the Maoists had also committed themselves to 'absolute democracy' and a 'nationwide storm of democratic protests'. In that agreement, it was also agreed to establish 'permanent peace along with a positive solution of the armed conflict' (Paragraph 3 of the Agreement), wherein there was commitment to 'competitive multiparty system of governance, civil liberties, human rights, the concept of the rule of law, fundamental rights etc.' (Paragraph 4). One of the points of the agreement clearly said: '*Undertaking self-criticism and self-evaluation of past mistakes, the CPN (Maoist) has expressed commitment not to repeat such mistakes in future*' (Paragraph 6, emphasis added). The theoretical basis for the mainstreaming of the Maoists had thus been prepared, at least partially, even before the outbreak of *Jan Andolan-II.*

MANAGEMENT OF ARMS

On the basis of the 12-point Agreement, the SPA and the Maoists moved to make the ceasefire permanent so that the very basic demand of *Jan Andolan-II*, that is, peace, could be restored and stabilized. This was done under two additional agreements signed between the interim government, headed by G.P. Koirala that took office soon after *Jan Andolan-II,* and the Maoists. Under an agreement concluded on 25 May 2006 the two sides signed a code of conduct promising not to attack each other or lay landmines, to allow the political activities of each other, allow developmental work, not to collect donations by force and to return properties seized during the insurgency to the original owners. In another 8-point Agreement signed within a month, on 16 June 2006, the two sides agreed to get the United Nations (UN) to monitor the ceasefire and manage arms and armed personnel of both the sides, that is, the Maoists and the Nepal Army (name changed from the Royal Nepal Army). There was an initial hitch in getting the UN involved because India had strong reservations. But these reservations were eventually given up when Nepal, during the first official visit of Prime Minister Koirala to India in June 2006, pleaded that if the UN was not acceptable then India should itself undertake the responsibility to manage arms and armed personnel of the Maoists because Nepal's security structure was not capable or resourceful enough to handle this task.[6] There was also an agreement on preparing an Interim Constitution.

The conclusion of these two agreements led to the negotiation and signing of yet another accord, the Comprehensive Peace Agreement (CPA), in November 2006. This agreement had diverse features wherein broad political and socioeconomic dimensions of the new Nepalese state were clearly spelled out. The procedure for the 'management' of arms and armed personnel of the Maoists and the Nepal Army were laid down. The peoples' war waged by the Maoists and the parallel administration and courts run by them in the areas under their control were formally called off, and setting up of two Commissions, one of Peace and Rehabilitation and another of Truth and Reconciliation, was agreed upon. The commitment to human rights, non-use of force in political activities, etc., was reiterated.

Within the framework of the CPA, the UN was approached to help in the management of arms and armed personnel. Accordingly, an Agreement on Monitoring and Management of Arms and Armies was concluded between the Maoists, the government and the UN Mission in Nepal (UNMIN) on 8 December 2006. With UN help, while the Nepal Army was confined to its barracks, a total of 31,152 Maoist Peoples Liberation Army (PLA) cadres were put in cantonments and 3,475 pieces of their weapons (including a variety of them) along with 6.7 tonnes of explosives were put under lock and key, in '7 main and 21 satellite sites'.[7] Questions were raised about the large number of armed personnel and small number of arms registered by the UNMIN. However, the types and numbers of arms handed over by the Maoists tallied with the numbers and descriptions provided by the Nepal Army from where the Maoists had looted a large number of weapons. It must also be kept in mind that not all Maoists PLA cadres had individual arms with them. Most of them also used explosives and the arms of the forward ranks were used by the subsequent rows in their various military operations.

And yet the possibility of the Maoists retaining and hiding arms may not be ruled out until the peace process is brought to its logical conclusion. This is how most insurgent groups behave. In Nepal itself, the Nepalese Congress kept their arms for a long time, even after abandoning their armed struggle against the monarchy and reconciliation with the King, first in 1968 and then in 1976. The Liberation Tigers of Tamil Eelam's surrender of arms to the Indian Peace Keeping Force in Sri Lanka in 1987 was also a token gesture. Insurgent groups always fear the possibility of a revival of the struggle and retain arms for the so-called self-defense and fall-back position to deal with unexpected contingencies. In the case of Nepal, the possibility of SPA leaders conniving in the retention of some arms by the Maoists was also real. There were no official objections or protests from the SPA government against the Maoists for the alleged cheating on arms registration. This silence could have been to remain prepared to deal with the possibility, however remote, of the Army striking against them again at the behest of the Monarch while political transition in Nepal was still under way. It is, however, least likely that the Maoists will resort to armed struggle again and wage a war to capture political power. The commitment not to go back to the 'jungle' seems to be permanent. They know that the odds against them arc too heavy if they go back on this commitment.

The Maoists were initially deceptive about the number of PLA cadres placed in cantonments. Many of the under-age and non-fighting cadres were registered with the UNMIN as PLA members. There could be two reasons behind this. One was to get money because the government had agreed not only to look after the cadres in the cantonment by providing food and shelter, but also to pay them wages at the rate of Rs 3,000 per month. Therefore, the more the cadres, the more the wages handed over in a lump sum to the Maoist party for subsequent disbursement to the PLA cadres. The Maoist party, like other left organizations, generally keeps a share of this money but the cadres also get a part of the wages. The second reason is to keep the trained cadres free for political activities. The Maoists raised their Youth Communist League (YCL), a typical left-wing group, to manage political constituencies, as we shall note later. As such, these senior and well-trained cadres could also be kept free from the watchful eyes of the UN and the government.

The UNMIN subsequently verified the background of all those registered in the cantonments and found that nearly 12,000 of these cadres were either under-age or not part of the Maoist PLA before April 2006. They were accordingly scrutinized and sent back to their homes. The Maoists have by and large accepted this, though there is dispute on some 600 of such cadres remaining to be sorted out finally.[8] There were occasional instances of indiscipline in the cantonments when the PLA cadres left the cantonments, participated in political activities and even brandished arms. The most serious of such violations occurred during the elections of April 2008 at the connivance of the party leadership which has used these cadres for political mobilization and electoral support. Except for this electoral misuse, by and large, the Maoists cadres have behaved, notwithstanding extremely poor sanitary conditions, inadequate ration supplies and irregular payment in the cantonments. The interim government on its part erred in delaying the payments of monthly wages to the Maoists PLA cadres under the pretext of one technical difficulty or another. The question of non-payments to the PLA cadres in cantonments contributed to the crisis in the peace process when the November 2007 the election was postponed and the Maoists threatened to walk out of the peace process.

AS PARLIAMENTARIANS AND MINISTERS

Following the management of arms and armed cadres, the Maoists joined the interim Parliament, with 83 members, and the interim government with four Ministers. Their conduct in the Parliament and as ministers has been normal, with clear signs of learning on the job on their part from the democratic processes.[9] However, the Maoists gave a serious jolt to the peace process in September 2007, by leaving the government and refusing to participate in the elections as their two demands of declaration of Nepal as a Republic even before the Constituent Assembly elections and fully proportional elections were not being conceded. The Maoists' fears were that in the absence of these two demands being granted, they would have nothing much to show as their achievement, would have weak political support and would be routed in the elections. They also argued that the King would not allow the smooth conduct of Constituent Assembly elections and to deter him from doing so, Nepal had to be declared a republic before the elections. The instances of bomb blasts in Kathmandu were cited by them as acts of palace-supported sabotage. Their grouses against the SPA went beyond these demands. The PLA cadres in cantonments were not being looked after well and they had not been paid except for a couple of initial months as noted earlier. They were also asking for compensation for those families who lost their members at the hands of the Royal Nepal Army. There were a number of disappearances of their cadres and supporters whom they wanted the Nepal Army to account for. The Prime Minister refused to concede to their demands and the international community was extremely unhappy with the Maoists' stance.

To come out of the stalemate, the Maoists seemed prepared to compromise if at least one of their two demands could be accepted by the SPA. Having failed in persuading the dominant SPA component the Nepalese Congress to do that, the Maoists joined hands with the Communist Party of Nepal [CPN (UML)], toned down their demands and got a non-binding parliamentary resolution adopted in favor of their demands. This political maneuver also underlined their resilience to use parliamentary methods in pursuance of political goals. The spirit of the resolution adopted by Parliament, after some resistance from the Nepalese Congress, was accepted by the SPA. It was accordingly decided that 'Nepal will be a federal, democratic republic and the decision will be implemented after the first meeting of the Constituent Assembly'. On the proportional representation issue also, the earlier agreed 50:50 formula was changed to 60:40, wherein the Constituent Assembly would now have 240 directly-elected members (first-past-the-post) and 335 to be nominated on the basis of proportional representation. 26 were to be nominated by the Prime Minister in the interests of inclusive representation. In all, the Constituent Assembly will now have 601 members. The interim Parliament on 28 December 2007 adopted the Third Constitutional amendment to incorporate the changes and also fixed the date of the Constituent Assembly elections for 10 April 2008. This has brought the Maoists back into the electoral process. They now seem to be serious in going forward on this road map, perhaps in the hope that their electoral prospects have considerably improved even with the notional acceptance of republican demand. The Maoist leader, Prachanda, has projected himself as the first President of a republican Nepal.

Notwithstanding the participation of the Maoists in Nepal's peace process thus far, there exists a trust deficit between them on the one hand and the SPA (which has now become a Six Party Alliance following the merger of two Nepalese Congress factions in August 2007), as well as sections of the international community on the other. Maoist activities in three specific areas reinforce this trust deficit. One is regarding the return of property (land and houses) captured by them during the insurgency period. Ignoring repeated assurances and agreements, such property is not being returned to the original owners. The Maoists' difficulties arise from the fact that they have settled their landless cadres and supporters on these properties and fear that evacuating these people will be politically counterproductive in the long run. It may also not be easy for the leadership to execute such evictions without the use of force and alienation of their cadres and supporters. The Maoists argued in defense of their defiance on this issue by saying that many other components of the CPA, like setting up of a Peace and Rehabilitation Commission, were not implemented by the interim government.[10] They also contend that such issues are linked to the overall question of socio-economic transformation, land reforms and economic justice to the depressed and discriminated people. They are asking for alternative resettlement proposals for the people to be vacated from the properties. But other political groups are not satisfied by these arguments, which are taken as fragile excuses.

Second, there are innumerable complaints against the YCL which is seen as Maoist muscle power. These complaints include the use of threats, extortions, abductions, obstructions to other political parties' activities, etc., by the YCL. There is truth in many of these complaints. At times the Maoist leadership has apologized for these activities and given assurances that they will curb them, but without much visible impact.[11] A probe report by the SPA on violent activities in Darchula, Baitadi and Sindhuli involving the YCL found the Maoists guilty. This probe committee also had a Maoist representative who accepted that his party's cadres were involved. He, however, registered his dissent by saying that the cadres of other political parties were also involved in these unlawful activities.[12] The YCL activities during the elections came in for widespread criticism. The Maoist leadership also blamed the media for exaggerating YCL activities, but there was a realization deep down that the aggressive activities of the Maoists cadres were tarnishing the party's image and political prospects in the elections. The Maoist leadership's difficulties in this respect arise from a number of factors: some of the local cadres are beyond the control of the central leadership; there has been penetration of criminal and other anti-social elements at the lower rungs of the Maoist organization; and many of the Maoists' adversaries, including dissenters from within the organization as also royalists from outside, are organizing and inspiring such activities to discredit and malign the Maoists.[13] Some of the criminal gangs based in India and Thailand have recently been exposed as indulging in the activities of abductions, extractions and killings.

Third, there were questions about the Maoists' behavior in the event of their poor performance in the elections. The Maoist chief, Prachanda, his second-in-command, Dr Baburam Bhattarai, and other important leaders occasionally issued statements asserting that they would capture power if they lost the elections. 'If we don't win elections, we will take power by force', Prachanda was quoted to have told his cadres at an organizational meeting.[14] In contrast to this, he was also quoted in personal interviews to journalists to have said; 'When we participated in the peace process, we said if an election was held, any result we would respect. Time and again we have stated that.' He then added, 'We will win this election in a peaceful way and in a free and fair manner. We think that only then we will see that they were wrong and we were right.'[15] Such assertions and the confidence exuded by the Maoists was questioned and disputed by almost everyone, the journalists and media analysts, the political parties and members of the international community. Many of them did not really want to see the Maoists emerge as victorious. The elections in Nepal were extensively observed, both by national as well as international observers. Among the latter were the Carter Center of the US and the European Union. The possibility of rigging elections at some places was there and the Election Commission ordered re-polling in more than 100 polling booths. The international and national observers, by and large, endorsed the elections as 'free and fair'. The Maoists did not win an absolute majority, but performed exceedingly well, beyond the expectations of most. They secured 120 seats in the directly contested constituencies and, after adding the proportionate vote, they hold more than 220 seats in a Constituent Assembly of 600. There strength is comparable to that of the two major mainstream parties, the Nepalese Congress and the CPN (UML), put together. No Constitutional amendment can be accepted without the Maoists' endorsement. Since August 2008, they have also been leading a coalition government with the CPN (UML) and Madhesh Janadhikar Forum (MJF).

The role of the Maoists in the peace process has so far been broadly acceptable. The jury may still be out on the question whether the shift in the Maoist line is tactical or strategic, but the Maoists know and realize very well that there is no way they can capture power by force and retain it in the face of internal as well as international opposition. The only option left for them is to jostle around in democratic, competitive politics and make room for themselves by actions that are legitimate and acceptable within the framework of democratic political competition in the emerging Nepal, the more so since they have been able to assume power through open democratic elections. The possibility of consolidating their power through the support of the people is now a reality for them to build upon. This is the option that will fully mainstream them into Nepalese politics, hopefully.

BUILDING AN INCLUSIVE DEMOCRACY

Nepal has been trying to build a democratic state since the anti-Rana revolution of 1950–1. The model it had been pursuing prior to *Jan Andolan-II* has been of constructing a multi-party democratic structure under a Constitutional monarchy. But this attempt did not succeed. Initially, both the internal feudal vested interests and external strategic interests militated against the demand for a fully representative Constituent Assembly to draft a viable constitution. The King continued to play a central role in constitutional and political affairs. In December 1960, the King assumed direct power and established a guided non-party polity keeping the monarchy at the core of the power structure. The first *Jan Andolan* in 1990 did bring about a significant change by asserting that sovereignty belonged to the people, but the way polity evolved in subsequent years, the vested interests brought it back to the palace-centric process with the political parties and elected representatives only playing second fiddle to the King. It was this degeneration of what was conceived to be a multi-party system under constitutional monarchy that enabled the King to become more autocratic as witnessed in 2002 and 2005.

CONSTITUTIONAL MONARCHY OR REPUBLIC?

The issue of democracy post-*Jan Andolan-II*, if faced squarely, meant democracy with or without the King. The Maoists throughout their ten years of insurgency stuck to the demand for a republican Nepal as central to their agenda. Even while negotiating with the

King's regime, they continued to hold on to this agenda. The political parties had turned against the King following the dissolution of Parliament in 2002 and the direct rule of the King in 2005, but they still did not seem ready to say goodbye to the institution of the monarchy. So also was the case with the international community, including India. This was the reason behind the absence of the word 'republic' in the 12-point agreement between the SPA and the Maoists. While the SPA was happy to commit itself to the concept of full and complete democracy, the Maoists had to live with a compromise, after long discussion, by accepting the ambiguous notion of 'absolute democracy', which for them meant a republic, but for the parties, democracy with nominal monarchy. The interim Constitution, drawn up in the shadow of *Jan Andolan-II*, stripped the King of all effective powers and made the Prime Minister the virtual head of the state. The question of the republic was left to be decided by the elected Constituent Assembly.

The Maoists, however, kept up the pressure on the agenda of the republic. They referred to the 12-point agreement that vowed to end 'autocratic monarchy', and there was no way to do so except to end the monarchy itself as an institution because the experience of 1990–2006 had clearly underlined that the King would not remain confined to constitutional limits. For them, this was to be one achievement they could boast of as a result of their ten-year struggle and loss of thousands of lives. They repeatedly emphasized that the King would try to sabotage the Constituent Assembly process and therefore needed to be contained through the abolition of monarchy. As a result of their pressures and in view of growing popular disenchantment with the monarchy,[16] the second amendment to the interim Constitution approved that the monarchy could be abolished by two-thirds vote if proof of the King obstructing the Constituent Assembly election could be produced in Parliament.[17] We have noted earlier that the Maoists postponed the November 2007 elections on the question of the republic and managed to get yet another (third) Constitutional amendment wherein the Parliament agreed that Nepal will be a 'federal, democratic republic', but this decision was to be implemented only by the first meeting of the elected Constituent Assembly. Here again, the rider of implementation was inserted because of the reservations of SPA constituents, particularly the Nepalese Congress and the CPN (UML). The latter had shown a preference for a referendum if Nepal was to be declared a republic before the Constitution of the Constituent Assembly. This was not acceptable to the Nepalese Congress and the Maoists because a referendum would allow the King to become the central issue and enable him to mobilize public support. In the referendum, if the monarchy got even 20 to 25 per cent of votes, if not more, which was in the realm of possibility, the establishment of the republic would face greater political difficulties.

Reservations on the question of the republic reflect various constraints inherent in Nepalese politics. The Nepalese Congress (NC) and the Communist Party of Nepal were the first to raise the issue of a republican Nepal as early as 1950, during the anti-Rana struggle. They were then in favor of an elected Constituent Assembly, but in view of international influences, particularly of India, could not get it. The NC moved closer to the idea of a Constitutional monarchy in their reconciliation with the King during 1968 and 1976. The party's acceptance of a referendum in May 1980 on the issue of a party-less Panchayat system *versus* multi-party democracy under Constitutional monarchy was based on this reconciliation. The CPN has gone through a number of erosions and distortions. Its CPN (UML) incarnation was generally propped up and encouraged by the Palace during the seventies to counter the NC before its reconciliation with the King. It is widely perceived in Nepalese political circles that the CPN (UML) is much closer to the palace than the NC.

The institution of the monarchy was perceived in India as a symbol of Nepalese unity and stability in the context of turbulent politics. Since India had played a decisive role in the anti-Rana revolution, the republican agenda got seriously diluted. In the then prevailing context, India also looked at the institution of monarchy as a bulwark against any expansion of Chinese communist influence in the Himalayan kingdom. In 1990, as noted earlier, multi-party democracy was accepted within the framework of a constitutional monarchy. The post-1990 political processes have evolved around the core of monarchy, making political parties dependent upon the palace. For the past sixteen years, mainstream Nepalese parties have played politics with reference to the palace. They have used palace patronage in their power struggle against each other and the palace has used their rivalries to entrench itself in the polity. In the process, the interests of the palace have deeply penetrated within the party organizations and leadership. Therefore, mainstream political parties are finding it painful and difficult to accept the republican agenda wholeheartedly. While organizational lethargy inhibits them from giving up the institution of monarchy, the popular aspirations and pressures from the rank and file force them to adopt the republican agenda. Almost all the mainstream political parties have by now done so, notwithstanding the voices of reservations being raised from within the organizations.[18] In this dilemma, they find it convenient to leave the issue for the elected Constituent Assembly to decide as that would also have popular sanction. Some among these parties entertained the thought that if the Maoists fared badly in the Constituent Assembly elections, efforts could be made to scuttle or postpone the republican agenda. The Maoists openly articulated such fears in the course of their campaign for Constituent Assembly elections. There also seems to be a compulsion to leave the republican issue to the elected Constituent Assembly as the Nepal Army, which stood loyal to the King all these decades, assured support to the interim government and the peace process only on the condition that the King's status would be changed, if at all, only by the elected Constituent Assembly. The international community has also been used to pursuing its strategic and economic interests in a monarchical Nepal. In India there are powerful interests, including the old princely households and Hindu religious groups, that looked towards the Nepalese monarchy with support and sympathy. Officially, however, Indian policy gradually moved in the direction of supporting a republic in Nepal if the Nepalese people so decide.

The King naturally had a vested interest in sabotaging the republican agenda. Encouraged by the confusion among the SPA on this issue and the periodic tensions between the SPA and the

Maoists, the King tried to raise his voice. Some sympathetic and sponsored public opinion surveys were also used by the royalists to underline the continuing relevance of the institution of the monarchy.[19] The tensions in Tarai, as we discuss below, also encouraged the King and the royalists to assert their political relevance. However, the resolution of the Tarai crisis led all the Madhes groups to declare their support for a republican Nepal. There is a gradual build-up of popular support for republican Nepal at the grassroots level. At the popular level, both King Gyanendra and his son, Crown Prince Paras, were extremely unpopular. There have been no public protests against the stripping of all the King's powers. Even the royalist parties are not going beyond referring the republican issue to the elected Constituent Assembly. In view of all this, and in the context of the Maoists' impressive electoral performance, it was a matter of formality for the elected Constituent Assembly to declare Nepal a Republic in its first meeting on 27 May 2008.

INCLUSIVE DEMOCRACY

The question of inclusion was also stirred up by the Maoist insurgency during which the marginalized ethnic and regional groups were promised self-determination and autonomy. The Maoists have subsequently diluted their position on self-determination under the fear that their Marxist concept when applied to prevailing conditions in Nepal may encourage forces of secession and national fragmentation. The people of the southern flat belt, the Tarai, called Madhes, the ethnic and tribal groups called the Janjatis, the Dalits, and women have been clamoring for their rights and share in the power structure for a long time. The coalition of hill-based feudal rulers and the upper castes (Brahmans and Chetries) that dominated the Nepalese political and social order for the past two and a half centuries never treated these marginalized groups with equality and dignity. These groups are very poorly represented in the administration, the political power structure including within the party organizations, army and police, economic and business sectors, etc.[20] Even after *Jan Andolan-II*, the SPA was not sufficiently sensitive to the long-standing grievances of these sections because politically the parties are also dominated by the upper castes. Their top organizational bodies have an abysmally poor representation of all these marginalized sections, not withstanding the fact that Madhesis constitute a sizable section of the entire population. The Maoists are only a shade better but not truly inclusive. According to one estimate, of the 28 appointments at the Secretary level in the government made after April 2006, 'only two were women and one Madhesi, but twenty were Brahmins'.[21] There is however, a strong rhetorical commitment to the concept of inclusion by the SPA and the Maoists following the April 2006 uprising. In the section on socio-economic transformation, the CPA committed all parties to:

> [A]ddress the problems related to women, Dalits, indigenous people, *janjatis*, Madhesis, oppressed, neglected minorities and the backward by ending discrimination based on class, caste, language, sex, culture, religion and region and to restructure the state on the basis of inclusiveness, democracy and progression by ending present centralized and unitary structure of the state.[22]

The elements of inclusiveness were reflected in the interim Constitution under the provisions related to the establishment and composition of political parties.[23] Under the Right to Equality (Art. 13), the state promised not to discriminate on the basis of 'religion, race, caste, tribe, sex, origin, language or ideological conviction', but allowed for special provisions to be made for the hitherto neglected and discriminated groups. But the much talked about demand for federalism was not included in the interim Constitution even after the Madhesi-dominated Sadbhavana Party members raised the issue and noted their dissent. Even the Maoists did not strongly support the Madhes demand and went along with the SPA in this respect.

The issue gradually gathered momentum with the ethnic groups staging demonstrations on the streets of Kathmandu. The Sadbhavana Party in December 2006 launched its agitation in the Tarai in favor of its demand for federalism. Another group, the MJF, during its rally ran into conflict with the Maoists whose adventurist involvement resulted in the killing of a young boy in Lahan. This added fuel to the Madhes fire which was initially encouraged by the SPA, royalists and even sections of the international community, in the interest of eroding the Maoist base in Tarai.[24] Thus by January 2007, the Madhes agitation had taken a serious turn. The Prime Minister had to address the public twice and announce an immediate amendment in the interim Constitution (first amendment) to incorporate the provision of a federal state. To calm tempers, the Prime Minister also instituted talks with the MJF. However it took the government nearly six weeks to get the talks initiated. After a slow process of two rounds of talks, in which the MJF gave up its demands for the resignation of the Home Minister and dissolution of the interim Parliament, there was a 22-point understanding between the government and the agitators in August 2007. The agreement included compensation for the persons dead and injured during the agitation. But months passed without any action on implementing the promises made by the government. The government, instead, was preparing special security plans for dealing with the situation in Tarai. Therefore, the Madhes agitation continued.

In the wake of the agitations in Tarai, widespread violence and anarchy, causing disruption of normal life, affecting movements of people and goods within Tarai as also between Tarai and the hill areas, including Kathmandu, has been witnessed for nearly one year. Various factors contributed to this situation. To begin with, the government lacked sincerity as the Pahari (hill people) mind-set of the ruling parties continued to guide them in taking the Madhes issue lightly. The internal constraints in the ruling coalition where the Maoists were against conceding any ground to the agitating groups also led to apathy and inaction. There was a near complete lack of leadership in Madhes. The cause of Madhes could, therefore, not be put forth assertively and in an organized manner. The lack of leadership also allowed for the mushrooming of groups to claim the leadership of the Madhes movement through acts of violence and vandalism. Many of the criminal groups had a field day, indulging in abductions, extractions and wanton killings under the cover of the Madhes agitation. Violence was also perpetrated by the extremist Tarai groups led by defected Maoists like Jwala Singh and Goit who run their respective factions of Jantantrik Tarai Mukti Morcha. Various other groups like the Tarai Tigers and Tarai

Cobra also entered the fray. Vested political interests, including the royalists, encouraged such groups to keep instability and anarchy, to discredit the government and erode the political base of the ruling alliance in Tarai. There were also reports of some of these groups getting support and encouragement from across the Indian border from vested interests like criminals, smugglers and Hindu fundamentalists who wanted to use Tarai's instability in getting the elections postponed in the interest of the Hindu monarchy of Nepal.

In December 2007, some of the Madhesi members of the interim Parliament defected from their mainstream parties to form the Tarai Madhes Loktantrik Party under the leadership of Mahanta Thakur who had a long association with the Nepalese Congress. In order to provide proper leadership to the Madhes movement, this party formed a united front, called the United Democratic Madhesi Forum (UDMF), with the MJF and a breakaway group of the Sadbhavana Party led by Rajendra Mahato. This front put forward six demands that included the creation of an autonomous Madhes province and raising the minimum percentage of the proportional representation system for inclusion from the existing 20 to 50 per cent. They gave the government a notice for agitation if their demands were not addressed in six weeks. In the absence of any response from the government, the agitation was launched by the Front on 12 February 2008. This resulted in severe scarcity of petrol and essential commodities in Kathmandu as the movement of goods through Tarai came to a virtual halt. The government had to repeatedly impose curfew to ease the situation but that was no solution. The agitation by the UDMF also raised a question mark on the conduct of the Constituent Assembly elections in Tarai. The government threatened to hold the election through the deployment of force, but without the participation of Madhes, which meant that the Constituent Assembly elections would have no credibility since the Madhes constitute nearly half of Nepal's population (32 per cent according to the latest census, which is disputed by Madhesis). Eventually the government and the Madhes Front had talks and arrived at an eight-point agreement. This agreement signed on 28 February 2008 raised the 'inclusive' limit from

20 to 30 per cent and endorsed the concept of an autonomous Madhes. It said:

> [T]he structure of Madhes and other autonomous regions, power devolution between the Centre and the provinces and the allocation of resources will be done through the Constituent Assembly by keeping intact the sovereignty, unity and integrity of the country.[25]

This agreement also called on 'all the armed groups of Tarai to come to the negotiating table' and help in the peaceful conduct of the Constituent Assembly polls. The front called off the agitation and promised to participate in the Constituent Assembly elections. It reiterated that the government should move fast to implement the agreement. Though some of the agitating groups have refused to endorse this agreement, there has been a broad-based positive response from the people in Tarai. The government also moved fast to conclude a similar understanding with the Federal Republican National Front (FRNF) of the other agitating ethnic groups. The way for the smooth conduct of the Constituent Assembly elections was thus prepared, though the challenge of getting the armed Madhesi groups on board still remains.

The issue of inclusiveness has thus been shifted to the elected Constituent Assembly. The challenge to resolve it to the satisfaction of all the groups involved remains because Madhes is a diversified region. In terms of religion, Madhes has 4.2 per cent Muslims who may want special provisions. Linguistically, groups speaking Maithili, Bhojpuri and Awadhi constitute 12.3, 7.5 and 2.4 per cent of Nepal's population, respectively, and they all live in Madhes. Then there is a tribal group of Tharus who constitute 5.1 per cent of Nepal's population but 6.8 per cent of Tarai's population. They had opposed one autonomous province for the whole of Madhes and want separate autonomy for themselves.

While the Madhes constitutes the biggest component in the search for an inclusive democracy, the Janjatis, Dalits and women also are its essential aspects. The question of women's representation has been addressed in the interim Constitution. In May 2006, the interim Parliament adopted a resolution unanimously according 33 per cent reservation to women in all 'state bodies'. There are, however, problems in implementing this provision, not only in the 'state bodies' but also in political parties. In the Constituent Assembly elections, not a single party has been able to field even 30 per cent women as their candidates. The Maoists have done comparatively the best but with only 20 per cent women candidates. To some extent the gap may be filled through proportional representation, but to reach the 33 per cent figure mandated by the Constitution would be nearly impossible. The explanation by the parties is that there are not enough active, competent and eligible women available to occupy political and administrative positions.

The ethnic groups have also been agitating for proportional representation in New Nepal. There are about 100 ethnic and tribal groups organized to put forth this demand. Some of the major ethnic groups from the hills and Tarai had joined together under the Federal Republican National Front (FRNF) and have been agitating for their rights.[26] Soon after clinching the peace deal with the larger Madhes groups, the government also reached a five-point agreement with FRNF on 1 March 2008. However, the smaller Madhes groups of the FRNF boycotted the agreement.[27] A faction of the Federal Limbuwan State Council, led by Palungwa, had also refused to abide by the 1 March 2008 agreement with the government and has been carrying on with its agitation.[28] The electoral process was facilitated by the government's agreements with the major Madhes and FRNF groups, and the task of knitting Nepal's social and cultural diversity into a viable federal structure poses a daunting challenge to the elected Constituent Assembly, the more so as not many of these groups are territorially homogenous.[29]

PERSPECTIVE

As Nepal gets engaged with the process of Constitution-making through the elected Constituent Assembly, the two dimensions of its state restructuring, that is, the mainstreaming of the Maoists and the building of an inclusive democracy, appear to be set on track. The Maoists have, for the past two years, shown considerable resilience and pragmatism in dealing with the question of getting into the mainstream. They have their radical ideological jargon, they have their muscle power in terms of undisclosed arms, trained cadres and the YCL and they have their aspirations to control the state. Shrill rhetoric and aggressive statements are flaunted at times to motivate war-hardened uneducated, radicalized cadres. But at the same time, it also needs to be kept in mind that the Maoists have made several compromises and adjustments as well. In a way, the Maoist leaders, Prachanda and Baburam Bhattarai, were not far off the point when they asserted prior to the elections that no other party will pursue the agenda of change and transformation advanced by them and therefore, their emerging victorious is essential if this agenda has to be carried forward.[30] This agenda of socio-economic transformation has been widely endorsed in Nepal except for feudal vested interests. Notwithstanding the implied threats in many of their statements, the Maoists will continue to be engaged with the evolving democratic dynamics of Nepal as long as they have a feeling that they are a critical, even if not the dominant, partner, in the process. A reasonable share in power, as is evident in the post-elected representative coalition government, will ensure this engagement. It also depends upon the rest of the players in the power game that the Maoists are treated sensitively and carefully, and not the way they were dealt with—with scorn and contempt—during the first Parliament after 1991. The Maoists' perception is that they were also treated shabbily by the SPA in the post-Andolan phase in the areas of distribution of positions of power and influence like ministers, ambassadors, secretaries, etc. Even now, threats of disturbing the present Maoist-led coalition are constantly flaunted by the Nepalese Congress and a section of the CPN (UML) leadership. The responsibility of keeping the Maoists engaged with the mainstream political process, therefore, is as much that of the other political forces and the international community as of the Maoists themselves.

Building an inclusive democratic state structure is a slow, difficult and long-drawn process. The parameters of this process have broadly been laid down and there appears to be a basic consensus on these parameters. The task, therefore, cannot be completed just after the Constituent Assembly elections or even after the new Constitution is finalized through a series of unexpected and unanticipated compromises and adjustments, give and take. 'Inclusiveness' will take a long period of evolution through the implementation of the Constitution and evolution of a culture of mutual accommodation and coexistence. The Nepalese and its federal structures are still evolving. The additional problem in Nepal is that it has had 250 years of a feudal political culture and deeply entrenched stakeholders. There is a near complete absence of rational and secular identity icons of nationalism and unity. The Nepalese involved in the restructuring of the state and the international community will have to have considerable patience, sagacity and ingenuity to carry forward the task at hand. Many hurdles like the recent crisis of Madhes agitation will have to be confronted and resolved. Even temporary breakdowns cannot be wished away. However, there is little doubt that the direction of democracy and inclusion is irreversible, unless unforeseen calamity besieges Nepal.

The change that has been witnessed in Nepal could not have taken place without the help and cooperation of the international community. The constructive engagement of the international community will have to continue to ensure that Nepal's peace process reaches its culmination. There are signs of change in the US attitude towards the Maoists. Former President Jimmy Carter talked to the Maoist leadership and was positive about their role and, in February 2008, even President Bush expressed the hope that the Maoists would work with other parties to build a democratic order in Nepal. India has also shifted its ground on questions like the constitutional monarchy and the Maoists' role. India, in particular, and the rest of the international community, China included, have stakes in a stable, peaceful and progressing Nepal. During Prime Minister Prachanda's first official state visit to India in September 2008, the Indian response was constructive.[31] The UN has also offered US$10 million support to help the peace process after the coming to power of the Maoist-led elected coalition. There may be areas where strategic interests of some of the members of the international community do not perfectly tally with the unfolding events and developments in Nepal. But the international community will have to adjust to these developments, keeping in mind that Nepal has gone through an unprecedented experience in the assertion of peoples' power. It will not accept directions or impositions contrary to the aspirations of its people. At the same time, it will heavily depend upon the generous and creative cooperation of the international community in discovering and harnessing its potential of prosperity. India, which is the closest and most effective neighbor, has so far been remarkably responsive to Nepal's emerging aspirations and its transitional travails. It is in India's own interests to see that Nepal regains its self-confidence and innovative acumen to chart its destiny in harmony with regional stability and peace.

NOTES

1. For one of the recent accounts of political change in Bangladesh, see Krishnan Srinivasan (2007). *Jamdani Revolution: Politics, Personalities and Civil Society in Bangladesh: 1989–92.* New Delhi: Har Anand Publishers.
2. Text of the Agreement, as in *Kathmandu Post*, 22 November 2005.
3. Shyam Saran's press conference in Kathmandu on 22 April 2006. For the text of this press conference, see http://www.mea.gov.in/pressbriefing/2006/04/22pb01.htm.
4. Text of the Proclamation, *BBC News*, 24 April 2006.
5. One of the documents adopted at their third plenum in May 2003 included 'Present situation and our historical task'. http://cpnm.org/new/English/worker/ 9issue.document.htm.
6. Author's personal interviews with Indian and Nepalese officials in New Delhi on 8–11 June 2006.
7. UN Secretary General's Report, S/2007/235, 26 April 2007. For the quantity of explosives, see *Nepal: Peace Postponed*, International Crisis Group Report, Asia Briefing No. 72 (p. 7), Kathmandu/Brussels. 18 December 2007.
8. Interview with UNMIN officials in Kathmandu, 20 February 2008.
9. *Nepal Maoists: Purists or Pragmatists?* International Crisis Group Report, Asia Report No. 132 (pp. 17–18), Brussels and other offices. 18 May 2007.
10. It may be noted in this context that landless communities from about 50 districts gathered in Kathmandu to demand the immediate setting up

of a Land Commission with their proper representation to ensure the rights of the landless people. Nepalnews.com, 5 March 2008.

11. C.K. Lal, 'Throwing justice to the wind', *The Nepalese Times*, 7 December 2007.
12. *The Himalayan Times*, Kathmandu, 6 March 2008.
13. Interview with Maoists leaders in Kathmandu, July 2007.
14. Liam Cocharne, 'Nepal elections: Will the third time be the charm?' http://www.worldpoliticsreview.com/articlePrint.aspx?ID=1610
15. Interview by Mark Williams in *The Herald*, http://www.theherald.co.uk/misc/ print.php?artid=2082475.
16. King Gyanendra and his son, Crown Prince Paras, were very unpopular following the Royal massacre in June 2001 and the King's autocratic moves in 2002 and 2005. Many in Nepal did not see King Gyanendra's coming to power as legitimate.
17. *Gorkhapatra* (Kathmandu), 14 June 2007.
18. For instance, even after the Nepalese Congress adopted the goal of a Republican Nepal, the Prime Minister's daughter and Central Committee Member, Sujata Koirala, has been publicly asking for the retention of Constitutional monarchy. Her stand has been endorsed by other Central Committee members like K.B. Gurung. But she has recently changed her position in favor of a republic. The Central Committee member, K.P. Oli, of the Communist Party (UML) has also taken a similar position of reservations on the question of abolition of monarchy. This category of people is also present in other constituents of the SPA, though all of them are in the extreme minority.
19. Such a survey recently projected 49 per cent support for the monarchy. Sudhindra Sharma and Pawan Kumar Sen (February 2008). *Nepal Contemporary Political Situation V: Nationwide Opinion Survey*, Interdisciplinary Analysts, Kathmandu. A more scientifically conducted survey completed under the auspices of the International IDEA (Institute for Democracy and Electoral Assistance) projected 59 per cent support for the republic. *State of Democracy in Nepal*, International IDEA, Kathmandu, June 2007.
20. Harka Gurung (2006). *From Exclusion to Inclusion: Socio-Political Agenda for Nepal*, Social Inclusion Research Fund, Kathmandu. Krishna Bhatchan (24–6 April 2003). 'Expected Model and Process of Inclusive Democracy in Nepal' (unpublished paper), Social Science Baha, Kathmandu. Dilli Ram Dahal (2002). 'Madhes, regionalism and national integration: A case of the Nepal Tarai', *Nepal Journal of Contemporary Studies*, 2, 1. Kathmandu.

21. *Nepal Peace Postponed.* Crisis Group Asia Briefing No. 72 (p. 11), 18 December 2007. Kathmandu/Brussels.
22. Paragraph 3.5, Comprehensive Peace Agreement, November 2006.
23. See Articles 141 and 142; also *Nepal's Constitutional Process*, International Crisis Group Asia Report No.128 (pp. 24–5, fns 204–6).
24. *Nepal's Troubled Terai Region*, International Crisis Group Policy Report, Asia Report No.136, 9 July 2007.
25. Text of the deal, Paragraph 2. *The Himalayan Times*, Kathmandu (p.1). 29 February 2008.
26. FRNF comprises the joint Tharu National Front, Dalit Janjati Party, Tamangsaling Autonomous State Council, Federal Limbuwan State Council, United Tharu National Front, Madhes People's Rights Forum, Madhesi Loktantrik Morcha and Loktantrik Madhes Morcha.
27. See *The Himalayan Times* (Kathmandu), 2 March 2008 for details.
28. *The Himalayn Times* (Kathmandu), 15 March 2008.
29. Lok Raj Baral, 'Nepal: The Restructuring of a Neo-Patrimonial State', unpublished paper presented at a national seminar on 'Restructuring the Nepalese State' in Kathmandu, 29–30 June 2007.
30 nepalnews.com 5 March 2008; *The Himalayan Times* (Kathmandu), 3 April 2008.
31. See the joint statement issued at the end of the visit on 15 September 2008. MEA website.

6

Old Conflicts, New Futures: Understanding Nepal's Political Transformation

ANINDITA DASGUPTA

INTRODUCTION

AT A TIME when people's movements for restoration of democracy are raging across parts of Asia, it is in the small South Asian country, Nepal, that some of its most significant achievements, or challenges, can be observed. This relatively little-known country has recently come out of a ten-year armed Maoist insurgency (1996–2006), experienced thousands of civilian deaths, challenged and abolished an autocratic monarchy, and organized a powerful people's movement leading to an eventual restoration of peace and parliamentary democracy. The move towards peace and reconstruction, after ten years of unprecedented political upheaval, began in April 2006 when the beleaguered king agreed to hand over power to the political parties, and the Maoist leaders formally ended the 'People's War' and entered mainstream politics as part of a Seven Party Alliance (SPA). In the Constituent Assembly elections held in April 2008, the Communist Party of Nepal (Maoist) [CPN(M)] was elected as the largest single party in the newly restored Parliament, and the Maoist leader Pushpa Kamal Dahal (better known as 'Prachanda') became the first Prime Minister of the newly declared Republic of Nepal. Thus Nepal seemed to be poised for a new beginning and what many hoped would be the start of a process of reconstruction, national reconciliation and economic development. Yet, there still remained forces within and outside the country with the potential to destabilize Nepal's resolute march towards a 'new' and different future. Many of these forces, ironically, are Nepal's own dogged old conflicts which have surfaced over and over again in its recent past. The new republic will now have to handle these fault lines with sensitivity and political acumen to keep them from resurfacing in the near future, especially if the new—and purportedly more inclusive—constitution fails to meet the high expectations that it has raised among Nepal's diverse population at this time.

One such conflict which threatened to derail Nepal's ongoing peace negotiations at the last minute was a spontaneous upsurge of identity assertion in the winter of 2006–7 along Nepal's southern borders, or the Tarai. In the Tarai, the plains people known as the Madhesis, made a powerful resurgence to ascertain their rights as bonafide citizens of Nepal. As a result, the Constituent Assembly election, which was an integral part of the peace process in terms of mainstreaming the Maoists and writing a new constitution, had to be postponed from November 2007 to April 2008. Analysts had warned at that time that if the movement was not properly and urgently addressed by the Nepal government and the Constituent Assembly when elected, a whole new form of conflict could start in the already troubled South Asian country (International Crisis Group, 2007). For the Madhesis, on the other hand, the run-up to the elections was the most opportune moment to articulate their deepest grievances in relation to access to state power and identity, and carve out a space for themselves in the new constitution. Given Nepal's vastly diverse population with its complex ethnic/caste/regional differences, and the high expectations from the new constitution, the Madhesis may not yet be the last ones to voice their demands for inclusion in Nepal's 'new' future.

Nepal has experienced a wave of identity-based assertions since what many call the 'spring awakening' of Nepal in 1990, a year generally associated with the opening of the floodgates of both identity and democratic politics in Nepal with the passing of a new and inclusive constitution. Nepal's recent history has been characterized by a conflict of various degrees between two sets of opposing forces. The first conflict was between a state-sponsored nation-building project and Nepal's numerous Tibeto-Burman speaking small communities trying to preserve their diverse cultures. The second conflict was between the national political elite consisting of a minority of hill people and Nepal's numerous politically marginalized plains communities or Madhesis on the other. This dual conflict is present throughout much of Nepal's recent history, and is located against the backdrop of a two-phased *Jan Andolan* (people's movements), led mostly by a vibrant Nepalese civil society. In its first phase (1990), the aim of the *Jan Andolan* was to establish a parliamentary democracy with a constitutional monarchy in Nepal. In its second phase (2006) its aim was to disarm and draw the Maoists into mainstream politics, abolish monarchy altogether and restore representative parliamentary democracy in Nepal. In fact, the identity assertions in Nepal were outgrowths of, and complementary to, the two phases of *Jan Andolan.* Such resistance picked up after the 1980s—due to the gradual loosening of restrictions on political activities, the spread of education and a growing political discourse within Nepal's diverse communities—and received a huge boost with the passing of Nepal's 1990 constitution that allowed for the creation of a more plural and inclusive society than ever before. It is this dual conflict, this paper suggests, that continues to run through much of Nepal's post-1990 history, reappearing periodically in different garbs, backed by different communities and guided by different ideological under-pinnings. Nepal's popular movements since 1990 have attempted to challenge this state-elite domination—using region, ethnicity or caste (or a mix of class and ethnicity as the Maoists have done)—and create a new social order that would give equal recognition to the aspirations of the country's diverse populations and provide economic advancement for all.

This paper attempts to understand Nepal's ongoing political transformation from a historical perspective which is necessary in order to understand how Nepal arrived at a stage in the spring of 2008 when it become a federal republic and conducted Constituent Assembly elections with the intention of drafting a new constitution.

I begin by presenting a brief historical background of Nepal, and then attempt to explain against the backdrop of the two-phased

Jan Andolan: (a) how the Janajati movements after 1990 were some of the initial instances of identity assertion in Nepal; (b) how the weaknesses within these movements allowed the Maoist leaders to appropriate the major Janajati demands into the Maoist discourse; and (c) how the Madhesis were successful in forging a strong ecological identity forcing the country to take note of their voice, leading to the postponement of the Constituent Assembly elections at the last minute. I will conclude with a discussion on the evolved situation in the larger Nepalese polity and point out some of the major challenges that the newly created republic will have to face even as it starts the much-awaited, though undoubtedly uphill, task of building a 'new' future for Nepal. Doing so, I hope to make the point that a peace settlement or constitution in contemporary Nepal which ignores this dual conflict may not be able to stand the test of time. Tackling this complex issue, however, will be one of the biggest challenges yet for a country which is just coming out of a decade or more of violence and political upheaval.

NEPAL'S SMALL COMMUNITIES

Nepal's unique demography makes it a country of small communities. All of Nepal's 103 caste and ethnic groups (mostly of Indo-Aryan and Mongoloid origin), speaking a hundred-odd different languages and dialects (mostly Indo-Aryan and Tibeto-Burman), are small. Most of these groups constitute between 5 and 7 per cent of the country's total population, with the largest constituting not more than about 17 per cent. Even when it comes to religion, a great deal of diversity exists in Nepal. The Census of 2001 listed Hinduism, Buddhism, Islam and other local faiths, but in reality there is far greater diversity and syncretism on the ground. Such a demographic composition is apparently not favorable for the polarization or constellation of people along ethnic or class lines. At the same time identity-based loyalties in Nepal tend to lurk close to the surface because almost every small community carries a burden of historical grievances and seeks some sort of a change in the existing socio-political order which, to them, continues to privilege a handful of high caste communities.

It is against this backdrop of small communities that the so-called 'conglomerate of communities' like the Nepal Federation of Indigenous Nationalities and the Madhesi People's Rights Forum often find a new space and voice. When they come together under an umbrella in spite of internal conflicts, they often emerge as powerful power camps that are taken notice of by other power camps and are involved in the negotiation process or dialogue on any national issue. They also seem to capture the attention of political parties, international donor agencies and the media.

The emergence of such conglomerates is also likely to make the national debates in the forthcoming Constituent Assembly a lot more focused because several local issues are sorted out at the level of the conglomerates, which are expected to put forward only the most important issues before the Assembly. The leaders of the constituent communities, belonging to both Janajati and Madhesi groups, are also able to see the space unfold in front of them when they come under an umbrella organization and how the space vanishes when they are not together. Even the Dalits are now taking a cue from these two large and politically significant groups, but their backward economic condition, social disabilities and distribution all over the middle-hills make it difficult for them to come together. But the very fact that each conglomerate represents a large number of groups, ideologies and aspirations, consensus at the Constituent Assembly debates can be highly elusive, which may further delay the process of democratization of this erstwhile hereditary and theocratic kingdom.

A BRIEF HISTORY OF NEPAL

The unification of Nepal as we know it now took place as late as the close of the eighteenth century when the Shah dynasty from the small hill kingdom of Gorkha brought much of the neighbouring territories both in the hills and the adjoining Indian plains under its control. Before the 1770s, numerous Tibeto-Burman language-speaking groups, which practised shifting cultivation in the middle hills and pastoralism and trade in the higher mountains, inhabited the elongated tract of land which now came to be known as Nepal.

Most such communities till the unification of Nepal by King Prithvinarayan Shah in the 1770s were, in today's parlance, non-caste, non-Hindu, and egalitarian communities (Hamilton 1971: 24). Historical sources suggest that the successors of King Prithvinarayan Shah pursued the agenda of nation-building quite forcefully, which essentially meant promotion of the Nepalese language, Nepalese dress and Hindu culture among the newly subjugated areas and peoples (Pradhan 2002: 7). This can be said to be the start of a nation-building project that was to play a significant role in influencing the nature of Nepal's politics in the forthcoming years.

From the 1770s till the Anglo-Nepalese War of 1814–16, Nepal displayed expansionist tendencies and conquered Sikkim as well as extended its western frontier up to the Kangra Valley. This resulted in large-scale immigration of the Mongoloid Nepalese to the neighbouring Indian plains in search of livelihood as well as to work for the British army. As they migrated southward, the hills of Nepal were increasingly occupied by the caste Hindus, from the surrounding plains in the south and the west, gradually pushing themselves towards the east.

In 1846, Jang Bahadur Kunwar (later taking the title 'Rana') took over as the absolute ruler of Nepal, turned the Shah kings into titular heads and established a new Rana dynasty. The Ranas, who were less tolerant of cultural plurality, initiated a new and more vigorous process of nation-building which was particularly imposed on the speakers of 20-odd different Tibeto-Burman speaking communities practising various forms of animism or Buddhism. In this process, the Nepalese state took the help of the *Tagadharis* (sacred thread-wearing high-caste Hindus) whose settlement in the east was facilitated by the nation state by changing the land laws and even putting an end to communal forms of ownership that existed there till the middle of the previous century, at least in Limbuan in the extreme eastern hills of Nepal.

In 1854, Jang Bahadur Rana imposed the *Muluki Ain* or national civil code in Nepal, which completely redefined the land tenure system, rules of inheritance, and food, including a ban on eating beef. Above all, under this code, he categorized the people of Nepal into five hierarchical groups with the *Tagadhari* on the top; the *Namasine Matwali* or 'unenslavable drinking castes' like the Magar and Gurung; the *Masine Matwali* or 'enslavable drinking castes' like the Limbu and Rai; the 'touchable but impure castes' like the Tamang and Sherpa; and finally 'untouchable and impure castes' like Kami, Sarki, and Damai. Though all groups within these broad five categories were not 'castes', the *Muluki Ain* prescribed caste status for them based on Hindu notions of purity and pollution in many domains of social life (Pradhan 2002: 8–9). There is now scattered information available to show how the various small indigenous communities protested against the nation-building process in Nepal since as early as the eighteenth century. Harka Gurung (2003) for instance provides information on protests made by different Janajati groups against the state from 1770 to 1964. Anne de Sales (2000) also provides a riveting account of Lakhan Thapa's resistance, while Lionel Caplan (1970: 175–82) describes some of the Limbu protests in the east.

As long as the British controlled India, the rulers in Nepal and India were in tandem, which made it difficult for democratic aspirations to grow in Nepal. But with India's Independence in 1947, the Nepalese state lost its political ally in the British and was thereafter unable to stop the growth of democratic aspirations in Nepal. Thus, it saw the birth of the Nepalese National Congress Party in 1947 and the CPN in 1949 (Nickson 1992: 358–86). In 1951, the Rana rule ended in Nepal. This, however, did not bring about any major changes in the policy of nation-building in the country.

In the first-ever election held in May 1959, the Nepalese Congress won 74 out of 109 seats and formed a government under the prime ministership of the legendary B.P. Koirala. However, Koirala was soon deposed by King Mahendra Bir Bikram Shah who changed the Constitution from a parliamentary democracy to a Panchayat 'non-party' democracy, in which, as it turned out, he reserved all powers to himself. The new system was mandated to be party-less in order to avoid ideological conflict. Although argued by the king as best suited for a country like Nepal (Nickson, 1992: 365), it was not accepted by all as a truly democratic system. The party-less Panchayat regime of Nepal, which lasted from 1960 to 1990, also tried to evolve a uniform national culture, language and religion (Rana et al. 2003: 11).

THE *JAN ANDOLAN* OF 1990: THE BEGINNING OF PEOPLE'S POWER IN NEPAL

The year 1990 remains a significant year in the history of Nepal as it saw disparate civil and political society elements come together in a massive *Jan Andolan* to demand a return to parliamentary democracy, and for the king to come under the purview of the highest laws of the country as a constitutional monarch. The sudden collapse of the Panchayat system in 1990 was precipitated, according to Whelpton (2005: 113), in the first place by India's decision in March 1990 to impose a semi-blockade of Nepal following differences over the signing of a new treaty with Nepal. This, coupled with the rising discontent with the government and the dramatic changes in Eastern Europe, led the members of various communist factions to ally with the Nepalese Congress in a struggle for the restoration of the parliamentary system. A Movement for Restoration of Democracy was announced by this alliance on 10 January 1990 which called for a *Jan Andolan* or People's Movement in Nepal. It was the first time that various communist factions and the Nepalese Congress came together to form the United Left Front.[1] Whether or not this movement was inspired by the break-up of the Soviet Union or the fall of com-munist regimes like that of Ceausescu[2] in 1989 as Millard (2003: 281–304) claims, the movement for the abolition of the Panchayat system and restoration of multiparty democracy gained unprecedented momentum and magnitude in a very short time. Thirty years of a party-less Panchayat system, the fact that King Birendra fell short of being a dynamic leader, that the country remained poor throughout this period and a realization that the world as a whole was going democratic led the Nepalese Congress and the Left forces, traditionally at loggerheads, to unite in their fight against the Panchayat system under the leadership of the Congress stalwart Ganesh Man Singh and the dynamic Left leader Madan Bhandari. Soon a number of intellectuals and professional groups joined the movement, and even Chandrashekhar, the one-time prime minister of India, exhorted the people of Nepal to take the movement to the streets.[3] The movement used some of the popular tactics of people power movements like public protests and demonstrations, using international radio networks to convey their messages, and 'lights out' (Whelpton, 2005: 114) by protesters led by party workers and students. There were, however, several incidents of violent clashes recorded.

Finally, on 16 April 1990 the King, who was under huge popular pressure by this time, dissolved the National Panchayat making way for the formation of an interim government which was represented among others by the Nepalese Congress, the United Left Front, and the independents, and headed by Krishan Prasad Bhattarai. While the United Left Front was willy-nilly party to its decisions, Mashal, a Maoist faction, stood alert to the designs of the palace and even denounced the new Constitution that the king promulgated on 9 November 1990.[4] The new constitution of 1990 defined Nepal as a 'multi-ethnic, multi-lingual, democratic, independent, indivisible, sovereign Hindu and Constitutional Monarchical Kingdom'. Though many celebrated this as the beginning of recognition of Nepal's cultural diversity, others were disappointed because the term 'Hindu' was retained and because they had hoped for more wide-ranging changes. The main weakness of the Constitution was seen to be that the country was declared a 'Hindu kingdom', which failed to recognize the cultural and religious plurality on the ground. Thus, even the second coming of democracy in Nepal can be said to have been half-hearted in the sense that the aspirations of several political parties and many of the hitherto marginalized communities, like the Janajatis, Dalits, and Madhesis did not find adequate space in the 1990 Constitution.

JANAJATI MOVEMENTS IN THE 1990s: IDENTITY ASSERTIONS IN NEPAL

Whatever might have been the shortcomings, there is little doubt that the 1990 Constitution was a significant leap forward without which the country might not have seen the emergence of the subsequent popular movements. The new constitution, thus, marked the beginning of mass politics in Nepal. Even the Maoists afterwards took advantage of the relative space provided by a democratic polity in order to organize itself.

Following the promulgation of the new constitution, Nepal entered a new phase of its history with almost every single community living in its territory mobilizing its members, reviving its age-old customs and traditions, and organizing itself for fulfilment of its demands (Subba 1999: 104–23). The various ethnic groups began their search for roots, identifying what they considered as their traditional and 'authentic' customs and rituals, and abandoning those they thought were imposed upon them during the past two centuries or so. Committees were formed at various levels, and some of them even established their networks outside Nepal, in areas like Assam, Sikkim, and Darjeeling in India, for garnering financial and moral support to the cause of their 'identity' which they were forced to submerge till the restoration of democracy in 1990.[5]

The story of this identity mobilization—called the Janajati Movement in most of the concerned literature—is important to recount here primarily because the later Maoist Movement benefited from both the successes and failures of this movement. It is also important to understand the Janajati Movement in order to place the later Madhesi Movement in its historical context. The period 1990–5 was the Janajati period in Nepal, which saw issues of caste and ethnicity everywhere, and few, if any, talked about class. It is significant that after 2005 the Maoist leadership itself stopped talking about class and pushed the ethnic card instead after realizing its inherent potential to mobilize popular support. Throughout the 1990s, however, each ethnic community was involved in mobilizing its members and building networks across ethnic boundaries for greater strength and solidarity. Although ethnic consciousness was quite old in Nepal, as it was nurtured by geographical conditions of the country and forced by the nature of its rule, the politicization of ethnic groups was something new. Once the initial hesitation to accept the new ideas subsided, the people started responding enthusiastically. Soon, however, many became disillusioned with some of the leaders who often lacked leadership qualities. Some of those who possessed such qualities had already been co-opted by the Panchayat regime purportedly to appear to be inclusive and thus they maintained a studied distance from the Janajati Movement (Dasgupta 2007).

A look at the relevant literature shows that the Janajatis were trying to differentiate themselves from the high-caste Hindus on several counts.[6] First, the Janajatis considered themselves 'Mongols', which is understood as a racial category (short for Mongoloids), and the caste Hindus are described as Aryans, which is a cultural rather than a racial category, but understood in the latter sense. Second, the Janajatis represented themselves as non-Hindu, hence different from the high-caste Hindus. The term 'non-Hindu' mostly represented people with animist and Buddhist beliefs and practices but who were 'Hinduized' to different degrees during the past two centuries or so. Third, the Janajatis used folk history to both empower and separate themselves from the high-caste Hindus, who, they said, were of 'Indian' origin. This is not only mentioned by several authors on Nepal, but also supported by the kind of rituals some of the *Tagadharis* still practise, though Whelpton (2005: 3) points out that this is an 'oversimplification' as migration and assimilation of immigrants into existing populations has been going on for thousands of years. However, the folk history of the Mongols which constructs them as being the 'original' inhabitants of Nepal and the high-caste Hindus as later immigrants had a powerful appeal and was not completely denied by all high-caste Hindus who had moved into parts of Nepal during the past two centuries. Finally, the Janajatis, Dalits and Madhesis projected themselves as an oppressed and marginalized lot, and the high-caste Hindus as oppressors, although such a construction did not take care of the poor and oppressed among the high-caste Hindus. One cannot, however, deny that there exists a lot of Hinduization among the Janajati which, over the years, have become intrinsic parts of their respective cultures. Participation in the *Dasain* festival, for instance, has become a part of the culture of some Janajati groups but not of others. Conversely, some Nepalese writers have pointed out that there exists a great deal of syncretism among high-caste Hindus. In all, it is important to bear in mind that Nepal's communities were amidst an ongoing identity discourse and recent self-discovery, and it cannot be denied that such a differentiation did serve a political purpose for the moment.

JANAJATI AND MAOIST DEMANDS

Of the various demands made by the Janajatis, the most significant were the end of monarchy (though quite a few of the Janajati elders were monarchists and part of the Panchayat system cadre), establishment of a secular state, federalism, and facilities for teaching in Tibeto-Burman languages. Significantly, these demands also turned out to be the most important demands in the later phase of the Maoist movement (1996–2006). Again, if the Janajati Movement saw the palace as the symbol of high-caste Hindu power and hence sought its end, the Maoists saw it as the seat of state feudalism to justify its abolition. The Maoists had thus carefully incorporated the demands based on caste and ethnicity without ever openly talking about them and taken over the demands made by the Janajati Movement. Gellner shows how in April 2002 the Maoists had established a Magar-dominated 'special district', and later divided their heartland areas into nine autonomous regions, six of which were named on an ethnic basis (Gellner 2007: 1827).

THE MAOIST 'PEOPLE'S WAR' (1996–2006)

The spread of the Maoist 'People's War' in Nepal was so slow and stealthy that few recognized its initial rumblings as early as the mid-1990s. Therefore, there are not only interesting debates on why Nepal turned red from 1996, but also whether or not anyone had foretold that the country would actually turn red as it did from 1996. Perhaps the only social scientist who saw it coming well ahead of time was Andrew Nickson of the University of Birmingham,[7] who, in his article 'Democratisation and the growth of communism in Nepal: A Peruvian scenario in the making?' in the *Journal of Commonwealth & Comparative Politics* in 1992 had predicted that Nepal would turn red if it did not make itself more inclusive. He had also foreseen the Peruvian situation unfolding in Nepal, which shared several commonalities with Peru[8] besides the inspiration that Nepal's Maoist leaders drew from the Peruvian leadership and the *Sendoro Luminoso.*

A quick replay of the story of the Maoist 'People's War' is necessary to see if one can spot any tendency, no matter how weak, at any stage for Nepal to turn red. Deepak Thapa traces the history of the Left Movement in Nepal from the Biratnagar Jute Mills strike in 1947 that took place with the active participation of Ratan Lal Brahman, better known as *Maila Baje*, and whose legendary leadership turned most of the tea gardens of the Darjeeling hills red (Thapa 2001: 77–99). Later, on 15 September 1949, Pushpa Lal Shrestha formed the Nepal Communist Party in Calcutta (Thapa 2001). It held its first conference in 1953 when Man Mohan Adhikari was elected as its secretary general. The party held its second convention in 1957 in which Keshar Jung Raimajhi replaced Adhikari as the party's secretary general. But the party fared rather badly in the first-ever multiparty election held in 1959 due to its ambivalent stand on monarchy. In the elections held in 1963, the Nepal Communist Party, although banned like any other political party, could put up an impressive show of strength when six of its candidates won the election from Kathmandu.[9] After that, factions developed within the party over issues of their allegiance to the monarchy as well as to the Soviet or Chinese camps.

One of the most significant developments after the first coming of democracy in 1959–60 was the launching of a short-lived guerilla movement in April 1972 by the Marxist-Leninist group led by young communists like Mohan Chandra Adhikari, Chandra Prakash Mainali and Radha Krishna Mainali, and inspired by the Cultural Revolution of China and the Naxalite Movement in adjoining West Bengal under the leadership of Charu Majumdar (ibid.). This is described as the 'Jhapa Uprising' after Jhapa, which is the south-eastern-most district of Nepal adjoining the Naxalbari area of Darjeeling district of West Bengal. Although their guerilla activities were quelled quickly by the King's government, there was little scope of the uprising sustaining itself for long especially in view of the heavy clamp-down on the Naxalites in West Bengal under the chief ministership of Siddhartha Sankar Ray. Besides, the Jhapa uprising was condemned even by Pushpa Lal Shrestha's party, calling the uprising 'semi-anarchy' for their use of 'terrorist tactics' (ibid.). The young and educated leaders subsequently formed the Nepal Communist Party (Marxist-Leninist), locally known as *Maale*, which was at one point of time in Nepal's communist history one of the best organized political parties.

The first seed of the Maoist Movement was actually sown in 1974 when Mohan Bikram Singh along with Nirmal Lama formed the Nepal Communist Party (Masal). But this party also split in 1983 with the formation of the Nepal Communist Party (Mashal) under the leadership of the hardliner Mohan Baidya, alias Comrade Kiran (who was arrested in India during the 'People's War', which paved the way for Pushpa Kamal Dahal to climb up the hierarchy of its leadership). In 1989, Dahal, better known by his *nom de guerre*, Prachanda, became the joint secretary of the Nepal Communist Party (Mashal). The other well-known Maoist leader today, Baburam Bhattarai, chose to stay with Mohan Bikram Singh at that time (ibid.).

In 1990, Masal and Mashal (both of which mean 'torch') united under the banner called Unity Centre and fought the 1991 parliamentary elections together, emerging as the third-largest party of the country by winning nine seats. In the same year, they convened the United General Conference in which Masal, which believed in transformation through mass uprising, was voted out by Mashal, which chose *Prachandapath*, which prescribed transformation through guerilla warfare. In 1992, the Mashal faction was formally named the Nepal Communist Party (Maoist). But it split again in 1994. Incidentally, the group led by Bhattarai was not recognized by the Election Commission of Nepal during the mid-term election that year. He had no option but to give a call for boycott of the elections, which he did, whereas the other faction was recognized by the Election Commission and, therefore, fought the election. According to Thapa (2001) the present leadership structure of the CPN(M) took shape as late as March 1995. This explains why the

Maoists overtook the *Janajati* Movement in 1996 and soon become the largest political force in Nepal.

This then is a brief history of the communist movement in Nepal till the declaration of the 'People's War' in 1996. This brief history shows, first of all, that the Communist Movement in Nepal is not only quite recent but also that clashes of orientation, strategy, and personalities have played significant roles in splitting the communists. Even now, the communists of Nepal are divided into several splinter groups. Second, on the basis of available information regarding the geographical base, it appears that the movement was centered on Kathmandu: the only other place mentioned until the declaration of the 'People's War' in 1996 was Jhapa. Thus, it was never really a pan-Nepal phenomenon. Third, while little is known about the social and economic background of the supporters, the leadership, including that of the CPN(M), has almost always been in the hands of high-caste Hindus, who control more than 90 per cent of the resources of the country (Blaikie et al. 1980: 91–8). This implies that even if the Maoists succeeded in establishing the dictatorship of the proletariat, it is reasonable to assume that the high-caste Hindu domination would remain in place.

JAN ANDOLAN, 2006: PEACE AND DEMOCRACY IN NEPAL

The events that followed the outbreak of the Maoist insurgency in Nepal are far too many and complicated to be narrated here in detail. The most important fallout was a spiralling of violence all over Nepal for almost ten years, particularly in the rural areas, starting sporadically in 1996 and continuing vigorously until 2006 when a peace deal was finally achieved. In this long-drawn armed combat between the Maoists on the one hand and the police and security forces on the other, thousands of civilians were wounded, killed and displaced resulting in unimaginable human loss and suffering. In the meantime, on 1 June 2001 the entire royal family of King Birendra was gunned down in circumstances shrouded in mystery. Perhaps the tragedy was a premonition of the eventual end of the monarchy, just as the Kot massacre that took place on 14 September 1846 paved the way for the supremacy of the Rana dynasty and titularization of the monarchy till 1951. The ascendancy of the new king, Gyanendra, soon after the Palace massacre of 2001 marked the beginning of a new phase of despotism in the country. Matters came to a head in April 2006 with the failure of the King's attempts to reinstate the autocratic monarchy and the outbreak of a powerful second people's movement also known as the Democracy Movement or *Loktantra Andolan* in Nepal. An eminent Kathmandu intellectual called this movement 'South Asia's first countryside show of people-power in decades' and pointed out that the people protested without the benefit of charismatic leadership, each citizen responding to their inner convictions and with a refined understanding of how only conflict-free democracy could deliver social and economic progress (Dixit 2007: 567). A broad alliance was now formed under the SPA against the royal takeover encompassing about a majority of the seats in the old, dissolved Parliament. Nepalese civil society carefully moderated a dialogue between the SPA and the Maoists, which brought the decade-long 'People's War' to an end with the signing of a 12-point agreement. The 2006 *Jan Andolan* thus provided the final push to the king to retreat and to return power to Nepal's political parties. These parties now re-emerged as champions of multiparty democracy under the very able leadership of the veteran politician Girija Prasad Koirala, successfully convinced the Maoists to join an interim government that took over power from the king on 24 April and cleared the way for Constituent Assembly elections to be held first in June 2007 and then postponed to November 2007. However, in a highly charged atmosphere of political uncertainty and high expectations of radical political transformation, the peace process faced several challenges as the election dates came closer. The biggest challenge, however, that threatened to indefinitely derail the process at the eleventh hour came over the winter of 2006–7 from Nepal's southern borders, or the Tarai, where one of Nepal's persistent old fault lines once again came to the forefront.

THE *MADHESI* MOVEMENT, 2006–2007: OLD WINE IN A NEW BOTTLE?

Nepal's Tarai, or what is also called *Madhes* (*Madhyades* or middle country), stretches the length of Nepal's southern border with India. This fertile stretch of land is generally considered to be crucial to Nepal's economy and its location is vital for access to Nepal's hills from the south. It has been the traditional base for Nepal's mainstream parties, particularly the Nepalese Congress which was the main opponent of Nepal's Rana regime which fell in 1950. While in theory anyone living in the Tarai could be considered a Madhesi, it has come to have an ethnic meaning referring to plains dwellers of Indian, Hindu origin though its usage may sometimes differ (Gellner 2007: 1825). In the fast-changing political landscape of Nepal, however, there is now a great deal of debate as to who actually constitutes a Madhesi.

The Tarai plains are home to many different ethnic, linguistic and religious groups, who are often seen as the 'Other' by the hill-people because of the resemblance of their culture to that of the neighbouring states of India in the south. The Madhesis are allegedly discriminated against and remain under-represented across all spheres in Nepal, even as their resources have been used and exploited by the national political elite (Jha 2007). Many of those who had been born in the Tarai but had no documentary proof of their status were denied citizenship certificates (Whelpton 2005: 186). There are other burning issues like that of language, economic discrimination and the Tarai's changing demographic profile due to a state-sponsored migration of Pahadis, which, many claim, has increased fivefold since 1951. A leader of the Madhesi Movement recently pointed out in an interview that the primary problems faced by the Madhesis were over identity and citizenship (Wann 2007).

It is generally believed that the Madhesi discontent, which had been quietly on the rise over several years—some say that that the first rumblings began as early as 1951—came suddenly to the forefront when it became apparent to them that the April 2006 *Jan Andolan* may not lead to a rapid addressing of their longstanding grievances. Under the Constitution of 1990 the hill ethnic groups or the Janajatis could at least lay claim to the national identity subsumed within the hill-centric notion of being 'Nepalese' in Nepal. The Madhesis on the other hand were too far removed from the state—geographically, politically and emotionally—to be able to find an organized voice even after 1990. Consequently, the feeling of being neglected remained strong among the people of Tarai-origin who were differentiated by language (Awadhi, Maithili, Bhojpuri) by caste, by religion (many are Muslims, others animists, etc.), region-ethnicity (Madhesi-Tharu), and so on.

Matters came to a head with the publication of the draft interim constitution prepared by the SPA and the Maoists that led to massive protests and even outright violence in many parts of the *Madhes*. The Madhesi agitators warned that unless the prevailing election guidelines were changed, the proposed Constituent Assembly would continue to represent the interests of the traditional power elites of Nepal. The Madhesis were also worried as the interim constitution had failed to announce a federal system of government in Nepal ahead of the elections. This led to a perception among them that the proposed electoral system would most likely discriminate against them. This was followed by a sparking of agitation in the Tarai, and the Madhesi Janaadhikar Forum (MJF) was the organization which was there at the right time to channelize the Madhesi disaffection over the winter of 2006–7. Since the Madhesis within the mainstream political parties (the Nepalese Congress had a strong base in the Tarai) were unable to speak up on the matter, and the Maoists were increasingly discredited as a hill-centric party, the MJF took over the populist mantle of the savior of the people.

In the southern Tarai plains, there appeared to be fault lines all over: between the hill-people and the Madhesis, the Maoists and the MJF, and the police and the public, and many more divided and overlapping loyalties. Journalists wrote of the complete failure of the Nepalese government to control the violence in Tarai where there is no law and order but a lot of 'raw anger' (MJF op. cit. 2006) and frustration. Official records of the Madhesi Movement of the winter of 2006–7 put the total number of deaths at about 100, though the resonance of the violence was felt by a much larger population far beyond the plains. Weeks of demonstrations and protests highlighted some major demands of the Madhesis, which included proportional electoral representation, increased representation in the army, police and the bureaucracy, affirmative action for margin-alized groups, and federalism, none of which had been adequately addressed in the draft constitution.

There is little doubt that the Madhesi Movement (2006–7) was a genuine uprising of people's power and anger, and not instigated by outside forces or royalist elements, though these forces may have tried to take advantage of the situation. Initially even the established Madhesi leaders of the political parties were forced to bow down to populist pressure and, as a whole, the Madhesi populism was channeled towards MJF. But soon a group splintered off from the Maoist and then separated into two, namely, Janatantrik Madhes Mukti Morcha (Goit) and (Jwala Singh). As the government procrastinated, their demands became more strident and even unrealistic, including self-determination and the declaration of the 500 × 20 mile Tarai plains as a single province (Dixit 2007). There are reports of displacement of many Pahadis from the *Madhes* where they had been settled for years. However, the brunt of the agitation was, without doubt, felt by the local Madhesis themselves. On the positive side, there is no doubt that the movement drew attention to the Madhesi situation at the national level and that the *Madhes* would perhaps never again be neglected the way it had allegedly been in the past.

Fortunately for the peace process, Madhesi leaders who had initially been in favour of another poll postponement agreed to suspend the agitations in the Tarai following a series of talks with the Prime Minister. The much-awaited Constituent Assembly elections were finally held on 10 April 2008 and, proving most social scientists and civil society activists wrong, saw the CPN(M) placed first in the election with 220 out of 575 elected seats. While on the one hand, this may be lauded as a successful transition of an armed group into a mainstream political party engaged in democratic politics that keeps them from returning to armed revolution, on the other hand, it is undeniable that such a scale of victory was largely unexpected. In any case, true to the election promises, the altogether 335 members of the 601-member Constituent Assembly were elected from proportional elections (half of them women) and they represented Nepal's various communities through the medium of the political parties. Another important force that emerged from this election was the MJF which went on to win 53 seats in the Assembly. Thus, the Constituent Assembly now became a powerful platform on which the demands of Nepal's diverse communities could be debated and discussed because almost every such community was represented within it.

The Madhesi Movement may be said to be complementary to the 2006 *Jan Andolan* in that it brought to the fore the demands of 'inclusion' in addition to the demand for democracy and peace which was the *raison d'être* of the 2006 people's movement. While the Madhesi Movement had served to postpone Constituent Assembly elections and delayed the peace process, it was perhaps not a grave loss in a historical perspective, because the identity assertion represented by the Madhesi Movement was something that was required in Nepal's national sphere at this time, particularly as a new vision for Nepal was being progressively evolved. The Janajati and Madhesi assertions as well as continuous civil society and non-governmental organization actions shook up Nepal's state establishment and the elite communities in the last two decades to the extent that the future political leadership is expected to be more inclusive than in the past. The people's movements since 1990 sent a consistent message to Nepal's political leaders that there is an immediate need to create an equitable social and political system in Nepal. The Madhesi Movement was a manifestation, once again, of the middle-hill Nepalese *versus* plains people conflict in Nepalese politics, and needs to be handled with urgency and sensitivity by the new government in order to pre-empt similar assertions in Nepal's 'new' future.

'NEW' NEPAL'S UNCERTAIN FUTURE

As the year 2008 draws to an end, most of Asia's ongoing civil society and people's movements, from Pakistan in the east to Thailand in the west, seem to slowly settle down on their laurels and begin questioning their respective failures. In the history of any country which has had to put up a fight for an inclusive democracy, the most challenging task yet is to consolidate those gains, and convince the elites and people alike that it is indeed the most suitable form of government for them. It is important to bear in mind that some of the hard-won gains of these popular movements may be challenged and even lost during the consolidation process due to external and internal pressures. Such a challenge now awaits Asia's newest republic as it goes about doing its daunting business of governance, national reconciliation and reconstruction after ten long years of political upheaval and violence. The transition to democracy in Nepal was unexpectedly swift and equally nerve-wracking, as few could have imagined not only the landslide election victory by the CPN(M) ex-rebels, but also the end of the centuries-long institution of monarchy and simultaneously the traditional Hindu character of the state. The civil society response to political high-handedness paved the way for a massive demonstration of popular will against the King and the institution of monarchy, and facilitated the emergence of a secular, democratic, republic. But far too much, it appears, has happened in too short a time.

The future of Nepal seems uncertain and several factors are working together to create this uncertainty. It is not yet clear how inclusive a constitution the Constituent Assembly can finally come up with and to what extent the new constitution will be able to cater to the aspirations of the Janajati and Madhesi popu-lations in particular. Even if Nepal gets one of the most inclusive constitutions, it is still difficult to imagine how the state will be able to deliver without adequate human as well as economic resources like land and capital, especially as it simultaneously recovers from war, violence, spiraling poverty and tremendous human suffering.

There is serious concern that the already limited resources due to natural population growth may be under further stress if some of the political demands in both Nepal and India, like abrogation of the 1950 treaty (which allowed for free movement across the India-Nepal border) and halting recruitment of Nepalese into the Indian army and paramilitary forces, are conceded. Prachanda, the rebel-turned-Prime Minister of Nepal, himself has gone on record saying that the recruitment of Nepalese in the Indian army should be stopped and the 1950 treaty between India and Nepal should be reviewed, because this is an 'unequal' treaty and the circumstances have changed significantly during the past 60 years. Many Nepalese in India are also demanding the abrogation of the treaty because they hold the treaty responsible for the continued migration of the people of Nepal to India and dilute their aspirations for an Indian identity. It may be recalled that the Gorkha National Liberation Front that fought for a separate statehood called Gorkhaland within the union of India burned copies of the treaty because the leaders of this organization desired a separate identity for Indian Nepalese from the identity of Nepal's Nepalese. Even nativist organizations like the Khasi Students' Union in India's northeast (which has a large Nepalese population) are demanding this abrogation because the Union is of the opinion that the influx of Nepalese to the coal-mining areas or its quarries cannot be stopped as long as the 1950 Indo–Nepal treaty is in place. It looks like the abrogation of the treaty is in the interest of several stakeholders in both Nepal and India, but one of the most important consequences of this demand being fulfilled may be on Nepal which will now need to create more avenues for employment of its people within the country.

Till the country is able to build its infrastructure and industrialize its economy in order to be able to sustain its growing population despite large-scale out migration, especially during the past four decades, the oft-recommended affirmative action may lose much of its meaning and purpose. While there is an urgent need to bridge the gap between various castes and ethnic groups of Nepal with affirmative action, this will require the country to divert all its development resources towards fulfillment of this goal. If the country is not able to create jobs, it will make little difference what percentage of jobs is reserved for which caste or ethnic group. The historically marginalized communities of Nepal need special support to come at par with the high castes but this cannot be achieved without adequate resources in the hands of the state to facilitate this.

The role of the two organizations—the Nepal Federation of Indigenous Nationalities and the Madhesi People's Rights Forum—

despite internal squabbles will be important for Nepal. These two organizations will have to be watched carefully, as they represent a large number of assorted organizations and have a lot of bargaining power. The former, representing 59 'indigenous' people's organizations, is not ignored by international donor organizations either if the Janajati Empowerment Project funded by the Department for International Development in the United Kingdom is anything to take seriously, not to ignore the government's compulsion in the face of the Nepal Federation for the Development of Indigenous Nationalities Act, 2002. Even the Maoists have to think before they take any step that is detrimental to the interests of the Madhesis because the latter have successfully challenged the Maoist sway in the plains of Nepal.

Representing the voice of the 100-odd caste and ethnic groups of Nepal is one of the greatest challenges the Constituent Assembly faces, especially when classifying its population has been one of the most difficult tasks social scientists can think of. In the absence of any credible classification of its population by the state, the various communities are engaged in self-classification. While self-classification has its own merit, the state may find such classifications too cumbersome for the purpose of affirmative action and too demanding for the scant resources the country has at its disposal. Yet, no political settlement will be lasting if the most important aspirations of the Janajatis, Dalits, and Madhesis for an inclusive democracy are not taken care of. The historical discrimination against the Dalits cannot be ignored simply because they have not been able to unite effectively until now. At the same time it is important to keep in mind that there also exists abject poverty among some sections of high-caste Bahun-Chhetris of Nepal, so as not to introduce yet another new fault line in the already precarious political scenario.

One of the biggest uncertainties the country faces is: Will the 601 members of the Constituent Assembly with diverse political, educational, religious, linguistic, caste and ethnic backgrounds be able to arrive at any decision on any important national issues? Not many observers of Nepal's political situation are hopeful about it, especially in view of the fact that the necessary homework towards preparation of draft resolutions after due consultation with stakeholders has not yet begun. Without these, the Constituent Assembly discussions can be unending and inconclusive. Such a situation will indeed be unfortunate for the country but there is a fair possibility that the country is in for more frustrating times than it is prepared for. One, however, wishes that the members rise above their primordial loyalties and debate on the best interests of the country.

In fact, Nepal has a huge task ahead to put the country back on the rails and this is possible only if the leaders of various political parties are united, which is difficult to expect in view of their past records. The country has already taken the first step towards making itself a federation. It must now take up affirmative action to raise a large number of communities spread all over the country to a certain level of development. It must also develop its infrastructure. But all this cannot happen together. The country must decide what to experiment with first and what next. Prioritization is difficult, but prioritize it must, because of the simple fact that resources are limited. Nepal's articulate civil society, which had played a remarkable role in initiating the process of democratization and in moderating a political dialogue between the Maoists and the mainstream political parties in April 2006, seems to have withdrawn from the forefront for the moment. But it is important that it continues to play a watchdog role and make timely and constructive interventions to guide this infant republic to the right path whenever it falters or requires guidance.

If the political developments during the past two years in Nepal are any indication of what is likely to happen in future, the predictions are rather worrying. If the political party of the Prime Minister has not detached itself from its guerilla army as yet, or if the Prime Minister himself has not yet dissociated himself completely from the ideology of violence for political transformation, the task of reconstruction may still experience more than a few hiccups. The Maoists themselves have a tough feat to accomplish, having raised high expectations of the creation of a fair and a more just society in Nepal. They now have to build bridges with people whose lives have been deeply wounded by the ten long years of war and violence. With their limited experience of governance, the Maoists will also have to deliver on the high hopes that the Nepalese people have reposed upon them by giving them a stunning electoral victory. Another daunting task would be to reach an understanding with the Nepalese army which is largely opposed to the proposed integration of ex-Maoist fighting forces into their midst. Trying to achieve a balance between the influence of its immediate neighbors, India and China, will be another tough act to achieve for Nepal's newly anointed politicians and diplomats. But most important of all, the people of Nepal have not forgotten the loss of over 14,000 persons killed and more maimed. These are not just figures for the people of Nepal, but the loss of their own fathers, brothers, or sisters killed in the 'People's War'. It might be unfair to expect too much too early from a country that was devastated almost completely in the recent past. Yet, one must do whatever is possible to prevent yet another ethnic insurgency to rise from the ashes of history.

CONCLUSION: A CHALLENGE OR AN OPPORTUNITY?

Historians writing with the benefit of hindsight will pronounce in years to come if this was Nepal's biggest challenge, or if it was its biggest opportunity to rebuild and unite a devastated country. Nepal's recent history has highlighted some of the country's long-standing fault lines that have surfaced several times to dog its history, the latest instance being as recently as the winter of 2006–7. Identity issues have refused to go away. Parallel to these identity assertions, Nepal has also witnessed two powerful people's movements to contain the power of the King and to establish a representative parliamentary democracy. As the country now stands close to achieving a whole range of demands ranging from inclusion to a representative democracy and a secular republic, it must indeed tread cautiously. At this moment, the entire world's attention is drawn to this new Asian republic as it steers itself along uncharted waters. It is also significant that its Himalayan neighbor, Bhutan, is simultaneously experiencing the birth-pangs of democracy in the form of an unexpected 'gift' from its wise and 'enlightened' King. How these two countries deal with the challenges of democratization will perhaps determine the lure of democracy for numerous other marginalized peoples and ethnicities in the region.

Acknowledgement: Some of the material for this paper was gathered and used as part of the Kodikara Fellowship of the Regional Centre for Strategic Studies, Sri Lanka.

NOTES

1. Blaikie, p. 365.
2. The government of Nicolae Ceausescu was the only government in the Eastern Bloc to be violently overthrown in the Romanian Revolution of 1989.
3. Nickson, p. 365.
4. Ibid., pp. 370–1.
5. Ibid., pp. 104–23.
6. For a discussion see Dasgupta (2007). *The Maoist 'People's War'*. Colombo: Regional Centre for Strategic Studies.
7. Nickson, pp. 358–86.
8. Ibid., pp. 378–80.
9. Ibid., p. 359.

REFERENCES

Blaikie, Piers, John Cameron and David Seddon (1980). *Nepal in Crisis: Growth and Stagnation at the Periphery*. New Delhi: Oxford University Press.

Caplan, Lionel (1970). *Land and Social Change in East Nepal: A Study of Tribal–Hindu Relations*. London: Routledge & Kegan Paul.

Dasgupta, Anindita (2007). *The Maoist 'People's War'*. Colombo: Regional Centre for Strategic Studies.

De Sales, Anne (2000). 'The Kham Magar country: Between ethnic claims and Maoism', *European Bulletin of Himalayan Research*, 19. www.mfo.ac.uk/recherche/chercheurs/ethnicclaim accessed 18 March 2008.

Dixit, Kanak (7 March 2007). 'India and Nepal's Constituent Assembly', *The*

Hindu, online edition. http://www.hindu.com/2008/03/07/stories/2008030755531000.htm. Accessed 27 March 2008.

Gellner, David N. (2007). 'Caste, ethnicity and inequality in Nepal', *Economic and Political Weekly*, 1823–8.

Gurung, Harka (2003). 'Trident and Thunderbolt: Culture Dynamics in Nepalese Politics'. Mahesh Chandra Regmi Lecture at the international conference on 'The Agenda of Transformation: Inclusion in Nepalese Democracy', Kathmandu, Social Science Baha.

Hamilton, Francis (1971). *An Account of the Kingdom of Nepal*, rpt. New Delhi: Manjushri Publishers.

International Crisis Group (ICG) (2007). *Nepal's Troubled Terai Region.* http://www.newssafety.org/index.php?view=article&catid=122per cent3Anepal-security&id=7488per cent3Aicg-report-nepals-troubled-tarai-region&option=com_content&Itemid=100399. Accessed 25 May 2009.

Madhesi Jonaadhikar Forum (MJF) (2006) Madhes Rises http://mjfn.org/index2.php? optn=com—content&task=emailform&id=21. Accessed March to May 2008.

Millard, Collin. 'Democracy and dissent in Nepal: An overview with some perceptions from the valley of Dhorpatan'. In David Gellner (ed.), *Resistance and the State: Nepalese Experiences* (pp. 281–304). New Delhi: Social Science Press.

Nickson, R. Andrew (1992). 'Democratisation and the growth of communism in Nepal: A Peruvian scenario in the making?' *Journal of Commonwealth & Comparative Politics*, 30, 3, 358–86.

Pradhan, Rajendra (2002). 'Ethnicity, caste and a pluralist society'. In Kanak Mani Dixit and Shastri Ramachandaran (eds.), *State of Nepal* (pp. 7–9). Kathmandu: Himal Books.

Rana, Pashupati S.J.B., Prabhakar S.J.B. Rana and Gautam S.J.B. Rana (2003). *The Ranas of Nepal.* New Delhi: Timeless Books.

Subba, T.B. (1992). *Ethnicity, State and Development: A Case Study of Gorkhaland Movement in Darjeeling.* New Delhi: Vikas Publishing House.

Subba, T.B. (1999). *Politics of Culture.* Hyderabad: Orient Longman.

Thapa, Deepak (2001). 'Day of the Maoist', *Himal Southasian.* Kathmandu: Himal Media. http://www.himalmag.com/may2001/cover.html. Accessed 25 December 2007.

——— (2002). 'The Maobadi of Nepal'. In Kanak Mani Dixit and Shastri Ramachandaran (eds.), *State of Nepal* (pp.77–99). Kathmandu: Himal Books.

Wann, Emily (2007). *Violence in the Terai Region and the Madhesi Movement: Prospects for Peace in Nepal.* United States Institute of Peace. http://www.usip.org/pubs/usipeace_briefings/2007/0803_violence_nepal.html. Accessed 25 March 2008.

Whelpton, John (2005). *A History of Nepal.* Cambridge: Cambridge University Press.

7

Politics of Sri Lanka: 2007–2008

JAYADEVA UYANGODA

INTRODUCTION

Sri Lanka's political developments in 2007 and 2008 have primarily been centered on the escalation of the 'undeclared' war between the government and the Liberation Tigers of Tamil Eelam (LTTE). The resumption of war has made the negotiation option largely irrelevant to the immediate agenda of both the government and the LTTE, although both sides had used the rhetoric of a political solution amidst a commitment to unilateral military outcomes. In 2007 and 2008, the language of war and hostility, rather than the language of peace and reconciliation dominated the news headlines and public debates in Sri Lanka.

During the past few years, developments in Sri Lanka's ethnic conflict process have been characterized by a particular puzzle: Relapsing into civil war seems to have been much easier for the government and the LTTE, rather than sustaining political engagement. It almost appeared that the parties were utterly exhausted by the kind of peace that the United National Front (UNF)–LTTE political engagement had produced in 2002–3 through a ceasefire agreement, negotiations and international facilitation. Against this backdrop, events in the years 2007 and 2008 have highlighted the relative ease with which Sri Lanka further entangled itself in what one may call the 'war trap'. They also draw attention to the difficulties in exploring a political settlement to the ethnic conflict in a new context of war escalation and re-militarization. In exploring this twin process, this essay will discuss the following themes: (i) resumption of war between the Sri Lankan government and the

LTTE; (ii) human rights and humanitarian issues linked to war escalation; (iii) the international dimension in both peace and conflict processes; (iv) the question of a 'political solution'; (v) issues of governance; (vi) intra-party and inter-party conflicts; and (vi) the peace and war traps that define the new dynamics of the conflict. I conclude the essay by showing how the United People's Freedom Alliance (UPFA) government under President Mahinda Rajapakse has substantially altered the parameters of the Sri Lankan discourse on the ethnic conflict and the approaches to its resolution.

RESUMPTION OF WAR

The resumption of war occurred in mid-2006 in the aftermath of the breakdown of talks between the new Rajapakse administration and the LTTE. Before mid-2006, there were of course clashes between the LTTE and the government armed forces on a somewhat regular basis. The LTTE was blamed for initiating many of these military confrontations. In the official discourse, these clashes have been described as 'ceasefire violations' and not as acts of war. Even after mid-2006, there was no formal declaration of war by either side. What actually happened was the escalation of violence and clashes on a regular basis in the context of the failure of talks between the two sides held in early 2006. 'Intensification of an undeclared war' is a sober way to describe this development.

The escalation of undeclared war, as suggested above, did not occur suddenly. Almost like a well-rehearsed piece of theater, the failure of talks acted as the necessary prelude to the intensification of war. President Rajapakse, who was elected to office in November 2005 with the backing of Sinhalese nationalist parties, the Janatha Vimukthi Peramuna (JVP) and Jathika Hela Urumaya (JHU), attempted to revive talks with the LTTE in his first few months in office.[1] Two rounds of talks were held in Geneva in early 2006. They were facilitated by Norwegians who had earlier helped the UNF government and the LTTE to engage in talks. In any case, the Norwegians still remained the official facilitators of talks between the government and the LTTE. The Geneva Talks, held in the first quarter of 2006, did not produce any major outcome in breaking the peace deadlock. By this time the peace process initiated in 2002 with international backing and Norwegian facilitation had exhausted all its energy. Moreover, there was no political commitment on the part of either the government or the LTTE to give the negotiation process another chance to succeed because each side had a very negative assessment of the outcome of the 2002 peace initiative. In fact, they had come to the conclusion that war was the best option to further their own interests. In retrospect, one can say that reviving the 2002 peace process in the changed political circumstances of 2006 was not a realistic option. If at all, it should have been a new peace initiative. But in early 2006, no one appeared to have a clear idea about what a new peace initiative should entail.

One peculiar feature of the war resumption was that both the government and the LTTE formally remained signatories to the Ceasefire Agreement (CFA) of 2002. This CFA was signed by the LTTE and the Sri Lankan government of the UNF on 22 February 2002 as a prelude to peace negotiations. Brokered by the Norwegian peace facilitators, the functioning of the CFA was monitored by a Scandinavian monitoring team, the Sri Lanka Monitoring Mission (SLMM). One key clause in the CFA made it necessary for either party to formally withdraw from the CFA only after giving two weeks' notice of such withdrawal.[2] To avoid international blame, neither the new Sri Lankan government nor the LTTE formally abrogated the CFA despite the resumption of hostilities in mid-2006 which was fairly large in scale. This explains the 'undeclared' nature of Sri Lanka's ethnic war in 2006 and 2007.

The developments in Sri Lanka's war since mid-2006 offer rich material for analysis of intra-state civil war. The challenge in Sri Lanka from early 2002 to mid-2004 was the transition from civil war to stable peace, making the best of an existing framework of 'limited peace'. This phase of limited peace consisted of the CFA and direct negotiations between the UNF government and the LTTE. In 2005 the task changed dramatically. It was about transition from limited peace to the resumption and escalation of war. In 2006–7, the task took another form—transition from undeclared war to declared war. The 'peace' established through ceasefire in 2002 as well as subsequent negotiations had not produced a settlement agreement as such. It was a peace of a limited scope and depth. The transition towards sustainable and comprehensive peace required a movement beyond the ceasefire and towards a credible peace agreement acceptable not only to the government and the LTTE, but also to a host of other actors in the conflict, both direct and indirect. The four rounds of negotiations between the UNF government and the LTTE in 2002 had produced a vague commitment for them to explore a federal solution, but when the idea of a solution had to be worked out in concrete detail, the entire exercise of political engagement ran into a crisis in March-April 2003.[3] The LTTE withdrew from direct talks in April 2003, and attempts made by the facilitators as well as international sponsors of the peace process to revive the talks throughout that year failed completely.

In the public debates as well as intense controversies and political disputes on the peace process as it unfolded in 2002 and after, negotiated peace became less and less attractive as an option. Among the key reasons were the failure of negotiations to produce a peace treaty, lack of consensus among major political parties about the path to and content of a peace agreement, the absence of a clear economic dividend of peace as promised by the UNF government, the assertion of Sinhalese nationalist opposition to the peace process, and the gradual erosion of public confidence in the particular peace process which the UNF government and the LTTE initiated in 2002. The dismissal of the UNF government in December 2003 by President Chandrika Kumaratunga and the electoral defeat of the UNF in April 2004 further contributed to the political context that was not conducive to carry the 2002 peace initiative forward. In fact, when President Rajapakse assumed office in November 2005, the peace process had reached a point of extreme crisis. Even the complex humanitarian disaster of December 2004 had failed to provide any new incentive for re-working the process of political engagement for negotiated peace. The two rounds of talks held in Geneva in February and March 2006 between the Rajapakse government and the LTTE did not produce any significant outcome to rescue the peace process that was in deep trouble due to continuing violations of the CFA. The acrimonious ending of the second round of Geneva talks in March 2006 demonstrated that retrieving the 2002 peace initiative was not on the immediate agenda of either party. Thus, the developments in 2004 to 2006 had merely marked Sri Lanka's inevitable relapse to a full-scale civil war.

The Rajapakse administration seems to have accepted the challenge of being locked into another protracted and intense phase of war with two outcomes in mind. Either the LTTE would be militarily defeated and totally destroyed as a fighting force, or decisively weakened so that it would no longer be a threat to the Sri Lankan state in any significant way. In the thinking of the government, either of these two outcomes would create conditions for a 'political solution' without the LTTE. The thinking of the Rajapakse government seems to be that the LTTE is the primary obstacle to peace and the removal of that obstacle by military means, despite the heavy cost such a course of action would entail, is of paramount importance. Thus, the present government has chosen the option of a full-scale military offensive. As long as the CFA was in force, the government's public posture has been that its military campaign was a mere defensive response to the LTTE's aggression. Once the government withdrew from the CFA, such a defensive posture was no longer necessary. Meanwhile, the military establishment of the government has begun to express confidence that by the end of 2008 the war would end with the 'extinction of Tigers', meaning that the LTTE would be defeated on the battle front.

The sections of the government that have conceptualized and begun to execute the present phase of war appear to believe that the war against the LTTE is winnable and should be won. They also seem to believe that in the past the Sri Lankan armed forces could have won the war against the LTTE, but were prevented from doing so not by military factors, but by extra-military, or political, factors. Among them are: (i) interference in the strategy and execution of war by politicians; (ii) pressure from the internationals to move away from a military solution; and (iii) concerns for human rights and humanitarian consequences. Meanwhile, the

Rajapakse regime, quite in contrast with the previous Sri Lankan regimes, seems to have given a great deal of autonomy to the Ministry of Defence and the military establishment in the planning, strategizing and the execution of the war against the LTTE. The fact that the President's own younger brother, an ex-Colonel in the military, has been appointed as the Secretary of the Ministry of Defence, while the President himself is the Minister of Defence, has also contributed to this 'relative autonomy' gained by the military establishment in the conduct of the present war against the LTTE.

This new development stands in contrast to the experience of previous governments which maintained the traditional practice of strict political control over the military. In fact, the Rajapakse administration seems to be responding to a critique that emerged within the military as well as the Sinhalese nationalist and journalistic circles about the undesirability of political control of the military. A pervasive belief among the Sinhalese nationalist forces has been that politicians should not interfere with the war against the LTTE and that the military establishment, in effect, should be given a free hand in all aspects of the war. In this argument, politicians have allowed themselves to be subjected to pressures from domestic and international lobbies and interfered with the military's war efforts. The nationalist media has often made the point that in the past the war had been conducted to suit political agendas and political time-tables of government leaders and not in accordance with professional military advice. The present Rajapakse regime seems to be the first government in Sri Lanka to insulate the military from political pressure in the conduct of the war. The broader political consequences of this policy shift are yet to be seen.

The LTTE on the other hand appeared to be ready for a protracted war too. The LTTE's war commitment seems to emanate from a different framework of strategic calculus. This thinking may be summarized as follows: A long drawn out war would create grave humanitarian and human rights problems for the government, isolating the regime from the international community. An intense war that escalates the cost of war and spreads violence would seriously damage the economy, eroding the support base of the regime and weakening the capacity of the economy to fund the war. A war that damages the economy while producing serious human rights issues, weakening the rule of law and the democratic process would also sharpen the contradictions in the Southern polity. Eventually, such a scenario will make the war unsustainable for the government and that will open strategic opportunities for the LTTE to secure battleground victories leading to a new equilibrium. This thinking is also governed by a particular strategic calculation that the LTTE appears to have made. Unlike the government, the LTTE does not seem to aim at a military victory. The LTTE perhaps knows that a military victory over the Sri Lankan state is not possible, in view of both the superior military strength of the state and the configuration of regional and international forces in favor of the state. Therefore, the LTTE's military-strategic aim seems to focus on preventing the Sri Lankan state from obtaining a military victory, eventually leading to a military and political stalemate. In the LTTE's thinking, a strategic stalemate would also create new conditions for the international community to intervene in Sri Lanka's conflict. The LTTE seems to envisage that international intervention in such a scenario would be a prelude to acknowledging a new political reality as well.[4]

However, the LTTE seems to have suffered quite significantly from the present phase of war to the inauguration of which it has made a substantial contribution with great enthusiasm. The loss of control in parts of the Eastern province was a major setback, both militarily and politically. In the Northern stronghold too, as the developments in the battled field by mid-2008 indicate, the LTTE has been losing much of the territory under its control. Contrary to the LTTE's propaganda about its military capacity, it has had no defense against the air attacks by the Sri Lankan Air Force. Many LTTE cadres and Tamil civilians have been killed in regular air raids over Killinochchi and Mulaitivu for many months. S.P. Thamilselvam, the head of the LTTE's political wing, fell victim to air force bombing in November 2007. Thamilselvam died inside a bunker when its walls collapsed on him due to the explosion of a bomb dropped by a jet.

Thamilselvam has been replaced by Nadesan as the head of the

LTTE's political wing. Nadesan is also the head of the LTTE's police. Under conditions of the escalating war, the LTTE's political wing, or even the Peace Secretariat in Killinochchi, has very little to do with peace. In both Colombo and Killinochchi, the years 2006 and 2007 were significant in the sense that the military wings effectively displaced the 'political' wings.

EASTERN PROVINCE

The war in the Eastern Province during late 2006 demonstrated the working of the competing strategic calculations of the government and the LTTE to a great extent. The government, using the forces of the LTTE's breakaway Karuna faction, sought to dislodge the LTTE from the province through a series of conventional battles. The LTTE, facing the superior fire-power of the state, decided to withdraw from the Eastern Province. This was similar to what the LTTE did in Jaffna peninsula in December 1995. Faced with a massive conventional offensive by the state, the LTTE withdrew all its fighters, cadres and military assets to the Vanni jungles without resisting the advancing army. In 1995 the LTTE also evacuated several hundred thousand civilians to the Vanni, south of the Jaffna peninsula. In early 2007, the LTTE resisted the military onslaught in the Eastern province for a while and then retreated to the north, without sacrificing much of the men and war material, which of course were scarce resources.

Meanwhile, the de-merger of the Eastern Province from the Northern Province by the government in January 2007 was a significant event in the context of the changes in the military balance there. The de-merger was facilitated by a Supreme Court decision made in October 2006. The Northern and Eastern provinces were temporarily merged in 1987, following the Indo–Lanka Accord. Sinhalese nationalist as well Muslim political parties have opposed the merger, yet no government took steps to separate the two provinces. The Supreme Court verdict was made in response to a petition filed by the JVP. In the Supreme Court determination, it was held that the merger of two provinces effected in 1987 was unconstitutional.

The government, claiming to have 'liberated' the Eastern Province from the LTTE, has launched massive development programs in the province with international assistance. The government seems to be quite keen to project the Eastern Province as a model in which 'terrorism' has been militarily defeated and that getting rid of the LTTE by military means is the most essential prerequisite for democracy and development in the region. But skeptics contest the government's triumphalist claims in the Eastern Province. As media reports indicate, the LTTE activities continue in the province. A more serious issue is the continuing conflict between the armed factions. In the year 2007, the Karuna faction also split, leading to violent clashes between the two groups. The breakaway group is led by Sivanesathurai Chandrakanthan, better known as Pillayan, Karuna's former deputy in the Batticaloa district. While Karuna, whose real name is Vinayagamoorthi Muralitharan, fled to England, Pillayan consolidated his power as the new regional war lord in the province. The government's stand seems to be one of indifference to the reported atrocities against Tamil civilians by the cadres of the Karuna and Pillayan factions.

The holding of the Provincial Council elections in the Eastern Province in May 2008 was a significant political event that has the potential to lay the basis for managing Sri Lanka's ethnic conflict in a new direction as preferred by President Rajapakse. The government has been very keen to showcase the success of the Eastern province in both the military and political fronts. One of the key military successes of the government against the LTTE in recent years has been the successful exploitation of the LTTE's internal split. The government, on the heels of this military success in the Eastern Province, swiftly moved in the direction of politically consolidating that gain by holding Provincial Council elections for the province. The ruling party even entered into an electoral coalition with the Thamil Makkal Viduthalai Puligal (TMVP). At the provincial elections held on 10 May 2008, the government-TMVP coalition won a majority in the Council. The UPFA in alliance with the TMVP won 20 seats in the Provincial Council while the United National Party (UNP), in alliance with the Sri Lanka Muslim Congress (SLMC), won 15 seats. President Rajapakse wasted no time in appointing Pillayan, the ex-LTTE leader of the TMVP, as the Chief Minister of the Province. He took oaths before the President in Colombo on 16 May 2008.[5]

There is a secondary narrative of the developments in the Eastern Province that warrants at least a brief acknowledgement. It is about the fate of Karuna, the LTTE's former military commander of the Province who led the initial split in 2004. Karuna helped the Sri Lankan military to flush the LTTE out of the Eastern Province. During the last phase of the war in the Eastern Province serious differences developed within the TMVP. Karuna's deputy leader, Pillayan, began to assert leadership in the group and in fact managed to oust him. After a series of bloody clashes between the two factions, Karuna seemed to have sought the help of his friends in the government for his security and survival. In November 2007, the news suddenly spread that Karuna had been arrested in London on charges of entering the UK on a forged diplomatic passport. This created a huge controversy about how he got a diplomatic passport and official visa from the British High Commission in Colombo. It appeared that somebody with the Sri Lankan government had played a direct role in this episode, but both the Sri Lankan and British governments decided to ignore that aspect of the incident. Karuna was tried in London and jailed for six months. Although a number of human rights groups in the UK and United States (US) asked the British government to indict Karuna on alleged war crimes committed during his days with the LTTE and after, no such action has been taken. Having completed his jail term in London, Karuna returned to Sri Lanka in July 2008. His claim to regain the TMVP leadership has been resisted by its new leader Pillayan who is now the Chief Minister of the Eastern Province.

WAR, HUMAN RIGHTS AND HUMANITARIAN ISSUES

A major consequence of the resumption of war has been its exceedingly negative impact on Sri Lanka's human rights and humanitarian conditions. In the previous phases of the war too, military actions by both the government armed forces and the LTTE led to grave violations of human rights and serious humanitarian issues.

This generated much international concern as well. The main aspects of the recurring and cyclical humanitarian crisis were the large-scale displacement of civilians, and the destruction of communities and their livelihoods in the areas where the war is concentrated. In response to international concerns and pressure from local and international human rights groups, governments in the past took steps to minimize both human rights and humanitarian consequences of the war. After the mid-1980s, improvement of human rights conditions was also linked to aid conditionality, along with democratization and good governance. The strategy of the present government on these issues seems to be at variance with the policies of previous governments. The Rajapakse administration seems to be willing to disregard both international and local concerns on human rights and humanitarian issues on the argument that paying heed to such external concerns would 'weaken the morale of the troops' and be in the service of the LTTE. The government has also been justifying this position on the argument that winning the 'war against terrorism' should take priority and precedence over human rights and political concerns, for which there is interest only in the United Nations (UN) and the Western countries.

In reports by the International Crisis Group (ICG), Human Rights Watch, Amnesty International and the Asian Human Rights Commission, the human rights and humanitarian issues came to be highlighted in the government's offensive against the LTTE in the Eastern Province in late 2006 and early 2007. In this offensive, large numbers of Tamil and Muslim civilians, who were living in the areas controlled by the LTTE in the Batticaloa and Trincomallee districts, were displaced. There were also reports of many atrocities against civilians that included abductions and extra-judicial killings. The ICG, in its report on the human rights situation in Sri Lanka in the context of the escalating war since 2006, noted that 'more than 1,500 have been killed and more than 250,000 displaced since early 2006'. Similarly there have been 'hundreds of extra-judicial killings' while 'more than 1,000 people are still unaccounted for, presumed to be the victims of enforced disappearances' (ICG 2007).

One shocking incident was the execution in August 2007 of 17 local aid workers belonging to Action Against Hunger, a French non-government organization (NGO), in Muttur in the Trincomallee district, a former stronghold of the LTTE. This massacre occurred when the Sri Lankan army troops entered the Muttur town which was being abandoned by the LTTE. This incident created a great deal of controversy bringing to sharp focus the question of responsibility as well as impunity in times of war intensification. While the government initially denied the culpability of the armed forces in this murder, the government spokesperson suggested that the LTTE may have been involved in these killings. But the SLMM, human rights groups and the independent media pointed to the possible culpability of the government soldiers. The gravity of this incident and the international attention it received eventually compelled the government to initiate a judicial inquiry by a Presidential Commission under the supervision of an international monitoring team called the International Independent Group of Eminent Persons (IIGEP).[6]

The mandate of the Commission of Inquiry, appointed on 3 November 2006, was to investigate 15 alleged incidents of violations including the Muttur killings of 4 August 2006, the killing of six Tamil youth in Trincomallee on 2 January 2006 and the assassination of former Foreign Minister Lakshman Kadirgamar in August 2005. The Commission is headed by a retired Supreme Court judge. Among its members are five civil society activists prominent in the human rights field. However, the Commission's inquiry process has been quite slow. Procedural difficulties in setting up actual inquiries, disputes between the government and the IIGEP over inquiry methodology, and the absence of witness protection mechanisms led to initial delays. This contributed to a bitter debate between the agencies of the Sri Lankan government and the IIGEP. In an interim report issued on 18 December 2007, the IIGEP questioned the independence of the Commission Inquiry as well as the usefulness of the role of the IIGEP. The report alleged that the Commission of Inquiry process 'fell short of international norms and standards' and that it 'lacked transparency and independence, was ineffective with its witness protection measures' with 'shortcomings in the investigations' (*Daily Mirror*, 19 December 2007). In 2008, the Commission has been hearing evidence on the Trincomalee and Muttur killings. It became clear in 2008 that lack of adequate resources, the issue of witness protection and acrimonious public debates between the IIGEP and the government agencies on the functioning of the Commission have hampered the progress of the inquiries.

One crucial component of the government's strategy for the success of its war against the LTTE—the 'war against terrorism' as the government prefers to call it—is the blocking of the presence of resident UN human rights monitoring missions in Sri Lanka. The present Sri Lankan government, unlike the previous governments, has been openly hostile to international scrutiny and criticism of the country's human rights situation. Visits by senior UN officials on human rights missions made in 2007 received both hostility and attacks by the government as well as its Sinhalese nationalist allies, the JVP and JHU. In these attacks, the government and the allies put forward three arguments. In the first, international human rights monitoring is part of a strategy to interfere with the national sovereignty of Sri Lanka by Western and colonial powers. In the second, blaming the government for human rights violations only helps the LTTE in its terrorist war against the Sri Lankan state. Third, the Western concern for alleged human rights violations by the armed forces is based on wrong reporting by partial and incompetent local human rights monitoring groups whose political sympathies are with the Tamil minority and the LTTE terrorists. Despite the obvious weakness of these arguments, the Sri Lankan government has succeeded in preventing any major UN initiative to open an office in Sri Lanka to monitor the human rights situation.

INTERNATIONAL DIMENSION

The way in which the international actors responded to Sri Lanka's relapse into civil war is a theme the examination of which helps us to understand the changing contexts and dynamics of the international dimension in Sri Lanka's conflict process. One defining aspect of the 2002–3 peace process was that it had been built around 'heavy international involvement' which was expected to 'create the pre-conditions for peace negotiations' (Goodhand and Klem 2005: 88). The international involvement was in two specific areas: peace facilitation through political and diplomatic means and 'post-conflict' economic development through economic assistance. The activities in the first area included facilitation of the CFA as well as direct negotiations through Norway, ceasefire monitoring through the SLMM and mobilizing international support for negotiations as well as for a possible settlement agreement. In the second area, the US, Japan and the European Union (EU) played a leading role in mobilizing bi-lateral and multilateral economic assistance for post-conflict development and re-building. However, when the negotiation process reached a deadlock and the possibility of war resumption loomed large in 2004, the role of the international actors largely centered on the task of persuading the LTTE to return to negotiations. The Tsunami of December 2004 opened up another opportunity for the international community to advance the agenda of negotiations in Sri Lanka. International economic assistance for post-Tsunami re-building was the incentive offered to both the Sri Lankan government and the LTTE to return to talks so that a joint effort between the two parties for post-Tsunami recovery could provide a new framework for peace building. However, the failure of the government to effectively move forward in institutionalizing the Memorandum of Understanding (MoU) signed with the LTTE for a joint post-Tsunami administrative mechanism brought these efforts to an end.

Meanwhile, the election of President Rajapakse to office in November 2005 opened up another opportunity for the international actors to revive their engagement in Sri Lanka's stalled peace process. The two rounds of talks in Geneva held in the first quarter of 2006 also revived hopes of saving the fragile CFA from total breakdown. Although the two sides jointly agreed to honor the terms of the CFA in its full implementation, there was very little progress achieved. There was a major reason that constituted the backdrop for this failure of Geneva commitments. The LTTE by this time had suffered a major split, with its military commander in the

Eastern province, Karuna Amman, having left the movement along with his fighters and then joined with the government against the mainstream LTTE leadership. The LTTE viewed the 'full implementation of the CFA' as a tactical move to disarm the Karuna faction and regain control of its military machine in the Eastern province. On the other hand, the government saw no reason to fully implement the CFA, because it saw in the LTTE split a rare and unprecedented opportunity to weaken the LTTE militarily and then push the LTTE out of the Eastern Province. The continuing clashes between the mainstream LTTE and the Karuna faction, the latter openly backed by the armed forces of the Sri Lankan government, eventually led to the intensification of the 'undeclared war'.

These developments that constituted the context in which the war between the government and the LTTE escalated in 2007 demonstrated the limits of international engagement in the process of civil war management in Sri Lanka. In 2002, when the UNF government and the LTTE actively solicited the assistance of international actors to begin the ceasefire and negotiation process, both sides, from their individual perspectives, had seen the strategic advantage of internationalization of the new peace process. For the UNF government, internationalization meant achieving a political as well as an economic objective. The political objective was to establish what came to be known as an 'international safety net' for the government's risky policy of entering into a ceasefire agreement with the militarily strong and secessionist LTTE and eventually signing a settlement agreement. Its economic objective was to obtain international economic assistance to ensure that the peace initiative will bring about a rich peace dividend in the form of increased foreign investment, development aid and post-conflict reconstruction. From the LTTE's perspective, the internationalization in 2002 had two primary objectives. The first was to obtain international legitimacy for its project of national self-determination in the post-9/11 global context. The second was similar to the UNF government's notion of an international safety net. It envisaged a role for the international actors to provide guarantees that the Sri Lankan government would abide by the CFA and decisions made at the negotiation table. What was quite noteworthy in the developments that occurred in and after 2003, and became clearer in 2007, was that both the Sri Lankan government and the LTTE sought to de-internationalize the peace process and then reduce the space for international actors on the new context of undeclared war.

It was the LTTE that took the first steps towards reducing the role of the international actors in the peace process in early 2003, alleging that the 'excessive internationalization' of the peace process had led to a strategic imbalance in favor of the Sri Lankan government (Balasingham 2004). Once the LTTE suspended its participation in the negotiation process, they even resisted the massive economic incentives offered by international actors, notably Japan and the EU, to return to the negotiation table. The LTTE's strategic objective in 2003 was probably to resume political engagement with the government in a new context where the global state system had little or no role to influence the negotiation outcome.[7] Although the UNF government, which was dissolved in January 2004, stood for greater internationalization of the peace process, the new UPFA alliance that came to power at the parliamentary election of April 2004 shared the LTTE's perspective of de-internationalization but from a completely different standpoint. In the policy of the newly established United People's Freedom Alliance—a coalition of Sinhalese nationalist parties led by the Sri Lanka Freedom Party—internationalization of the peace process under the UNF government was seen as a wrong approach that jeopardized the national sovereignty of Sri Lanka, created space for undue external intervention in an essentially internal problem and allowed the LTTE to get unwarranted international legitimacy.

The steps towards de-internationalization of the conflict management process taken by the UPFA government as well as the LTTE in 2005 and 2006, eventually led to de-internationalization of the renewed conflict process as well. Sri Lanka saw the culmination as well as consequences of the de-internationalization of the renewed conflict in dramatic form in 2007. The de-internationalization of the conflict as it occurred in 2005 and after indicated that both the government and the LTTE sought to redefine, and indeed minimize, the space and ability of international actors to influence their conflict behavior. The government and the LTTE had their specific reasons to arrive at this perspective. In the thinking of the government, the new phase of war, the objective of which is to defeat the LTTE by means of an all-out military campaign, would invariably result in human rights violation of the Tamil civilians and even a serious humanitarian crisis. In the past and in such situations, the international community had come down hard on the previous governments. The present Sri Lankan government's thinking is that when the past governments came under international pressure on human rights and humanitarian issues, the armed forces could not continue to fight the war against the LTTE to its successful conclusion. Thus, as the government's thinking goes, insulating the government as well as the armed forces from international actors, notably the UN agencies, the Western governments and international NGOs, is a crucial prerequisite for the successful prosecution of what is viewed as the 'final' war against the LTTE. The LTTE's objective of relative isolation from the international community emanates from the assessment that the global state system was still backing the Sri Lankan nation state at the expense of their own secessionist project. Thus, in the LTTE's present thinking, the isolation of Sri Lanka's war from the international community is a strategic necessity until the military ground situation favors direct intervention by the powerful global actors, possibly similar to the developments in Kosovo.

The preference of the main parties to Sri Lanka's conflict for de-internationalization stands in sharp contrast to the active international engagement in two successful Asian instances of negotiated conflict management—Nepal and Aceh in Indonesia. The peace agreement in Nepal signed on 21 November 2006 was facilitated by the UN. The Indian government played a major role in persuading King Gayanendra to give up power and Maoist rebels to give up the armed struggle. Strategies for eventual de-commissioning of weapons and demobilizing the guerilla units by the Maoist rebels were worked out with the assistance of a special body set up by the UN. It was headed by Ian Martin, former Secretary General of Amnesty International. In Aceh, both the Indonesian government and the Free Aceh Movement rebels accepted the peace facilitation offered by an international team, an international NGO called Crisis Management Initiative, headed by Marti Ahtissari, former President of Finland. They signed the Helsinki Peace Agreement on 15 August 2005. The Association of South-East Asian Nations (ASEAN) and the EU helped the negotiation process and participated in the monitoring of the peace agreement. The experience of both Nepal and Indonesia shows how creative utilization of international assistance can facilitate transition from civil war.

Meanwhile, there have been some subtle shifts in the UPFA government's foreign relations under President Rajapakse since the war escalation began in 2006. These policy shifts became clearer in 2007. There were two major tendencies in this foreign policy shift. The first is the policy of looking beyond India as the government's major regional ally. The second is the shift away from the West and looking to the East—notably China and Japan—and West Asia—primarily Iran—as the main sources of support in case relations with the West became severely strained. Re-working the relations with India began to take shape in mid-2006 when the Rajapakse administration failed to obtain direct military assistance from India in its envisaged war with the LTTE. In the aftermath of the breakdown of the Geneva talks, President Rajapakse visited New Delhi seeking closer military and defense cooperation. The Sri Lankan government expected India to sign a defense pact in order to formalize the military cooperation. But, the Indian government was reluctant to enter into a closer military alliance with Sri Lanka which would lead to a military solution to Sri Lanka's ethnic conflict. The Indian government insisted on a political solution to the ethnic conflict. In the face of the Indian government's reluctance to be the key external partner in the envisaged war against the LTTE, the Sri Lankan government sought the military assistance of Pakistan and China. In view of the traditional tension that had existed between India and its two major neighbors, this move by the Sri Lankan government had the element of a small state exploiting regional geo-political realities. It appeared that while India's enhanced military assistance to Sri Lanka was to be conditional on the Sri Lankan government's commitment to a political solution to the ethnic conflict that would address what Indian leaders see as 'legitimate minority grievances', military cooperation by China or Pakistan would be devoid of any such political conditionality.

The Colombo government's willingness even to take the risk of challenging the UN human rights and humanitarian agencies and resist the pressure from some key Western governments on human rights issues can only be understood in terms of the Rajapakse regime's experiment in trying to re-configure its global relations. When the Rajapakse administration embarked on its undeclared war against the LTTE, the government leaders appeared to expect the full backing of the Western governments in its own 'war against terrorism'. However, Western backing for the war against the LTTE came with human rights conditionality. This ran counter to the government's stand on the war against the LTTE which assumed that concerns for human rights would blunt the effectiveness of the military campaign. Against this backdrop, the Sri Lankan government indicated closer economic cooperation with China and Japan and closer military cooperation with China, Pakistan and, later, Iran.

THE QUESTION OF A 'POLITICAL SOLUTION'

Amidst war escalation, the government continued its efforts towards searching for a political solution to the ethnic conflict, which some critics saw as with lukewarm enthusiasm and half-hearted commitment. The mechanism for the formulation of a political settlement was the All Party Representative Committee (APRC). Established in May 2006, the Committee was composed of representatives of most of the political parties in Parliament. Notable absences in the Committee were the UNP, the Tamil National Alliance (TNA) and the JVP. The UNP, the main opposition party in Parliament, and the JVP, a leading member of the UPFA coalition government, decided to boycott the APRC proceedings. The UNP's decision was made in the context of political disagreements with the government when President Rajapakse engineered a split in the UNP despite an MoU signed by President Rajapakse and the UNP leader in October 2006 to work together in finding solutions to urgent national issues, including the ethnic conflict. Meanwhile, the TNA was not present in the APRC process due to a government policy decision not to invite 'pro-LTTE' parties. The government considered the TNA as a front of the LTTE, although it was the biggest Tamil party in Parliament.

The APRC process met many challenges and complexities throughout the years 2006 and 2007. The trouble for the APRC began when its Committee of Experts submitted an interim report in December 2006 proposing a political solution with enhanced province-based devolution. The essence of the interim proposals was to further strengthen the existing system of power-sharing in Sri Lanka in order to address Tamil aspirations for regional autonomy. The President and the ruling party immediately dissociated themselves from the report of the Committee of Experts. Sinhalese nationalist partners of the ruling coalition, the JVP and JHU, were particularly harsh in denouncing the proposal of the Committee. Although this was a political setback to the APRC process, its proceedings continued throughout 2007 with little progress in terms of any concrete proposals.

The international community, notably the EU, the US and India, watched the APRC process in 2007 with both enthusiasm and anxiety. Their enthusiasm was rooted in the belief that the Rajapakse administration, despite the LTTE's rejection of the negotiation option, would be ready to offer a credible political framework that would satisfy the moderate Tamils.[8] The claims made by the government in 2006 suggesting that President Rajapakse favored a solution along the Indian model of power-sharing had further encouraged the international community to believe that there was actually a real willingness on the part of the government to break the political deadlock. The global and regional powers were also anticipating a valid political excuse to support the Rajapakse regime's war against the LTTE on the premise that the Sinhalese leadership would treat the Tamils fairly in a post-LTTE dispensation. However, when the Sri Lanka Freedom Party (SLFP), the political party led by President Rajapakse, presented its proposals to the APRC in May 2007, it appeared that the main party of the ruling coalition was not in favor of a settlement framework based on any enhanced power-sharing arrangement with the minorities.

There were two key features in the SLFP proposals—recognition of the smaller administrative unit of the district, as opposed to the larger unit of the province, as the unit of administrative decentralization, and greater emphasis on local government. Reforming the power structures of the central government was not on the agenda. In fact, the idea of district-based devolution, which the SLFP proposals emphasized in 2007, had earlier been associated with the Sinhalese nationalist parties that were opposed to devolution and ethnicity-based power sharing. Similarly, strengthening of local government as a solution to minority grievances had also been a Sinhalese nationalist idea, based on the assumption that the Tamil and Muslim grievances could best be addressed by means of decentralization of administration. The fact that the main party of the ruling coalition had put forward a minimalist framework of a political solution led to much unease among the international actors who backed the war against the LTTE with the hope that a credible political solution was actually being worked out by the government.

The much-awaited interim report of the APRC was presented to the President on 23 January 2008 by the Committee's Chairman, Tissa Vitharana. The Report almost reflected the SLFP proposals submitted to the APRC earlier. It merely proposed the full implementation of the existing 13th Amendment, holding of early elections to the de-merged Eastern Province, setting up of an interim council to the Northern Province and the full implementation of the official language provisions. Those who expected a report with proposals for substantial power-sharing arrangements for the ethnic minorities were disappointed with the Vitharana report. As Rohan Edrisinha noted, Vitharana proposed a framework of '13th Amendment minus', whereas it should have been '13th Amendment plus' (Edrisinha 2008). But Vitharana and the government defended these proposals on the grounds that they reflected the most realistic compromise achievable within the structure of the APRC. Vitharana has pledged to produce a final report of the APRC after another phase of consultation with the political parties represented in the Committee. Since the balance of power within the APRC favors the Sinhalese nationalist position on the ethnic conflict, the final report might not be substantially different from the interim report, unless President Rajapakse decides otherwise.

In an overall assessment of the possibilities for a negotiated political settlement to Sri Lanka's conflict, there are two equally tenable perspectives. The first is a negative assessment of actually existing possibilities for a political solution. In this perspective, Sri Lanka has lost the momentum for a negotiated political solution and it is not yet clear how a new momentum can be built. It also views the APRC process as incapable of generating new political momentum towards a constitutional settlement of the ethnic conflict, primarily because of the minimalist framework of solution it is likely to propose. The second is a pragmatic assessment of what is actually possible in view of the insurmountable barriers to enhanced devolution. In this approach, President Rajapakse's formulation, 'maximum devolution within a unitary framework', constitutes a political solution that can be acceptable to the Sinhala nationalist forces, whose endorsement is crucial for any political solution to be viable. This perspective also asserts that a workable political solution should be one that does not require the amendment of the existing constitution. Neutralizing of the LTTE's military capability is an essential precondition for this pragmatic path to limited devolution.

Meanwhile, the intense political debates on the nature of a political solution to the ethnic conflict have highlighted the sharp differences that continue to resurface in Sri Lankan society on such key issues as the nature of the conflict and the post-conflict state. Concerning the nature of the Sri Lankan conflict, the discourse of terrorism seems to have triumphed over the discourse of ethnic conflict. The Rajapakse regime, ideologically backed by the Sinhalese nationalist JVP and JHU, defines the island's conflict primarily as a terrorist problem. In the early years of the ethnic war, particularly in the early- and mid-1980s, the dominant and official understanding of the conflict, as articulated by the Sinhalese political class at the time, was that the Tamil ethnic insurgency was primarily a terrorist challenge leveled against the legal and legitimate state of Sri Lanka. This view changed after the mid-1980s primarily as a result of the Indian intervention in Sri Lanka's political debates on the ethnic conflict. The Indo–Lanka Accord of July 1987, signed by the Indian Prime Minister and the Sri Lankan President, was the first official acknowledgement in Sri Lanka that the Tamil rebellion was a political problem that required a political solution through political reforms. All subsequent governments generally shared this perspective. During the People's Alliance regime (1994–2001) headed by President Kumaratunga and the UNF administration led by Prime Minister Ranil Wickramasinghe (2002–3), the ethnic conflict discourse became the official discourse. The terrorism discourse still continued, but it was limited to small and extreme Sinhalese nationalist groups. This situation underwent a radical change in 2006–7. Under the Rajapakse administration, the terrorism discourse became official and dominant, and the ethnic conflict discourse lost political support.

Parallel to the re-emergence of the terrorism discourse has been the question of how the post-conflict state in Sri Lanka should be characterized. Until about 2006, there was a consensus built in Sri Lanka that the post-conflict state in the island should be one in which state power is shared among majority and minority communities within a framework of devolution. In 2002–3, the devolution discourse took a further step towards federalism. The Sinhalese nationalist forces in turn resisted the federalist discourse. In the context of the breakdown of negotiations between the UNF government and the LTTE in 2003 and then between the UPFA government and the LTTE in 2006, the federalist vision of the post-conflict state took a severe beating. In his presidential election campaign in late 2005, the present President Rajapakse, in alliance with the JVP and JHU, revived the unitary state vision through a new slogan, 'maximum devolution within a unitary framework'. Thus, since 2005, unitarism has been the official vision for Sri Lanka's post-conflict state. Quite interestingly, the UNP, which had been associated with the federal idea since 2002, decided to abandon its commitment to federalism on the argument that the party lost electoral support in Sinhalese society in the 2004 and 2005 elections because of its association with federalism. Although this claim may be disputed, what remains significant is that no major political party at present seems to project a federalist vision for the post-conflict state in Sri Lanka.

The events in 2007–8 seem to suggest that the trajectory of a political settlement to Sri Lanka's conflict has reached a blind alley, because the two dominant visions of a solution emanating from the Sinhalese and Tamil polities are so far apart that a common ground between them is even inconceivable. However, if President Rajapakse's vision of implementing 'maximum devolution within a unitary framework' were to work, it should enjoy the endorsement of the majority of Tamil and Muslim political parties. Many of them, except the TNA and SLMC, are members of the ruling coalition. In a situation where the LTTE is either defeated or decisively weakened, the minority parties, who now seem to have settled down to the reality of living with the Sinhalese majoritarian state while adjusting to the dominance of Sinhalese nationalism, are most likely to accept even limited devolution offered as a 'concession' and not as a 'right' to the minorities. This is a new situation which was unthinkable ten years ago. In a post-LTTE scenario, the spoils would be too huge to lose in the name of equality.

The decision arrived at by both the present Sri Lankan government and the LTTE in 2006, for different reasons though, to give the war another chance, has radically re-defined the political debate on the ethnic conflict and even politics in general in Sri Lanka. The government has quite successfully made use of the 'war against terrorism' argument to acquire for its war strategy a certain degree of distance from the internationals as well as the domestic and international peace and human rights communities. The government leaders have also succeeded in presenting the case for the war against the LTTE in a reasonably convincing manner at home. The LTTE, through its own preference for war, has contributed in no small measure to the government's political success in pursuing the war. The present Sri Lankan government seems to have presented its case in a fairly simple argument: what is the point in a democratic government talking to an entity that uses terrorism to pursue its unreasonable goal of secession? In the post-9/11 world which has simplified many of the world's problems, such simple arguments do work.

ISSUES OF GOVERNANCE

The trends in governance, inter-party and inter-group relations and institutional linkages of regular politics in Sri Lanka are also shaped by the turns and twists of the politics relating to the ethnic conflict. This constitutes what may be called the 'sub-plot' of the conflict process. In terms of governance and state power, Sri Lanka continues to represent a unique and mutually hostile existence of duality. In the provinces and districts where the Sri Lankan state is present without facing the direct challenge of the Tamil secessionist insurgency, the state presence is accompanied by the presence of formal institutions and formal practices of democratic governance. In contrast, in areas where the civil war is concentrated, the Sri Lankan state is present there primarily through its military apparatus.

Sri Lanka continues to have a coalition regime which reflects both the fragmented nature of the polity and the way in which the system of Proportional Representation (PR) works. Sri Lanka has a multi-party system, but only two parties—the SLFP and the UNP—can win majorities in Parliament. Yet, under the PR system neither of the two major parties has been able to command even a simple majority, as the PR system favors small and ethnic minority parties to win representation. This has necessitated the formation of coalition regimes centered on either the UNP or the SLFP. The main partner of the present UPFA coalition is the SLFP. Two other partners, JVP and JHU, have been exercising considerable influence on the UPFA policies. The JVP has been functioning independently without accepting any cabinet positions. The JHU, in contrast, is a member of the UPFA government. The continuing support of the JVP with 39 MPs in Parliament is crucial for the survival of the Rajapakse regime. The JVP's influence on the policy of the government is felt on two major areas: the ethnic conflict and economic policy. On the ethnic conflict, the JVP has been in the forefront of a campaign to abolish the ceasefire agreement, to sever links with the Norwegians and the SLMM, and to initiate an all-out war against the LTTE. The JVP has also been objecting to the government's initial willingness to design a power-sharing formula as the basis for a constitutional settlement to the ethnic conflict. In the area of economic policy, the JVP has been objecting to further privatization, and advocating a policy framework of economic nationalism. The JHU's influence is primarily on government policy on the ethnic conflict with some commitment to redistributive justice and social welfare. With only nine members in Parliament, the JHU has been quietly shaping the 'War for Peace' strategy as well as the Sinhalese–Buddhist orientation of the Rajapakse administration.

While the government has been preparing for war, the question of economic management of war escalation has emerged as a significant governance issue. The government has so far been able to politically manage the economic and social consequences of rising war expenditure. The defense expenditure has been rising sharply in recent years. The budgetary allocation for defense for the year 2007 was US$1.4 billion, which was a 46 per cent increase from the previous year. This was almost 24 per cent of the annual government income and 17 per cent of the annual government expenditure. This tendency of increasing defense expenditure has been a regular facet in Sri Lanka's economic life throughout the civil war. Some analysts even describe Sri Lanka as the 'most militarised country in South Asia' (Balachandran 2006).[9] Amidst this spiraling economic cost of war, interest rates, inflation and cost of living have also been rising. Continuous rise in fuel and food prices have been key to the rising cost of living throughout 2007 as well. Labor unions linked to the JVP have been agitating for wage increases. In 2007, the plantation unions got a marginal wage increase through strike action. The fact that the trade unions are largely controlled by political parties linked to the ruling UPFA alliance has enabled the government to keep the labor front relatively peaceful. One strategy the government has resorted to with some success to manage the public discontent against increasing economic hardships is to portray its military campaign against the LTTE as a goal worthy of sacrifices by the people. Relentless media campaigns by the government have been projecting its war against the LTTE as requiring the patience and support of the people until the final victory is achieved before the end of 2008. The government seems to have succeeded at least for the moment to convince the people that there will be economic and security dividends of war before long.

Increasing re-militarization of politics is a tendency that has continued apace in 2007. The relatively stable functioning of the CFA during the period of 2002–5 had set in a tendency towards mild de-militarization of politics in Sri Lanka. However, the resumption of hostilities between the government and the LTTE in 2006 and its subsequent intensification has seen the emergence of the Ministry of Defence and the military establishment as the key institutions of state power. The continuation of Emergency Regulations and the introduction in early 2007 of the Prevention of Terrorism legislation have contributed to this tendency in considerable measure. There have been a few incidents that exposed the ethnic insensitivity of the defense establishment in exercising its newly gained powers to maintain security. In two occasions in 2007, the military and police authorities in Colombo arrested large numbers of Tamil civilians. On the first occasion, the Defence Ministry was planning to deport nearly three thousand Tamil civilians arrested in Colombo to Vavuniya in the Northern Province, in one security swoop. On the second occasion, in December 2007, about two thousand Tamil civilians were arrested and detained in a major security operation in Colombo. Due to a major public outcry and judicial intervention, the defense authorities released most of these Tamil civilians. Yet, what became quite clear is that for the defense establishment, arbitrary arrest of Tamil civilians on suspicion as potential terrorists is a legitimate national security measure. In this approach, the civil rights of ethnic minorities are secondary or even subservient to national security needs.

The year 2007 also saw the continuation of the tendency towards increasing concentration of political power in the hands of the President. Under the Rajapakse administration, this process has taken a peculiar form in which the President heads a government with over one hundred ministers, deputy ministers and non-cabinet ministers. In order to ensure parliamentary majority to the ruling coalition, President Rajapakse has given ministerial appointments to a large numbers of MPs. All opposition MPs who have joined the government have also been given ministerial portfolios as an inducement to cross over and as a reward for supporting regime stability. What is still peculiar about this arrangement is that all the key ministries and departments are controlled by the President and his brothers who are also either ministers or key government officials. Many of the ministers of this large ensemble have only insignificant departmental responsibility. This has implications for governance in a number of ways. Firstly, the institution of cabinet of ministers has lost its public esteem. People associate the ministerial office with corruption and political opportunism. Secondly, presidential control of the legislature is now maintained by means of an elaborate system of patronage, with both rewards and punishment. The punishment is the removal of the security detail provided by the Defence Ministry at a time when assassination of politicians has become an almost regular feature. Thirdly, although the cabinet of ministers has been expanding in numbers, the cabinet is no longer the institution that makes major public policy decisions. Such decisions are made by a small group headed by the President, and consisting of the President's three brothers—two of whom are ministers and the other the Defence Secretary—and a few ministers, officials and advisors. This indeed is a consolidation of a process that continued under previous Presidents as well. Sri Lanka's executive presidential system of government, political expediencies of civil war and imperatives of economic liberalization have provided its broad context for policy-making by a small caucus that advises the President.

All these have a direct implication for the nature of the Sri Lankan state at present. Developments during the past two years suggest that Sri Lanka has already made the transition to a national security state. The defining feature of a national security state is the primacy given to the security of the state at the expense of the rights-based security of its citizens. The national security state also privileges emergency and exceptional laws designed to ensure the security and stability of the state over the civil and political rights of its citizens. In such a situation, civil and political rights, including freedom of expression and media freedom, are often treated as excessive luxuries that can easily be dispensed with in order to ensure the security of the state. One may even call this process 'securitization of governance'.

INTER-PARTY AND INTRA-PARTY POLITICS

Although there were no dramatic changes in inter-party and intra-party politics in Sri Lanka in 2007, there were some developments worth noting. The split in the SLFP, the main party in the ruling UPFA coalition and headed by President Rajapakse, added some excitement to the otherwise dull process of party politics. This split occurred in February 2007 when President Rajapakse removed Mangala Samaraweera from the position of Foreign Minister. Samaraweera has been a close associate of former President Kumaratunga. He was one of the key campaigners for Rajapakse when he contested the presidential election in November 2005. Rajapakse also sacked another minister, Sripathi Suriyarachchi, a close associate of Samaraweera. The two of them later formed a breakaway party called the Sri Lanka Freedom Party (Mahajana) [SLFP(M)]. The SLFP(M) has been closely aligned with the main opposition UNP in public campaigns against President Rajapakse's regime. The UNP and SLFP(M) eventually formed a new political front called National Congress.

The way in which serious differences between Rajapakse and Samaraweera had developed, leading to Samaraweera's sacking from the cabinet, is symptomatic of some of the dynamics of party politics in contemporary Sri Lanka. Sri Lanka's political parties, particularly the SLFP and the UNP, which are the two main parties, are exceedingly family-centric. For example, the SLFP from its inception of 1953 has been led by members of the Bandaranaike family—father, mother and daughter. When Rajapakse became the SLFP's presidential candidate and then the party leader, it marked a radical shift in the party leadership away from the monopoly held by the Bandaranaike family. Rajapakse received the SLFP's candidacy for presidency in 2005 after a bitter power struggle with the then President Kumaratunga, who is a Bandaranaike. After becoming the President, Rajapakse brought his own family members into the party as well as the government in order to secure his own position against possible threats from Bandaranaike loyalists. In this process of consolidation of his own personal power, Rajapakse seems to have antagonized Samaraweera, who was a Bandaranaike loyalist as well as a stalwart in the SLFP's old guard. Interestingly, Samaraweera's campaign against Rajapakse after the split focused primarily on the alleged monopolization of power within the party as well as the government by President Rajapakse and his brothers.

The intra-party rivalry of the SLFP thus led to inter-party rivalry in 2007. It reached a high point in November–December 2007 when the Rajapakse regime presented its annual budget proposal to Parliament. The opposition UNP in association with the SLFP(M) made an attempt to defeat the government at the voting of the budget. With increasing dissatisfaction among ethnic minority parties within the ruling coalition and the dissent building up within the SLFP, there was some possibility of the plan of the UNP–SLFP(M) to succeed. But, President Rajapakse managed to convince the JVP, which had voted against the Budget at the first reading, to change their tactics at the second reading. The abstention by the JVP with 39 MPs ensured the survival of the Rajapakse government for another year.

As for the SLFP(M), it has so far failed to generate any momentum towards effectively challenging President Rajapakse's government. Its alliance with the UNP does not provide any particular strength to the opposition either. The sudden death of Sripathy Suriyarachchi, Samaraweera's deputy, on 9 February 2008 in a road accident, has been a major setback to the SLFP(M). Suriyarachchi was a capable party worker and organizer, and along with Samaraweera the co-leader of the party. The relative failure of the SLFP(M) suggests something peculiar about the political party system in Sri Lanka. No breakaway group seems to be able to effectively challenge an established party, either the UNP or the SLFP(M). The option available to dissidents is to join the other rival party, as many UNP-ers have been practising over the past few years. This re-affirms the logic of the bi-centric multiparty system in Sri Lanka.

The UNP, meanwhile, has managed to continue in 2007 and 2008 as well, its record of being a weak and ineffective opposition with repeated failures to mobilize much public opposition to the government, even under conditions of the rising cost of living and increasing economic difficulties faced by the majority of the populace. Although there have been many challenges to his leadership from within the party, Ranil Wickramasinghe, the UNP leader, has survived in his position. The UNP's second-level leadership has been keen to reform the party and even remove its present leader, yet the UNP seems to go on under the same leader and without any internal reforms.

Among the significant political developments in Sri Lanka in 2008 is the surprising split of the radical-Sinhalese nationalist JVP. The media had earlier speculated about a possible rift within the JVP. But the story of an actual break-up of the party became public on 5 April 2008, the day when the JVP was commemorating the 27th anniversary of the 1971 insurgency which the JVP led. In his Hero's Day address, the JVP leader, Somawansa Amerasinghe, announced that Wimal Weerawansa, the party's Propaganda Secretary, was suspended from all positions in the party on disciplinary grounds. The next day, Weerawansa made an emotional speech in Parliament—Weerawansa was also the JVP's parliamentary group leader—accusing the party leadership of stabbing him in the back. He walked away with 10 out of 39 JVP MPs, indicating that he was ready to launch a new party. In subsequent charges and countercharges that the two factions have been exchanging, there are numerous conspiracy theories, attributed to some foreign and reactionary forces, to explain each faction's behavior.

The JVP's breakaway faction is led by the party's propaganda secretary, a brilliant public speaker and a charismatic young leader of the Sinhalese nationalists. While being a leading office holder of a party which still calls itself Leftist—the English media in Colombo continue to deliberately call the JVP 'reds' and 'Marxists' though these labels are quite dubious—Weerawansa in fact founded and led a Sinhalese-Buddhist nationalist movement called the Patriotic National Movement (PNM). Thus this split seems to reflect the mainstream JVP's unease with Weerawansa's Sinhalese–Buddhist nationalist project.

To place the recent split in some context, it is useful to recall at least briefly some aspects of the history of the JVP. The JVP is one of the most remarkable political entities to have emerged in Sri

Lanka. It has a history of nearly 40 years. An off-shoot of the Maoist Communist Party of Ceylon, led by N. Shanmugathasan, the JVP first emerged in the late 1960s as an underground radical movement. Its founder leader, Rohana Wijeweera, began his political career as a youth activist in the Maoist Communist Party in 1965. The defining feature of the JVP as a radical movement has been its serious and uncompromising commitment to capturing state power. The JVP made two attempts to fulfill that objective, first in April 1971 and then in 1987–9. Both ended not just in failure, but in the annihilation of large numbers of its leaders, members, sympathizers and even their family members. The 1971 attempt was a brief affair, spread over a few weeks. Many of the movement's leaders, including Wijeweera, survived death and prison sentences to re-launch the movement in the early 1980s.

The second JVP 'insurgency' of 1987–9 developed in a new political context. The civil war between the Sri Lankan state and the Tamil secessionist groups had erupted after the anti-Tamil riots of 1983. The Jayewardene regime proscribed the JVP in July 1983 alleging, falsely though, that the 'Left' parties were behind the anti-Tamil riots. The JVP, which had been engaged in parliamentary and electoral politics for a few years, went underground again. The Indian involvement in Sri Lanka's ethnic conflict, particularly through the Indo–Lanka Accord of July 1987, gave a new opportunity for the JVP to re-emerge. And re-emerge the JVP did with a bang. The day Rajiv Gandhi and Junius Jayewardene signed the Accord on 27 July 1987 there were organized riots in Colombo. Gandhi himself escaped possible death at the ceremonial guard of honor when a naval rating attempted to hit Gandhi's head with the butt of his rifle. Those were the unmistakable signs of the second coming of the JVP's 'revolution'.

India's political and military intervention in Sri Lanka in the mid-1980s seems to have re-defined the JVP's political agenda. To capitalize on the public anger generated by what many Sri Lankans thought at the time as the high-handed behavior of the Indian government as well as the fears generated by the huge Indian military presence in the north-east of the island, the JVP launched a 'patriotic war' against the 'Indian imperialist state' and its 'local agents'—the Jayewardene regime. That turned out to be a bloody campaign of violence, directed against the UNP regime, the armed forces and the police and even the Left parties who supported the Indo–Lanka Accord and the devolution of power to the Tamils. Nearly three years of intense violence forced the Sri Lankan government to send the IPKF back home, forge a new alliance with the LTTE and then launch, in early March–April 1989, the bloodiest counter-insurgency war Sri Lanka has experienced in such a short time span. It may have killed nearly 30,000 JVP-ers in just a period of six months. It also resulted in the rounding up and the cold-blooded killing of the entire top JVP leadership, including Wijeweera, except one Polit Bureau member. This only survivor was Somawansa Amerasinghe, the JVP's present leader. Legend has it that he hired a fishing boat off the coast of Negombo and escaped to the Kerala coast to later proceed to Italy. Eventually, he led the life of a political exile in Italy and England, until returning to Sri Lanka in 2001 to take up the powerful position of the new JVP's leadership.

What has been remarkable about the JVP is that even after the annihilation it suffered at the hands of the state in 1988–9, the movement re-emerged in the early 1990s as a parliamentary party. Amerasinghe and his colleagues, who were exiled in Europe and Japan, kept the red flag flying till a new generation of leaders emerged from among the survivors of the terror of 1988–9. Wimal Weerawansa, the leader of the new dissident group, is one among them. Most of the JVP's present top leaders are survivors of 1988–9. They also successfully steered the JVP away from the armed struggle and towards parliamentary and electoral politics.

The golden opportunity for the new JVP began in 2000 when President Kumaratunga sought its support to form a parliamentary majority. Interestingly, the JVP did not accept cabinet positions, but supported the Kumaratunga regime from outside, calling the regime a 'probationary government'. Then the JVP entered into a formal coalition with Kumaratunga's People's Alliance in 2004 to win 39 parliamentary seats and be in a position to dictate terms to the government. Amerasinghe, the exiled leader, had returned in 2000. Quite interestingly, it was the PA-JVP coalition, with its powerful appeal to Sinhalese nationalist fears and anxieties that largely succeeded in politically undermining the UNP–LTTE peace attempt of 2002–3. Out of power, and therefore in a self-critical mode, ex-President Kumaratunga now admits that she made two fatal mistakes by aligning with the JVP and then pushing the Ranil Wickramasinghe administration out of power, at the JVP's behest. That was in October–December 2003.

The JVP's break-up is probably the manifestation of a general crisis among political parties and movements in Sri Lanka. Interestingly, the JVP has remained for quite some time the only entity that did not suffer a major internal crisis in recent years. All the others—the LFP, UNP, SLMC, the Ceylon Workers' Congress, LTTE, People's Liberation Organisation of Tamil Eelam and Eelam People's Revolutionary Liberation Front—have suffered splits, leading to declining party fortunes, re-alignment of party loyalties, shifts in the party leadership and even re-configuration of politico-military balance in the country. The JVP's split seems to be of considerable political consequence, too.

The split also indicated the crisis which the JVP encountered by trying to maintain two faces—Sinhalese nationalism and class politics. The JVP has always had these two faces, but it was its radicalism and the politics of class struggle that gave it a niche in the political process. The JVP's shift to nationalism as a means to state power occurred in the 1980s in the context of the Tamil secessionist insurgency and the Indian intervention in the ethnic conflict. In its post-1989 regeneration, the new leadership has given the nationalist agenda greater emphasis. This mixture of Sinhalese nationalism and radicalism paid the JVP dividends for some time, enabling it to emerge as the third largest party in Sri Lanka's Parliament in 2004. In the 1994 Parliament, the JVP had only one MP who used to wear a red shirt over his white trousers. Subsequently, all the JVP MPs began to wear the politician's uniform in Sri Lanka: white, grey or black trousers and white or light-brown long-sleeved shirts. That is how the Parliament had domesticated yesterday's rebels as respectable, 'national' and professional politicians with a very peculiar sartorial taste.

It appears that the present split is the outcome of the collision of Sinhalese nationalist and class struggle lines within the JVP. The nationalists wanted the party to extend uncritical support to President Rajapakse's war against the LTTE and be silent on economic and other issues. But the class politics line, based on trade union constituencies, had a different agenda, that is, to confront the regime on economic and social issues. In the short-run the Rajapakse administration is the immediate beneficiary of the JVP's split. The JVP cannot now mobilize trade unions on the street to protest against the spiraling inflation, rising cost of living, impending food crisis and the transfer of the economic burden of the war onto the poor and the middle classes.

FROM 'PEACE TRAP' TO 'WAR TRAP'

One of the recurring dimensions of Sri Lanka's protracted ethnic conflict has been the periodic swing from war trap to peace trap and then to war trap. The 'war trap' and the 'peace trap' have also been the connecting thread of the cycle of Sri Lanka's ethnic conflict. Sahadevan's (2006: 239) observation that peace negotiations have constituted an 'integral part of the long-drawn life cycle' of Sri Lanka's ethnic conflict is quite apt. The 'peace trap' refers to brief periods of political engagement between the government and the LTTE that initially produces political space as well as huge expectations for the civil war ending through a negotiated peace agreement, but soon leads to a deadlock and a crisis. Parties then abandon the political engagement in favor of the resumption of hostilities, violence and war. The metaphor of a trap becomes vividly visible when the parties try to get out of the 'peace process' unilaterally and in great haste, while other political forces too begin to behave in a manner which suggests that returning to war is the most prudent and rational alternative despite the potentially high cost of that option. The 'war trap' refers to phases of intense war spread over relatively longer periods. Usually a war trap emerges following the failure of political engagement between the state and the rebels.

This phenomenon of war trap has had a few defining features built up over the years. First, after the failure of every peace process, both the government and the LTTE have returned to war with great enthusiasm and fervor as if the brief period of political engagement and relative peace had been an unmitigated disaster and that the only path to recover the losses was all-out war. Second, the period of relative peace has been seen by the government, the LTTE as well as other indirect parties to the conflict, as a period of abnormality. Therefore, returning to war is a process of normalization. Third, parties see war as the only path to ensure unilateral outcomes and benefits.

The parties to Sri Lanka's conflict have now moved out of the peace trap and are back in the war trap. It is difficult to assess the outcome of this phase of war because the government as well as the LTTE appears to consider it as something akin to a 'final war'. Therefore, both sides will mobilize all their resources to impose a unilateral military outcome. What nevertheless has become clear is that in the year 2008, Sri Lanka's crisis is likely to deepen, with very serious political, economic and humanitarian consequences. The outcome of the present phase of war will thus be crucial in defining the future trajectories of Sri Lanka's conflict, including a limited space for reviving the track of political engagement.

CONCLUSION

As this survey indicates, the developments in Sri Lanka's politics in the year 2007 provide an immediate context for further escalation of the war between the government and the LTTE. To recapture the main trends, it has been a year during which the Rajapakse administration consolidated its power. The year 2007 also saw further intensification of the undeclared war between the government and the LTTE, leading to battlefield defeats for the LTTE in the Eastern Province. The government eventually consolidated its military and administrative control of the entire province. The war in the Eastern Province led to serious human rights and humanitarian issues, but the government succeeded in politically managing the fallout of these developments by adopting a confrontationist approach to pressures from local and international human rights bodies. The successes in the battlefield also enabled the government to manage public discontent arising out of rising inflation and the spiraling cost of living.

Against such a backdrop as developed in 2007, the government of Sri Lanka formally withdrew from the CFA on 2 January 2008. Following a cabinet decision made on that day, Sri Lanka's Foreign Minister informed the Royal Norwegian government in writing that it would be withdrawing from the CFA with effect from 16 January 2008. Thus, the year 2008 began for Sri Lanka with a very clear message that the new year would bring the war to a decisive phase. The government and the military establishment are confident that before the end of the year, the war will reach a successful conclusion. The signs in 2007 were that the LTTE had also been making preparations for a decisive showdown. While it is extremely difficult for independent observers to speculate with any degree of accuracy about the outcome of this decisive phase of the war, which may arrive towards the end of 2008, what one can say with some degree of confidence is that any opening for reviving the political engagement will depend on the outcome of the impending finale of the war.

The way in which the Rajapakse administration has re-defined the debate about a political solution is exceedingly interesting. In fact, as it became quite clear in 2008, President Rajapakse has altered the basic framework within which a negotiated political solution to the ethnic conflict has hitherto been conceptualized. He has changed three components of that framework and added two new elements. The first of the three components of the political solution framework is about the basic strategic path to peace in Sri Lanka. The government does not seem to believe that a political solution without a military victory will provide sustainable and durable peace in Sri Lanka. In the government's thinking, as articulated by the President and elaborated by the government's political theorists, a military solution, or a political solution paralleled with a military victory, is more likely to work. This differs from the argument held by governments some time ago that the LTTE needed to be militarily weakened in order to persuade its leadership to opt for a political settlement. The emphasis now is on *defeating*, rather than weakening, the LTTE.

The second, emanating from the first, is about the position concerning the LTTE's role in a possible negotiated solution to the ethnic conflict. The government does not believe in, neither does it hope for, any negotiations with the LTTE. The military defeat and the elimination of the LTTE from the politico-military equation seems to be the government's thinking, although there may be some who question the viability of this goal. Those who pursue the objective of peace without the LTTE treat the LTTE as the 'absolute enemy' of the Sri Lankan state. In this thinking, the LTTE is the main obstacle to peace in Sri Lanka, and that obstacle has to be removed and it has to be removed through military conquest.

The third concerns the unit of regional autonomy. With the help of the JVP and through judicial intervention, the government has achieved a goal which no other government would have dared: the de-merger of the Northern and Eastern provinces. Tamil nationalists for long held the belief that the merger of the two provinces was a non-negotiable principle in any political settlement. Acknowledging this Tamil nationalist claim, the Indo–Lanka Accord of July 1987 proposed the merger of the two provinces. They were temporarily merged a few months later. The de-merger occurred in 2006 when the Supreme Court, in a determination of a petition filed by the JVP, held that that temporary merger was illegal.

The fourth component is derived from all the three above. It entails pragmatic political deals with the non-LTTE Tamil militant groups while the military thrust against the LTTE is proceeding. The first phase of this new strategy has been successfully implemented in the de-merged Eastern Province, with the active participation of the group called TMVP which broke away from the LTTE a few years ago. In the north, the PDP heads the non-LTTE entity with which the government has already established a strategic partnership to replace the LTTE.

The fifth is the willingness demonstrated by minority political groups, except the LTTE and TNA, to accept under the Rajapakse presidency a political solution to the ethnic conflict that ensures a secondary status to ethnic minorities. What is remarkable about this is that some of major minority political parties have voluntarily given up the quest for inter-group equality and are now ready to accept the status of second-class citizens on the argument that confrontation and war with the Sinhalese-led state has not done any good for the minorities. In this new perspective, capitulation and collaboration are viewed as more acceptable and pragmatic than resistance to the state that produces no tangible benefit. The minority parties in Sri Lanka also seem to be conscious of the fact that in the post-9/11 world, the best course of action available for ethnic minorities is the path of least resistance and unilateral compromise.

Finally, what will happen to Sri Lanka's war and conflict in the coming months, during the remaining months of 2008? A sober answer to this question requires the ability to think in terms of a variety of possibilities.

NOTES

1. The main coalition allies of the President Rajapakse UPFA alliance were the JVP and JHU. Both the JVP and JHU are Sinhalese nationalist parties. They were opposed to CFA, negotiations with the LTTE and any political settlement based on ethnicity-based power-sharing. They were also the most vocal advocates of a military approach to the ethnic conflict, suggesting that the Sri Lankan state should defeat the LTTE in the battlefield before working out a political solution. At the parliamentary elections held in April 2004, the JVP won 39 seats and the JHU 9. All JHU members initially were Buddhist monks. While the JVP refused to accept any cabinet positions, the JHU accepted political office in the Rajapakse-led UPFA administration.
2. Section 4.4 of the CFA reads as follows: 'This agreement shall remain in force until notice of termination is given by either party to the Royal Norwegian Government. Such notice shall be given fourteen days in advance of the effective date of termination.'
3. The understanding to 'explore' a federal solution was reached in December 2002 when the government and LTTE delegations met in Oslo. The official statement issued by the Norwegian government on 5 December 2002 stated as follows: 'Responding to a proposal by the leadership of the LTTE, the parties agreed to explore a solution founded on the principle of internal

self-determination in areas of historical habitation of the Tamil-speaking peoples, based on a federal structure within a united Sri Lanka.'

4. Reliable indications about the LTTE's new strategic thinking are quite rare. A somewhat clear articulation of the LTTE's strategic thinking is available in the statement attributed to E. Balakumar, which appeared on the pro-LTTE Website, Tamilnet, in early January 2008. Balakumar's thesis may be summarized as follows: 'When the LTTE presented its proposals for a political solution, the government in Colombo or the international community did not respond to them adequately. Only the balance of power established in the developments in the battlefield have enabled the LTTE to be taken seriously. In that backdrop, the outcome of the present war will demonstrate once again that a military solution as envisaged by the Sri Lankan government would not be possible and that a new framework of political engagement would be needed.' In his annual hero's day speech made on 27 November 2007, the LTTE leader also hinted at a possible new role for the international actors in Sri Lanka after the outcome of the present phase of war. The LTTE probably thinks that under conditions of new military stalemate on the ground, their proposal for an Interim Self-Governing Authority (ISGA), made in October 2003, would provide the basis for a new phase of negotiations. The LTTE might also peruse international support for its secessionist goal if the outcome of the war favors that option.
5. According to the full results of the Eastern Province election, the JVP won one seat and Tamil Democratic National Alliance won another. In the Trincomalee district, the UNP received more votes and seats than the UPFA. The latter won the majority in the Amparai and Batticaloa districts.
6. The IIGEP consists of the following 11 eminent persons: Justice P.N. Bhagwati (India) (Chairman), Judge Jean-Pierre Cot (France), Marzuki Darusman (Indonesia), Arthur E. Dewey (US), Prof. Cees Fasseur (Netherlands), Dr Kamal Hossain (Bangladesh), Prof. Bruce Matthews (Canada), Andreas Mavrommatis (Cyprus), Prof. Sir Nigel Rodley (UK), Prof. Ivan Shearer (Australia) and Prof. Yozo Yokota (Japan).
7. An examination of the LTTE's approach to a possible solution suggests two options: a separate state or a regional sub-state within Sri Lanka with extensive regional autonomy in a confederal framework. The LTTE seems to have been extremely cautious about the role of international actors in terms of their potential role in defining what the solution should be. In all occasions when the external actors even appeared to suggest the framework of a solution, notably in 1987–8 and 2002–3, the LTTE has resisted the international engagement and adopted a policy of isolationism.
8. To give a sense of what the international actors expected from the APC

process, one may quote the US Ambassador in Colombo, Robert Blake: 'Sri Lanka now has an important opportunity finally to achieve peace. . . . The SLFP is in the final stages of crafting a proposal that will then be shared with the All Party Representative Committee.' www.lankanewspapers.com/ news/2007/ 12/22560_space.html

9. Balachandran cites a study conducted by the Mumbai-based Strategic Foresight Group (SFG) in 2006. The SFG report says that Sri Lanka has 8,000 military personnel per one million population, which is the highest among the South Asian countries. In terms of military expenditure as percentage of GDP, Sri Lanka records the highest figure in South Asia which is 4.1 per cent, whereas for Pakistan it is 3.5 per cent and for India 2.5 per cent.

REFERENCES

Balachandran, P.K. (2006). 'Lanka most militarized in South Asia: Study', *Hindustan Times*, September 21.

Balasingham, Anton (2004). *War and Peace in Sri Lanka: Armed Struggle and Peace Efforts of Liberation Tigers.* Mitcham: Fairmax Publishing Ltd.

Daily Mirror (19 December 2007). *IIGEP hits out at Government again.*

Edrisinha, Rohan (2008). 'The APRC process: From hope to despair', *Groundviews.* http://www.groundviews.org/2008/02/03/the-aprc-process-from-hope-to-despair/

Goodhand, Jonathan and Bart Klem (2005). *Aid, Conflict and Peacebuilding in Sri Lanka 2000–5.* Colombo: The Asia Foundation.

International Crisis Group (2007). 'Sri Lanka's human rights crisis', Asia Report No.135.

Sahadevan, P. (2006). 'Negotiating peace in ethnic wars', *International Studies,* 43, 3, 239–66.

Uyangoda, Jayadeva (2007). 'Ethnic conflict in Sri Lanka: Changing dynamics', Policy Studies 32. Washington DC: East West Center.

PART II

8

South Asia in Global Trade: Participation and Prospects

K.V. RAMASWAMY

INTRODUCTION

SOUTH ASIA contributes to less than 1.4 per cent of world exports. If one uses this measure, then South Asia can be seen to be one of the least integrated regions of the world. Based on an alternative index, that is, the ratio of trade to gross domestic product (GDP), South Asia is one of the fastest integrators in the 1990s. The average trade to GDP ratio of India and Bangladesh doubled between 1991 (18 per cent) and 2004 (36 per cent). At present South Asia's exposure to world trade ranges between a minimum of 35 per cent (Pakistan) to a maximum of 75 per cent (Sri Lanka). This attained greater interaction and integration with the world economy *per se* does not indicate or ensure gains from trade in terms of potential income growth or welfare. It is now widely recognized that successful participation in the world economy involves continuous upgrading of production structure. Greater participation also carries the higher risks of external shocks to developing economies resulting from changes in the importing countries. The rules of international trading have also undergone many changes under the World Trade Organization (WTO) agreement with respect to tariffs, quotas, and the rules of origin. How is South Asia faring in this context of changing rules of international trade and mechanisms of participation? Are there structural weaknesses on the supply side? This chapter focuses on these issues and also touches upon issues related to market access to round up the discussion.[1]

SOUTH ASIA: ECONOMY AND TRADE LIBERALIZATION

South Asia consists of seven economies at various stages of development and diversity. It has one large economy (India), two landlocked economies (Nepal and Bhutan), two island economies (Sri Lanka and Maldives, an archipelago), and two economies separated by India in the middle (Pakistan and Bangladesh). In this chapter we focus attention on five of them, namely, Bangladesh, India, Nepal, Pakistan, and Sri Lanka. Bhutan and Maldives (the two economies with relatively smaller population size within South Asia) are excluded as they require separate analysis given their special features and not because they are less important. Maldives is ranked 26th and Bhutan 54th when countries are ranked in terms of the size of their population, smallest to largest (FAO 2005). Maldives falls within the world's 31 small island developing economies. South Asia accounts for more than 22 per cent of the world's population and 2.4 per cent of world GDP. The bulk of South Asia's population (approximately 60 per cent) is in the age group of 15–64 years (working age) and largely unskilled. This is expected to give South Asia a comparative advantage in trade in agriculture, labor-intensive manufactures, and services. This is the basis for the expectation that South Asia has gained from international trade and investment. In terms of domestic market size, India is estimated to be the fifth largest economy in the world with a GDP of 2.3 trillion in terms of purchasing power parity (PPP) dollars according to the latest revised benchmark estimates for the year 2005 (Table 8.1). At market exchange rates, India's GDP was US$1.2 trillion in 2007–8 (Government of India 2007–8). The other South Asian economies are relatively small economies and lack the advantage of a large domestic market base. International trade and exports are relatively more important for their economies.

The South Asian countries are latecomers to the trade and investment liberalization process with the exception of Sri Lanka, which embarked on trade liberalization in 1977. In the beginning of the 1990s, South Asian tariff and non-tariff rates were among the highest in the world (Pigato et al. 1997). Bangladesh had the highest simple mean tariff for manufactured products (110 per

Table 8.1: Population and Income: South Asia

Country	Population (million)	GDP 2005		Per Capita Income 2005	
	2006	Current (US$ billion)	PPP (Current US$ billion)	Current (US$)	PPP
Bangladesh	144.3	61.2	173.8	446	1,268
India	1,009.8	778.7	2,341.0	707	2,126
Nepal	27.7	8.7	27.4	343	1,081
Pakistan	159	118.4	368.9	769	2,396
Sri Lanka	19.8	24.0	68.5	1,218	3,481
South Asia	1,492.5	991	2,979.5	NA	NA

Source: World Bank (2008), International Comparison Program: Tables of Final Results.

cent) followed by India (80 per cent). Sri Lanka and Nepal had the lowest mean tariff rates (24 per cent and 28 per cent, respectively). By the end of the decade tariff rates came down to 22 per cent and 32 per cent in India and Bangladesh, respectively. The tariff rate is below 20 per cent in Nepal and Sri Lanka. Pakistan brought down the maximum tariff rate to 35 per cent in 1998–9. In Bangladesh, the unweighted coverage of the non-tariff barriers (NTBs) went down from 57 per cent of the tariff lines in 1986 to 9 per cent in 1994. It dropped from 14 to 4 per cent in Sri Lanka over the same period. Pakistan reduced the NTBs coverage from 83 per cent in 1984 to 15 per cent in 1992 (Panagariya 1999). The dismantling of NTBs began relatively late in India, with a coverage of 61 per cent in 1996. Consumer goods remained under quantitative restrictions even at the end of the period. However, 95 per cent of the tariff lines were freed from NTBs in 2001. All the South Asian countries have made their currency convertible on the current account and simplified policy restrictions on foreign direct investment (FDI). The details of policy changes and simplifications are available in other sources (Pigato et al. 1997; RIS 2002).

It is useful in this context to record the trends in GDP growth rates in these five selected South Asian economies for the period 2001–6 (Figure 8.1). What are striking are the high average GDP growth rates of all except Nepal, particularly since 2003. Pakistan,

Figure 8.1: Annual Growth Rates of GDP, 2001–6

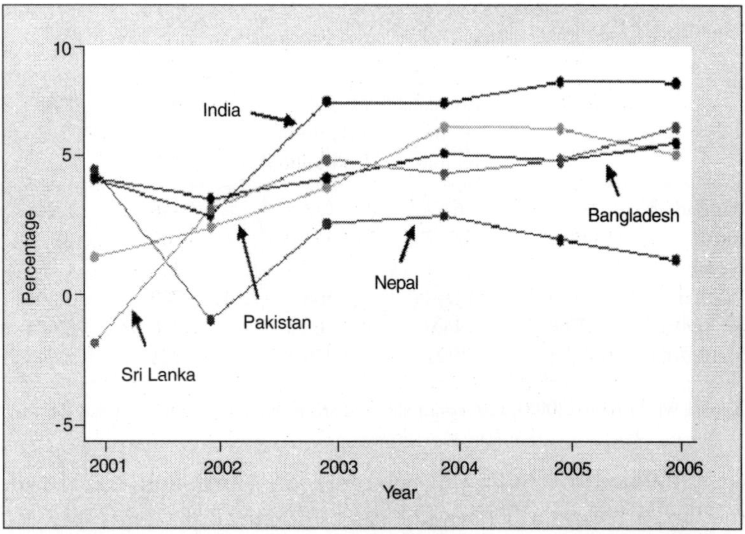

Source: World Development Indicators 2006, World Bank.

Bangladesh, and Sri Lanka have recorded an average growth of above 6 per cent since 2003 (the average is 5.1 per cent if one looks at the entire period from 2001 to 2006). This would make South Asia one of the fastest growing regions in the world, next only to East Asia. India outshines everybody else in the group with its high average growth rate of close to 9 per cent since 2003 (2001–6 average is 7.3 per cent). This leaves out Nepal as the slowest of the five with an average growth rate of just 2.8 per cent for the three years beginning 2003. It is important to keep in mind that world merchandise trade was growing at 5.5 per cent per annum during 2000–6 driven by the 6 per cent growth in world manufactures (WTO 2007). The recent International Monetary Fund (IMF) World Economic Outlook 2007 estimates of GDP growth suggest a slowdown or stagnation in the years 2007 and 2008 in these five economies except Nepal (that is expected to improve its growth rate to 4 per cent even though the reason for this is not clear) compared to the growth rate achieved in 2006 (IMF 2007). Bangladesh and Pakistan are estimated to grow at 6.5 per cent, while Sri Lanka is set to achieve 7 per cent. The global economy itself is estimated to slow down by 0.5 per centage points to 4.9 per cent in 2007 and 2008 from 5.4 per cent achieved in 2006. In brief, the external environment will not be all that rosy in the immediate future. In such years, economies like India with large domestic economies would be better off in absorbing the external shocks. The structural weaknesses in the South Asian economies excluding India need greater attention.

GAINS FROM TRADE AND GLOBALIZATION: MECHANISMS AND MARKET ACCESS

CHANGING MECHANISMS

Greater participation in international trade has been a key determinant of material well-being of many nations in the recent past. The economic growth and success of East Asian countries is a widely known example. However, the empirical evidence on gains from trade has not been unequivocal. A widely cited study is that of Frankel and Romer (1999) which finds that a 1 percentage point increase in the share of exports in GDP raises per capita income by up to 1 per cent. It needs to be recognized that improving a developing country's trade performance depends on several factors such as supply capacities, upgrading the production capacities, and conditions of market access to developed country markets.

In other words, the nature of international trade itself has been changing rapidly, bringing about changes in mechanisms of participation and market access. The latter is the outcome of WTO agreements modifying the extent of market access and setting new standards for participants, and the former due to slicing up of the production into a variety of stages, adding value at each stage. Globalization, often used to mean trade and investment without borders, is different from internationalization. Internationalization is defined as the spread of economic activity beyond national borders. Globalization has a much deeper connotation. It can be better understood using the framework of Global Value Chains (GVC) that presents a network-centered view of the world economy.[2] The GVC concept recognizes that in the global economy, economic activity is organized as a global network of different stages of production. FDI by multinational enterprises (MNE) in natural resource industries, such as oil, iron, bauxite and copper production, in post-World War II in the manufacturing sector of third world countries in the 1950s and 1960s capture the phenomenon of internationalization.

Under this process of internationalization, MNEs typically manufactured within host nations to reach host country consumers (cigarettes, autos, sewing machines, etc.). Their advantage was the ownership of intangible assets such as production knowledge and experience. The low marginal costs of transferring production methods that were already mastered gave MNEs an advantage that offset the costs of operating over distance in relatively unfamiliar areas. Internationalization merely involved transplantation of scaled-down versions of advanced (home country) productive organization to third world (host) countries. This soon made no economic sense due to the following reasons. First, world trade and investment barriers fell rapidly in the 1980s and early 1990s, under successive rounds of General Agreement on Tariffs and Trade negotiations. Developed country average tariffs on industrial products fell to 4 per cent under the Uruguay round. Second, dramatic declines in transportation and communications costs have been witnessed. For example, the sea freight unit real costs declined by 70 per cent between 1980 and 1996 and the per-minute cost of international phone calls fell by 4 per cent per year in the developing countries in the 1990s. Third, the role of knowledge (technology) and other intangible assets (trademark or brand name) became crucial and of strategic importance in world production. Geography and national boundaries are no longer over-binding constraints. A US toy manufacturer sets up a purchase contract with a firm in Hong Kong (China), which establishes a joint venture to manufacture labor-intensive toys elsewhere in China, using plastics shipped from Malaysia, and ships the final product to the United States (US). The new logic is to supply every national market by sourcing from whichever country in the world can ensure efficient supply. The system of global production networks has replaced the concept of simple cross-border production. In other words, integration of trade is associated with the disintegration or fragmentation of production. The drivers of global production networks are lead buyers in the buyer-driven value chains (in sectors such as textiles, apparel, and footwear) and lead producers in producer-driven value chains (in sectors such as automobiles and electronics).

In buyer-driven value chains, the lead buyers are often 'manufacturers without factories' as for example, Nike, Gap, and Wal-Mart. Greater benefits flow from participation in value chains if and only if the firms/nations move up the value ladder, that is, continuous upgrading of production. Industrial upgrading in low-cost locations such as South Asia is a process of restructuring by firms that enables them to produce higher value-added and sophisticated products. It may involve upgrading of the product, processes of production, and activity mix. The entry of a developing country firm into a global production network as a supplier is the first big step that signals upgrading. For a number of developing country firms this is a formidable step. The next step of moving up the value chain within the network is far more demanding (Sturgeon and Lester 2002). A change in supplier status from a simple cut, make and trim function to that of original equipment manufacturing (OEM) supplier is an example of upgrading. OEM suppliers in the apparel industry are also known as full-package suppliers. The next stage of upgrading is from OEM supplier to original design manufacturing supplier. To reach this stage the supplier will have to develop the capability to offer original design services to the buyers in addition to the manufacturing and delivery responsibilities at the agreed price and time.

A related set of papers in the area of trade and development highlights the importance of the quality of export structure and economic growth (see among others Haussmann et al. 2006; Lall et al. 2005). The classical and neo-classical trade theories emphasize differences in technology (Ricardo's theory of Comparative Cost Advantage) and factor endowments (Heckscher-Ohlin) as determinants of relative cost and patterns of specialization that characterize different countries. This framework implicitly assumes that all goods are alike in terms of their consequences for economic performance. On the contrary, it has been argued that it is not so. Economists argue that 'specializing in some products will bring higher growth than specializing in others' (Haussmann et al. 2006). The quality of export mix of a country can be measured by the level of 'sophistication of products' exported. How can the quality of export structure be measured? A standard approach takes the relative share of high-skill intensive and low-skill intensive industries in export production (Mayer and Wood 2001). However, trade fragmentation due to globalization has changed the logic of this approach. For example, a large proportion of hi-tech products in electronics (semi-conductors) are produced (assembled) in low-wage industries. If we consider the factor content, the Philippines turns out to have a more sophisticated export structure than the US or Japan (Lall et al. 2005: 4). Therefore, it is argued that we should take into account the income (implied productivity) level of the exporter to draw inferences on the level of sophistication of the product. On this basis, an export is more sophisticated the higher the average income of its exporter. Different authors have proposed variants of the sophistication or export quality index. The basic logic is similar. Two steps are involved. First, estimate the income/productivity level associated with a traded product. This can be estimated as weighted average of per capita incomes of countries exporting that product. In the second step, calculate the income level that corresponds to the export basket of a country as a weighted average of income/productivity level of each product estimated in Step 1. The weights are the share of each commodity in that country's total exports. The resulting estimate is an index of representative income associated with the country's exports. (For details, see Haussmann et al. 2006; Rodrik 2006.) Based on this reasoning, it is argued that China's export sophistication (associated income level) was much higher than its actual per capita income in 1992 (Rodrik 2006). In brief, China's export structure quality is much higher than that implied by its per capita income, and this explains its high economic performance. The implications of this strand of literature on export structure quality further strengthen the argument that countries need to move up the value chain to consolidate their gains from trade.

MARKET ACCESS ISSUES

The gains from global trade to South Asian countries are equally dependent on improved access to developed country markets. The products of export interest to developing countries, viz., agricultural products, textiles, clothing, and footwear continue to face relatively high tariffs and NTBs in developed country markets. An analysis of the evolution of the post-Uruguay round tariff structures, between 1994 and 2005, shows that the products of export interest to developing countries face the highest tariff barriers in developed country markets (UN 2006). It is important to note that between 1994 and 2005, developed countries reduced weighted average tariffs on their imports from other developed countries more in comparison with their tariffs on imports from other developing countries. The higher average tariffs are imposed on labor-intensive manufactures. The effective protection against developing country exports is higher than that revealed by average nominal tariffs. This is due to specific tariffs, tariff peaks, and tariff escalation in developed country markets. The average tariff rate of specific product lines in selected countries for the year 2002 are shown in Table 8.2.

Table 8.2: Average Import Tariffs in 2002

(*in per cent*)

Region/Country	Manufactures	Textiles	Clothing
OECD Countries	6.2	9.4	16.2
Japan	2.9	6.5	11.0
EU	4.4	7.9	11.4
USA	4.0	9.4	11.4
Developing Countries	13.5	18.1	23.0
Sri Lanka	8.0	3.4	11.0
India	34.1	39.0	40.0
Bangladesh	22.1	28.4	–
Pakistan*	16.6	NA	NA

Source: Centre for Trade and Development (Centad) (2005). *South Asian Year Book of Trade and Development.*

Note: *Applied rates for 2003 taken from USAID (2005), Tables 1–19, p. 71.

It is the 'peak tariffs' that are a major issue in multilateral trade negotiations on non-agricultural market access (NAMA). A significant proportion of South Asian exports have been denied market access in various developed countries, as is evident from Table 8.3.

Another major concern has been the issue of tariff escalation practised by developed countries, that is, the tariffs in increasing order to the different levels of processing of a product. In this strategy, the developed country imposes high tariffs on raw material, higher tariffs on semi-finished products, and the highest tariff on fully processed products. The fourth ministerial conference of the WTO held in Doha, Qatar, in November 2001, issued a mandate that has set out the issues for NAMA. Following the Doha mandate, negotiators are discussing various proposals that can reduce the high and peak tariffs on non-agricultural products in member countries. South Asian trade in agricultural products, such as rice, wheat, sugar, and cotton face a different type of problem, that is, low world prices due to the high level of producer subsidy given by the US, the European Union (EU), and Japan. The EU and the US are among the top five exporters of wheat, sugar and cotton (Naik 2005). These commodities also receive the highest level of subsidies in the US and EU. This high level of domestic support leads to over-production and lower domestic prices. The resulting surplus is sold in the world market, bringing down world prices and adversely affecting developing country exports (see Naik 2005

Table 8.3: South Asian Exports Facing Peak Tariff in Principal Trading Partners

Countries	Total no. of National Tariff Lines	No. of Tariff Lines Subject to Peak Tariff (that is 12%)	Per cent of Line with Peak Tariffs
USA	10,668	775	7.3
Japan	9,310	1,126	12.1
EEC	10,254	1,185	11.6
Australia	6,120	691	11.3
Canada	11,570	988	8.5

Source: Centre for Trade and Development (Centad) (2005). *South Asian Year Book of Trade and Development.*

for a detailed discussion and statistics). It is important to note that the US Farm Bill, 2002 provides for an increase of over 80 per cent in subsidies over a period of 10 years, leading to an estimated expenditure of US$180 billion. These are trade-distorting subsidies that adversely affect exports of wheat and other agricultural products of South Asian countries.

The Doha round of negotiations is supposed to correct some of these distortions. The gain from trade for South Asia depends on progress on these trade-distorting issues in the Doha round. With this background, we shall now turn to actual trade performance and structure in South Asian countries.

SOUTH ASIAN MERCHANDISE EXPORTS: GROWTH AND CHANGE IN COMPOSITION

In terms of absolute value, merchandise exports of the five South Asian countries were more than US$156 billion in 2006. This is a remarkable achievement considering the fact that it was less than US$30 billion in 1990. India's share in South Asian exports has risen over time from 65 per cent in 1990 to 77 per cent in 2006. South Asia, excluding India, exported goods worth more than US$36 billion in 2006.

The three countries that appear to be stagnating are Nepal, Pakistan, and Sri Lanka. Bangladesh has done relatively better (Table 8.4). The relative performance in terms of export intensity of aggregate output (export to GDP ratio) is shown in Figure 8.2. Sri Lanka, Pakistan, and Nepal have been performing poorly during the last three years of the period covered. The decline in Sri Lanka seems to have started much earlier, in the year 2000.

The share of South Asian countries in world merchandise exports increased to 1.3 per cent in 2006 from less than 1 per cent in 2000 (Table 8.5). This is largely due to India's increasing share, with the share of the remaining four countries stagnating or declining since 2000. Pakistan's share in world exports has not risen since 1990. This is in sharp contrast to the export performance of Asia whose share rose by 5 per centage points during 2000–6. The growth rate of exports decelerated in the period 2000–5

Table 8.4: South Asia: Value of Merchandise Exports

(*US$ billion*)

Year	Bangladesh	India	Nepal	Pakistan	Sri Lanka	South Asia
1990	1.7	18.0	0.2	5.6	1.9	27.4
2000	6.4	42.4	0.8	9.0	5.4	64.0
2001	6.1	43.4	0.7	9.2	4.8	64.2
2002	6.1	49.3	0.6	9.9	4.7	70.6
2003	7.0	59.0	0.7	11.9	5.1	83.7
2004	8.3	76.4	0.8	13.4	5.8	104.6
2005	9.3	99.5	0.8	16.1	6.3	132.0
2006	12.1	120.2	0.8	16.9	6.9	156.8

Source: World Development Indicators 2006, World Bank.

compared to that achieved in the 1990s, in Bangladesh, Nepal, and Sri Lanka (Table 8.6). The growth rate of exports accelerated in Pakistan and in India. The average rate of growth of exports in India (19 per cent) during the period 2000–5 is better than the growth rate for the group of Asian countries for the same period (15 per cent).

Figure 8.2: Merchandise Exports to GDP Ratios (1990–2006)

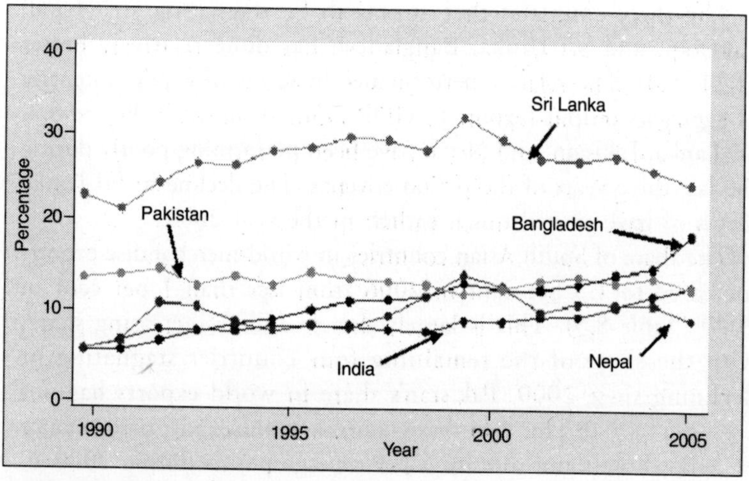

Source: World Development Indicators 2006, World Bank.

Table 8.5: Share in World Exports and Imports: South Asia

(*in per cent*)

Country	1980	1990	2000	2005	2006
			Merchandise Exports		
Bangladesh	0.037	0.048	0.099	0.089	0.102
India	0.422	0.517	0.658	0.953	1.009
Nepal	0.004	0.006	0.012	0.008	0.007
Pakistan	0.129	0.161	0.140	0.154	0.137
Sri Lanka	0.052	0.055	0.084	0.061	0.056
Above Five	*0.644*	*0.787*	*0.993*	*1.265*	*1.311*
ASIA	17.9	16.9	23.8	27.6	28.3
			Merchandise Imports		
Bangladesh	0.125	0.101	0.126	0.13	0.131
India	0.717	0.657	0.776	1.301	1.392
Nepal	0.017	0.019	0.024	0.017	0.021
Pakistan	0.258	0.205	0.164	0.237	0.233
Sri Lanka	0.098	0.075	0.095	0.082	0.085
Above Five	*1.215*	*1.057*	*1.185*	*1.767*	*1.862*
ASIA	13.1	15.9	20.8	24.2	24.7

Source: UNCTAD Handbook of Trade Statistics 2006–7.

South Asian countries had achieved the status of manufacturing exporters by the late 1980s. In 1990, South Asia was observed to have a merchandise export pattern that concentrated on labor-intensive manufactures, with few primary export and few skill-intensive manufactured exports. This pattern was well explained by the composition of South Asia's resource endowments, with low levels of skill per worker and land per worker (Mayer and Wood 2001). This structure has changed very little in recent years except in India, the country experiencing substantial structural change in its export pattern and competitiveness. This has turned out to be the key weakness of the trade structure of South Asia.

In a simple decomposition analysis framework, the sources of change in a country's exports between two periods can be attributed to four factors. These are as follows:

Table 8.6: Growth Rates of Exports and Imports: South Asia

(in per cent)

Country	1980–90	1990–2000	2000–5	2004–5	2005–6
		Merchandise Exports			
Bangladesh	7.8	15.7	8.6	14.1	32.1
India	7.3	9.5	19.2	30	21.5
Nepal	8.1	10.7	1.1	9.8	-1.5
Pakistan	8.1	4.3	12.7	20	2.6
Sri Lanka	5.4	11.3	4.1	10.2	6.1
ASIA	4.6	9.5	14.9	20.8	17.7
		Merchandise Imports			
Bangladesh	3.6	10.3	12	10.2	15.3
India	4.2	10.1	23.1	39.7	23.1
Nepal	6.9	9.3	5.2	-0.5	40.0
Pakistan	3.0	3.1	19.0	41.3	12.0
Sri Lanka	2.7	8.9	7.9	10.8	17.2
ASIA	6.5	8.2	15.1	16.8	16.7

Source: UNCTAD Handbook of Trade Statistics 2006–7.

i. *World Trade Effect*: This is the level of change in the exports attributed to growth in world exports with no change in the export share of the (reference) country;
ii. *Commodity Composition Effect*: The change in the country's composition of exports in favor of commodities for which world demand was growing relatively faster during the reference period;
iii. *Market Distribution Effect*: The country's exports would have changed in favor of fast-growing regions of the world; and
iv. *Competitiveness Effect*: The country would have improved its overall competitiveness, due to both price and non-price factors.

The last effect is actually the residual effect. A recent study of India (Veeramani 2007), using the method of constant market share analysis, showed that between 1993 and 2005, India's merchandise exports increased by US$80.5 billion, which was clearly above the potential offered by the growth of world trade (US$46.2 billion). This is shown to be due to improved world trade growth (57 per cent) and India's competitiveness effect (49 per cent) that offset the negative composition effect (-12 per cent).

South Asia, excluding India, suffers from lack of substantial change either in commodity composition or destination of markets. Recent data for the year 2006 on destination of exports shows the US and the EU to be the major destination for exports from Bangladesh (72.3 per cent), Pakistan (52.4 per cent), and Sri Lanka (63.2 per cent). These shares are more or less unchanged when compared to the year 1991 (RIS 2002). In the case of Nepal, the dominant export destination countries are India and the US (81.5 per cent). This is in contrast to India with only 39.4 per cent of its merchandise exports going to the US and the EU. More than 20.2 per cent of India's exports were absorbed by the United Arab Emirates, China, and Singapore in 2006. This sort of diversification strengthens India's position in the world economy.

Textiles and apparel exports have dominated the manufactured product mix of South Asian economies except India. India's manufactured export structure is more diversified than the other four countries in the group (Table 8.7). Agricultural exports are important for South Asian countries, with its share of more than 10 per cent. Agricultural exports are very important for India, Pakistan, and Sri Lanka with an absolute value of agricultural exports of 8.8, 1.7, and 1.3 billion US dollars, respectively, in 2005 (World Bank 2007b).

The major structural problem is the continuing over-dominance of textiles and apparel in the merchandise exports of Bangladesh, Pakistan, Nepal, and Sri Lanka (Table 8.7). A serious implication of this dominance is that total merchandise exports growth of these economies is being primarily driven by the trend of their textile and apparel sector exports (with the exception of India), as illustrated by Figures 8.4 to 8.8. This constitutes the basic structural weakness and makes them relatively more vulnerable to shocks both internal and external. This is accentuated by the fact that textile and clothing were the slowest growing sectors in world merchandise trade during 2006 (WTO 2007). India with its large diversified economy stands out with better growth prospects. Notice that in India the share of two relatively technology-intensive manufacturing industries, viz., chemicals and machinery, has increased markedly and not in other countries (Table 8.7).

Table 8.7: Structure of Exports: South Asia

(*in per cent*)

Country	Year	Food and Agricultural Products	Fuels & Ores	Manufactures	Of Total Manufactures		
					Chemicals	Machinery	Others including Textiles & Apparel
Bangladesh	1995	13.1	0.4	85.2	3.0	1.6	80.5
	2005	9.8	0.4	89.6	0.3	0.4	88.9
India	1995	20	5.3	73.2	8.1	7.5	57.5
	2005	10.4	18.7	69.8	11.6	10.9	47.3
Nepal	1995	9.6	0.1	90.2	1.3	0.2	88.8
	2005	21.7	4.3	74.0	6.8	0.4	66.8
Pakistan	1995	15.6	1.2	83.0	0.7	0.5	81.8
	2005	13.5	4.6	81.8	3.0	1.8	77.0
Sri Lanka	1995	23.1	1.1	75.7	0.9	3.6	71.2
	2005	24.3	0.7	70.2	1.3	4.5	64.4

Source: UNCTAD Handbook of Trade Statistics online at http: \\www.stats.unctad.org\Handbook\. Accessed 10 December 2007.

Figure 8.3: Share of Textiles and Garments in Total Exports (1995–2005)

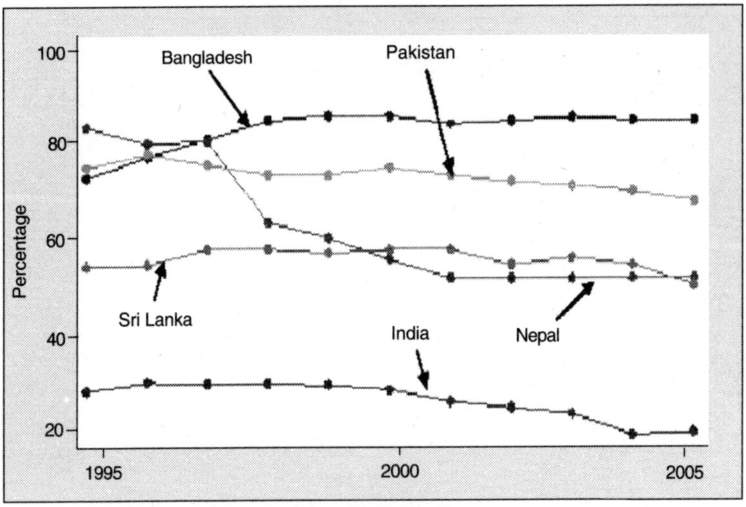

Source: UNCTAD Handbook of Trade Statistics 2006–7.

Figure 8.4: Bangladesh: Growth of Exports (1995–2005)

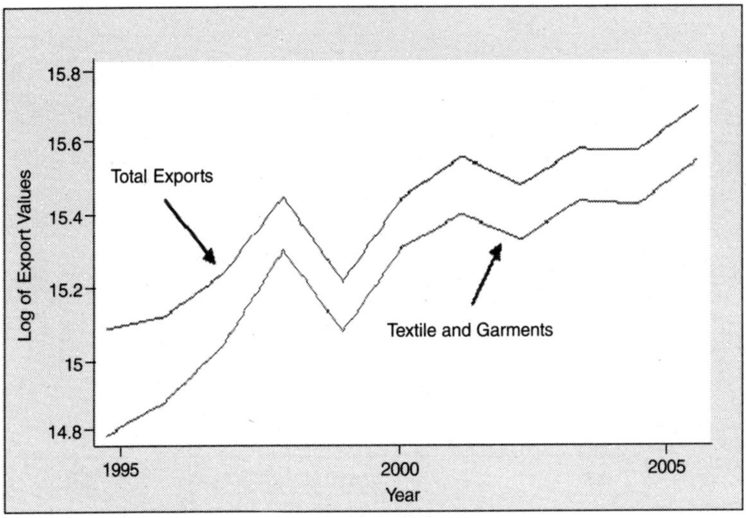

Source: UNCTAD Handbook of Trade Statistics 2006–7.

Figure 8.5: India: Growth of Exports (1995–2005)

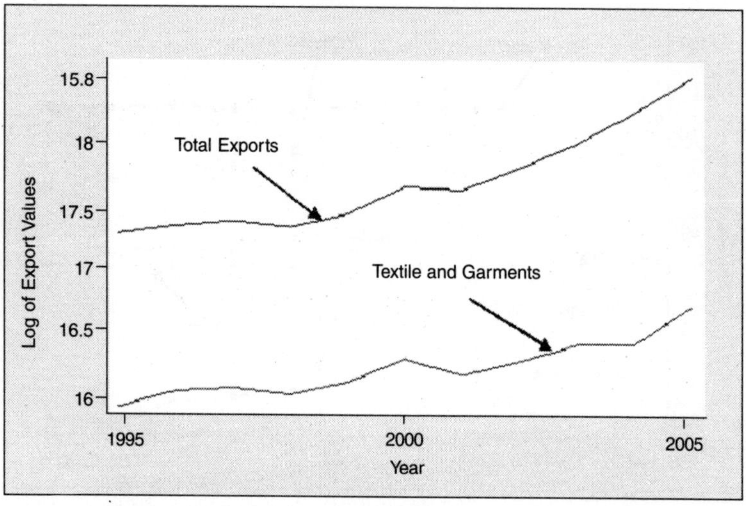

Source: UNCTAD Handbook of Trade Statistics 2006–7.

Figure 8.6: Nepal: Growth of Exports (1995–2005)

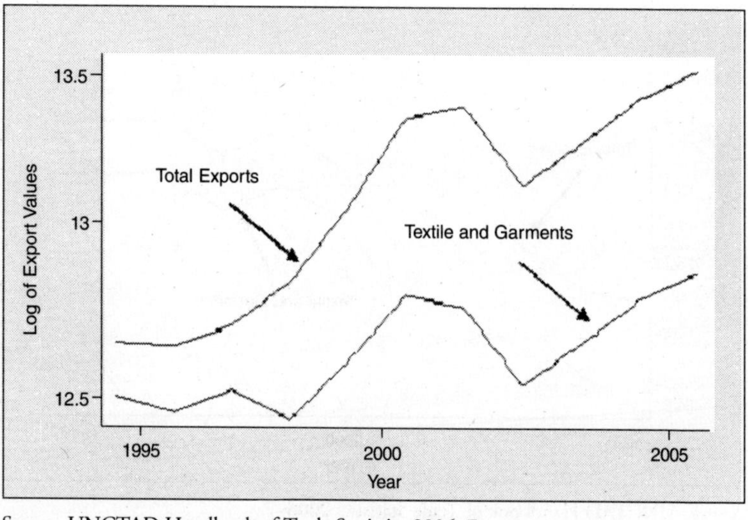

Source: UNCTAD Handbook of Trade Statistics 2006–7.

Figure 8.7: Pakistan: Growth of Exports (1995–2005)

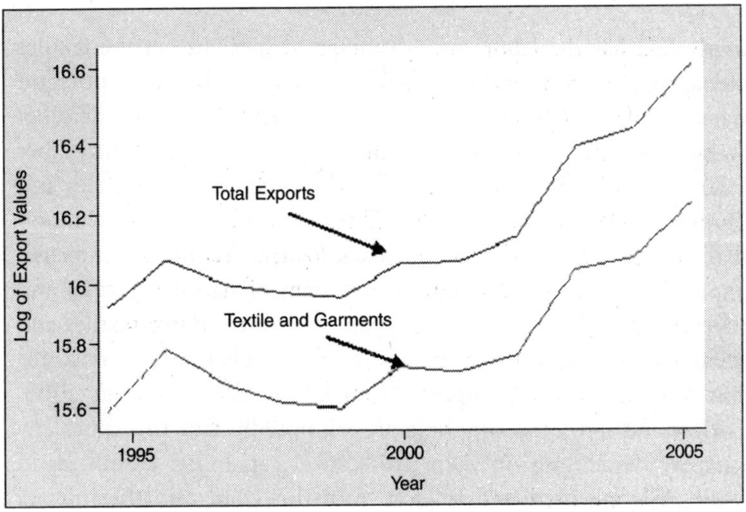

Source: UNCTAD Handbook of Trade Statistics 2006–7.

Figure 8.8: Sri Lanka: Growth of Exports (1995–2005)

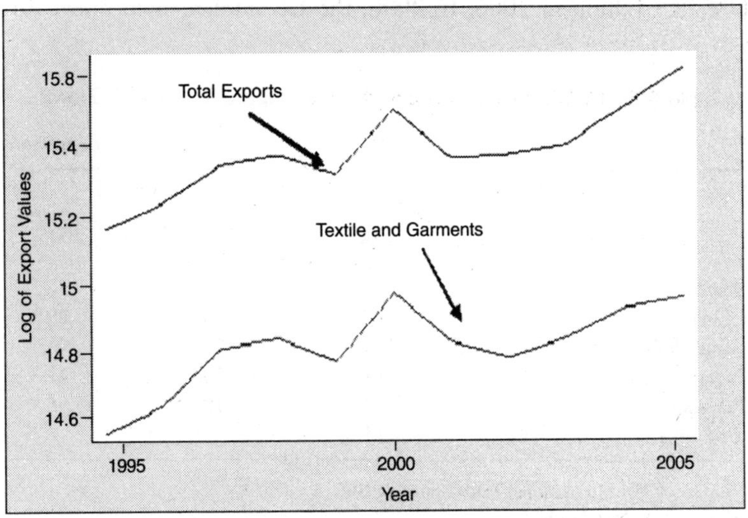

Source: UNCTAD Handbook of Trade Statistics 2006–7.

TEXTILES AND APPAREL INDUSTRY IN SOUTH ASIA: SALIENT FEATURES AND DOMESTIC CONSTRAINTS[4]

South Asia has the labor cost advantage to specialize in the textiles and apparel (T&A) industry, and its relative labor cost position matches that of China. World trade in T&A has undergone a sea change with the elimination of quotas [following the Multi-Fiber Arrangement (MFA)] under the WTO Agreement on Textiles and Clothing (ATC) from 1 January 2005. The stage-wise integration of textiles and apparels, that was back-loaded, has been completed. Imports are now subject only to a system of national tariffs, and buyers in the US, the EU, and Japan are free to source textiles and apparel in any amount from any country. There are restrictions that remain on T&A imports from China till December 2008. Correspondingly, the suppliers are supposedly free to export any quantity depending on their production capability. Countries in South Asia are predicted to gain from this change in the rules of world trade in textiles and garments. The data on T&A exports of South Asia after 2005 (post-ATC/MFA quota abolition period) would be revealing in this context. This is shown in Table 8.8 below. China increased its T&A exports by 19 per cent to reach US$48.7 billion in 2006. In 2006, the US implemented safeguard

Table 8.8: T&A Industry in South Asia: Comparative Export Growth

(*in per cent*)

	Textiles		Apparel	
	2005	2006	2005	2006
World	5	7	7	12
China	23	19	20	29
Bangladesh	17	NA	23	NA
India	21	10	39	11
Pakistan	16	5	19	8
Sri Lanka	-9	13	4	6

Source: WTO International Trade Statistics 2007.
Notes: NA: Not Available.
Data for Nepal was not available.

quotas on several categories of Chinese textiles and clothing, providing more room for other country suppliers. It is important to remember that India and Pakistan export both textiles as well as apparel. In 2006, India and Pakistan accounted for 4.3 and 3.4 per cent, respectively, of world exports of textiles. They could become full package suppliers. Bangladesh and Sri Lanka are import-dependent for their fabric requirements and are mainly exporters of apparel. India has out-performed other South Asian countries in the post-quota period (Table 8.8).

What were the facilitating factors that aided this transformation? First, India is well-endowed with an extensive fiber base in cotton and modest man-made fiber (MMF) production capacities. India is the third largest global producer of cotton yarn, the fifth largest producer of synthetic fiber, and second largest producer of silk, next only to China (Ministry of Textiles, Government of India 2006). This enables possible integrated production and greater domestic value addition. Second, the policy initiatives of the 1980s following the new textiles policy facilitated the structural transformation. Indian textile mills and looms have undertaken restructuring using the textile modernization fund initiated by the Indian government in 1999.

The available data indicates that the T&A exports of Pakistan increased by 5 and 8 per cent, respectively, in 2006 over 2005. This is in contrast to an increase of 16 and 19 per cent achieved in 2005 over 2004. Business paper reports suggest that textile exports had not recovered even by October 2007.[5] This is attributed to the concentration of low value added items in the product structure and the low-grade cotton used. Aggregate FDI inflow into Pakistan in 2006 is estimated to be US$4.3 billion but much of it is in tertiary sectors.

In the case of apparel exports from Bangladesh, total exports were estimated to be US$7.7 billion in 2005—an increase of 23 per cent over 2004 (WTO 2007). Official data is not available for the year 2006. It is reported that apparel exports have fallen sharply in recent months of 2007. In the period January to July 2007, apparel exports are reported to be growing at only 1.3 per cent compared to 16 per cent observed for the same period in

2006. This is entirely attributed to the political turmoil and labor unrest in Bangladesh since June 2006. This is supposed to have caused global buyers to shift orders to other countries like China and India with political stability. A leading expert on the garment industry in Bangladesh, Professor Mustafizur Rahman, is reported to have said, 'Business confidence in the country has been down since the interim government launched its anti-graft crackdown'.[6] FDI inflow into Bangladesh in 2006 is estimated to be marginally less at US$625 million compared to US$692 million in 2005 (UNCTAD 2007a).

Sri Lanka's apparel export was estimated to be US$3 billion in 2006, higher than the estimated value of US$2.87 billion in 2005 (WTO 2007). Sri Lanka's exports have also slowed down due to competition from India and China in the post-MFA quota regime and due to rules of origin applied in the case of Generalized System of Preferences offered by the EU. This scheme gives duty-free access to garments made in Sri Lanka. In order to qualify for this scheme local garments have to show over 50 per cent domestic value addition. This was not possible for Sri Lanka as it is highly import-dependent for its fabrics. The imports of fabric and accessories of the T&A industry were valued at around US$1.5 billion in 2005. The inflow of FDI into Sri Lanka fluctuated from 233 million in 2004 to 480 million in 2006 (UNCTAD 2007).

The emergence of new supplier countries such as Vietnam and Cambodia in addition to competition from established suppliers such as China and Hong Kong has hurt South Asian exports. Vietnam's T&A exports increased by 20.8 per cent in 2006 over 2005 to reach US$5.8 billion. Vietnam is reported to target T&A exports of US$10 billion by 2010. Vietnam has managed to attract a substantial amount of FDI from Taiwan, South Korea, and Hong Kong in the T&A sector. The total FDI into Vietnam increased to US$2.3 billion in 2006 over US$1.6 billion in 2004 (UNCTAD 2007a). The world's leading supply chain managing firm, Li & Fung from Hong Kong, is the main operator in Vietnam. Cambodia's apparel exports reached US$2.7 billion in 2006 from a value of less than a billion in 2000 (WTO 2007).

South Asia specializes in a narrow range of apparel products.

Recent data for 2004–5 shows that nearly 55 per cent of Bangladesh apparel exports originates from men's wear woven, while more than 50 per cent of India's apparel exports is contributed by women's wear; men's wear (woven and knit combined) has a share of more than 50 per cent in Pakistan, and in Sri Lanka the product group women's wear woven has a share of 30 per cent. This clearly suggests greater room for growth of South Asian exports through product diversification. A few specific points that need to be made about the T&A industry in South Asia are as follows:

- South Asia is a large producer of cotton and synthetic textiles. It is a leading producer of yarn with a strong spinning sector. Its fabrics weaving sector is the weakest. The textiles industry of South Asia is composed of two competing segments, namely, organized mill sector and the non-mill (also called unorganized sector) of handlooms and power-looms. The former consists of both large vertically integrated mills that do spinning, weaving, and finishing operations as well as small-scale factories that do only one of the above three operations. The non-mill segment sector consists of thousands of geographically dispersed fabric weaving, knitting, and dyeing units. Large variations in production capabilities exist within South Asia.
- Bangladesh and Sri Lanka are largely dependent on imported fabrics for apparel production, as they have not developed their textile industry. In the Bangladesh apparel industry, the proportion of imported fabrics is over 70 per cent and it is over 90 per cent in Sri Lanka.
- The spinning sector in Pakistan has stagnated since 1995. Only 16 per cent of the spindles were reported to be less than 10 years old as against 30 per cent in India. Modernization of spinning mills in India, using open-ended (OE) rotors, has been quite rapid in the 1990s. More than 68 per cent of the OE rotors are reported to be less than 10 years old (USITC 2001).
- The dyeing and finishing segment in South Asia is the least advanced in terms of technology and environmental standards. They are unable to meet the quality standards demanded by the apparel exporters.

- A large part of apparel-making in South Asia takes place in small-scale units having 50 to 60 machines. They are severely constrained by their inability to meet social and labor standards of large buyers in the global value chain. South Asian export industries in general suffer from the high cost of power supply for production and lack of good roads and port infrastructure; these create difficulties for exporters trying to meet tight delivery schedules of 'lean retailers and buyers'.

EXPORT OF COMMERCIAL SERVICES FROM SOUTH ASIA

It is well established that services exports are the most dynamic and fast growing component of world trade in recent years. We focus on commercial service that excludes government services. The years since 2000 have seen an acceleration in the growth rate of world export of commercial services that grew by 12 per cent relative to the growth rate (5 per cent) achieved between 1995 and 2000 (WTO 2007). South Asia's contribution to the services trade in terms of software services is much acclaimed and reported. Software services are part of the commercial services that consist of three components, namely transportation, travel, and other commercial services. The last category 'other commercial services' is further divided into (i) communication services, (ii) construction, (iii) insurance, (iv) financial, (v) computer and information services, (vi) royalties and fees, and (vii) other business services. Depending on the location of the supplier and the consumer, the General Agreement on Trade in Services (GATS) defines four modes of supply of services:

Mode 1: Cross-border supply of services (both the supplier and the consumer remain in their respective home territories)

Mode 2: Consumers are outside their home territory to consume services (consumption abroad)

Mode 3: Service suppliers are in the territory of the consumers to provide their services by establishing affiliates through direct investment abroad (commercial presence)

Mode 4: Service suppliers are in the territory of the consumers to provide their services through the presence of natural persons.

For South Asian countries Mode 1 and Mode 4 are the key categories.

Between 2000 and 2006 Asia's exports of commercial services doubled in value (Table 8.9). The value of services exports from South Asia rose by more than four times during the same period to reach US$78 billion. This growth of South Asia primarily reflects the growth of India's services exports that increased by more than 4.6 times the value in 2000. Software and IT-enabled services dominate India's services exports, valued at US$31.3 billion in 2006–7 (Reserve Bank of India 2007). The shares of South Asian countries in world exports of services are shown in Table 8.10. India has more than doubled its share in world commercial services exports between 2000 (1.1 per cent) and 2006 (2.7 per cent). Due to this strength India has succeeded in raising its penetration of world markets more rapidly in the case of services than for goods (Chanda 2005). If we exclude India, the share of the remaining four countries in South Asia has actually declined from 0.19 per cent in 2000 to 0.17 per cent in 2006. If we look at the performance of Bangladesh, Nepal, Pakistan, and Sri Lanka, we observe either decline (Nepal and Pakistan) or stagnation (Bangladesh and Sri Lanka) (see Table 8.10). A silver lining in this context for these

Table 8.9: Exports of Commercial Services: South Asia

(US$ billion)

	1996	2000	2005	2006
World	1270.60	1493.60	2458.80	2755.90
Asia	279.70	308.90	533.40	622.90
Bangladesh	0.22	0.28	0.47	0.49
India	7.18	16.03	54.38	73.84
Nepal	0.68	0.41	0.27	0.25
Pakistan	1.55	1.28	2.04	2.25
Sri Lanka	0.74	0.92	1.52	1.60
South Asia*	10.37	18.92	58.69	78.44
South Asia excluding India	3.19	2.89	4.31	4.60

Source: WTO International Trade Statistics 2007.
Note: *Sum of the above five countries.

Table 8.10: Share in Exports of Commercial Services: South Asia

	1996	2000	2005	2006
World	100	100	100	100
Asia	22	21	22	23
Bangladesh	0.02	0.02	0.02	0.02
India	0.57	1.07	2.21	2.68
Nepal	0.05	0.03	0.01	0.01
Pakistan	0.12	0.09	0.08	0.08
Sri Lanka	0.06	0.06	0.06	0.06
South Asia*	0.82	1.27	2.39	2.85
South Asia excluding India	0.25	0.19	0.18	0.17

Source: WTO International Trade Statistics 2007.
Note: *Sum of the above five countries.

four economies is their services export through movement of natural persons (Mode 4). One indicator of the significance of Mode 4 services is the dollar value of remittances into Bangladesh, India, Nepal, Pakistan, and Sri Lanka in recent years. This amounted to US$5.5, 25.7, 1.2, 5.4 and 2.1 billion, respectively, for these countries in 2006 (World Bank, 2007). While this inflow of remittances is good for South Asia in terms of improved balance of payments situation, they cannot be expected to ensure growth unless matched by domestic investment in physical/human capital and structural change. In information technology (IT) and IT-enabled services, new supplier countries such as the Philippines have entered the world market based on their large English-speaking population.

CONCLUDING REMARKS

South Asia has been one the leading trade-integrating and trade-liberalizing regions of the world in the 1990s. Its share in world merchandise exports did not undergo much improvement, with a gain of 0.32 per cent during 2000 and 2006. The absolute value of South Asian exports has increased five-fold during this period. In world commercial services exports, South Asia improved its share from 1.3 per cent in 2000 to 2.5 per cent in 2006. This gives us a misleading picture of South Asian trade performance. It essentially shows the improving trade performance of the largest country in the region, viz., India. Both in merchandise trade as well as in commercial services the South Asian performance, excluding India, is rather poor. This is a matter of serious concern because during this period (2000–6) world trade in manufactures and commercial services was expanding and the ATC restrictions on China's T&A exports were in place. In merchandise exports, the share of South Asia excluding India remained stagnant at 0.3 per cent and in commercial services the share declined from 0.19 to 0.17 per cent between 2000 and 2006. What constrained other economies (other than India) in South Asian exports? We highlighted the structural constraints in terms of commodity composition of exports that relies overly on T&A exports. In commercial services, the fastest growing segment is information technology (IT) and IT-enabled services and other business services. Other than India, South Asian countries have little presence in this segment and are confined to traditional segments like tourism.

Given South Asia's current level of participation in global trade in goods and services, the natural question to ask is: What are the prospects for South Asia in global trade in the near term? The short answer is the prospects are bright for India but not for others in the group. South Asia excluding India is likely to remain a marginal player in global trade for the following reasons:

(i) The prospects for rapid growth of food and agricultural exports (more than 10 per cent of merchandise exports) are moderate given the slow progress of the Doha round of negotiations that aims to reduce trade-distorting subsidies given by Western countries.

(ii) Restrictions on T&A exports from China will be removed in December 2008. Greater competition in world T&A markets after the quota removal and the emergence of new supplier countries will continue their adverse impact. The good news is that in China labor costs are reportedly rising (*The Economist*, 15–21 March 2008). This should work in favor of South Asia.

(iii) The bad news is that industrial upgrading in T&A industry within these countries has not taken off. They are yet to develop full-package supplier capabilities.

(iv) World trade and economic environment, in general, and for the T&A sector, in particular, are unlikely to show great improvement.

(v) The supply of skilled workers and educational upgrading of the population in these economies lag behind that in India and in other Asian countries. This will constrain trade in commercial services.

(vi) The world's leading buyers are likely to look to other alternative supplier countries due to the lack of full-package suppliers and the limited range of T&A goods.

The main constraint on growth, investment, and exports in these four countries (Bangladesh, Nepal, Pakistan, and Sri Lanka) is their present state of political instability, social conflict, and institutional environment. The case of South Asia perhaps strongly suggests that it is the institutional change-facilitating upgrading of domestic industrial structure and supplier capabilities that leads to greater global trade participation and not mere trade liberalization. Industrial firms in South Asian countries need to accelerate their investment efforts for technology and product upgrading. This calls for concentrated government policy support.

NOTES

1. Issues related to intra-regional trade and regional trade are not discussed. See Institute for South Asian Studies (2007) for a detailed discussion.
2. For a discussion of the concept, see Gereffi (1999).
3. See http://www.yarnsandfibers.com/news/. December11.2007. Accessed 13 December 2007.
4. This paragraph is partly based on Ramaswamy (2004).
5. This paragraph takes data from the country profiles available at http://www.bimstec.org/countryprofile.html.
6. http://www.centad.org/news/October10. Accessed 13 December 2007.

REFERENCES

Centre for Trade and Development (Centad) (2005). *South Asian Yearbook of Trade and Development 2005*. Centad, New Delhi.

FAO (2005). 'Small developing economies: Characteristics and vulnerability' (109), http://www.fao.org/DOCREP/005/Y3733E/y3733e0e.htm\ Accessed 5 December 2007.

Frankel, Jeffrey and David Romer (1999). 'Does trade cause growth?', *American Economic Review*, 89, 3, 379–99.

Government of India (2007). *Annual Report 2006–7*, Ministry of Textiles. http:\\www.texmin.nic.in/anuualrep/arep.htm/accessed 5 December 2007.

——— (2008). *Economic Survey 2007–8*, Ministry of Finance. http:\\ www.financemin.nic.in\finmin.nic.in/reports/index.html. Accessed 5 April 2008.

Gereffi, G. (1999). 'International trade and industrial upgrading in the apparel commodity chain', *Journal of International Economics*, 48, 1, 37–70.

Haussmann, R., J. Hwang and Dani Rodrik (2006). 'What you export matters'. http//www.ksghome.harvard.edu/drodrik/papers.html/. Accessed 10 December 2007.

International Monetary Fund (IMF) (2007). *World Economic Outlook 2007*, http://www.imf.org/.

Institute of South Asian Studies (2007). 'Regionalism and trade: South Asian perspectives'. Institute of South Asian Studies, Singapore.

Lall, Sanjaya, John Weiss and Jinkang Zhang (2005). 'The sophistication of exports: A new measure of product characteristics', Queen Elizabeth House Working Paper No. 123, http://www.qeh.ox.ac.uk/. Accessed 10 December 2007

Mayer, J. and Adrian Wood (2001). 'South Asia's export structure in a comparative perspective', *Oxford Development Studies*, 2, 1, 5–29.

Naik, Gopal (2005). 'Tackling agricultural subsidies in WTO negotiations'. In *South Asian Yearbook of Trade and Development 2005* (pp. 41–79). Centad, New Delhi.

Pigato, M., Caroline Farah, Ken Itakura, Kwang Jun, Will Martin, Kim Murrell and T.G. Srinivasan (1997). *South Asia's Integration into the World Economy*, Washington, D.C.: The World Bank.

Panagariya, Arvind (1999). 'Trade policy in South Asia: Recent liberalization and future agenda', *The World Economy*, 23, 3, 353–79.

Ramaswamy, K. V. and Gary Gereffi (2000). 'India's apparel exports: The challenge of global markets', *The Developing Economies*, 33, 2, 186–210.

Ramaswamy, K.V. (2004). 'Global opportunity and domestic constraints in textile and apparel industry in South Asia: analysis and strategic response of firms in India'. In Mita Bhattacharya, Russell Smyth and Marika Vicziany (eds.), *South Asia in the Era of Globalization: Trade, Industrialization and Welfare*. New York: Nova Science Publishers.

Reserve Bank of India (RBI) (2007). *Annual Report 2006–7*. http://www.rbi.org.in/scripts/Annual Report/Publications.aspx/ accessed 10 December 2007.

Rodrik, D. (2006). 'What's so special about China's exports?' http//www.ksghome.harvard.edu/drodrik/papers.html/Accessed 10 December 2007.

Research and Information System for the Non-Aligned and other Developing Countries (RIS) (2002). *South Asia Development and Cooperation Report 2001–2*. RIS, New Delhi: RIS.

Chanda, Rupa (2005). 'Trade in services and South Asia: An aggressive agenda'. In *South Asian Yearbook of Trade and Development 2005* (pp. 105–207). Centad, New Delhi.

Sturgeon, Timothy J. and Richard K. Lester (2002). 'The new global supply base: New challenges for local suppliers in East Asia', Working Paper No. 02002, Industrial Performance Center, Massachusetts Institute of Technology (MIT), Cambridge.

United Nations (UN) (2006). *Trade and Development Report, 2006*. New York and Geneva.

UNCTAD (2007a). *World Investment Report 2007: Transnational Corporations, Extractive Industries and Developments*. http:\\www.unctad.org\ Accessed 20 December 2007.

——— (2007b). *Handbook of Trade Statistics 2006–7*. http://www.stats.unctad.org/Handbook/ accessed 10 December 2007.

USAID (2005). *South Asian Free Trade Area: Opportunities and Challenges*. Washington, DC: USAID.

United States International Trade Commission (USITC) (2001). 'India's textile and apparel industry: Growth potential and trade and investment opportunities', Staff Research Study 27, Publication 3401. Washington DC.

Veeramani (2007). 'Sources of India's export growth in pre and post-reform periods', *Economic and Political Weekly*, 42, 25, 2419–27.

World Bank (2006). *World Development Indicators 2006*. CD_ROM.

——— (2007a). *World Development Indicators database 2007*. http://www.worldbank.org/, Accessed 20 February 2007.

——— (2007b). *World Development Report 2008.* World Bank, Washington, D.C.

——— (2008). *International Comparison Program 2005: Tables of Final Results,* http://www.worldbank.org/. Accessed 1 March 2008.

WTO (2007). *International Trade Statistics 2007.* http://www.wto.org/. Accessed 10 December 2007.

9

Indian Manufacturing: The Road Ahead

JAYAN JOSE THOMAS

INTRODUCTION

MANUFACTURING GROWTH in India in recent years presents somewhat of a mixed picture. After a period of recession between 1996–7 and 2001–2, India's manufacturing sector is currently recording high rates of growth of output. A number of Indian manufacturing firms in fields such as automobiles and pharmaceuticals are attracting global attention, best exemplified in a recent headline in Fortune magazine, 'Manufacturing takes off in India'.[1] India has gained a reputation as a center for manufacturing design and innovation. In January 2008, India's Tata Motors unveiled a US$2,500 passenger car 'Nano', claimed to be the world's cheapest car, giving ample signals of engineering excellence in the country. For all this, however, India's manufacturing sector is showing signs of weaknesses too. The appreciation of the Indian Rupee in 2007–8 significantly reduced the competitiveness of many export-oriented industries in the country such as textiles and engineering. Tirupur, the largest source of exports of knitwear garments from India, was badly hit. It was estimated that job retrenchments in this textile town would reach 50,000 by March 2008.[2]

This chapter reviews India's manufacturing growth experience in recent years. The next section is a short review of the long-term trends in India's manufacturing sector. Economic reform measures in India, especially those relating to the manufacturing sector, are also discussed. The third section studies India's manufacturing sector in some detail, focusing on its relative size and recent growth experience. The fourth section features three Indian industries that are today recording impressive growth performance: pharmaceuticals, automobiles and auto components, and manufacturing services. The fifth section features two sectors that might pose serious challenges to India's manufacturing growth in the coming years: i. ports, and ii. power and energy. The sixth section is on regional aspects of India's industrial growth, while the final section provides some concluding remarks.

LONG TERM TRENDS IN INDIAN MANUFACTURING

Scholarly analyses of industrial growth in post-Independence India have identified three important growth phases. The early years of Indian planning, from 1950 to the mid-1960s, constitutes the first growth phase. Indian industry grew at respectable rates during this period. In the second growth phase, between the mid-1960s and the late 1970s, Indian industry experienced a long period of stagnation. The third phase began with India's industrial sector staging a revival of growth in the 1980s. This revival continued through the mid-1990s. Industrial growth showed signs of deceleration after 1995-6 but picked up again after 2002–3 (see Table 9.1).

There are clearly two major strands in the literature on long-term constraints to India's industrial growth, particularly relating to the period of industrial stagnation between the mid-1960s and the late 1970s (Nayyar 1994). One set of explanations focused on

Table 9.1: Growth Rates of Manufacturing Incomes (at constant 1993–4 prices) in India, 1950–1 to 2004–5

(*in per cent*)

Time period	Rate of growth
1950–1 to 1964–5	5.67
1965–6 to 1979–80	3.88
1980–1 to 2004–5	6.66

Source: Calculations based on data from Central Statistical Organisation, available from EPW Research Foundation and www.rbi.org.in.

Notes: Rates of growth are calculated by semilogarithmic regression.
All growth rates are statistically significant at less than 5 per cent level.

the problems at the macroeconomic level, and argued that India's industrial progress was hindered mainly due to the slow expansion of domestic demand. This, in turn, was a consequence of the unequal income distribution and slow growth of agricultural incomes in the country (Bagchi 1970; Chakravarty 1979; Mitra 1977; Patnaik 1972). Unequal income distribution affected the overall level of demand and, therefore, savings in the economy, and, in this way, slowed down industrial growth (Bagchi 1970; Chakravarty 1979). Unequal income distribution also affected the pattern of domestic demand for industrial goods (Mitra 1977; Nayyar 1978). The demand for consumer durables and luxury goods kept rising fast, while the demand for goods of mass consumption, for textiles for example, remained stagnant.[3]

The other set of explanations on the slow growth of industrial incomes in India gave greater attention to questions at the microeconomic level and raised several criticisms on a number of control measures that characterized India's industrial policy framework. The controls led to economic inefficiency and resource misallocation, it was contended (Bhagwati and Desai 1970; Bhagwati and Srinivasan 1975). Price controls set by the government generated inefficiencies and growth constraints, particularly in those industries in which the leading producers enjoyed monopoly power (steel and machinery industries, for instance) (Bhagwati and Desai 1970). Imports were highly controlled in India: firms were required to obtain licenses for importing goods into the country; there were also limits on the amount of foreign exchange they were allowed to hold. Such controls resulted in inordinate delays in project implementation, substantial administrative and other expenses, barriers to entry of new firms, and constraints for competitive firms to exploit scale economies. There have also been criticisms on the early Indian Plans for the almost insignificant role they envisaged for the private sector (Bhagwati and Desai 1970).

Studies have pointed to several problems with the system of industrial licensing in India. The licensing system, which decided the pattern of investment down to detailed product level, was 'ill-designed' and concerned itself with 'excessive detail', according to Bhagwati and Desai (1970). The choice between alternative industrial projects was not based on any economic criteria, but was, in most instances, determined by political factors (ibid.). At the same time, studies have also shown that India's large business houses acquired sufficient oligopoly power to distort the industrial licensing system to their advantage. Large business houses managed to obtain licenses ahead of their smaller competitors. However, they invested largely in profitable and fast growing industries such as consumer durables. In slow-growing industries such as textiles, and in industries, such as cement where price control existed, they obtained licenses (and thereby prevented entry by others) but did not always translate their licenses into production capacities, resulting, among other things, in a mismatch between actual and planned production capacities (Chandrasekhar 1988).

After a long phase of stagnation, India's industrial growth revived from the early 1980s. It was argued that the rise in public investment in India during the 1980s was an important factor behind the revival of industrial growth (Chandrasekhar 1996; Nagaraj 1990). A significant improvement in investment in infrastructure was identified as particularly contributing to industrial growth revival in the 1980s. There was acceleration in investment in sub-sectors such as railways, electricity, and petroleum during the 1980s. Studies have confirmed that there was also a distinct improvement in performance and output growth of public sector enterprises in the 1980s (Ahluwalia 1991; Nagaraj 1990). Some studies noted that the revival of manufacturing growth in India in the first half of the 1980s was due to better productivity growth performance. According to Ahluwalia (1991), during the first half of the 1980s, total factor productivity in India's manufacturing sector grew at a rate of 3.4 per cent per annum compared to the negative growth rate (-0.3 per cent per annum) in the preceding 15 years of industrial stagnation (ibid.). Balakrishnan and Pushpangadan (1994) and Rao (1996) questioned the methodology in Ahluwalia's (1991) study, and their results showed that productivity growth in the 1980s was not faster, but in fact slower than in the previous decade. Patnaik and Chandrasekhar (1995) argued that the industrial growth revival of the 1980s left India's economy on a 'powderkeg': that is, the revival was associated with large debt build-up and the economy became vulnerable to currency speculations and inflationary upsurges.

ECONOMIC REFORMS

Early measures to liberalize India's industrial policies began in the late 1970s. However, it was after 1991–2 that wide-ranging measures for economic liberalization were initiated in the country. It is argued that the changes that the reforms after 1991 brought in were 'fundamental' in nature compared to the 'marginal' changes only in the previous decade (Ahluwalia and Little 1998: 4–5).

As part of the trade liberalization policies from the 1990s, quantitative and tariff restrictions on imports were progressively eased. In the early years of the reforms, the number of goods that could be imported through Open General License was increased. Capital goods and intermediates have been made freely importable since 1993. In 1993, India shifted to a flexible exchange rate regime, and this allowed the government to manage balance of payments impacts through exchange rate flexibility; stabilizing balance of payments was an important objective of import restrictions until then (Ahluwalia 2002). According to estimates by Mehta (1997), the percentage of products covered by non-tariff barriers (NTB) was around 90 per cent in the pre-reform period, which declined to 44 per cent by 1995. Measures for trade liberalization proceeded at a much accelerated pace in India after 1998. The removal of tariff and quantitative restrictions were in many cases more than what was required under World Trade Organization (WTO) commitments (Chandrasekhar and Ghosh 2004). On 1 April 2001, India finally removed quantitative restrictions on imports of manufactured consumer goods and agricultural products (Ahluwalia 2002).

Reforms also led to progressive reduction in tariff rates. According to Ahluwalia (2002), the weighted average import duty rate declined from 72.5 per cent in 1991–2 to 24.6 per cent in 1996–7. Import duties increased over the next four years, but the peak duty rate was reduced again to 30 per cent in February 2002 (Ahluwalia 2002). Ahluwalia (2002) notes that although India's tariff levels have been brought down by trade liberalization measures, they are still considerably higher than the corresponding tariff levels in China and the East Asian countries.

There have been major policy changes in India with respect to foreign direct investments (FDI). Nagesh Kumar (1995) identified four distinct phases in the Indian state's attitude towards FDI. The period from 1947 to the late 1960s was one of liberalized policy environment towards FDI. From the late 1960s to the late 1970s, the Indian government adopted a more restrictive stance towards FDI. The policy regime towards FDI began to be liberalized in the 1980s, and this marked the third phase. In the fourth phase beginning in 1991, the policies towards liberalization of FDI regime received a further impetus (Kumar 1995). The industrial Policy Statements of 1980 and 1982 made announcements in regard to liberalized rules for FDI investments. With the liberalization policies of the early 1990s, FDI involving 51 per cent equity was given automatic approval in 34 high-priority industries requiring large investments and advanced technologies. In the power sector, 100 per cent FDI was permitted. Over the years, limits on foreign ownership have been relaxed in several additional industries. Foreign equity participation of up to 74 per cent is allowed in many high-priority and infrastructure industries including telecom; 100 per cent foreign ownership on an automatic basis is permitted in ports and roads (Kumar 1995; Rao and Dutt 2006).

MANUFACTURING SECTOR IN INDIA: ITS RELATIVE SIZE AND GROWTH EXPERIENCE

This section studies India's manufacturing sector in some detail. The topics covered include: i. the manufacturing sector's relative importance in India's national economy; ii. India's manufacturing sector compared to manufacturing sectors in selected countries; iii. recent growth performance in India's manufacturing sector; and iv. employment generation in the manufacturing sector in India.

MANUFACTURING SECTOR IN INDIA'S DOMESTIC ECONOMY

National Accounts Statistics of India published by India's Central Statistical Organisation (CSO) is the source of information on industrial sector incomes in the country. As per the definition followed in this study, the industrial sector comprises mining and quarrying, manufacturing, and electricity, gas and water supply. According to the CSO data, the industrial sector accounted for 21.9 per cent of India's gross domestic product (GDP) in 2004–5. Manufacturing is the largest segment within the industrial sector, having shares of 77.3 per cent in total industrial sector income and 17.4 per cent in GDP in 2004–5. In turn, there are two important components within the manufacturing sector in India, namely, registered manufacturing and unregistered manufacturing (see Table 9.2).

In India, registered factories comprise all factories that employ more than 10 workers and operate with the aid of electric power as well as factories that employ more than 20 workers without the aid of electric power. In 2000–1, there were a total of 131,268 registered factories in India employing 8 million workers. All registered factories constitute the factory sector. Manufacturing activities of

Table 9.2: Shares of Major Segments within Industrial Sector in India's GDP at Factor Cost, 2004–5

	Per cent share of total industrial sector	Per cent share in total GDP
Mining & Quarrying	11.3	2.3
Manufacturing	77.3	17.4
Registered Manufacturing	52.7	–
Unregistered Manufacturing	24.7	–
Electricity, Gas & Water Supply	11.4	2.3
Total Industrial sector	100	21.9
Gross Domestic Product	–	100

Source: Central Statistical Organisation (CSO), from EPW Research Foundation and www.rbi.org.in.

Note: GDP at constant 1999–2000 prices.

registered factories are classified under registered manufacturing; all other manufacturing activities are classified under unregistered manufacturing. The Annual Survey of Industries (ASI), published by the CSO, is the major source of statistics on registered factories. The ASI also covers some factories that are engaged in activities other than manufacturing. They include electricity undertakings engaged in the generation, transmission, and distribution of electricity and registered with the Central Electricity Authority. They also include factories engaged in manufacturing service activities such as cold storage, water supply, and repair of motor vehicles.

Industrialization in India has not been highly successful as regards generating employment. Many scholars have written on the failure of Indian industry to provide employment to the large labor reserves in the country (Bhagwati and Chakravarty 1969; Patnaik 1994). The total number of workers employed in India's factory sector was 8 million in 2000–1. Factory sector employment was only 1.98 per cent of India's total working population of 402 million in 2001. The factory sector also accounted for only 15.6 per cent of the 51 million employed in the manufacturing sector (see Thomas 2005a). The rest of the manufacturing employees worked in the unregistered manufacturing sector. Studies have shown that the bulk of unregistered manufacturing in India employs traditional technologies. Also, workers in the unregistered manufacturing sector survive largely under exploitative and poor working conditions.

In India, the factory sector accounts for the dominant share of value added by the industrial sector, although, as discussed above, its share in employment is rather low. The value added by the registered manufacturing sector (that is, the factory sector minus manufacturing service activities) accounted for a share of more than 60 per cent in the total value added by manufacturing (that is, the industrial sector minus manufacturing service activities) in India in the 1990s. It is generally expected that the proliferation of activities in the factory sector leads to the creation of employment in the unregistered sector. For example, the operations of a large automobile plant, which falls within the factory sector, lead to the emergence of several small-scale, ancillary units in the unregistered sector. However, recent trends indicate a growing disconnect between the growth experiences of registered and unregistered manufacturing sectors in India.

India's Manufacturing Sector in a Comparative Perspective

This section compares India's manufacturing sector performance with the performance of other selected Asian countries for the year 2006 (see Table 9.3). The selected countries include China, the East Asian tiger economies of South Korea and Singapore, and three South Asian countries, namely, Bangladesh, Pakistan and Sri Lanka. The share of manufacturing value added in GDP is a good indicator of the relative importance of the manufacturing sector in the national economy. The share of manufacturing in GDP was 16.1 per cent in India, much lower than China's 30.9 per cent. China's success in generating large numbers of manufacturing jobs is often contrasted with India's failure in this regard. Other South Asian countries have not fared well either in building a large manufacturing sector. Per capita manufacturing value added (at constant year 2000 dollar prices) was US$91 in India, compared to US$530 in China and US$4,131 in South Korea. Per capita manufacturing value added for the three other South Asian countries were also less than US$150 (all at constant 2000 prices) (see Table 9.3).

In terms of growth of manufacturing value added, India's performance has not been spectacular. Growth rates for India for the periods 1995–2000 and 2000–5 were much lower than the corresponding growth rates for China, and also lower than the average rates of growth for South and East Asia and Oceania. At the same time, growth of non-manufacturing GDP for both the periods noted above was faster in India compared to the corresponding averages for South and East Asia and Oceania, although still considerably slower than the growth in China (see Table 9.4).

Table 9.3: Indicators of Manufacturing Performance in India and Selected Countries, 2006

Countries	Manufacturing value added as per cent of GDP	Manufacturing value added, constant 2000 US$ million	Population, numbers in millions	Per capita manufacturing value added, constant 2000 US$	Per capita GDP, constant 2000 US$
India	16.1	1,01,307	1,110	91	634
China	30.9	6,95,290	1,312	530	1,595
South Korea	27.8	1,99,997	48	4,131	13,865
Singapore	29.2	32,750	4	7,455	27,685
Bangladesh	17.2	10,639	144	74	454
Pakistan	18.3	17,184	159	108	623
Sri Lanka	15.1	2,959	20	150	1,076

Source: World Development Indicators, World Bank.

Table 9.4: Average Annual Rate of Growth of Manufacturing and Non-Manufacturing Sectors, India and Selected Countries, 1995–2000 and 2000–5

(*in per cent*)

Countries	Manufacturing value added		Non-manufacturing gross domestic product	
	1995–2000	2000–5	1995–2000	2000–5
India	4.4	6.6	6.0	6.6
China	9.2	10.4	8.0	9.0
South Korea	6.8	7.2	2.2	3.4
Singapore	7.2	5.0	5.2	3.4
Bangladesh	5.6	5.8	5.2	5.2
Pakistan	3.4	8.2	3.0	4.0
Sri Lanka	7.0	2.8	4.8	4.6
South & East Asia and Oceania	6.6	8.0	4.4	5.8
Developing countries	4.8	5.2	3.8	4.6

Source: Industrial Statistics from United Nations Industrial Development Organization (UNIDO), www.unido.org/statistics

Rates of Manufacturing Growth in Recent Decades

As discussed earlier, India's manufacturing sector has grown at relatively fast rates from the 1980s. In Table 9.5, we compare the growth of manufacturing incomes in India in two periods: 1980–1 to 1990–1 and 1991–2 to 2004–5. Annual rate of growth of manufacturing incomes in India is seen to have declined in the period between 1991–2 and 2004–5 compared to the period between 1980–1 and 1990–1.

If we closely study manufacturing sector growth after 1991–2, a clearer picture emerges (see Figure 9.1). Growth over the previous year of the manufacturing sector in India was negative in 1991–2 and only 4.1 per cent in 1992–3. Year-on-year growth of the manufacturing sector rose to very high levels in the next three years, peaking at 14.9 per cent in 1995–6. These were also the initial years of liberalization in India. However, India's manufacturing sector entered a period of relative stagnation in growth in the period between 1997–8 and 1999–2000. Growth of the manufacturing sector appears to have climbed to higher levels again after 2002–3 (see Figure 9.1).

Table 9.5: Annual Rates of Growth of Manufacturing Incomes (at constant 1993–4 prices) in India, 1980–1 to 2004–5

(*in per cent*)

Time period	Rate of growth
1980–1 to 1990–1	7.52
1991–2 to 2004–5	6.66

Source: Calculations based on National Accounts Statistics published by CSO, available from EPWRF and www.rbi.org.in

Notes: Rates of growth are calculated by semilogarithmic regression.
All growth rates are statistically significant at less than 5 per cent level.

Figure 9.1: Rate of Growth over the Previous Year of Manufacturing Incomes (at constant 1993–4 prices)

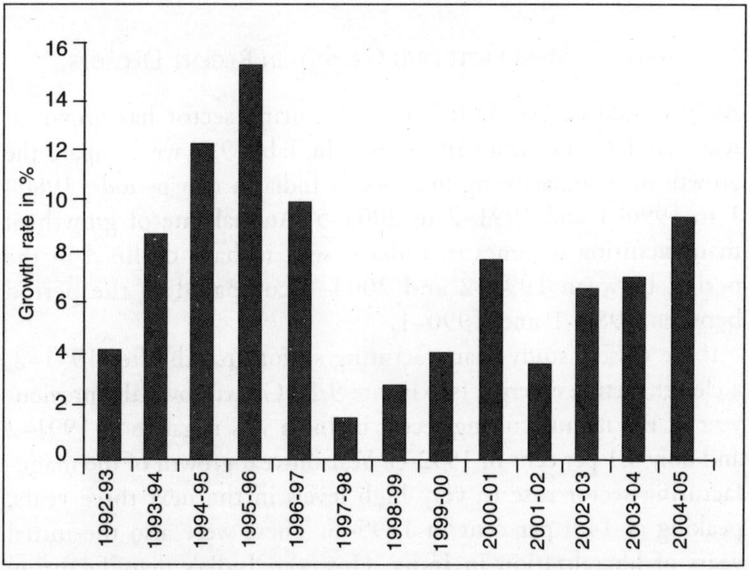

Source: Calculations based on National Accounts Statistics published by CSO, available from EPWRF and www.rbi.org.in.

Table 9.6: Indicators of Performance in Export of Manufactured Goods: India and Selected Countries

	Merchandise Exports, 2005 (US$ billion)	Manufactured exports as per cent of total exports, 2004	High-tech exports as per cent of manufactured exports, 2004
China	762	91	30
India	90	73	5
South Korea	285	92	33
US	904	82	32

Source: World Development Report 2007, World Bank.

It is generally perceived that India is set to emerge as a major manufacturing hub like China. Increasing levels of globalization, availability of cheap labor, and the rise in recent years of sophisticated industries such as automobiles and pharmaceuticals are factors that fuel this optimism. However, with respect to current levels of performance in export of manufactured goods, India is far behind China. As Table 9.6 shows, the export of manufactured goods from China was 8–9 times the export of manufactured goods from India. More importantly, in 2004, high-technology exports as a proportion of total manufactured exports was only 5 per cent in India compared to 30 per cent in China (see Table 9.6).

Generation of Employment in Indian Manufacturing

The 1980s is often called the decade of 'jobless growth' in Indian manufacturing. The revival in growth of output witnessed in this period was not accompanied by adequate generation of employment. Only 484,000 jobs were generated in India's registered factory sector between 1979–80 and 1990–1. Compared to the 1980s, manufacturing growth in the 1990s was more employment generating. 1,763,000 new jobs were created in India's registered manufacturing between 1991–2 and 1997–8 compared to only 484,000 jobs in the earlier decade (Thomas 2002). Table 9.7 shows India's experience with respect to the generation of factory employment between

Table 9.7: Employment in India's Factory Sector and Organized Sector (various years)

	Factory Sector	Organized Sector
1960	3.8	–
1970	5.0	17.8
1981–2	7.9	23.8
1991–2	8.3	27.1
1997–8	10.1	28.2
2003–4	7.9	26.5

Sources: Annual Survey of Industries, various issues; Handbook of Statistics on Indian Economy, Reserve Bank of India www.rbi.org.in

Note: Numbers in millions.

1960 and 2003–4. The growth of employment in India's factory sector was stagnant in the 1980s, showed some improvement in the 1990s, but declined again after 1997–8. There is clear evidence of a decline in manufacturing employment in India in recent years. Factory sector employment in India was 10.1 million in 1997–8 but it declined to 7.9 million in 2003–4. Correspondingly, employment in India's organized sector (of which the factory sector is a component) declined from 28.2 million in 1997–8 to 26.5 million in 2003–4 (Table 9.7).

AREAS OF GROWING MANUFACTURING EXCELLENCE

This section features three industries that are currently growing at high rates in India and promise much for the future. They are the pharmaceuticals industry, automobiles and auto components, and manufacturing services.

PHARMACEUTICALS INDUSTRY

India's pharmaceuticals industry is expanding rapidly. According to statistics available for the year 2007, there were 75 drug manufacturing units in India approved by the United States Food and Drug Administration (USFDA). This is the largest number of FDA-approved manufacturing facilities in any country other than the US. India's pharmaceutical industry consists of 24,000 firms (if small firms are also included) of which there are 300 large firms.[4] India's export of drugs, pharmaceuticals and fine chemicals was worth US$4.9 billion in 2005–6, and export destinations included the US, United Kingdom, Germany, Russia and China (CMIE 2006; Thomas in press).

Domestic pharmaceutical firms in India have benefited greatly from state intervention in the industry, notably from favorable government legislation: the Indian Patent Act of 1970, which disallowed product patenting on drugs and food products. By 2004, domestic firms supplied 77 per cent of the market for pharmaceuticals in India, multinational corporations accounting for only the remaining 33 per cent (Thomas in press). More importantly, domestic pharmaceutical firms were able to manufacture and sell generic drugs at low prices in India. Indian firms have been major exporters of active pharmaceutical ingredients and pharmaceutical formulations of several medicines, including vaccines and anti-retrovirals (Grace 2004: 13–15; Thomas in press).

Between 1995 and 2005, India introduced laws ensuring greater protection to intellectual property rights (including product patenting rules), in compliance with the WTO's Agreement on Trade-Related Aspects of Intellectual Property Rights. India's pharmaceuticals industry has responded well to the challenge of a stricter patent regime. Major domestic pharmaceutical firms have been allocating a larger share of resources for research and development (R&D) and trying to acquire patents abroad. In the case of Dr Reddy's Laboratories, an Indian firm, R&D charges as a proportion of sales revenue were 2.8 per cent in the three-year period ending in 1994–5, which rose to 11.0 per cent in the three-year period ending in 2005–6.[5] Ranbaxy made 698 patent filings in the first nine months of 2005.[6] Also, India's generic drug makers are exporting more, notably to the regulated markets of North America and Europe. They are challenging big pharmaceutical corporations in the market for generic drugs in the West. Many Indian drug firms have also been pursuing an aggressive strategy of overseas acquisitions during the past several months[7] (see Thomas in press).

At the same time, given India's cost advantages in pharmaceuticals R&D, global pharmaceutical corporations are keen to form research partnerships with Indian firms. There has been an especially fast growth of outsourcing of clinical trials to India. The number of ongoing clinical trials in India was 270 in 2007 (Yee 2007a). Leading Indian firms are carrying out cutting-edge research to develop new drug molecules, but, so far, none has succeeded in fully developing an original drug. Instead of venturing into the more difficult clinical trial and regulatory stages, they license out the molecule to bigger pharmaceutical companies (Chaudhuri 2005). It is too early to say whether Indian drug firms will grow in size to reach the levels of pharmaceuticals corporations in the West. There are also concerns that as Indian firms focus their energies on the market for global diseases in India and abroad, there will be a corresponding decline in their manufacturing and research efforts targeting neglected diseases among poor patients (see Thomas in press).

Automobiles and Auto Ancillaries

Production of automobiles and auto ancillaries has grown at spectacular rates in India in recent years (see Figure 9.2 for growth in the production of commercial vehicles in India). An important driver of this growth is the burgeoning domestic demand for automobiles. India and China are the two fastest growing markets for passenger cars and light commercial vehicles in the world. In 2006–7, more than 1.6 million light vehicles and 7.8 million motorbikes were sold in India. Given the low penetration of cars (seven to eight cars per 1,000 people in India compared with 750 cars per 1,000 in the US), India's market potential in the automobile industry will remain very high over the coming years (Yee 2008). A number of domestic and foreign automakers—including Maruti Udyog, Tata Motors, Hyundai, Honda Siel and Mahindra—are active in the Indian market. Maruti Suzuki and Tata are gearing up to expand their annual production capacities in India to one million vehicles each, while Mahindra, Renault and Nissan will each raise their production capacities to 0.5 million (Agali 2007). General Motors (GM) is looking to more than double its production capacity in India, to 225,000 vehicles a year, in their factories in Gujarat (Halol) and Maharashtra (Talegaon) (Timmons 2007).

Figure 9.2: Annual Production of Selected Industries in India, 1981–2 to 2006–7

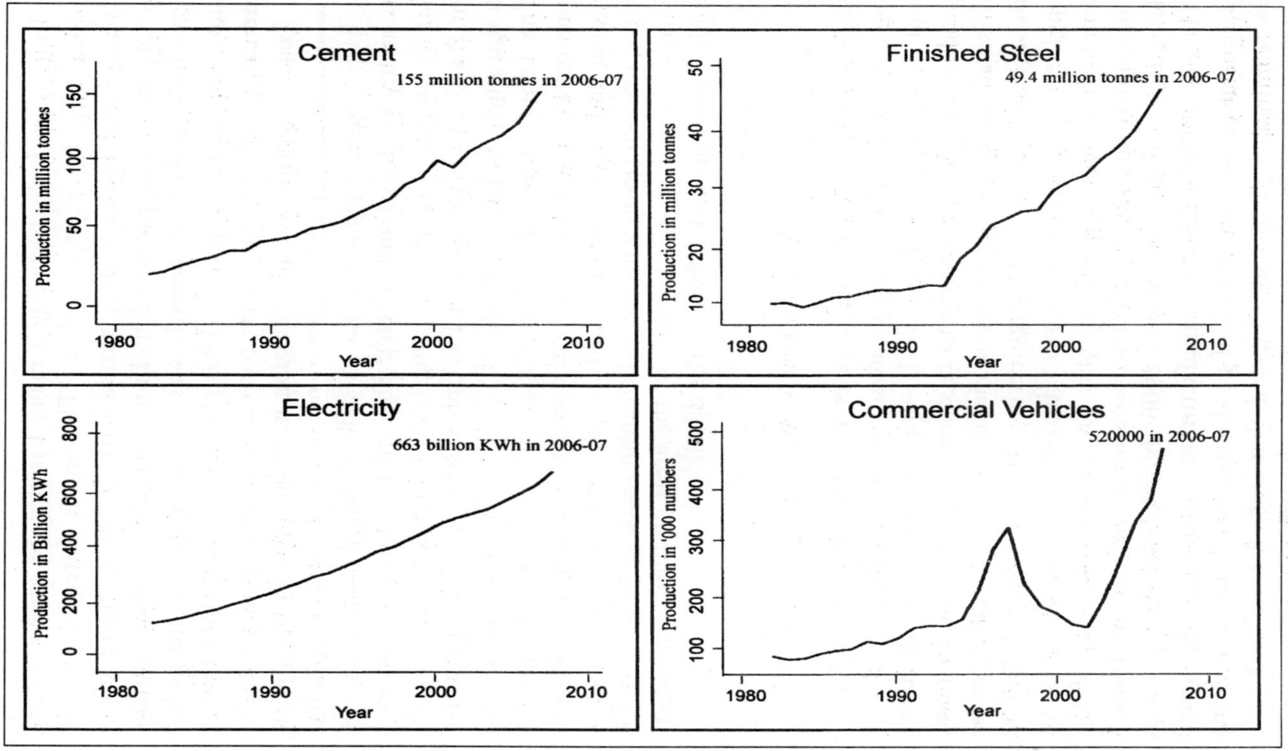

India is gradually becoming a major base for the production of automobiles for export markets. The South Korean company Hyundai and India's Maruti Suzuki have drawn up major plans for export of cars produced in India (Yee 2008). Many Indian firms have established themselves as leading players in the global auto components industry. GM has plans of spending US$1 billion annually on the purchase of car parts from India (Timmons 2007).

Major opportunities are emerging in India today in the area of automobile research and development. In the global auto industry, India is gaining a reputation for its skills in 'frugal engineering', or its ability to design and develop high quality, low-cost vehicles.[8] Suzuki Motors of Japan is investing US$1.8 billion in India, mainly for R&D and marketing. In December 2007, GM inaugurated a design studio in Bangalore, one of 12 such GM centers worldwide. The 1,000 employees at the Bangalore studio will design the interiors for new GM cars that the company will be launching in Indian and export markets. GM has also announced plans for a major research tie-up with the Indian Institute of Technology (IIT), Kharagpur to carry out research in the areas of automotive electronics, controls, and software (Yee 2008).

Manufacturing Services

India is increasingly known as a center for 'service-based manufacturing'. This refers to the country's advantages in manufacturing design and development, linkages with suppliers, and in small batch production adhering closely to customer requirements. In turn, these advantages originate from India's well-established expertise in software services and engineering. India produces 536,000 engineering graduates in a year (in 2007–8), and the costs of employing them in India are only one-third to one-fifth of the corresponding costs in advanced countries, such as the United Kingdom and the US (Marsh 2006; NASSCOM data cited in Thomas 2008). Globally, manufacturing services was considered peripheral to the central task of production, but is today growing in prominence. It is widely agreed that India has an edge over China in service-based manufacturing, while China retains a considerable lead in mass production.

Estimates in 2006 by consultancy Booz Allen Hamilton and India's National Association of Software and Services Companies show that engineering services, especially services for the automotive, telecommunications, and other high-technology sectors, could rise to a US$40 billion industry in India by 2020 (Yee 2008). According to Asea Brown Boveri, the Swiss-Swedish engineering group, India is an advantageous location for the manufacture of products such as automation equipment for factories and electricity transmission systems. Cisco, a leading producer of networking equipment and routers worldwide, has inaugurated its center in Bangalore and has allocated to it US$750 million for R&D. HCL Technologies, an Indian company, has 1,500 engineers carrying out R&D for big aerospace corporations such as Boeing and European Aeronautic Defence and Space Company. HCL was involved in the development of Boeing's 787 Dreamliner. The 450 or so aerospace projects outsourced to HCL involved the development of avionics such as landing gear, flight controls, power distributions systems, brake controls and other systems (Yee 2008).

Many leading Indian engineering firms are making forays into the international market. Mahindra & Mahindra, an Indian automaker, is setting up a chain of production units worldwide for supplying specialized auto components to major automobile companies in the West. Bharat Forge, a major Indian auto component manufacturer, is establishing manufacturing plants in the United Kingdom, Germany, and the US. Such tales of success are not limited to the automobile sector alone. Essel and Mahika Packaging, two Indian packaging firms, are setting up production plants outside the country (Marsh 2006).

GROWTH OF THE INFRASTRUCTURE SECTOR

Need for Improvement

Several basic and infrastructure industries in India have recorded considerably high rates of growth in recent years (see Figure 9.2 for growth in the production of cement, finished steel and electricity). For instance, India's cement industry has expanded much after the 1980s. The period after the 1980s was also one in which many of the regulations on the cement industry were relaxed. Annual production capacity of India's cement industry was 155 million tonnes in 2006–7. This must be compared, however, with China's annual cement production capacity of 1.06 billion tonnes (in March 2006). Over the years, the Indian cement industry has matured to the modern dry process technology, and the size of leading individual plants has risen to 3 million tonnes a year (Thombre 2007). While there are such clear indications of progress in some areas, several other infrastructure and basic industries are lagging behind, erecting serious constraints to overall manufacturing growth in the country.

Indian Railways has launched a new freight corridor with linkages to major ports, and construction work for the Golden Quadrilateral Road Project, linking the different corners of the country, is nearing completion. However, rail and road networks in the country still require massive modernization. In the remaining part of this section, we feature two major infrastructure sectors where India needs to build large capacities over the coming years, namely, ports and, energy and power.

Ports

Indian ports need to be modernized. Container traffic through Indian ports is still at relatively low levels even while some other regions in Asia witnessed fast growth of containerized cargo movement. Ten container ports in Asia, importantly the ports of Singapore, Malaysia, and Dubai, handle over 40 per cent of the container traffic worldwide. It is estimated that approximately 70 per cent of the potential transshipment business for India is today handled by the ports of Colombo, Salalah, Dubai, Aden, and Singapore (Rao and Kumar 2005).[9]

Between 1950–1 and 1980–1, cargo traffic through India's major ports increased from 20 million tonnes to only 80 million tonnes. After 1980, the traffic increased much faster, to 151 million tonnes in 1990–1, and 423 million tonnes in 2005–6. There has been a notable improvement in the growth of containerized cargo traffic too, although the volume of traffic is still very low. The combined container cargo traffic through all ports in India was estimated to reach 4.4 million TEUs (twenty-foot equivalent units) in 2005–6, even while this accounted for just 1 per cent of the world container cargo traffic and 5–6 per cent of the container cargo traffic through Asia.[10] It may be noted that container traffic through the port of Singapore, which operates four container terminals and maintains an excellent network of 200 shipping lines, is 22 million TEUs (Thomas 2007).

Container cargo traffic through India is heavily concentrated in Jawaharlal Nehru Port Trust (JNPT) and Mumbai port, which together handle around 60 per cent of the total container traffic through the country. The combined share of India's western and northern region in the total container traffic through India is estimated to be 69 per cent, while the shares of the southern and eastern regions are 26 and 5 per cent, respectively (ibid. 2007).[11] It is suggested that the efficiency levels in India's major and minor ports need to be raised considerably. JNPT can handle ships carrying containers with maximum capacities of only 2,500 TEUs. Chinese ports are equipped to handle larger ships with container capacities of 12,000 TEUs. Vessels serving Indian ports incur higher costs per container shipped. Also, given their small sizes, they cannot make long, intercontinental voyages, which mean that they need to be transshipped at ports such as Colombo in Sri Lanka or Salalah in Oman on their voyages to Europe or North America (Wright 2007).

Energy and Power

The energy situation in India is not very promising. At present, only 30 per cent of crude oil requirements in the country are met through local production, imports accounting for the remaining. Per capita energy consumption in India is going to rise to higher levels with faster economic growth. Some estimates show that India's energy requirement in 2030 will be in the range of 337–462 million tonnes of oil, 99–184 million tonnes oil equivalent (mtoe) of gas, and 602–954 mtoe of coal (Ramanathan 2007). There are several challenges to expanding the hydrocarbon reserves of a country like

India. It may be noted that 85 per cent of the known reserves in the world are concentrated in 10 countries. India's public sector oil companies, Oil and Natural Gas Corporation and Oil India, are in the race for new petroleum exploration licenses. However, Indian companies are late entrants in this field as some of the best hydrocarbon reserve acreages in the world were last auctioned in the 1990s (Butala 2007).

At the same time, India is gradually emerging as a hub for the export of petroleum products based on crude oil imported from West Asia, West Africa, and Latin America. There are 19 oil refineries in the country—17 of them in the public sector and 2 in the private sector—and their combined refining capacity is 149 million tonnes per annum. The country's western region boasts of world-class oil refineries. While India was an importer of petroleum products until 1999–2000, the country is today a net exporter (Acharya 2007; Butala 2007).

India has the fourth-largest coal reserves in the world. However, a number of factors, including social unrest in regions where coal mines are located, hinder the growth of the domestic coal-mining industry. In 2006, India produced 447.3 million tonnes of coal compared to China's 2.38 billion tonnes.[12] Coal accounted for 77.9 per cent of total electricity produced in China compared to 69.1 per cent in India (in 2004).[13] To meet the demand for coal from steel and energy industries, India had to import 61 million tonnes of coal in 2006. It is estimated that India will be consuming about 800 million tonnes of coal by 2015, and more than 25 per cent of this coal demand will have to be met through imports (Leahy 2007b).

The power generating capacity in India in January 2007 was 128,435 MW (Wadhera 2007). Per capita electric power consumption in India, at 457 kWh in 2004, is very low by East Asian country standards (8,170 and 7,391 kWh in Singapore and South Korea, respectively, in 2004), and also considerably lower than per capita electric power consumption in China, which was 1,585 kWh in 2004.[14] Power shortages and peaking power shortages currently facing the country are at the rates of 11 and 8 per cent, respectively (Wadhera 2007). Power cuts are common in many Indian cities.

There are many problems connected to electricity distribution in India; transmission and distribution 'losses' arising from poor maintenance and operations, electricity theft, and corruption are approximately half of the power generated. Faster economic growth will generate demand for more intensive consumption of electricity over the coming years. The country will have to nearly double its electricity generation capacity to 250,000 MW by 2015 and to 778,000 MW by 2032 to sustain an 8 per cent annual economic growth (Leahy 2007b; Yee 2007b). Therefore, more than 100,000 MW of power generation capacity will need to be added by 2015. The government's plan to install 'ultra mega power plants' across the country with a capacity of 4,000 MW each could go a long way towards the creation of new power generation capacity (Yee 2007a).

REGIONAL ASPECTS OF INDUSTRIAL GROWTH IN INDIA

There is a high degree of regional concentration in India's industrial growth.[15] The two western states of Maharashtra and Gujarat had a combined share of 34.9 per cent in gross value added by India's factory sector in 2003–4. Their combined share in India's population in 2001 was only 14.3 per cent (see Table 9.8).

Mumbai (previously Bombay), the capital of the state of Maharashtra, continues to be the pre-eminent industrial city in India. However, Mumbai has been witnessing some degree of de-industrialization over the past few years, starting with the closing down of large numbers of cotton textile mills in the city from the 1980s. At the same time, huge investments in chemical and petrochemical industries have been made in some other regions of Maharashtra and more significantly in Gujarat, markedly after the 1980s. Today, Jamnagar in Gujarat has one of the largest petrochemical complexes in the world. With investments by Reliance Industries and Essar Oil, two major private sector oil refiners, Jamnagar will have a combined refining capacity of 1.9 million barrels a day. It is noted that Jamnagar will then have the largest refining capacity in the world in a single location, ahead of refining hubs such as Rotterdam and Singapore and those in China and

Table 9.8: Shares of Indian States in Gross Value Added by Factory Sector and Total Population

	Gross value added 2003–4	Population 2001
Maharashtra	20.0	9.4
Gujarat	14.9	4.9
West	*34.9*	*14.3*
Tamil Nadu	9.6	6.1
Andhra Pradesh	6.7	7.4
Karnataka	6.9	5.1
Kerala	1.9	3.1
South	*25.1*	*21.7*
Uttar Pradesh*	7.0	17.0
Punjab	2.6	2.4
Rajasthan	2.7	5.5
Haryana	4.5	2.1
North-West	*16.8*	*27.0*
West Bengal	4.0	7.8
Bihar*	4.1	10.7
Assam	1.7	2.6
East	*9.9*	*21.1*
Madhya Pradesh*	5.1	7.9
Orissa	1.8	3.6
Cental East	*6.9*	*11.5*
Himachal Pradesh	0.9	0.6
Jammu & Kashmir	0.1	1.0
North	*1.0*	*1.6*
India	*100*	*100*

Source: Annual Survey of Industries, various issues.
Notes: All numbers in per cent.
* As they were before the reorganization of Indian States in the year 2000. The shares shown for the year 2003–4 against Bihar, Uttar Pradesh and Madhya Pradesh in this table are, respectively, the sum of the shares for the reorganized states of Bihar and Jharkhand, Uttar Pradesh and Uttaranchal, and Madhya Pradesh and Chhattisgarh.

South Korea.[16] Ulsan in South Korea with a refining capacity of 1.35 million barrels a day will be the second largest. The plants at Jamnagar will handle crude imported from the Middle East for refining and re-export (Leahy 2007a).

The southern states of Tamil Nadu, Karnataka and Andhra Pradesh are also highly industrialized (see Table 9.8). Chennai, the capital of Tamil Nadu, is likely to become the leading manufacturing center in India. Manufacture of automobiles and auto ancillaries has grown very rapidly in this city from the 1990s. Leading automobile corporations such as General Motors, Ford, Daimler Chrysler, BMW, Volvo, Nissan, Hyundai and Mitsubishi have established their presence there. Multinational corporations such as Dell, Nokia, Motorola, Cisco, Samsung, Siemens, Flextronics and Foxconn are setting up manufacturing plants in the Sriperumbudur electronics Special Economic Zone. Ericsson, Alcatel, Texas Instruments, and semiconductor companies like SPEL and Tessolve are the other firms with plans to set up manufacturing or R&D facilities in Chennai (Chuang 2007). Tirupur and Coimbatore, two other cities in Tamil Nadu, have become major producers of cotton textiles, garments and engineering goods.

CONCLUDING REMARKS

This chapter provides a review of India's manufacturing growth experience in recent years. Beginning in the early 1980s, and more clearly after 1991–2, India's industrial regulatory framework began to be liberalized. Licensing was done away with for most industries. Restrictions on imports were eased greatly; and foreign investment was encouraged except in a few sectors. In India, the period after the 1980s has been one of faster industrial and economic growth compared to its three previous decades, yet there are significant yearly variations in growth. India's manufacturing sector recorded very high rates of growth during the four years between 1993–4 and 1996–7. However, the country's manufacturing sector entered a period of relative stagnation in growth in the period between 1997–8 and 2001–2. The growth of the manufacturing sector appears to have climbed to higher levels again after 2002–3. Despite the fast rates of growth of output, the record with respect to growth of employment in India's factory sector has been very poor; in fact, factory sector employment fell after 1997–8. In terms of per capita manufacturing value added, share of manufacturing in GDP, and size of manufactured exports, India is clearly behind China. There is evidence of growing regional concentration in India's manufacturing growth, as the western and southern Indian states, especially Maharashtra, Gujarat, and Tamil Nadu, are advancing much ahead of other regions in industrial growth.

A number of Indian industries, especially pharmaceuticals, automobiles and auto ancillaries, and manufacturing services, have witnessed remarkable rates of expansion in recent years. However, the growth of the infrastructure sectors, for instance, ports and energy and power, has been tardy, and this could pose serious challenges to the future of India's manufacturing growth. Shortage of skilled workers is another problem looming ahead for Indian manufacturing, as it fails to match the rising salary levels in other booming sectors in the country (such as the information technology sector). While this chapter has focused on the supply-side constraints facing Indian manufacturing, demand-side problems, particularly those arising from slow growth of agricultural and rural incomes, are also important and require much policy attention in the future.

NOTES

* The author is grateful to P.L. Beena and Jesim Pais for their valuable suggestions on this paper.

1. John Elliot, 'Manufacturing takes off in India', *Fortune*, 19 October 2007.
2. See the report 'Tirupur Exporters Seek More Sops', 25 November 2007 in www.newindpress.com.
3. For a review of this literature, see Ahluwalia (1985: 54–7) and Chaudhuri (1998).
4. See 'Pharma industry aims high: headed for a place in the global top 10: country focus: India', *Chemical Week*, 21 November 2007, p. 38.
5. See Dr Reddy's Laboratories Ltd. Annual Reports, various years.
6. www.ranbaxy.com, accessed 15 January 2006.

7. Information obtained from various issues of *Indian Industry: A Monthly Review* for the year 2007, published by Centre for Monitoring Indian Economy, Mumbai.
8. According to Carlos Ghosn, Chief Executive of Nissan and Renault. See Yee (2008).
9. Also see a container shipment economics study conducted by Infrastructure Leasing and Financial Services Ltd. (IL&FS) and Hauer Associates. According to this study, 61 per cent of India's export/import containers are transshipped through the ports of Colombo, Singapore and Salalah (Oman). ww.thehindubusinessline.com/2005/08/30/stories/2005083000410 700.htm.
10. Speech by M.P. Pinto, 'Connecting India: Asia Pacific business summit 2006', Singapore, 12–13 April 2006. Also see 'Docking at Port India', *Financial Express*, 23 December 2005.
11. See the container shipment economics study conducted by IL&FS and Hauer Associates. www.thehindubusinessline.com/2005/08/30/stories/2005083000410700.htm.
12. http://en.wikipedia.org/wiki/Coal.
13. Data from World Bank, *World Development Indicators.*
14. Ibid.
15. On some aspects of regional industrialization in India, see Thomas (2005a).
16. According to figures compiled by Fesharaki Associates Consulting and Technical Services, Singapore. See Leahy (2007a).

REFERENCES

Acharya, K.K. (2007). 'Petroleum products: A potential regional hub', *The Hindu Survey of Indian Industry 2007.* Chennai: Kasturi and Sons Ltd.

Agali, Prasen (2007). 'Auto components: Global focus to the fore'. In *The Hindu Survey of Indian Industry 2007.* Chennai: Kasturi and Sons Ltd.

Ahluwalia, Isher Judge (1985). *Industrial Growth in India: Stagnation since the Mid-Sixties.* New Delhi: Oxford University Press.

——— (1991). *Productivity and Growth in Indian Manufacturing.* New Delhi: Oxford University Press.

Ahluwalia, Isher Judge and I.M.D. Little (1998). 'Introduction'. In Isher Judge Ahluwalia and I.M.D. Little (eds.), *India's Economic Reforms and Development: Essays for Manmohan Singh* (pp. 1–20). New Delhi: Oxford University Press.

Ahluwalia, Montek S. (2002). 'Economic Reforms in India since 1991: Has gradualism worked?', *Journal of Economic Perspectives*, 16, 3, 67–88.

Bagchi, Amiya Kumar (1970). 'Long-term constraints on India's industrial growth 1951–68'. In E.A.G. Robinson and Michael Kidron (eds), *Economic Development in South Asia* (pp. 170–98). London: Macmillan.

Balakrishnan, P. and K. Pushpangadan (1994). 'Total factor productivity in manufacturing industry: A fresh look', *Economic and Political Weekly*, 29, 31, 2028–35.

Bhagwati, Jagdish and Padma Desai (1970). *India: Planning for Industrialization.* London: Oxford University Press.

Bhagwati, Jagdish and T.N. Srinivasan (1975). *Foreign Trade Regimes and Economic Development: India.* New York: Columbia University Press.

Bhagwati, Jagdish and Sukhamoy Chakravarty (1969). 'Contributions to Indian economic analysis: a survey', *The American Economic Review*, 59, 4, 2–73.

Butala, R.S. (2007). 'Oil: Time for a bolder strategy', *The Hindu Survey of Indian Industry 2007.* Chennai: Kasturi and Sons Ltd.

Byres, T.J. (ed.) (1994). *The State and Development Planning in India.* New Delhi: Oxford University Press.

Byres, T.J. (1998). *Indian Economy: Major Debates since Independence.* New Delhi: Oxford University Press.

Centre for Monitoring Indian Economy (CMIE) (2006). *Foreign Trade and Balance of Payments.* Mumbai: CMIE.

Chakravarty, Sukhamoy (1979). 'On the question of home market and prospects for Indian growth', *Economic and Political Weekly*, 14, 30/32, 229–42.

Chandrasekhar, C.P. (1988). 'Aspects of growth and structural change in Indian industry', *Economic and Political Weekly*, 23, 45–7, 2359–70.

——— (1996). 'Explaining post-reform industrial growth', *Economic and Political Weekly*, 31, 35/37, 2537–45.

Chandrasekhar, C. P. and Jayati Ghosh (2004). *The Market That Failed: Neoliberal Economic Reforms in India.* New Delhi: LeftWord Books.

Chaudhari, Sudip (1998). 'Debates on Industrialisation'. In T.J. Byres (ed.), *Indian Economy: Major Debates since Independence.* New Delhi: Oxford University Press.

——— (2005). *The WTO and India's Pharmaceuticals Industry: Patent Protection, TRIPS, and Developing Countries.* New Delhi: Oxford University Press.

Chuang, Peck Ming (11 January 2007). 'Gateway to South India has lots to offer investors', *Business Times*, Singapore.

Grace, Cheri (2004). 'The effect of changing intellectual property on pharmaceutical industry prospects in India and China: Consideration for access to medicines'. Department for International Development (DFID) Health Systems Resource Centre, London, June. http://*www.dfidhealthrc.org/shared/publications/Issues_papers/ATM/Grace2.pdf*, accessed 28 December 2005.

Kumar, Nagesh (1995). 'Industrialisation, liberalisation and two way flows of foreign direct investments: Case of India', *Economic and Political Weekly*, 30, 50, 3228–37.

Leahy, Joe (22 November 2007a). 'Refining hub to be largest in world', *Financial Times*, London.

——— (25 November 2007b). 'India's looming power struggle', *Financial Times*, London.

Marsh, Peter (16 May 2006). 'A new manufacturing mantra: India's industrial revolution—Part I', *Financial Times*, London.

Mehta, Rajesh (1997). 'Trade policy reforms, 1991–2 to 1995–6: Their impact on external trade', *Economic and Political Weekly*, 32, 15, 779–84.

Mitra, Ashok (1977). *Terms of Trade and Class Relations*. London: Frank Cass.

Nagraj, R. (1990). 'Industrial growth: Further evidence and towards an explanation and issues', *Economic and Political Weekly*, 25, 41, 2313–32.

Nayyar, Deepak (1978). 'Industrial development in India: Some reflections on growth and stagnation', *Economic and Political Weekly*, Special Number August. Reprinted in Deepak Nayyar (ed.) (1994), *Industrial Growth and Stagnation: The Debate in India* (pp. 219–43). New Delhi: Oxford University Press.

Patnaik, Prabhat (1972). 'Disproportionality crisis and cyclical growth', *Economic and Political Weekly*, 7, 5/7, 329–36.

——— (1994). 'Critical reflections on some aspects of structural change in the Indian economy'. In T.J. Byres (ed.), *The State and Development Planning in India* (pp. 109–31). New Delhi: Oxford University Press.

Patnaik, Prabhat and C.P. Chandrasekhar (1995). 'Indian economy under structural adjustment', *Economic and Political Weekly*, 30, 47, 3001–13.

Ramanathan, S. (2007). 'Energy security policy: Areas for focussed attention', *The Hindu Survey of Indian Industry 2007*. Chennai: Kasturi and Sons Ltd.

Rao, J. Mohan (1996). 'Manufacturing productivity growth: Method and measurement', *Economic and Political Weekly*, 31, 2, 2927–36.

Rao, J. Mohan and Amitava K. Dutt (2006). 'A decade of reforms: The Indian economy in the 1990s'. In Lance Taylor (ed.), *External Liberalization in Asia, Post-Socialist Europe, and Brazil* (pp. 139–79). Oxford and New York: Oxford University Press.

Rao, N. Janardhan and Deepak Kumar (2005). 'Vallarpadam Container Terminal Project: Enabling Port Infrastructure'. Hyderabad: The ICFAI University Press. http://129.3.20.41/eps/urb/papers/0505/0505007.html accessed 25 February 2006.

Thomas, Jayan Jose (2002). 'A review of Indian manufacturing'. In Kirit Parikh and R. Radhakrishna (eds.), *India Development Report 2002* (pp. 84–101). New Delhi: Oxford University Press.

——— (2005a). 'Labour in the new economy: The Indian perspective', *Indian Journal of Labour Economics*, 48, 4, 821–35.

——— (2005b). 'Kerala's industrial backwardness: A case of path dependence in industrialization', *World Development*, 33, 5, 763–83.

——— (2007), *Kerala: Economic Growth and Investment Opportunities*, Monograph published by Institute of South Asian Studies (ISAS), Singapore.

——— (forthcoming). 'Innovation in India and China: Challenges and prospects in pharmaceuticals and biotechnology'. In Govindan Parayil and Anthony P. D'Costa (eds), *The New Asian Innovation Dynamics: China and India in Perspective.* Basingstoke: Palgrave Macmillan Ltd.

Thombre, Deepak (2007). 'Cement: Changing growth dynamics', *The Hindu Survey of Indian Industry 2007.* Chennai: Kasturi and Sons Ltd.

Timmons, Heather (18 April 2007). 'GM says it will make more vehicles and buy more parts in India', *New York Times*, New York.

Wadhera, Shyam (2007). 'Ultra mega power projects', *The Hindu Survey of Indian Industry 2007.* Chennai: Kasturi and Sons Ltd.

Wright, Robert (8 May 2007). 'Shipping: Ports await shipment of fresh investment', *Financial Times*, London.

Yee, Amy (8 May 2007a).'Power: Switching on to progress', *Financial Times*, London.

——— (5 September 2007b). 'Rule changes ease pharma pain', *Financial Times*, London.

——— (25 January 2008). 'Moving up the value chain', *Financial Times*, London.

10

Financial Sector Reforms in South Asia: A Perspective

D.M. NACHANE AND
M. SHAHIDUL ISLAM

INTRODUCTION

THE FINANCIAL sectors in the various economies of South Asia prior to the initiation of structural reforms in the 1990s constitute typical examples of what McKinnon (1973) and Shaw (1973) have dubbed as 'financial repression'. The financial repression thesis maintains that governmental restrictions on the financial sector, by reducing the quantum as well as the quality of investment, have a retarding effect on a country's economic growth prospects.

Financial liberalization is viewed as an integral component of overall liberalization, in the twin beliefs that (i) liberalization in the real sector cannot proceed satisfactorily in the absence of financial liberalization, and (ii) financial liberalization is an 'enabling condition' of faster economic growth, as it increases competition, transfer of know-how, and transparency. The process of financial liberalization is usually viewed as encompassing four dimensions:

1. *Financial Deregulation*: This refers to (i) the dismantling of existing restrictions on the prices of various types of credit instruments (the so-called P-restrictions); (ii) the removal of quantitative and other restrictions (the so-called Q-R restrictions) on banks, stock markets, insurance, pension funds, etc.; and (iii) allowing for freer movements in domestic and international flow of funds.
2. *Financial Innovation*: This encompasses both new financial instruments (swaps, credit derivatives, collateralized debt obliga-

tions, etc.) and the adoption of new practices by financial institutions.

3. *Market Making*: This is viewed as an integral part of financial liberalization, involving the promotion of greater competition among financial market participants and occasionally the setting up of new institutions and markets (primary dealers, money market mutual funds, etc.)
4. *Financial Supervision*: As financial liberalization proceeds, it is expected that the central bank (and other regulators, if any) will move away from direct intervention in financial markets to indirect measures (such as provisioning norms, capital adequacy, etc.).

Financial liberalization seems at best a double-edged weapon. On the one hand, there does seem to be a positive association between financial liberalization, savings (domestic plus foreign) investment, and growth (though the causal nexus seems to run both ways). On the other hand, financial liberalization poses several problems for monetary and fiscal policy and increases the vulnerability of developing economies to banking and currency crises.

This chapter examines the progress of financial liberalization in four South Asian economies, viz., India, Pakistan, Bangladesh, and Sri Lanka. The next section examines the pros and cons of financial liberalization. The literature on the various issues under this rubric is vast and burgeoning, so our discussion should be seen as nothing more than an overview. The third section is devoted to a study of the financial liberalization process in India, while the fourth, fifth, and sixth sections are devoted to Pakistan, Bangladesh and Sri Lanka, respectively. Where appropriate, comment is made on the adequacy of various safeguards in operation in these four economies. The final section provides some concluding remarks.

FINANCIAL LIBERALIZATION: THEORETICAL CONSIDERATIONS AND EVIDENCE

This section examines four important and interrelated aspects of the financial liberalization process in developing countries (DCs) and emerging market economies (EMEs), viz., (i) the impact on growth; (ii) likely consequences for income distribution, poverty, and inequality; (iii) the challenges posed for monetary policy; and (iv) the possibility of increased vulnerability to financial crises.

FINANCIAL LIBERALIZATION AND ECONOMIC GROWTH

The relationship between financial liberalization and economic growth has been extensively debated in the academic literature as well as in policy circles. The McKinnon-Shaw case for financial liberalization is based on the perception that financial repression (arising as a consequence of government control over important parameters of bank behavior) tends to result in low (and often negative) real interest rates and an excess demand for credit. The resultant credit rationing leads to credit allocation to favored sectors by administrative fiat rather than through the purview of a market mechanism. Following financial liberalization, real interest rates would rise to their natural levels and economic growth would result from an increased quantum of domestic savings and a rise in total factor productivity (TFP) due to an improvement in the quality of bank credit for investment purposes. Additionally, if foreign capital inflows were to be liberalized, the quantum of aggregate investible funds would rise because of the flow of foreign direct investment (FDI). To these basic considerations, several others have been added in the more recent literature. For example, Acemoglu and Zilibotti (1997) suggest that liberalization fosters specialization and efficiency in capital allocation by leading to a diversification of risk across countries. Levine (2001) and Klein and Olivei (1999) draw attention to the possibility of foreign investment improving the functioning of the domestic financial system by increasing competitive pressures and inducing adoption of international best practices. On the other hand, some authors have underscored the likely harmful effects of financial liberalization in triggering financial crises and in misdirecting the allocation of capital (see Eichengreen 2001; Saidane 2002).

The empirical literature, while undoubtedly throwing a great deal of light on the *conditioning* factors determining the way financial liberalization affects growth, has compounded the theoretical controversies. It would be pointless to attempt to survey the vast empirical evidence, but some of the more important and interesting conclusions need to be pointed out. The literature mainly seems to have addressed three sets of issues, namely:

(i) Does financial liberalization spur growth?
(ii) What are the channels through which financial liberalization is likely to affect growth?
(iii) What factors account for the cross-country differentials in the effects of financial liberalization?

On the first of these issues, the evidence can at best be described as mixed. Some studies have uncovered a beneficial association between financial liberalization and growth[1] (see among others, Bekaert et al. 2001; Bonfiglioli and Mendicino 2004; Levine 2001), others have found the effect to be detrimental (Eichengreen and Leblang 2003), while some find no association at all (Grilli and Milesi-Ferretti 1995; Kraay 2000; Rodrick 1998).

The lack of unanimity is even more evident when we turn to an examination of the likely channels via which financial liberalization impinges on growth performance. We confine ourselves to a very brief discussion of some of the important channels that have received varying shades of emphasis in the literature. Bonfliglioli (2005) finds that the main channel via which financial liberalization spurs growth is the impact on TFP. This beneficial impact on productivity derives in considerable measure from the fact of financial liberalization driving up the competition for international funds, thereby forcing capital into the most productive channels. Hubbard (1998) and Gilchrist and Himmelberg (1998) maintain that by reducing the premium on external finance and correcting capital market imperfections, financial liberalization acts as a spur to economic growth. Rajan and Zingales (1998) and Love (2000) find that financial constraints act as less of an impediment to growth in financially developed economies. Bhattacharya and Daouk (2000) show how equity market liberalization not only allows in additional foreign capital but also often results in better corporate governance at the insistence of foreign investors.

It is also being increasingly realized that cross-country studies slur over the differential effects of financial liberalization and, hence, much of the new literature is addressed to isolating the factors responsible for such differential effects. Two sets of factors have been broadly distinguished. On the one hand, there are country-specific factors such as local conditions, internal policies, size of the government, the structure of the legal system, levels of education and other human capital variables (La Porta et al. 1997) and, on the other, there are factors that are outside the control of individual countries such as the diversification potential of the local equity market for world investors, regional, trading and investing agreements (Bekaert et al. 2001). Empirical models are then constructed which try to decompose the effects of financial liberalization on growth attributable to each of these various factors separately. The general conclusion to emerge from these studies is that these factors are important conditioning variables that should figure prominently in the design of a sustainable strategy of financial liberalization.

FINANCIAL LIBERALIZATION AND EQUITY

Inequality is possibly one of the most neglected dimensions of the on-going liberalization program in South Asia. It becomes one of the crucial factors determining sustainability of financial sector reforms, because of the following three features identified by Nancy Birdsall (2005):

(i) Inequality inhibits growth in countries with weak markets and governments.

(ii) Inequality undermines good public policy, by undermining collective decision-making and social institutions critical to healthy societies (the so-called 'vanishing middle class' syndrome).

(iii) A cross-country correlation analysis reported in Birdsall (2005) indicates a low but positive correlation (0.33) between inequality (as measured by the Q5/Q1 index) and the poverty headcount ratio (US$1 per day threshold).

A distinction is usually attempted between two kinds of inequality, viz. (i) within-country inequality across regions and federal states, and (ii) within-country interpersonal inequality.

REGIONAL INEQUALITY

The study by Ahluwalia (2002) (covering 14 major states) showed a sharp increase in the Gini coefficient from 0.175 (1991–2) to 0.233 (1998–9), based on the state domestic product (SDP) per capita. Deaton and Dreze (2002) reiterate similar conclusions but based on per capita consumption across states. Singh et al. (2003), however, challenge the robustness of these conclusions by noting the sensitivity of the results to the attainment indicators used with, in particular, the use of the human development index (HDI) tempering the inequality conclusion considerably. Most of these studies seem to point to an important role for private investment and FDI in explaining the divergence of per capita SDP or consumption. However, the fact that private investment and FDI emerge robustly as important determinants of a state's economic performance could be interpreted as indirectly pointing to the importance of financial liberalization in aggravating inequalities between states (since both private investment and FDI would be strongly driven by the extent of financial infrastructure in a state). By and large, econometric evidence of financial liberalization per se leading to an aggravation of regional inequality seems to be weak.

INTERPERSONAL INEQUALITY

Perhaps this facet of inequality is the one which attracts the maximum attention of policy makers and academics alike. For India, the central features from major studies such as Mundle and Tulasidhar (1998), Ravallion and Datt (1999), and Jha (2000) are that in the 1990s, while there has been a moderate rise in both rural and urban inequality (in contrast to the two previous decades when inequality remained constant), accompanied by a decline in urban poverty, the widening of the rural-urban income gap has implied a significant increase in overall inequality. Ravallion and Datt (1999) also point to a decline in the poverty alleviation elasticity of growth.

Three explanations have been advanced to explain the re-emergence of income inequality in the 1990s, viz., (i) traditional causes (such as land concentration and unequal access to education and health); (ii) technological change (increasing wage differentials, as between skilled and unskilled workers); and (iii) domestic and external liberalization. Given the current focus of the chapter, the last of the three aspects is analyzed in greater detail. While domestic and external liberalization includes, *inter alia*, trade and investment liberalization, labor market reforms, taxation reforms and privatization, this chapter focuses on the consequences for equity of financial sector reforms.

So far as reforms in the domestic financial sector are concerned, they tend to raise the share of financial services in the GDP. A particularly puzzling feature, for which there seems to be no analytical explanation, is the relative rise in financial sector salaries as compared to salaries in the manufacturing sector (even after correcting for standard conditioning factors such as education levels, hours worked, non-salary incentives, etc.). Another factor contributing to inequality is the redistributive impact of the budget, which, in a largely deregulated financial environment, could transfer labor incomes to holders of state bonds. The liberalization of cross-border direct investment flows, as well as bank loans and portfolio investments has three potential consequences for inequality. First, there is the 'disciplining' effect on domestic policy, involving tax reforms and restraints on organized labor. Second, capital inflows are likely to lead to real exchange rate appreciation, which shifts resources to the non-tradeables sector and encourages sub-contracting and wage cuts in the tradeables sector to preserve profit margins (see Taylor 2000). Third, increasing openness of the capital account increases the vulnerability of the domestic economy to financial crises (Caprio and Klingebiel 1996). This aspect is discussed at greater length below, but it is important to note here that such crises have pronounced disequalizing effects, especially in countries with weak institutions and social safety mechanisms. Galbraith and Lu (1999), for example, document that in Latin America financial crises (1998-99) raised inequality by 73 per cent and in the Asian financial crisis (1997) inequality rose by 62 per cent. Diwan (2000) also notes the marked permanent decline in labor shares following financial crises. In the detailed study by Behrman et al. (2000) for wage inequality in Latin America, it is found that the strongest disequalizing effects seem to be attributable to domestic financial reform, capital account liberalization, and tax reforms (in that order).

MONETARY POLICY IN THE ERA OF FINANCIAL LIBERALIZATION

Prior to the onset of financial liberalization, the prevailing paradigm for monetary policy rested on the famous triad of instruments, intermediate targets/indicators, and objectives.[2] The guiding principles behind the triad were essentially threefold:

(i) The intermediate targets (usually simple-sum or Divisia monetary aggregates) were 'controllable' via the instruments (either a short-term interest rate or the monetary base) within tolerable margins of error.
(ii) The monetary targets bore a stable relationship with macroeconomic aggregates (such as output, inflation, and long-term interest rates), so that the intermediate targets served both as early warning signals of portending changes in the macro-aggregates, as well as guideposts for the intended trajectories of these aggregates.
(iii) The flexible exchange rate regime in operation in much of the developed world implied a certain independence for the pursuit of national monetary policies [in the case of the European Union (EU), this statement has to be suitably qualified].

Financial liberalization seems to have irreversibly jeopardized all three of the above premises. To facilitate the discussion we analyze the consequences of the domestic and global aspects of financial liberalization on the conduct of monetary policy in a separate fashion, though this separation is somewhat artificial.

So far as the consequences of domestic financial liberalization are concerned, as noted by Tobin (1983), the leverage exerted by the monetary authorities on non-financial variables was precisely because money bore an exogenously fixed nominal interest rate, inducing portfolio substitution between 'money' and 'nonmoney' assets in response to changes in interest rate levels. The process of financial liberalization implies a greater role for market forces in the pricing of bank deposits, whose demand thus becomes more dependent on the spread (between nominal rates on money and near money assets) than on the level of nominal rates. Since monetary authorities are much better at influencing short-term rate levels than the spread, this factor seriously erodes their ability to control monetary aggregates.[3]

Another feature, critically germane to the matter, is the blurring of the distinction between the liabilities of banks and non-bank financial institutions (NBFIs). There is in evidence a massive increase in money substitutes, although most central banks have tried to accommodate this development by continuous revisions of the definitions of money supply.

Such a development poses serious difficulties for the conduct of monetary policy, as traditionally a central bank's control over banks has been far more effective than over NBFIs.[4] Since the products offered by the banks and NBFIs overlap to varying degrees, with respect to their money-ness and other characteristics (such as interest paid), it is becoming increasingly difficult to measure or define a given monetary aggregate over time (Akhtar 1983).

It has also to be noted that the link between monetary aggregates and important macroeconomic magnitudes (especially nominal income) has been rendered tenuous (in the wake of financial liberalization) due to a host of factors such as:

(i) the blurring of the distinction between money and near-money;
(ii) the breakdown of the money demand function (ibid.; Cotula 1984);[5]
(iii) the easing of credit and liquidity constraints [owing to the emergence of variable rate lending and large-scale 'liability management' (see Goodhart 1986, 1989)]; and
(iv) the rising role of arbitrageurs in financial markets, which has introduced considerable volatility in the yield curve (Brown and Manasse 1989).

Finally, the international dimension of financial liberalization is reflected in a greater integration of global capital markets in recent years. International capital flows, always on the lookout for profitable portfolio opportunities, are quick to respond to domestic interest changes, setting up a tendency for real interest differentials between countries, to become insignificant. This implies, of course, that the pursuit of domestic monetary policy is seriously circumscribed by the unpredictable responses of global capital flows. As a matter of fact, a famous trilemma succinctly sums up the various issues involved. The trilemma in question (see Bernanke 2005 for a recent exposition) refers to the impossibility of maintaining in simultaneous operation (for a given country) all three of the following policy regimes: (i) an open capital account, (ii) a fixed exchange rate, and (iii) an independent domestic monetary policy. Of course, in practice, concepts like 'openness', 'fixity' or 'independence' are not absolute, but relative or even fuzzy. Hence the trilemma needs to be interpreted as a move in one direction having to be compensated by a countervailing move along another dimension.[5]

For the advanced economies the choice seems to be clear (at least to most academics and policy makers), viz., the benefits of capital mobility and independent monetary policy exceed whatever costs may be associated with a system of freely floating exchange rates. For the LDCs and EMEs, the picture becomes hazier. One view (see Bernanke 2005; Dornbusch and Warner 1994; Vegh 1992) maintains that the best course for such economies is to overcome their deeply ingrained 'fear of floating' and let the exchange rate float freely. A firm central bank commitment to gear monetary policy exclusively to maintaining a low and stable inflation rate would then provide the much needed 'nominal anchor' for the macroeconomic system. There are two major arguments against a 'free float' for such economies.

1. First, as Sargent (1982) has noted, a fixed (or heavily managed) exchanged rate can be a suitable guard against high inflation, and can even act as a strong brake on persistent hyperinflations.[6] A fixed exchange rate commands visibility and is more credible than a direct inflation target (both because the former is observable instantaneously unlike the inflation rate which suffers from a lag of at least a few weeks and also because its measure-

ment is noncontroversial in contrast to the several competing measures suggested for the inflation rate in the literature).

2. Second, Calvo and Reinhart (2000) have drawn attention to the low credibility of policy makers in several LDCs, which could mean that a flexible exchange rate could exhibit high volatility (both short-term and long-term). The latter is usually recognized as exports-inhibiting and could also lead to volatility in capital inflows and domestic interest rates (if these are unregulated) via the covered interest parity (Calvo 1996; Cavoli and Rajan 2006; Kwack 2003).

In the Indian context, the problems confronting monetary policy in the wake of capital inflows (and financial liberalization generally) have been discussed extensively in Rangarajan (2000), Reddy (2008), Mohan (2007), Nachane and Raje (2007), etc. There has been in evidence a general movement away from the heavily managed exchange rate system of the 1980s and early 1990s towards a more flexible policy of letting the exchange rate gravitate towards its equilibrium value (as determined by market fundamentals). Today the concerns over exchange rate management are limited to short-term considerations such as the need to smoothen out excessive volatility and foreclose the emergence of destabilizing speculative activities and are usually subsumed under the rubric of 'overall financial stability'. Even though the Reserve Bank of India (RBI) does not have a target exchange rate band in mind, it has not hesitated from proactive intervention to prevent undue nominal exchange rate intervention. However such episodes of 'leaning against the wind' are becoming increasingly less frequent now as the economy is showing signs of a robust growth and successful integration with the international economy. But, as the following quotation illustrates, India's exchange rate policy is in a state of evolution and may undergo a substantial transformation in the foreseeable future:

> . . . the Dutch disease syndrome has so far been managed by way of reserves build-up and sterilization, the former preventing excessive nominal appreciation and the latter preventing higher inflation. However the issue remains how long and to what extent such an exchange rate management strategy would work given the fact that we are faced with large and continuing capital flows

apart from strengthening current receipts on account of remittances and software exports.[7] (Mohan 2007: 13)

FINANCIAL VULNERABILITY

The theoretical case for financial liberalization derives from the textbook models of efficiency in financial markets. That such models may be inappropriate for LDCs and EMEs was forcefully pointed out in an influential paper by Diaz-Alejandro (1985). The asymmetric information literature also highlights that the behavior of financial markets is often irrational, propelled by animal spirits on successive waves of optimism and pessimism (see, for example, Greenwald et al. 1984). The Latin American crises of the 1980s, the Asian financial crisis of 1997 and the Russian crisis of 1998 provided a fresh impetus for economists to examine afresh the relationship between financial liberalization and financial crises. Two types of financial crises may be distinguished, viz., domestic (bank failures) and external (balance of payments). A growing body of empirical evidence seems to be pointing towards an inexorable link between financial liberalization and financial crises.

How does this link operate? Domestic financial liberalization opens up new avenues for risk-taking via the development of complex derivative products and securitization, which can get excessive in the face of lax supervision and irresponsible credit rating. The opening up of the capital account aggravates the risk further by permitting the opening up of huge short-term foreign exposures. Broadly speaking, the risks attendant on financial liberalization may be classified into five categories: (i) currency risk, (ii) capital flight risk, (iii) fragility risk, (iv) contagion risk, and (v) sovereignty risk. [These risks are discussed in detail in Nachane (2007).]

An increasing amount of empirical evidence seems to be strongly indicating that financial liberalization increases a country's vulnerability to both banking and currency crises. The literature has been critically evaluated and empirically tested in Wyplosz (2001), whose four main lessons are worth noting:

(i) By increasing exchange rate volatility, financial liberalization contributes towards increased financial fragility.

(ii) There is a clear boom-bust cycle for developing countries, with a peak-to-trough gap that can be as high as 20 per cent. The boom exceeds the bust in magnitude but not in duration.

(iii) Financial restrictions (including primarily restrictions on capital flows) by slowing down market reactions can make all the difference between a temporary turmoil and a long-drawn meltdown.

(iv) The consequences of a financial crisis are more pronounced in LDCs and EMEs because of poor financial supervision and regulation, corruption, opaqueness in legal provisions, etc.

Having examined the important dimensions of financial liberalization and their interface with important macroeconomic aspects, we now turn to an examination of the progress of financial reforms in South Asia.

INDIA: FINANCIAL SYSTEM AND REFORMS

Financial System

The Indian financial system comprises the Reserve Bank of India (RBI) at the apex, numerous financial intermediaries, the money market, the debt market, the foreign exchange market, and the equity market. Financial intermediaries include commercial banks, cooperative banks, and NBFIs.

The RBI plays an instrumental role in the Indian financial sector. Being the country's monetary authority, it formulates, implements, and monitors India's monetary policy. As a prime regulator and supervisor of India's financial system, it uses and prescribes broad parameters of banking operations within which the country's banking and financial system functions. The RBI supervises, among others, commercial banks, cooperative banks, development finance institutions (DFIs), and non-banking financial companies (NBFCs). Through its monetary policy, the RBI aims to secure stability in the internal and external value of the Indian currency and manages the foreign exchange market. Besides performing the traditional role of acting as the banker to the government, it also provides merchant banking services to both central and state governments.

The RBI also does other traditional central banking activities such as currency issuance and promotional functions.

Banks are the oldest form of financial intermediaries in India and they are segregated into various categories, viz., commercial banks, regional rural banks, local area banks, and cooperative banks. Commercial banks constitute the largest segment of India's financial system. India had 179 commercial banks as of September 2007. Of them, 175 were scheduled commercial banks (SCBs) and 4 were non-scheduled commercial banks (NSCBs); of the 175 SCBs, 95 are regional rural banks.[8] The country has 73,836 bank offices that are located in the rural (30,560), semi-urban (16,484), urban (13,840), and metropolitan areas (12,952). Its population to bank branch ratio is roughly 16,000:1.

One important aspect of India's commercial banking is the dominance of public sector commercial banks (PCBs) in terms of branch offices and banking operations. Of the 73,836 bank branches, nationalized banks (excluding the State Bank of India group) have the largest number of branches at 36,927, followed by regional rural banks (14,773), State Bank of India and its associates (14,465), other SCBs (7363), foreign banks (276), and NSCBs (32). The balance sheet of the SCBs shows that the share of public sector banks is much higher than private and foreign banks in terms of total assets, deposits, advances, and investments. Of all assets, the shares of the public sector banks, private sector banks, and foreign banks are 70.5, 21.5, and 8.0 per cent, respectively, as of 2007.

Cooperative banking is an integral part of India's banking system. It comprises two major components, viz., urban co-operative banks (UCBs) and rural co-operative credit institutions (RCCIs). Of them, RCCI has the largest number of branch networks and its structure is more diverse and complex than UCBs that maintain a single-tier structure. The numbers of branches at end-March 2007 for UCBs and at end-March 2006 for RCCIs were 1,813 and 107,497 respectively.

NBFIs are an important segment of India's financial system. NBFIs consist of a heterogeneous group of diverse institutions that includes development finance institutions (DFIs), insurance companies, NBFCs, primary dealers (PDs), and capital market intermediaries such as mutual funds. NBFIs offer a variety of products and services and play an important role in broadening the access of a vast section of the population to financial services. As of March 2005, there were 8 DFIs and 13,187 NBFCs in India.

The money market is another key component of India's financial system, as it is the pivot of the RBI's monetary operations. The RBI employs short-term interest rates as a key instrument of monetary policy. The abolition of ad hoc treasury bills (T-bills) and introduction of regular auctions of T-bills paved the way for the emergence of a risk-free rate, which has become a benchmark for pricing the other money market instruments (RBI 2006–7). The average daily turnover in the India's money market increased from Rs. 427 billion[9] in 1997–8 to over Rs. 888 billion in 2006–7.

The Indian debt markets are one of the largest in Asia and include the government securities (G-Secs) and corporate bond market. The G-Sec market consists of central and state government securities, zero coupon bonds, floating rate bonds, securities with embedded options, and T-bills. The corporate securities market comprises FI bonds, public sector units (PSU) bonds, and debentures/corporate bonds. The G-Sec market is the oldest and the largest component of the Indian debt market in terms of market capitalization, outstanding securities and trading volumes. The G-Sec market plays a critical role in the Indian economy as it provides the benchmark for determining the level of interest rates in the economy through the yields on the government securities. However, the market has remained predominantly a wholesale market. The corporate debt market remains undeveloped *vis-à-vis* other segments of India's financial markets. The market for debt derivatives has not yet developed appreciably; nevertheless, a market for over-the-counter (OTC) derivatives in interest rate products exists. The outstanding bond volume over gross domestic product (GDP) was roughly 35 per cent at the end of 2006.

The Indian equity market has witnessed unprecedented growth in recent years. There are a total of 23 stock exchanges in India, but the Bombay Stock Exchange (BSE) and the National Stock Exchange (NSE)[10] comprise 83 per cent of the total volumes. The Securities and Exchange Board of India (SEBI), among others, regulates the country's equity market. In the Indian stock markets, the most popular indices are the BSE Sensex (Sensitive index) and the

S&P CNX Nifty. The BSE Sensex, also called the 'BSE 30', is a widely used market index in India. It consists of the 30 largest and most actively traded stocks, representative of various sectors, on the BSE. These companies account for around one-fifth of the market capitalization of the BSE. Nifty is a well diversified 50–stock index accounting for 23 sectors of the economy. It accounted for 56.52 per cent of total market capitalization of the capital market segment of NSE as of end-March 2006.

India is already the fourth largest financial market in Asia after Tokyo, Hong Kong, and Shanghai. The NSE has become the world's second fastest growing bourse in terms of number of listed companies, while BSE has consolidated its position as the biggest bourse as of July 2007 with 1,274 and 4,853 listed companies, respectively. Over 9,000 companies are listed on the Indian stock exchanges, which are serviced by approximately 7,500 stockbrokers. The market capitalization in the Indian equity market amounted to US$1.58 trillion as at November 2007, which is higher than the country's GDP. The daily average turnover in the cash and derivative segment of the Indian equity markets were Rs. 118 billion and Rs. 298 billion, respectively (as of 2006–7).

The foreign exchange market in India has grown exponentially in recent years. Full convertibility on the current account and gradual liberalization of capital account transactions have resulted in a large increase in transactions in the foreign exchange market. Financial innovation in the foreign exchange market such as the Rupee-foreign currency swap market, introduction of additional hedging instruments (foreign currency-Rupee options), and other products like cross-currency options and forward rate agreements have transformed the market over the years. The daily average turnover in the foreign exchange market amounted to over Rs. 1,950 billion as at the end of December 2007.

FINANCIAL SECTOR REFORMS IN INDIA

Financial sector reforms in India were initiated as part of the structural adjustment programs in the early 1990s. Prior to reforms, this sector was characterized *inter alia* by administered interest rates guided by social concerns, high intermediation costs, a low base of capital, directed credit programs for priority sectors, a high degree of non-performing assets, low intensity of technologies, stringent entry barriers for new entrants, and excessive regulations. To sum up, the environment in the financial sector in these years can be best characterized by segmented and underdeveloped financial markets coupled with paucity of instruments (Reddy 2004).

With the objective of developing a market-oriented, competitive, well-diversified, and transparent financial system, the concerned authorities, in particular the RBI and the newly established SEBI, introduced a wide-range of reforms in the Indian financial sector. The first phase of these reform programs was initiated in the early 1990s. It was based on the recommendations of various committees, notably the Chakravarty Committee (1985), the first Narasimham Committee (1992),[11] and the second Narasimham Committee (1998).[12] The reform measures that have been undertaken since the 1990s in the various sub-sectors and areas of the Indian financial sector will be discussed below in some detail.

Since the early 1990s financial sector reforms have focused on (i) removing the restrictions on pricing of assets; (ii) building institutional and technological infrastructure; (iii) strengthening risk management practices; (iv) fine-tuning the market microstructure; (v) making changes in the legal framework to remove structural rigidities; and (vi) widening and deepening of the market with new participants and instruments (RBI 2006–7).

The private sector was allowed to set up banks, mutual funds, general insurance companies, etc. A reduction of public ownership in public sector banks was encouraged by allowing them to raise capital from the equity market up to 49 per cent of paid-up capital. Foreign banks were allowed to set up their offices subject to certain guidelines. The share of public sector banks in the aggregate assets of the banking sector declined from 90 per cent in 1991 to around 75 per cent in 2004. The share of wholly government-owned public sector banks sharply came down from about 90 per cent to 10 per cent of aggregate assets of all scheduled commercial banks during the same period. Since 1993, 12 new private banks have been set up. Foreign direct investment in the private sector banks is now permitted up to 74 per cent.

Consolidation in the financial sector is another important landmark of India's financial reforms. Detailed guidelines for mergers between NBFCs and banks have been laid down. During 2006–7 and the first half of 2007–8, four banks were merged/amalgamated with other banks.

Institutional and legal reforms in the financial sector have been beefed up. A Board for Financial Supervision (BFS) was constituted in 1994. Reforms in the supervisory areas have also been initiated. The RBI had instituted a state-of-the-art off-site monitoring and surveillance (OSMOS) system for banks in 1995 as part of a crisis management framework for the so-called Early Warning System (EWS). A Board for Regulation and Supervision of Payment and Settlement Systems (BPSS) was formed in 2005 to prescribe policies with regard to the regulation and supervision of all types of payment and settlement systems. Accounting standards and disclosure norms have been strengthened.

Financial sector reform is a continuing process. The RBI, SEBI, and other regulators in India are currently carrying out reforms, among others, in the area of banking sector consolidation, capital account convertibility, risk management capabilities, capital adequacy rules, Basel II[13] implementation, corporate debt market development, and other evolving areas in the capital markets.

BANKING SECTOR REFORMS AND INTEREST RATE DEREGULATION

The deregulation and rationalization of interest rates has been one of the key aspects of India's financial sector reforms. Prior to reforms, the entire structure of interest rates was complicated and had multiple layers. Following the recommendations of various committees [notably the committees headed by Chakravarty (1985), Narasimham (1991), Reddy (2001), and Rakesh Mohan (2004)], the interest rates structure in India transformed from highly administered to a market-determined one with some exceptions.[14]

The key rates in the banking sector, especially deposit and lending rates, have undergone a rapid process of liberalization. The process commenced with the consolidation of different categories of lending rates and slabs in 1992–3. Subsequently (in 1994–5), banks were released from the obligation to adhere to minimum lending rates and were granted complete freedom to fix interest rates on loans above Rs. 2 lakh. Interest rates on term deposits have been completely deregulated since 1997.

To reduce interest rate spreads, banks have been required to announce the maximum spread over the prime lending rates (PLR) since 1996. Banks were allowed to offer a fixed rate or a floating rate linked to an anchor rate on deposits. Banks have been allowed to charge fixed/floating rate loans at or above PLRs for a credit limit of over Rs. 2 lakh. The tenor linked prime lending rates (TPLRs) was introduced in 1999 to give the SCBs more operational flexibility. Banks were given the flexibility to charge interest rates without reference to the PLR with respect to certain categories of loans/credit such as discounting of bills, lending to intermediary agencies, etc. To provide further operational flexibility to commercial banks in deciding their lending rates, it was decided to make the PLR a benchmark rate. The export credit interest rates were rationalized by linking them to the ceiling rate related to the PLR. In 2003–4, in order to enhance transparency in banks' pricing of their loan products, the RBI advised banks to announce a benchmark PLR with the approval of their Boards.

Thus, the inherited administered interest rates structure stands largely liberalized except for certain specific classes of deposits [savings deposit accounts, non-resident Indian (NRI) deposits) and loans (small loans up to Rs. 2 lakh and export credit)]. Direct restraints on lending through the use of the cash reserve ratio (CRR) and the statutory liquidity ratio (SLR) by the RBI have been reduced. Attempts were made to reactivate the Bank rate by linking it to all other refinance rates in 1997 but, in recent years, seems to have fallen into disuse again. Interest rates on all money market instruments have been market-determined since 1992. In the money market, repos were introduced in 1992 for maturity up to 14 days. Subsequently repos were allowed against all Central government dated securities and T-bills (since 1997), the reverse repo facility with the RBI in government dated securities was extended to the Discount and Finance House of India (DFHI) and the Securities Trading Corporation of India (STCI) in 1995–6, access to call/

notice market was liberalized through PDs in 1997–8, and interest rate swaps (IRS) was introduced in 1998–9. The liquidity adjustment facility (LAF) was introduced in 2000 to stabilize short-term interest rates and has emerged as an important tool both for liquidity management and as a signaling device for interest rates in the overnight market.

In the money market, Zero Coupon Bonds were introduced in January 1994 and Floating Rate Bonds were introduced on 29 September 1995 with rates linked to the 364-day TB rate. Capital Indexed Bonds were floated on 29 December 1997 on a tap basis.

The RBI specifies an interest rate ceiling for NRI foreign currency deposits and NRI rupee deposits. Since July 2003, these have been linked to the London Interbank Offered Rate (LIBOR) for selected international currencies, less 25 basis points for NRIs' foreign currency deposits and plus 250 basis points for NRI rupee deposits.

All these measures have been of help in reducing interest rates over the years. The nominal deposit rate for 1–3 year maturities dropped from 12.0 per cent in 1991–2 to 4–5.25 per cent in 2004–5, and the nominal lending rate over the same period dropped from 16.0 to 10.25 per cent. The incremental CRR of 10 per cent was removed and the average CRR reduced from 15 per cent in 1991–2 to 10 per cent in 1995–6, and it was further reduced to 4.75 per cent in 2003. The SLR has been gradually reduced from a peak of 38.5 per cent to 25 per cent in 1997. Nevertheless, in recent years there has been in evidence a hardening of interest rates as well as an increasing resort to the CRR with a view to reining in inflation whenever there have been indications of the economy getting overheated.

GOVERNMENT SECURITIES MARKET

Several measures have been taken to reform the G-Sec market. The switchover to an auction-based system of issuance of government securities in the early 1990s was a major step towards the development of the G-Sec market. Administered interest rates on G-Secs were replaced by an auction system for price discovery. Automatic monetization of the government deficit has been phased out. As a result, the RBI was prohibited from subscribing to primary issuance of G-Secs from April 2006. 364-day T-Bills replaced the 182-day T-bills in 1992–3 and the auction of the 91-day T-bills commenced from 1993. The primary dealer (PD) system was introduced in 1996 to facilitate the development of the G-Sec market. The Delivery *versus* Payment (DvP) system was introduced in 1995. Repo and reverse repo were launched as tools of short-term liquidity adjustment. The introduction of the LAF in 2000 has been one of the most important recent changes in the money market. Zero Coupon Bonds, Floating Rate Bonds, and Capital Indexed Bonds were issued, and exchange traded interest rate, futures and OTC interest rate derivatives like IRS and forward rate agreements (FRAs) were introduced. Foreign Institutional Investors (FIIs) are allowed to invest in G-Secs subject to certain limits. The Negotiated Dealing System-Order Matching (NDSOM) system in the G-Sec market was introduced in August 2005.

A major development in the Indian money market is the establishment of the Clearing Corporation of India Limited (CCIL) which was set up in April 2001. It provides exclusive clearing and settlement for transactions in money, G-Secs, and foreign exchange. The CCIL introduced a new product, Collateralized Borrowing and Lending Obligations (CBLO) in 2003 with the objective of providing an alternative avenue for managing short-term liquidity for market players who have been restricted and/or are being phased out of the call market. The operationalization of the CCIL has ensured guaranteed settlement of trades and has, therefore, imparted considerable stability to the G-Sec market (RBI 2006–7).

CORPORATE DEBT MARKET

The corporate debt market in India has not developed in tandem with other segments of its financial sector. The fixed income market (both the primary and the secondary markets) in India is dominated by government securities, and the size of the corporate bond segment is only 14 per cent of the total debt market. Nevertheless, the reform process in the corporate bond market was initiated in the early 1990s. A major stimulus to the development of the corporate bond market has been the withering away of the development banks that were traditionally a major source of external long-term finance for industrial projects (Patil 2005).

In the primary market, the Public Sector Undertakings (PSUs) have been issuing bonds since 1985–6 which are subscribed to mainly by large investors, including banks. The presence of retail investors in the market is low. Nevertheless, falling interest rates have encouraged the corporate sector to reduce their heavy reliance on the banking sector. Bond issuance by the corporate houses has increased steadily, though there have been some fluctuations in recent years. Bond issuers generally prefer private placement due to its flexibility and operational ease. The financial institutions furnish about 80 per cent of the funding resources, whereas other private corporate entities account for the remaining 20 per cent. SEBI has mandated that all trading of corporate bonds must proceed through the order-matching screens of the stock exchanges. The RBI has instructed banks and PDs that their investments in unlisted corporate bonds should not exceed 10 per cent of their investment portfolio of non-SLR securities. In the secondary debt market, activity in the corporate bonds segment is very low as the market is highly dominated by a limited number of players, being a pure OTC market.

However, all these reforms did not deliver the expected results. As Reddy (2007c) has observed, 'while primary issuances have been significant, most of these were accounted for by public sector institutions and were issues on a private placement basis to institutional investors. The secondary market, therefore, has not developed commensurately and market liquidity has been an issue.' (Reddy 2007c: 2166).

With a view to examining the entire gamut of issues involved in developing a sound corporate debt market, the Government of India (GOI) constituted a high-powered committee (the Patil Committee) in 2005. The committee identified some areas for the concerned authorities to focus on if the market was to be made active and vibrant. The committee made several useful suggestions. First, it highlighted the importance of rationalization of stamp duty across the country. Second, the committee was of the opinion that for improving liquidity in the market, there was an urgent need to limit the fragmentation of issues. Third, the committee felt that the development of a centralized counter-party to the trades in the secondary market, and an appropriate hedging mechanism were imperative for developing an active corporate bond market. Fourth, the committee drew attention to the fact of trading and issuance taking place in a totally non-standardized way and called for a single standardized method for interest day count conventions.

The Patil Committee also highlighted that in order to develop a sound primary corporate debt market there is a need for enhancement of the issuer and investor base, development of a market maker, consolidation of privately placed bonds and development of a bond primary issuance database. For development of the secondary market, the Committee also recommended some measures, notably in the areas of the trade reporting system, clearing and settlement system, bond issuance, and securitization.

The RBI, SEBI, and the Government of India have accepted these recommendations and many of them are now in different phases of implementation.

EQUITY MARKET

India has had a long history of stock trading, dating back to 1875, with the Indian equity market being one of the oldest in Asia. However, it remained underdeveloped until the late 1980s. The reform process in the Indian securities market began with the establishment of SEBI in 1988, which became a fully autonomous body in 1992.[15] Subsequently, the equity market in India underwent a series of reforms in the wake of the infamous securities scam (Harshad Mehta) of April 1992. The SEBI Act, 1992 was enacted to empower SEBI with statutory powers for protecting the interests of investors in securities, and for promoting and regulating the securities market. Apart from the SEBI Act, 1992, three major legislations governing the securities market are the Company Act, 1956 (revised 2004), the Securities Contracts (Regulation) Act,

1956 (SCRA), and the Depositories Act, 1996. The government's control over the issue of capital, pricing of issues, fixing of premia and rates of interest on debentures, etc., effectively ceased with the removal of the Capital Issues (Control) Act, 1947 in May 1992.

The NSE was established during the early 1990s. With a view to providing efficiency, transparency, and liquidity, NSE introduced a nation-wide online fully-automated screen-based trading system (SBTS). To assist market participants to manage risks better through hedging, speculation, and arbitrage, SC(R)A was amended in 1995 to lift the ban on options in securities. The demutualization process has been initiated where ownership, management, and trading are with three different sets of people. To reduce settlement risk, the Depositories Act, 1996 was passed to provide for the establishment of depositories in securities with the objective of ensuring free transferability of securities with speed and accuracy. To avoid any kind of market failure, the regulators and the exchanges have developed a sophisticated risk management system. To integrate the Indian exchanges with other global markets Indian companies have been permitted to raise resources from abroad through the issue of American Deposit Receipts (ADRs), Global Depository Receipts (GDRs), Foreign Currency Convertible Bonds (FCCBs), and External Commercial Borrowings (ECBs). Moreover, FIIs are allowed to invest in all types of securities, including G-Secs. Such investments are entitled to full convertibility on the capital account. The Indian Stock Exchanges are also permitted to set up trading terminals abroad, which are now globally accessible through the Internet.

Another important milestone in India's equity market reforms has been the development of the derivative markets. Reforms of the derivative markets took place based on various recommendations, principally those of the Dr L.C. Gupta Committee (1996) report. The trading of derivatives products started in India in 2000, and a variety of products are traded now at the NSE and the BSE.[16] This segment of the equity market has witnessed substantial product innovations since its inception. The trading in BSE Sensex options commenced in June 2001 and the trading in options on individual securities commenced in July 2001. Futures contracts on individual stocks were launched in November 2001. The derivatives trading on NSE commenced with S&P CNX Nifty Index futures in 12 scrips in 2000. The trading in index options commenced on 4 June 2001 and trading in options on individual securities commenced on 2 July 2001. Single stock futures were launched on 9 November 2001.[17] Trading in interest rate derivative instruments was approved by the RBI and the SEBI in 2003. Another notable development is the NSE's introduction (in 2003) of trading in futures contracts on 91-day Notional T-Bills.

FOREIGN EXCHANGE MARKET

The Indian foreign exchange market is ahead of many other segments of India's financial system in terms of product innovation. Reforms in the foreign exchange market have been undertaken to transform the market from being a heavily controlled one to a market-driven one. India has moved gradually from a fixed exchange rate to a market-based exchange rate system. The Rupee, India's currency unit, was made convertible on the current account in August 1994. The Indian exchange rate regime gradually moved from a single currency fixed-exchange rate system to fixing the value of the Rupee against a basket of currencies to a market-determined floating exchange rate regime. The exchange rate regime is officially described as market determined, with no target rate, but the RBI reserves the right to intervene in the market to resist speculative attacks and to guide the exchange rate in the directions of 'appropriate' competitiveness.

The reform measures in the foreign exchange market were further augmented based on the recommendations of the Sodhani Committee (1994) report, which suggested relaxing the regulations with a view to vitalizing the foreign exchange market. With the replacement of the Foreign Exchange Regulation Act (FERA) by the market-friendly Foreign Exchange Management Act (FEMA), 1999, the RBI delegated powers to authorized dealers to release foreign exchange for a variety of purposes. Capital account transactions were also liberalized in a calibrated manner, notably following the Tarapore Committee reports.[18] The financial liberalization in the early 1990s provided the economic rationale for the introduction of foreign exchange (FX) derivatives. The facility of hedging transaction risks through foreign currency rupee options was introduced by the RBI with effect from 7 July 2003. Authorized dealers have been permitted to use innovative products like cross-currency options, interest rate and currency swaps, cap/collars, and FRAs in the international forex market. OTC interest rate derivatives, such as Interest Rate Swaps (IRSs) and Forward Rate Agreements (FRAs) were introduced. Exchange traded interest rate derivatives (IRDs) was introduced in 2003 to enable better risk management in the Indian market.

COMMODITY DERIVATIVES MARKET

India had a flourishing commodity derivatives market in the early twentieth century. However, in the early years of Independence a feeling gained ground that commodity derivatives fuelled excessive speculation, and accordingly, commodity options trading and cash settlement of commodity futures were banned in 1952. For the next 50 years a commodity derivatives market in India was virtually non-existent, except for some minuscule OTC operations. The situation, however, changed drastically in 2003 with the emergence of three important national electronic exchanges, viz., the Multi-Commodity Exchange of India Ltd. (MCX), National Multi-Commodity and Derivatives Exchange of India Ltd. (NCDEX), and National Multi-Commodity Exchange of India Ltd., Ahmedabad (NMCE). In addition, there are 21 regional commodity exchanges. Currently, commodity futures (but not options) are permitted in 108 commodities, and the volume of trading has already crossed the US$1 trillion mark. The MCX offers futures trading in bullion, ferrous and non-ferrous metals, pulses, oils and oilseeds, crude oil, spices and several other agricultural commodities, whereas the NCDEX engages in futures trading of commodities such as wheat, cashew, castor seed, chana, chilli, coffee, cotton, cotton seed oilcakes, gold, and silver. The regulation of commodity futures is governed by the Forward Contracts (Regulation) Act, 1952, which envisages a two-tier system of regulation with the Forward Markets Commission (FMC) providing overall supervision on a day-to-day basis, but the ultimate regulatory power residing with the Ministry of Consumer Affairs, Food and Public Distribution, Government of India (see Ahuja 2006).

MARKET MAKING

Market Making is viewed as an integral part of financial liberalization, involving the promotion of greater competition among financial market participants and occasionally the setting up of new institutions and markets. Primary dealers (PDs) play an important role in making markets for financial products, especially in the primary stage of a country's financial development. Nevertheless, cross-country experiences show that the role of market makers does not always decline as markets mature.

The RBI introduced the system of PDs[19] in the G-Sec Market in 1995 with the following objectives:

(i) to strengthen the infrastructure in the government securities market in order to make it vibrant, liquid, and broad based;
(ii) to ensure development of underwriting and market making capabilities for government securities outside the RBI so that the latter will gradually shed these functions;
(iii) to improve the secondary market trading system, which would contribute to price discovery, and enhanced liquidity and turnover, besides encouraging voluntary holding of government securities amongst a wider investor base; and
(iv) to make PDs an effective conduit for conducting open market operations (RBI 2007).

Banks that do not have a partly or wholly-owned subsidiary undertaking PD business and which fulfill some criteria [Minimum net owned funds (NOF) of Rs.1,000 crore, minimum Capital to Risk-Weighted Assets Ratio (CRAR) of 9 per cent, and net NPAs of less than 3 per cent of their assets and a profit-making record for the last three years] are eligible to apply for a PD licence.

PD obligations are, among others, giving annual bidding commitment, underwriting primary issuances and offering two-way quotes, achieving prescribed success ratios for dated securities and T-bills and realizing a minimum turnover in government securities. The RBI takes into account both the bidding commitment and the performance of PDs in the primary and secondary markets. The RBI provides liquidity support to the PDs through LAF against collateral of government securities and through repo operations. They are also permitted to borrow and lend in the Call Money market and to trade in all money market instruments. They are granted favored access to open-market operations and also allowed to underwrite for a commission the offerings of dated government securities.

Moreover, currently PDs are permitted to operate in the stock and derivative markets. In June 2003, they were allowed to transact in exchange traded interest rate futures in order to make available a wide array of products for banks to hedge their interest rate risk effectively. While earlier PDs were allowed to hold trading as well as hedging positions in interest rate futures (IRFs), banks were allowed only to hedge their underlying government securities in the 'available for sale' (AFS)/'held for trading' (HFT) category portfolio through IRFs. In order to broad-base the PD system, the permitted structure of PD business was expanded in 2006–7 to include banks.

The periodic supervisory returns being submitted by PDs were rationalized and simplified. A new quarterly return (PDR-IV) on certain balance sheet and profit and loss (P&L) indicators was introduced from 31 March 2004. Revised 'capital adequacy standards and risk management guidelines' for PDs were issued in January 2004.

The share of turnover of PDs in outright market for G-Secs has declined in recent years, reflecting increased participation by banks. There were 17 PDs in operation in India at the end of 2006. However, due to interest rate reversal, all the PDs except one made losses in the previous financial year. The RBI set up a committee that recommended that PDs may be merged with their parent banks. Consequently, most of the PDs floated by banks merged with parent banks and there are only eight standalone PDs in India today.

TECHNOLOGICAL UPGRADING

An integral dimension of financial liberalization is the increasing role of technology, especially information technology. Reflecting this thrust, the RBI has consistently encouraged banks to adopt advanced technologies to enhance their global competitiveness with a special focus on information technology in order to keep pace with the rapid strides occurring in banking systems worldwide such as branch-banking, e-banking, off-site ATMs, anywhere banking, credit cards, debit cards and smart cards. Several initiatives have been launched in this connection notably Society for Worldwide Interbrain Financial Telecommunication (SWIFT), Real Time Gross Settlement System (RTGS), and Automated Clearing House (ACH) (Sharma 2004). Additionally, considering that banks have been moving away from 'plain vanilla' lending to commercial and industrial lending, customers now have more options in terms of cash management, channel financing, and foreign currency loans. Product innovations and process re-engineering are being designed to meet these newer customer requirements that ultimately reduce costs and improve efficiency.

CURRENT AND CAPITAL ACCOUNT LIBERALIZATION

India has made substantial progress in terms of current and capital account convertibility. The current account was made convertible in August 1994 by accepting Article VIII of the International Monetary Fund (IMF). Consequently, the rupee has been convertible on the current account. The capital account has been witnessing gradual liberalization; however, there is a strong debate in India whether the capital account should be fully convertible.

In 1997, a committee was set up for charting a course towards full capital account convertibility under the Chairmanship of S.S. Tarapore (henceforth Tarapore I). Tarapore I adopted a threefold approach. First, it enumerated the major kinds of restrictions that were in force in India for capital account transactions. For this purpose, it grouped these restrictions according to the sector that they were applied to, viz., (i) corporates (domestic/resident), (ii) corporates (foreign/non-resident), (iii) banks (domestic/resident) (iv) banks (foreign/nonresident) (v) NBFIs (resident), (vi) NBFIs (non-resident) (or what are now popularly called foreign institutional investors), (vii) individual (residents), (viii) individuals (non-residents), and (ix) financial markets. Second, the committee laid down a framework for the progressive dismantling of each of these restrictions over a short span of three years (that is, by April 2000). Third, it laid down a series of macroeconomic conditions that needed to be fulfilled before capital account convertibility was finally attained.[20] Nevertheless, the Asian financial crisis cast the entire issue of capital account liberalization in a fresh perspective. As Goldstein (1998), Singh (2002), and Bhalla and Nachane (2001) have noted, the extent of capital account liberalization made a big difference to the incidence of the crisis on individual countries, and countries like India and China managed to avoid the worst consequences of the crisis mainly because their capital accounts still had a number of restrictions in place. The recommendations of Tarapore I had been shelved for a few years subsequent to the crisis.

However, following the high growth phase of the past few years, Indian policy makers once again revived the capital account convertibility issue. A new committee was set up once again under the Chairmanship of S.S. Tarapore in March 2006 (henceforth Tarapore II). The recommendations of Tarapore II are discussed in some detail in Nachane (2007). Tarapore II essentially marked a follow-up to Tarapore I. It began by reviewing the extent to which the earlier Committee's recommendations had been actually implemented. It then laid down a detailed timeframe for achieving full convertibility and also drew up a new set of safety guidelines. As discussed in Nachane (ibid.), the major recommendations of Tarapore I have been either followed or even exceeded. So, one may say that there has already been a 'creeping movement' in the direction of capital account convertibility. However, Tarapore II is far more ambitious in the scope of its recommendations, and intends to take India quite a bit further along the road to full (or almost full) capital account convertibility. This it proposed to do progressively in three phases: Phase I (2006–7), Phase II (2007–9) and, Phase III (2009–11). The major recommendations of Tarapore II are set out below:

1. Removal of overall ECB ceiling of US$22 billion and removal of restrictions on end-use of ECBs.
2. Limits on corporate investments abroad to be doubled from the current limit of 200 per cent of net worth.
3. Banks to be allowed to borrow overseas up to 50 per cent of paid-up capital and reserves in Phase I, which amount can be raised to 75 per cent in Phase II and 100 per cent in Phase III.
4. As against the current limit of US$25,000, individuals to be allowed to remit abroad (annually) up to US$50,000 in Phase I, US$100,000 in Phase II and US$200,000 in Phase III.
5. Currently only NRIs are allowed to invest in companies listed on Indian stock exchanges. The Committee recommended extension of this facility to all non-residents (through SEBI-registered entities, such as mutual funds and other portfolio management schemes).
6. FIIs to be prohibited from raising money through Participatory Notes (PNs).

Except for the issue of PNs which seems to be still under discussion, most of the other recommendations have already been accepted. For example in September 2007, the limit on direct investment abroad was raised to 300 per cent of net worth (for companies incorporated in India). Similarly in October 2007, the annual limit on individual remittances was raised to US$200,000 in line with the recommendations of Tarapore II.

FINANCIAL SUPERVISION AND REGULATION

One feature which sometimes escapes proponents of financial sector reforms is that a precondition for the success of reforms is a strengthened and highly effective system of supervision and a reorientation of regulation. One of the strengths of the Indian financial reforms story has been the emphasis placed by the RBI and other concerned authorities on these aspects right since the inception of reforms. This emphasis seems specially justified in the aftermath of the bank runs experienced in several EMEs in the 1980s and during the Asian financial crisis in 1997–8. To supervise the country's financial sector the Board for Financial Supervision (BFS) was set up in 1994. It consists of a four-pronged approach that includes a restructuring system of inspection, setting up of off-site surveillance, enhancing the role of external auditors, and strengthening corporate governance, internal controls, and audit procedures. The Department of Supervision was split into the Department of Banking Supervision (DBS) and Department of Non-Banking Supervision (DNBS) in 1997. A new approach was adopted for the on-site inspection of banks based on the Capital adequacy, Asset quality, Management, Earnings appraisal, Liquidity and Systems and controls (CAMELS) model. A rating system for domestic and foreign banks based on the international CAMELS model combining financial management and systems and control elements was introduced in 1998. An off-site monitoring system for surveillance over banks was set up by the RBI in 1996.

New draft guidelines on restructuring/rescheduling were issued in June 2007 with a view to aligning the existing guidelines on restructuring of advances with the provisions under the revised corporate debt restructuring mechanism. To develop a healthy secondary market for NPAs, guidelines on sale/purchase of NPAs were issued in July 2005. The issue was reviewed in response to concerns expressed by banks and the guidelines were partly modified in May 2007.

To minimize the adverse impact of fraud activities on the financial system, a Fraud Monitoring Cell (FrMC) was instituted in June 2004 for centralized monitoring of frauds detected in entities regulated by the RBI.

The RBI endorsed the Narasimham Committee I's[21] recommendations on endorsing internationally accepted norms for capital adequacy standards, developed by the Basel Committee on Banking Supervision (BCBS). The BCBS initiated Basel I norms in 1988, which can be considered as the first global initiative towards risk-weighted capital adequacy norms. The BCBS framework on capital adequacy in India was introduced in 1992. As a result, all scheduled commercial banks were required to maintain a CRAR of 8 per cent in a phased manner, which was revised to 9 per cent from 2000 onwards. Basel I, though a major step forward in capital regulation, had serious shortcomings that became increasingly evident with time. Subsequently, the Basel committee proposed a New Capital Adequacy Framework in June 1999 incorporating three major elements or pillars.[22] After the first proposal of June 1999, there were two subsequent consultative packages, released in 2001 and 2003. Finally, on 26 June 2004 the central bank governors of the G-10 countries endorsed the revised framework for the 'International Convergence of Capital Measurement and Capital Standards', commonly known as the new Basel Capital Accord or 'Basel II'.

The RBI's reaction to the Basel accord has been discussed at some length in Nachane et al. (2005). First, while the RBI agreed with the view that the focus of the New Accord might be primarily on internationally active banks, it contended that after a period of time, all 'significant' banks would be expected to adhere to it. The RBI recognized that even this simplified approach is likely to be more extensive and complex than the 1988 Accord, and hence recommended that the New Accord may be applied in phases.

Second, a basic difference of view between the New Accord and the RBI lies in the relative roles of supervisors *vis-à-vis* external rating agencies. The RBI (2001) categorically reiterates that External Credit Assessment Institutions should not be assigned the direct responsibility for risk assessment of banking book assets. Furthermore, the RBI pointed out that unsolicited ratings by external agencies are generally superficial, and could lead to a potential trade-off between competition and quality in the rating industry. Consequently, it favored the view that preferential risk weights should be assigned only on the basis of solicited ratings. In a similar spirit, the RBI pointed out that the risk weighting of banks should be de-linked from the credit rating of the sovereign in which these banks are incorporated.

The RBI has initiated several measures to implement certain important components of the Basel Accord as well as to beef up the risk management practices in banks and other financial institutions. It issued guidelines on the Asset Liability Management (ALM) system in 1999, which covered interest rate risk and liquidity risk measurement/reporting framework and prudential limits. The Risk Based Supervision (RBS) process was introduced from April 2003.

To assist banks in setting up appropriate risk management frameworks, guidelines on credit risk management, market risk management, and risk-based internal audit were issued. The Risk Profile Template (RPT) for use in commercial banks was forwarded to all banks. Further, guidelines on country risk management and provisioning have been issued to banks. These guidelines require banks to formulate appropriate Country Risk Management (CRM) policies. In tandem with these developments, the third pillar of the New Accord is being strengthened by broadening the range of disclosures of information that banks have to disclose as part of 'Notes on Accounts' to their balance sheet. As per the guidelines issued in June 2007, banks were required to put in place appropriate stress test policies and the relevant stress test framework for the various risk factors by 30 September 2007. Banks were obliged to ensure that their formal stress testing frameworks are in operation from 31 March 2008.

The final guidelines on the revised capital adequacy framework were issued to banks in India in 2007. According to the guidelines, internationally active Indian banks were expected to migrate to Basel II with effect from March 2008 and other commercial banks (excluding local area banks and regional rural banks) advised to migrate to the new capital accord by March 2009. It has been decided that banks in India will initially adopt the Standardized Approach[23] for credit risk and the Basic Indicator Approach[24] for operational risk. After adequate skills are developed, at both bank and supervisory levels, some banks may be allowed to migrate to the Internal Ratings Based (IRB) Approach[25] subject to the specific approval of the RBI.[26]

The RBI advised a 'three track' approach for Basel compliance to the Indian banks. The commercial banks are Basel I-compliant with respect to credit and market risks; the urban cooperative banks maintain capital for credit risk as per Basel I and for market risk through surrogate charges; and the rural banks have capital adequacy norms that are not on par with the Basel norms (Leeladhar 2006; Reddy 2006).

Banks have also been advised to formulate and operationalize the Capital Adequacy Assessment Process (CAAP) as required under

Pillar II of the New Framework. The RBI has also placed emphasis on the post-Basel II migration impacts. In order to assess the impact of Basel II adoption in various jurisdictions and re-calibrate the proposals, the BCBS is currently undertaking the Fifth Quantitative Impact Study (QIS 5). India will be participating in the study, and has selected 11 banks that form a representative sample for this purpose (Leeladhar 2006). A parallel run of the revised framework is being conducted by the banks, which will allow them to streamline their systems and strategies so as to ensure a smooth transition to Basel II.

To assess the state of India's financial stability, a Committee on Financial Sector Assessment (CFSA) was constituted by the Government of India in 2006 under the Chairmanship of Rakesh Mohan. The assessment is based on three mutually reinforcing pillars, viz., (i) financial stability assessment and stress testing; (ii) legal, infrastructural, and market development issues; and (iii) assessment of the status and progress in implementation of international financial standards and codes. The CFSA completed its assessment by the end of 2008.

PAKISTAN: FINANCIAL SYSTEM AND REFORMS

FINANCIAL SYSTEM

The financial system in Pakistan comprises the State Bank of Pakistan (SBP) at the apex, various financial intermediaries, the money market, and the capital market. Financial intermediaries include commercial banks and NBFIs. Being the country's central bank, the SBP regulates and supervises Pakistan's banking sector along with all NBFIs, except for *Mudarabahs*[27] and leasing companies. It conducts monetary policy, and manages public debt and foreign exchanges. It is also the banker to the government and performs other traditional central banking functions.

Banks, with a share of 72 per cent in total assets, dominate the asset base of Pakistan's financial sector. Currently, there are 47 scheduled banks, six DFIs, and two microfinance banks (MFBs) operating in Pakistan. The banking system comprises four public sector commercial banks, four specialized banks, 26 domestic private banks, and 13 foreign banks.[28] As of June 2007, there were 7,755 bank offices in Pakistan. In terms of deposits, advances, and investments, domestic private banks predominate over public sector and other banks. Currently, 80 per cent of the banking assets are held by private sector banks.

NBFIs are classified into eight different groups of institutions, namely DFIs, investment banks, leasing companies, mutual funds, housing finance companies, discount houses, *mudarabahs*, and venture capital companies. The DFIs hold more than 30 per cent of the overall assets of NBFIs.

FINANCIAL SECTOR REFORMS IN PAKISTAN

As in many developing countries, the financial sector in Pakistan in the pre-reform era was characterized by the typical features of a highly regulated system, such as administered interest rates, directed and subsidized credit, dominance of nationalized commercial banks as financial intermediaries, and excessive regulations. The capital market was thin with low capitalization and rampant insider trading. The foreign exchange market was probably the most controlled one among all financial segments.

The financial sector restructuring programs in Pakistan started in the late 1980s with the twin objectives of strengthening the existing financial institutions, on the one hand, and developing an efficient financial system, on the other. The IMF and the World Bank provided the technical and financial assistance to carry forward the reforms.[29] Later the Asian Development Bank (ADB) joined the reform bandwagon by providing a loan for the development of Pakistan's capital market.[30]

BANKING SECTOR REFORMS AND INTEREST RATE DEREGULATION

The reform programs focused on, *inter alia*, privatization of public sector banks, licensing to new commercial banks, merger and acquisitions of various financial institutions, rationalization of interest rate structure, non-performing loan (NPL) resolution, monetary and credit management, current and capital account liberalization, capital market development, and autonomy of the SBP and its restructuring.

By an amendment to the State Bank of Pakistan Act, 1956, the SBP was granted autonomy in February 1994. The SBP now enjoys complete independence in matters such as prescribing liquidity ratios for banks and fixing their cash reserves. The SBP's autonomy was further strengthened in 1997 by promulgation of three ordinances.

Privatization of nationalized commercial banks was started in the early 1990s. State-owned banks' domination in the banking sector was targeted to be reduced from almost 100 per cent in 1991 to 20 per cent by 2003. Consequently, four major state-owned banks[31] have been de-nationalized. The government relaxed the entry barrier on private and foreign banks in 1991. Major state-owned commercial banks and DFIs were re-structured and downsized in terms of branches and employees. In order to reduce the dependency on the banking sector for credit, a number of NBFIs were granted entry and allowed to conduct lending operations.

To solve the problem of NPL, a multi-track strategy was adopted which included creation of new institutions and enactment of new laws. As a result, the Corporate and Industrial Restructuring Corporation (CIRC) and Committee on Revival of Sick Industrial Units (CRSIU) were set up. The Financial Institutions (Recovery of Finance) Ordinance, 2001 was promulgated and amendments were made to the Banking Companies Ordinance, 1962.

The SBP liberalized the Branch Licensing Policy (BLP) in 2002 which led to the growth of small and medium-sized banks. However, the rapid growth in private commercial banks and NBFIs resulted in balance-sheet strains and other administrative problems for many financial intermediaries. Consequently, the SBP and other concerned regulatory agencies undertook several reform measures to consolidate the sector. To accelerate the mergers and acquisitions (M&A) activities, the SBP increased the capital requirements from Rs 500 million[32] in 2001 to Rs 3 billion by end of 2005, which is expected to increase further to Rs 6 billion in December 2009. The Banking Companies Ordinance, 1962 was amended to facilitate the merger of banks and NBFCs. Both banks and NBFIs have witnessed around 50 cases of financial consolidation/M&A since 2000.

The interest rate deregulation process in Pakistan started in the 1990s. Restrictions on banks' maximum lending rates (except on concessionary finance schemes) were removed in 1995. Since 26 July 1997, the minimum lending rate has also been abolished. Banks and other financial institutions have been allowed to determine their own deposit rates since June 1998. The credit ceiling as an instrument of credit control was abolished in 1992 and it was replaced by the credit deposit ratio (CDR). Subsequently, the CDR was removed in 1995. The lending rates which remained stagnant at around 11 per cent during 1985–92 increased to 13.6 per cent in 2000–1. However, the average deposit rate moved in the opposite direction, which resulted in higher interest rate spreads. The increase in spreads is attributable to several factors, chief among which are the gradual increase in NPLs and high administrative cost of financial institutions.

The banking sector has also witnessed a limited degree of product innovation in the wake of financial liberalization, though most of the innovations have been confined to technological developments.

CAPITAL MARKET REFORMS

Pakistan has made some progress in the direction of capital market reforms since the 1990s. The regulatory, legal, and institutional frameworks for the capital market have been beefed up, a large number of state-owned institutions have been privatized, and the financial health of many ailing financial institutions has been restored. Nevertheless, the role of the capital market in Pakistan is still substantially lower than its potential. Several reform measures have been initiated since the 1990s under the auspices of the government and the ADB, among others. The Capital Market Development Program (CMDP) was initiated in 1997 under an ADB loan. The program resulted in several fresh initiatives, including the establishment of the Securities and Exchange Commission of Pakistan (SECP), a modernized infrastructure for stock exchanges, full operationalization of an automated trading and a central depository system, establishment of a national clearing and settlement system, liberalization of mutual fund investment policies and harmonization of taxation for private and state-owned mutual funds, barring of institutional investment in National Savings Schemes (NSS) instruments to support corporate bond market development, and establishment of basic regulatory frameworks for insurance, leasing, and asset backed securities (ADB 2007). The reform measures undertaken in the corporate debt and the equity market are discussed below in some detail.

GOVERNMENT SECURITIES MARKET

The fixed income securities market in Pakistan includes both debt and debt-like securities issued by the government, statutory corporations, and corporate entities. The share of government securities in total bond issuance is much higher than that of the corporate sector. More than 92 per cent of debt securities are sovereign bonds in the form of long-term Pakistan Investment Bonds (PIBs) or as short-term T-bills. The PIBs remain the longest tenor sovereign bonds which provide the benchmark yield curve for private issuances. National Savings Schemes provide risk-free investment options to retail and institutional investors. The size of the fixed-income market in Pakistan was US$32,410 million at the end of 2006, which was equivalent to 25.2 per cent of the country's GDP.

In the G-Sec market, a full-fledged auctioning system of T-bills was introduced in March 1991, and the system of *ad hoc* T-bills was abolished. In order to create a long-term yield curve of government securities and to provide benchmark pricing for private sector securities, the SBP launched the Pakistan Investment Bond (PIB) in December 2000, available in maturities of 5–10 years. PIBs with 15-year and 20-year maturity were introduced in January 2004.

CORPORATE BOND MARKET

The corporate bond market in Pakistan exists in the form of Term Finance Certificates (TFCs). TFCs are based on legislation enacted in 1984, which authorized the issuance of redeemable capital securities. As a debt instrument, the TFC is different from the traditional corporate bond to some extent, as it was specifically designed to comply with Sharia law. The key difference is that the TFC substitutes the words 'expected profit rate' for 'interest rate.' (Leonardo 2000). Commercial and investment banks are the two main investors in private sector TFCs. In 1997, listed TFCs became 'approved securities' for the purpose of meeting statutory liquidity requirement (SLR) for NBFIs.

Like many developing markets, the corporate debt market in Pakistan remains underdeveloped in comparison to other segments of the financial sector. To develop a vibrant corporate bond market, several initiatives have been launched by the concerned authorities. Development of the corporate bond market has been constrained *inter alia* by the distortions caused by the high yields on NSS instruments. To remove the anomalies, the rates on NSS have been linked with the yields on market-based instruments. Institutional investors have been barred from investment in NSS since March 2000. To increase the investor base, investment restrictions on institutional investors have progressively been liberalized.

Nevertheless, the market remained undeveloped and to identify impediments to the development of the debt market, a working group on 'Debt Market and Commercial Paper' was formed in 2005 comprising representatives from SBP and SECP, among others. Various recommendations of the working group regarding reduction in initial listing fee for debt instruments, reduction in stamp duty on various debt instruments, and withholding tax on profits of TFCs have already been implemented. The debt market is currently undergoing a second phase of reform under the Second Generation Capital Market Reform Program sponsored by the ADB.

EQUITY MARKET

The equity market in Pakistan has undergone significant reforms in recent years. The reform programs have focused on the areas of *inter alia* market development, investor's protection, risk management, and governance and transparency. The SECP regulates the equity market. There are three mutual stock exchanges of which the Karachi Stock Exchange (KSE), founded in 1947, is Pakistan's largest and oldest stock exchange. As of 20 December 2007, 671 companies were listed on the KSE with a market capitalization of Rs. 4,364.312 billion (US$73 billion) and a listed capital of Rs. 717.3 billion (US$12 billion). There are 278 registered brokers, and numerous mutual funds. The Central Depository Company of Pakistan Limited (CDC) was incorporated in 1993 to manage and operate the Central Depository System (CDS). The CDS is an electronic book entry system that records and transfers securities. The National Clearing Company was set up in 2001 to manage and operate the national clearing and settlement system. It acts as a centralized clearing house for the stock exchanges and promotes efficiency in clearing and settlement operations. To enhance the level of liquidity in the market, Continuous Financing System (CFS) was introduced in 2005.

While derivatives have long been traded in Pakistan, the trading was usually confined to OTC instruments. The formal market of derivatives started in Pakistan in 2003, with trading in future contracts introduced with a view to providing hedging instruments and investment alternatives to investors. Since then, the derivatives market in Pakistan has shown significant growth. New products like FX options, IRS, cross-currency swaps (CCS), FRAs and Cash Settled Stock Futures Contracts have been introduced. In order to facilitate provision of financing to the market in a transparent and efficient manner, a new leverage product called Continuous Finance System (CFS) MK II has been initiated by the SECP.

The volumes of IRSs and CCS were Rs 162 billion and Rs 101 billion, respectively, in March 2007. To develop the derivatives market, the SBP circulated the Financial Derivatives Business Regulations (FDBR) in 2004. Authorized derivatives dealers (ADD) or non-market maker financial institutions (NMI) no longer require any prior approval from the SBP to launch/trade financial derivative products like IRS, foreign currency options, and FRAs. The concept papers with regard to other derivative products, namely, Index Futures and Options, are under deliberation and these products are also expected to be launched soon.

New indices have been introduced in the stock markets. Of all, the KSE Index is the most popular index in the country's stock market which began as a 50-share index. Subsequently, the KSE-100 was introduced and remains the most generally accepted measure of the exchange. The KSE-100 is a capital weighted index and consists of 100 companies representing about 86 per cent of market capitalization of the exchange. Two other active indices, the KSE All Share Index and the KSE30 Index, were introduced in 1995 and 1996, respectively.

Special emphasis has been placed on the development of risk management capabilities in Pakistan's equity market. Capital adequacy standards for brokers are being introduced in line with international standards. To avoid excessive volatility in the equity market, appropriate control measures of 'Circuit Breakers' have been introduced. To increase the level of transparency and disclosure in corporate reporting, a code of corporate governance was introduced in March 2002. As part of the ongoing liberalization program, the capital market has been gradually opened to foreign investors. Foreigners and overseas Pakistanis have been allowed to make new investment in all industries with some exceptions.

FOREIGN EXCHANGE MARKET

Since the early 1990s the foreign exchange market in Pakistan has gradually been deregulated. The foreign currency accounts (FCAs) scheme was launched for resident Pakistanis, money changers were authorized to deal in foreign exchange, forward cover for imports and exports was shifted to banks, and forward cover for FC loans was also transferred to banks. Phased approaches were adopted in 1998 to gradually move towards market-based exchange rates.

The foreign exchange market in Pakistan is regulated by the SBP. Commercial banks that hold authorized dealer (AD) status, the SBP, corporate treasuries, and inter-bank brokerage houses are, among others, the major participants in the foreign exchange market.

MARKET MAKING

With a view to developing a market for government securities, the Primary Dealer System was introduced in 2000 in the G-Sec market.

Initially seven banks were chosen by the SBP on the basis of their treasury expertise, infrastructure, and past performance. In order to make the system more broad-based and meaningful, the rules concerning PDs were revised in 2003. The minimum paid-up capital requirements were relaxed to allow brokerage houses to act as PDs. It is mandated by the SBP that only PDs are eligible to participate in the auctions of government securities. However, they can sell the securities (on a market-based auction system) to other banks and financial institutions. In order to allow an effective price discovery mechanism, each PD is allowed to short sell 5 per cent of the target amount before the auction. They are also obliged to underwrite the auctions of long-term paper offered by the SBP. PDs are allowed to carry a short position in securities, managing it through repos up to a maximum of four consecutive weeks for bonds and one week for T-bills.

To keep the G-Sec market liquid, PDs are mandated to work actively both in the primary and secondary markets. As a price maker, they are required to offer two-way quotes on marketable government securities. The PDs have been entrusted with the explicit responsibility of developing an active secondary market by supplying non-PDs and institutional investors with PIBs. All security trading activity by the PDs in the secondary market shall be done in spot value unless otherwise specified. As the PDs are the main source of market information for the regulators, a consultative mechanism between the SBP and the PDs has been put in place.

CURRENT AND CAPITAL ACCOUNT LIBERALIZATION

The process of foreign exchange market liberalization in Pakistan started in 1991. Since May 1999, following a prolonged period of a managed float regime (1982–99), a market-based exchange rate system has been adopted. To make the current account fully convertible, all restrictions concerning the current account have been removed and several measures have been initiated to liberalize the capital account. The Pakistani Rupee was made convertible on current international transactions in 1994 as per the obligations of the IMF Article VIII. Section 23 of the State Bank of Pakistan Act, 1956 was amended in 1999 to empower the banks to trade (buy and sell) foreign exchanges. Non-residents are permitted to invest freely in all but some specified industries. They are also allowed to remit dividends and disinvestment proceeds, and transfer shares without approval. Since 1996–7, non-resident investors have been allowed to trade in shares in the futures market through Special Convertible Rupee Accounts. Resident Pakistanis are allowed to open and maintain Foreign Currency Accounts (FCAs) with banks in Pakistan. Permission was given to Authorized Dealers (ADs), DFIs, and housing finance institutions to grant rupee loans to Pakistani nationals working overseas to purchase real estate properties in Pakistan. Foreign investors are allowed to bring in and take back their capital, as also to remit profits, dividends, and fees directly through their banks. Similarly, foreign portfolio investors can also enter and exit the market at their own discretion.

FINANCIAL SUPERVISION AND REGULATION

The supervision of the financial sector in Pakistan has been invested with two regulators, namely the SBP and the SECP. Until December 2002, the SBP was responsible for regulating both the scheduled banks and the NBFIs. However, the SECP's responsibilities overlapped with those of the SBP in some circumstances. Subsequently, the SECP, which was initially concerned with the regulation of the corporate sector and the capital market, was also empowered to supervise the NBFIs (except DFIs and House Building Finance Corporation) from December 2002. In addition, the SECP has been empowered to oversee various corporate and financial sectors service providers, including chartered accountant firms, credit rating agencies, corporate secretaries, brokers, and surveyors.

The SBP conducts both on-site and off-site supervision of all banks, using different tools and methodologies, notably the CAMELS approach for on-site supervision and the CAELS framework for off-site supervisions.[33] A new department called Off-Site

Supervision and Enforcement Department (OSED) has been instituted in the wake of the re-organization of the former Banking Supervision Department under SBP restructuring. The OSED is responsible for off-site supervision of banks and other financial institutions.

As the central banking supervisory focus around the world has shifted from a 'compliance-based approach' to a 'risk assessment-based approach', the SBP has evolved a uniform bank rating system in line with international benchmarks. In 2004, it instituted a new system of monitoring, surveillance, and supervision called the Institutional Risk Assessment Framework (IRAF). The new framework envisages a collaborative and flawless supervisory focus amongst the various supervisory departments within the SBP. The IRAF stipulates four criteria for evaluation of banks/DFIs, viz., (i) compliance with standards, codes, and guidelines, (ii) supervisory and regulatory information, (iii) financial performance and conditions, and (iv) market information and intelligence.

The risk-based capital framework was institutionalized with the adoption of Basel I in the late 1990s. Most banks in Pakistan maintain a higher capital adequacy ratio than the Basel II requirements.[34] The average capital adequacy ratio (CAR) (capital-to-risk weighted assets) was 13.3 per cent in June 2007. To ensure a smooth transition to the new capital accord, a number of steps have been taken by the SBP, banks, and DFIs. To assess the existing capacity of the banks to meet additional capital requirements, a quantitative impact study (QIS) of Basel II (concerning the Standardized Approach) was conducted by the SBP in July 2004. Based on the QIS results, it was observed that 'there would not be any significant increase in required capital and most of the banks will be able to meet capital requirement under Basel II rules' (SBP 2005). To implement the Basel II framework, the role of credit rating agencies has been defined. In this regard, the SBP issued detailed eligibility criteria for the recognition of External Credit Assessment Institutions (ECAIs) in July 2005. Banks' internal plans for Basel II are reviewed and monitored continuously by the SBP.

The SBP issued a road map for Basel II implementation in March

2005. A parallel run of the Basel II framework has been underway in order to ensure a smooth transition to Basel II. A parallel run of one and a half years for the Standardized Approach commenced from 1 July 2006 and of two years for the Internal Ratings Based (IRB) Approach started from 1 January 2008. The assessment of capital requirement on the basis of returns under the Basel II framework shows that, 'while adopting the Basic Indicator Approach (BIA), the Pakistani banks were required to allocate an additional capital charge of around Rs 29 billion for operational risk during 2006' (SBP 2007).

Detailed instructions for the adoption of various approaches for calculation of capital adequacy requirements for credit risk, market risk and operational risk were issued on 27 June 2006. Banks in Pakistan are required to adopt the Standardized Approach for credit risk. For operational risk, the banks are allowed to adopt either the Basic Indicator Approach or Standardized Approach from 1 January 2008. Banks can adopt the IRB Approach from 1 January 2010.

Capital reporting formats concerning capital calculation under Standardized Approaches for credit and market risk, and BIA and Standardized Approaches for operational risk were prescribed in March 2007. The gap between disclosure practices and requirements under market discipline (Pillar III) of Basel II were identified and detailed requirements for public disclosure were issued in February 2006. These instructions provide for the disclosures to be made by the banks under different approaches of the Basel II adopted by them. A detailed survey to assess the level of preparedness of the banks regarding Basel II implementation was conducted in February 2007 (SBP 2007).

To institutionalize the risk management practices in the banking system and other segments of the financial sector, the SBP and the concerned banks are upgrading their capacity pertaining to information technology and human resources. Banks have also been mandated to set up a risk management team.

Further, in order to gauge the vulnerability of the banks to various shocks, the SBP has instituted a framework of stress testing. Under the framework, exposures of all the banks towards five major risks—interest rate risk, credit risk, real estate price risk, equity price risk and exchange rate risk—are assessed after giving unusual but plausible shocks to the underlying risk (IMF 2005).

BANGLADESH: FINANCIAL SYSTEM AND REFORMS

FINANCIAL SYSTEM

The financial system of Bangladesh comprises the Bangladesh Bank (BB) at the apex, numerous financial intermediaries, the money market, the debt market, and the stock market. Financial intermediaries include commercial banks, specialized banks, NBFIs, and MFIs, the last constituting a very special feature of the Bangladesh financial system. The BB, being the central monetary authority of Bangladesh, performs most of the traditional functions of a central bank such as the supervision and regulation of banks and NBFIs, formulation and implementation of monetary policy, management of foreign exchange reserves, and note issuance, besides being the banker to the government. The financial sector in Bangladesh is highly bank-dominated. There are four nationalized commercial banks (NCBs), five government-owned specialized banks (SBs), 30 domestic PCBs, and 10 foreign private commercial banks (FCBs).[35] The total number of scheduled bank offices was 6,576 as of March 2007, of which 3,839 branches were in operation in the rural areas and 2,737 in the urban areas. Out of 6,576 scheduled bank branches, the NCBs operate 3,384 branches, whereas SBs, PCBs and FCBs account for 1,358, 1,785 and 49 branches, respectively. With four branches per 100,000 people, Bangladesh exhibits a rather low penetration of the bank network within the country. The breakdown of the share of assets and deposits of the various categories of banks (as of March 2007) was as follows: NCBs (assets 52.21 per cent, deposits 35.0 per cent), PCBs (assets 35 per cent, deposits 52.4 per cent), SBs (assets 7.5 per cent, deposits 5.6 per cent), and FCBs (assets 5.29 per cent, deposits 7 per cent). A problematic feature of NCBs is the substantial NPL overhang in their portfolios, accounting for 75 per cent of total classified loans of the commercial banking system.

NBFIs are an integral part of the financial system of Bangladesh. As of March 2007, there were 29 NBFIs in Bangladesh, consisting of investment, finance, leasing companies, etc., with their operations regulated under the Financial Institutions Act, 1993. Only one NBFI is state-owned, 15 being privately owned (local), and the remaining 13 joint ventures with foreign participation.

MFIs are one of the fastest growing financial intermediaries in Bangladesh, offering micro-credit programs (MCPs) to approximately 25 million borrowers, located primarily in the rural areas. These micro-credit programs are implemented by various formal financial institutions, viz., nationalized commercial banks, specialized banks, specialized government organizations, and semi-formal financial institutions that include nearly 1,000 NGO-MFIs.

There are 62 insurance companies in Bangladesh, of which 18 companies provide life insurance and 44 entities offer general insurance services. The insurance sector is regulated under the Insurance Act.

FINANCIAL SECTOR REFORMS IN BANGLADESH

As in almost all other countries of South Asia, the financial sector in Bangladesh prior to reforms was a highly repressed one. Banks and other financial institutions were owned by the government, and an active capital market was missing. As observed by Ahmed (2005), 'banks at early stages of history of Bangladesh were nationalized and there was mismatch between assets and liabilities. The central bank of the country had limited tools to manage monetary policy. Direct tools namely determination of SLR/CRR, administered interest rate policy and moral suasion were the main instruments of monetary policy. Most banks pursued a policy of financial deepening through extending bank branches to the remote and rural areas without considering financial viability.'

The liberalization process in the financial sector started in the 1980s with the privatization of two NCBs. Subsequently, several programs were initiated to carry the reforms forward. Among the many initiatives launched with a view to laying out a road-map for reforms, special mention needs to be made of the following: The National Commission on Money, Banking and Credit (NCMBC) constituted in 1984, the Financial Sector Reform Programme (FSRP) undertaken in active collaboration with the International Development Agency (IDA) in 1990, the high-powered Banking Reform Committee (BRC) set up by the government in 1996, and the Central Bank Strengthening Project (CBSP) undertaken in 2003 in order to achieve a strong and effective regulatory and supervisory system for the banking sector.

The reform programs initiated under various auspices focused on several dimensions, most notably, privatization of state-owned banks, recovery of NPLs, interest rate deregulations, increasing autonomy of the BB, enhancing prudential regulation and supervision, rationalization and merger of bank branches, and effecting improvements in the money and debt markets.

BANKING SECTOR REFORMS AND INTEREST RATE DEREGULATION

The privatization of the NCBs and relaxation of entry barriers to private sector banks were the priority of the banking sector reforms. As a result of this thrust, several new private banks commenced operations during the early 1980s and 1990s and some state-owned banks were privatized. Additionally, the authorities have also taken initiatives to merge/rationalize NCB and DFI branches that have been incurring losses on a continuous basis for five consecutive years.

Abandoning its traditional administered and sector-specific concessional credit facilities, the BB introduced a flexible interest rate policy in January 1990 under the FSRP. Under the new policy, interest rate bands were prescribed for different categories of loans, advances, and deposit rates. In 1992, the prescribed bands for lending rate were removed from all but three sectors, namely, agriculture, export, and the small-industry sectors[36] and NCBs, SBs, PCBs, and FCBs were allowed to set their lending rates in line with market conditions. Floors on savings and fixed deposits were continued, but ceilings were removed. In 1997, the floor rates on deposits were removed too. Currently, commercial banks adjust deposit and lending rates in response to changes in the National Savings Directorate (NSD) rates.

The money market in Bangladesh plays a somewhat limited role. Participants in the call money market are mainly commercial banks and NBFIs. The BB introduced repo, reverse repo, and the interbank repo operations from July 2002, April 2003, and July 2003, respectively, in order to manage day-to-day liquidity positions in the money market and to strengthen the indirect monetary operations.

Important steps have been undertaken to improve the functioning of the interbank and T-bill markets, including the establishment of a settlement system for secondary market bond trading and introducing detailed 'mark-to-market' guidelines for government securities. The government and the BB have also taken steps to strengthen debt management operations. Separation of government cash and debt management started from 1 July 2006. Repo facilities have been opened for investors and they can borrow up to 90 per cent of the value against T-bills.

Somewhat uniquely in the South Asian context, BB has also tried to implement various reform measures directed at improving the various legal aspects bearing on issues such as corporate governance, loan recovery, exchange and interest rates management, risk management, and efficiency of the financial system in general.

GOVERNMENT SECURITIES MARKET

The Ministry of Finance issues T-bills and T-bonds, which are auctioned by the BB on behalf of the government. The primary market in both T-bills and G-Secs is dominated by commercial banks. G-Secs are traded in the OTC segment and in the organized segment of the country's stock exchanges. The Central Depository Bangladesh Limited (CDBL) does the depository function for all securities including G-Sec and corporate bonds. Issues and turnover in G-Sec are dominated by T-bills, which account for 80 per cent of transactions and 67 per cent of trading volume. The system of *ad hoc* T-bills for financing the budget deficit was abolished and market-based auctions for treasury securities instituted in September 2006.

CORPORATE DEBT MARKET

At the end of 2006, the size of the total domestic debt (public and private) constituted a modest 15.58 per cent of the financial system, which is highly dominated by government bonds. The size of the corporate bond market in Bangladesh is very small. There are eight corporate bonds (debentures) available in the market.

The corporate debt market in Bangladesh can hardly be said to have developed in tandem with other segments of the country's financial sector. There is virtually no corporate bond market, and whatever does exist can more aptly be described as a debenture market. The corporate bond market development has been constrained by a few critical factors, viz., distortions and high costs in the market, poor performance by issuers in meeting payment terms, and poor enforcement of investor (bond holder) protection. Some efforts have been underway of late to establish conditions congenial for promoting investor confidence and participation, including household (retail) participation.

There are a number of impediments in developing a corporate debt market. One major impediment is the relatively high interest payments on the NSD certificates that have acted as a huge disincentive to investment in the market. However, in recent years this rate has been reduced significantly and NSD returns are now more closely aligned with market rates. Second, there is no benchmark yield curve for the term structure of interest rates. The absence of such a long-term risk-free yield curve for G-Secs constitutes a key obstacle to the development of an active bond market. The BB's recent switch to volume-based auctions has the potential to make the auction system more transparent. The government of Bangladesh introduced 5-year and 10-year Bangladesh Government Treasury Bonds (BGTB) in 2003, with the intention of facilitating the development of a long-term benchmark yield curve. Third, the Bangladesh bond market does not have a strong investor base. In addition to banks, the potential base for bond markets has typically included insurance companies, pension, provident, and mutual funds.

All these sectors continue to remain undeveloped in Bangladesh. Credit rating agencies are a crucial ingredient in the development of efficient debt instruments. Two credit rating agencies have been permitted to evaluate the credit qualities of different financial institutions in Bangladesh but, by and large, the penetration of credit ratings must be considered as low.

EQUITY MARKET

In spite of Bangladesh having had a long history of securities trading, the equity market still remains underdeveloped, which is reflected in a very low stock market capitalization *vis-à-vis* the country's GDP.[37] However, the market has shown some signs of revival in recent years in spite of the stock market crash in 1996. The Securities and Exchange Commission (SEC) regulates the country's capital market under the Securities and Exchange Commission Act, 1993. In addition, the BB is empowered to regulate institutions engaged in financing activities (including leasing companies and venture capital companies) under the Financial Institutions Act, 1993. Of the 29 NBFIs in the country, 12 are listed on the stock exchanges (as of 31 March 2007), including 19 merchant banks and portfolio managers and 8 issue managers and underwriters. The country has two stock exchanges, namely the Dhaka Stock Exchange (DSE) and the Chittagong Stock Exchange (CSE), established in 1954 and 1995, respectively. The DSE is the country's major bourse, with the total number of listed securities (as of May 2007) standing at 326, of which listed companies account for 260 and mutual funds for 14; of the remaining, there are 8 debentures and 44 treasury bonds. The market capitalization of the DSE at the end of 2006 was only 5.2 per cent of the country's GDP. The Investment Corporation of Bangladesh (ICB), established in 1976, underwrites issues of securities, provides substantial bridge financing programs, and maintains investment accounts, besides floating and managing closed-end and open-end mutual funds. It operates both in the DSE and the CSE as a dealer.

The securities market in Bangladesh has undergone some reforms since the 1990s. Entry barriers in stock trading have been relaxed, ownership restrictions on foreigners in the share market liberalized, and listing requirements and investor protection improved. The CDBL was incorporated as a public limited company in August 2000 to operate and maintain the Central Depository System (CDS) of electronic book entry for recording and operating securities accounts and for registering transfer of securities.

FOREIGN EXCHANGE MARKET

The foreign exchange market in Bangladesh currently plays a very limited role. There was virtually no foreign exchange market in Bangladesh till 1993. The BB supervises the market and the ADs are the only resident entities in the market who transact and hold foreign exchange. There are 32 banks who act as ADs. The inter-bank foreign exchange market is still in its nascent stage and the average daily transactions of foreign exchange (US$/Bangladesh Taka) in the inter-bank market amounted to a meager US$16 million in 2006.

MARKET MAKING

In order to develop a vibrant market for government securities, the BB introduced the Primary Dealer System in 2003. Eight banks and one NBFI were selected as PDs. However, the PDs could not make any substantive difference in the G-Sec market. Subsequently, the PD guidelines have been amended and various incentives have been offered. According to the new guidelines, each of the bank and non-bank PDs are expected to underwrite a minimum of 12 and 4 per cent of the auction amounts, respectively. Apart from underwriting commissions, they are eligible to avail of collateralized liquidity support from the BB through repurchase agreements.

CURRENT AND CAPITAL ACCOUNT LIBERALIZATION

On 24 March 1994, the Bangladesh Taka (domestic currency) was declared convertible for current transactions in terms of IMF Article VIII. As a result, current external settlements for trade in goods and services and for amortization payments on foreign borrowings can be made through the approved ADs to deal with foreign exchange, without prior central bank permission. However, because resident-owned capital is not freely transferable abroad (the Bangladesh Taka is not yet convertible on capital account), some current settlements beyond certain indicative limits are subject to approval.

FINANCIAL SUPERVISION AND REGULATION

The BB assesses the performance and soundness of the banking sector under the CAMEL framework, which involves analysis and evaluation of the five crucial dimensions of banking operations, namely capital adequacy, asset quality, management soundness, earnings, and liquidity. An Early Warning System (EWS) was introduced in 2004 to streamline the BB's supervision of banks under threat of incipient crises. Measures have been undertaken to beef up risk-based supervisions and, finally, a Money Laundering Prevention Act was enacted in 2002.

Loan defaulting is one of the key areas where the BB has initiated several supervisory measures, including provisioning, which has become necessary as a cushion against increased loan defaults. The BB introduced new accounting policies on loan classification, provisioning, and interest suspense in 1989 in line with international standards. This policy was successively revised in 1994, 1999, and 2001, with increasing stress on independent assessments of each loan on the basis of qualitative factors and objective criteria.

Risk-based supervision has been beefed up since the mid-1990s. Banks in Bangladesh were required to adopt Basal I norms in January 1996, with capital adequacy requirements on scheduled banks imposed at a minimum of 9 per cent of risk in different types of assets (inclusive of off-balance sheet items) (with at least 4.5 per cent in core capital) or BDT 1 billion whichever is higher.[38] As of December 2006, the DFIs, PCBs, and FCBs in Bangladesh had managed to attain the prescribed CAR. However, several NCBs fell short of the target, largely owing to shortage in owner's equity, provisioning shortfall and high operational costs. In 2003, the BB issued guidelines on managing core risks to banks, which were also asked to build up their own risk management manuals on the basis of the prevailing guidelines. Since 2007, banks have also been mandated to have their credit portfolios rated by an approved credit rating agency.

Bangladeshi banks have been advised to implement the new Basel Accord in early 2009. To expedite the process, a high-level national steering committee was constituted in 2005. Furthermore, a coordination committee and a Basel II implementation cell have been established in the BB. A quantitative impact study (QIS) was carried out in April–May 2007 to assess the banks' preparedness for Basel II implementation as well as to note banks' views on the optional approaches for calculating minimum capital requirements. Banks have been recommended to adopt the Standardized Approach for calculating risk weighted amount (RWA) against credit and market risk and the Basic Indicator Approach (BIA) for providing against operational risk. As a preparatory step towards the implementation of Basel II, banks have been required to maintain a CAR of 10 per cent from December 2007 onwards.

SRI LANKA: FINANCIAL SYSTEM AND REFORMS

Financial System

The financial system in Sri Lanka comprises the Central Bank of Sri Lanka (CBSL) at the apex, numerous financial intermediaries, the money market, the bond market, the foreign exchange market, and the equity market. Financial intermediaries include licensed commercial banks (LCBs), licensed specialized banks (LSBs), registered finance companies, specialized leasing companies (SLCs), authorized PDs, insurance companies, and venture capital companies.

The task of supervising and regulating banks, finance companies, leasing companies, and primary dealers vests with the CBSL. The Securities and Exchange Commission of Sri Lanka is responsible for supervising the stock exchanges, stock broking and dealing firms, unit trusts, venture capital companies, investment managers, margin providers, and credit rating agencies. The major objectives of the

CBSL are primarily two-fold, viz., maintaining of economic and price stability, and stability in financial markets. But as with most other central banks, it performs a host of other functions including currency, foreign exchange, and public debt management.

The banking sector in Sri Lanka comprises 23 LCBs (of which 11 are local and 12 foreign) and 14 LSBs[39] (6 regional development banks, 3 private savings and development banks, 2 housing finance institutions, 2 long-term lending institutions, and 1 national savings bank). With a share of about 82.5 per cent of banking assets, LCBs dominate Sri Lanka's banking sector (with the LSBs accounting for the residual of about 17.5 per cent). The country has 3,931 bank offices, of which 3,516 outlets (89 per cent) are operated by LCBs. The six major LCBs are known as systematically important banks (SIBs) and comprise two state-owned commercial banks and four domestic private commercial banks, with the major share of financial assets resting with the state-owned banks.[40]

NBFIs still constitute only a small segment of Sri Lanka's financial system.[41]

FINANCIAL SECTOR REFORMS IN SRI LANKA

The financial sector reforms in Sri Lanka can be divided into two phases: the 1977–88 period and the post-1989 period. The first phase of reforms focused on banking sector reform, interest rate deregulations, and foreign exchange market liberalization. The reform process was flagged off in 1979 with the removal of operational restrictions on foreign banks. The period also witnessed an expansion of bank branches and, additionally, several new banks and credit institutions were set up in the 1980s. The National Development Bank was instituted in 1979 to supplement the work of the Development Finance Corporation of Ceylon. The Sri Lankan Export Credit Insurance Corporation was set up in the same year for provision of insurance coverage to the export sector. Finally, the Regional Rural Development Board was instituted in 1985. The second phase, by contrast, emphasized issues of stabilization of the financial system and relaxation of the remaining regulations. Emphasis was placed on the development of specialized financial institutions. Most of the new merchant banks, leasing companies, PDs, etc., have been instituted during this latter phase.

GOVERNMENT SECURITIES MARKET

The G-Sec market in Sri Lanka has undergone significant reforms since the early 1980s. In 1981, a secondary market window was opened for T-bills by the CBSL. Weekly T-bill auctions commenced in 1986[42] and T-bills with 6- and 12-month maturities were introduced in 1989. The repo and the reverse repo windows for T-bills were introduced by the CBSL in 1993 and 1995, respectively. In the G-Sec market, the CBSL acts as an agent of the government, and PDs have been assigned the role of market makers (see below). Banks and NBFIs are the major investors in the G-Sec market that offers both short- and long-term tradeable debt instruments, namely, T-bills (91–364 days) and T-bonds.

T-bonds issuance began on a modest scale in 1997. In 2001, US$-denominated Sri Lanka Development Bonds were issued and in 2003, the 10-, 15-, and 20-year T-bonds were initiated. In 2004, the Registered Stock and Securities Ordinance (RSSO), the Local Treasury Bills Ordinance (LTBO) and the Monetary Law Act (MLA) were amended to enable the trading of scripless securities. The Scripless Securities Settlement System (SSSS) and Central Depository System (CDS) have already commenced operations. Secondary market transactions in T-bills amounted to Rs. 443 billion for outright transactions and Rs. 652 billion for repurchase transactions in 2005.[43]

The money market in Sri Lanka consists of the inter-bank call money and the T-bill market. Commercial banks participate in this market to cover their short-term liquidity needs. The stability in the market is supported by the CBSL's Repo and Reverse Repo instruments. The daily inter-bank call money market transactions averaged about Rs. 8 billion in 2007.

CORPORATE DEBT MARKET

The debt market in Sri Lanka consists of the G-Sec market, the commercial paper market, and the corporate bond market. While the size of the bond market in Sri Lanka was 50.8 per cent of its GDP in 2006, the market is highly dominated by the government bonds.

The issuance of corporate bonds in Sri Lanka began in 1996. However, the market remains underdeveloped[44] owing to several factors, such as the lack of an institutional investor base, availability of bank credit at attractive rates for high net worth companies, high cost of debt issues, lack of investor information on the quality of debt, and, finally, the non-availability of a longer term benchmark yield curve.

With a view to overcoming some of the deficiencies noted above, the Debt Trading System (DEX) was launched at the initiative of the Colombo Stock Exchange (CSE) in March 2004 for trading in both corporate and government securities. At present, 69 corporate debt securities are listed on the CSE and Government Debt is tradeable exclusively through the DEX system.

EQUITY MARKET

Securities trading in Sri Lanka dates back to 1896. However, the establishment of a formal stock exchange took place only in 1985 with the incorporation of the CSE. The CSE has two indices, namely, the All Share Price Index and the Milanka Price Index (MPI). The latter was introduced in January 1999, replacing the earlier Sensitive Price Index (SPI). In January 2004, the CSE launched a Total Return Index (TRI) series in addition to the Price Indices. There are 235 listed companies on the CSE and its market capitalization stood at Rs. 816 billion as of 25 February 2008.

Recent years have witnessed several attempts to introduce important reforms in the capital market. To regulate the equity market, the Securities and Exchange Commission (SEC) of Sri Lanka was set up in 1987. In 1988, the Colombo Securities Exchange Limited adopted new rules for listed companies, replacing the bye-laws of the Colombo Brokers' Association. To attract foreign capital in the market, several incentives were provided such as abolition of wealth tax on listed companies' shares, and elimination of the 100 per cent transfer tax on share purchases by non-nationals. In the wake of these initiatives, the number of listed companies, market capitalization, turnover, and number of investors increased rapidly. In 1991, the CDS was established to serve as the depository for all securities traded on the Exchange and to assume responsibility for the post-trade clearing and settlement of transactions. An OTC market for trading of unlisted shares was introduced in 1996.

FOREIGN EXCHANGE MARKET AND LIBERALIZATION OF FOREIGN TRANSACTIONS

The foreign exchange market in Sri Lanka consists of the CBSL, authorized dealers, and the offshore market. In the inter-bank foreign exchange market, transactions are conducted both on spot and forward basis. Major steps have been undertaken in recent years to liberalize the country's foreign exchange transactions by allowing commercial banks and other authorized dealers to determine the exchange rate freely. The daily average turnover in the inter-bank FX market (including the forward market) was US$32 million in 2007.

In accordance with Article VIII of the Articles of Agreement of the IMF, Sri Lanka removed all restrictions on current external transactions on 15 March 1994. As a result, the Sri Lankan rupee is fully convertible on the current account. However, the capital account is far from fully convertible, with several restrictions in place on capital flows.

MARKET MAKING

In order to develop and lend depth to the market for government securities, a PD system was installed in 1992. Under the initial arrangement, the CBSL appointed 18 accredited PDs comprising 11 commercial banks and 7 NBFIs to bid for G-Secs at the primary auctions. The PDs have been assigned the major functions of: (i) participating in the primary market to help create a stable demand for T-bills and T-bonds, and (ii) keeping the secondary market liquid by trading in G-Secs.

The PD system has undergone several changes since its inception in 1992. The current PD system was established in 2002 with two types of PDs in operation (9 dedicated PD companies and 3 PD units of LCBs). All assets of these PDs are collateralized against government securities. To minimize the settlement risk, the SSSS was introduced in 2004, with the settlement based on a delivery *versus* payments (DvP) mechanism. PDs have access to the secondary market windows operated by the CBSL to meet any urgent liquidity needs. As of end-September 2006, all PDs were maintaining the CAR above 8 per cent and the leveraging level below 20 times, which are the statutory required levels. PDs are subject to regular and continuous surveillance as well as periodic on-site examinations.

FINANCIAL SUPERVISION AND REGULATION

The CBSL supervises banks and other financial institutions based on a two-pronged approach of off-site and on-site surveillance. Under the off-site surveillance system, the financial condition of the LCBs and the LSBs is monitored on the basis of a few select variables.[45] The off-site surveillance works as an early warning system in identifying significant and critical changes in the financial condition of banks, which might require further investigation and examination. The on-site supervision is a risk-based examination process, which focuses on identification of banking risks, the management of these risks and the assessment of adequacy of resources to mitigate these risks, which is supplemented by an examination based on the internationally accepted CAMELS model.

Banks in Sri Lanka adopted Basel I norms in 1993. Since then, risk-based supervisory measures have been further strengthened. Several measures have also been initiated to move over to the New Basel Capital Accord. In 2005, the CBSL increased the minimum capital requirement for commercial banks to Rs. 2500 million from Rs 500 million and for specialized banks (except regional development banks) to Rs. 1,500 million from Rs. 200 million. In 2006, the CBSL introduced a capital charge for market risk, which requires commercial and specialized banks to maintain a CAR of 10 per cent on account of risk-weighted assets for market risk, in addition to the CAR of 10 per cent for credit risk.

Banks in Sri Lanka have been advised to implement Basel II

with effect from January 2008. The CBSL has suggested that banks adopt the Standardized Approach for calculating credit and market risks, and the Basic Indicators Approach for calculating operational risk. However, the central bank may permit some banks to migrate to an IRB approach after adequate skills and a risk management infrastructure are in place, both at the bank and supervisory levels.

In order to maintain financial stability, a Financial System Stability Committee (FSSC) was set up in 2002 under the chairmanship of the Deputy Governor of CBSL with the following objectives:

(i) Assessment of the risks and vulnerabilities that may lead to financial system instabilities or imbalances and to recommend measures and policies to mitigate them to the Governor and the Monetary Board;
(ii) Monitor the financial system and submit periodic reports to the Governor and the Monetary Board, recommending policies necessary to promote financial system stability; and
(iii) Prepare the Financial System Stability Review.

CONCLUDING REMARKS

The process of financial liberalization impinged on the US and UK financial systems in the 1970s, on most other advanced countries in the 1980s and on the LDCs only in the past decade. The change has been unevenly distributed across countries, and even though the general direction of movement has been unambiguously forward, the pace has varied between countries owing to intrinsic structural differences rooted in 'contestability' of markets, structure of competition, industrial concentration, and 'financial literacy' in general.

After providing detailed discussions of the likely effects of financial liberalization on economic growth and social welfare, the sections above underlined some of the challenges posed for the conduct of monetary policy by the liberalization process. Finally, the chapter assessed the increased vulnerability of an economy to currency and banking crises in the wake of financial liberalization, especially capital account liberalization.

Considerable econometric as well as case study evidence seems to be accumulating on several of these aspects. While the results of different studies show considerable divergence, there is a consensus building around the following general consequences of financial liberalization.

By and large financial liberalization seems to promote growth in the long run, though the immediate and medium-term consequences can be sharply destabilizing. The immediate aftermath of liberalization is characterized by a boom, followed by a sharp contraction. The boom exceeds the bust in magnitude (and possibly in duration), so that the long-term income benefits are positive (Wyplosz 2001). However, the socio-political consequences of the bust can be serious, so that the overall welfare gains attributable to financial liberalization are questionable. It is important, therefore, to have adequate welfare systems in place before embarking on ambitious liberalization programs.

The choice of an exchange rate regime becomes crucial in determining an economy's vulnerability to financial crises. Eichengreen (1994) and Calvo and Reinhart (2000) argue in favor of taking either of the 'extremes', viz., a freely floating exchange rate or a 'hard peg'. Many development economists, however, feel that excessive exchange rate volatility associated with a free float erodes trade competitiveness and entails unnecessarily large hedging exposures. Hard pegs, on the other hand, are extremely costly and it is difficult to sustain their credibility for long. Perhaps the 'soft middle' option of a 'managed float' represents some kind of a golden mean option.

The sequencing of reforms is extremely important to the success of liberalization. The sequencing strategy advocated by McKinnon (1991), in which the domestic goods market is liberalized first, followed by opening up of the trade sector, with financial liberalization and capital account liberalization bringing up the rear, seems possibly to be the best, and the experience of most developed countries (especially in Europe) seems to be in conformity with this strategy.

Recent studies such as those by Rodrik et al. (2002), Alcala and Ciccone (2004), and Kaufmann et al. (2007) clearly indicate the importance of institutional features such as corruption, rule of law, and general governance issues (such as political accountability and quality of bureaucracy) in determining whether the outcomes of liberalization in general (and financial liberalization in particular) would be beneficial or otherwise. This could be an important part of the explanation as to why liberalization usually succeeds in the developed countries but often fails in the developing world. It also throws up in retrospect the fallacy implicit in the reform advocacy of the 1990s which urged developing countries with weak institutions to undertake economic reforms, under the implicit assurance that political progress and good governance would follow as a consequence.

This chapter, though no more than an overview of the financial liberalization process under way in four South Asian countries, unambiguously indicates that a considerable degree of liberalization has already occurred in this region, most of which seems irreversible. It is also important to stress that financial liberalization usually races ahead of liberalization in the real sector, mainly because it meets with far less political resistance than real sector reforms. The issue of 'unbalanced reforms' with a highly reformed financial sector co-existing with a largely unreformed real sector has hardly attracted much attention in either the theoretical literature or in policy circles. But the South Asian economies currently constitute prime examples of such 'unbalanced reforms'.

While it is too early to applaud the South Asian experience of financial liberalization as an outstanding success (or for that matter, to cynically dismiss it as a failure), our discussion points to the imperative of a much more cautious approach than the one hitherto followed. In particular, apart from the general issues discussed above, there are at least five others that deserve close attention in view of some of the factors that are specific to the South Asian context. These are (i) sequencing of reforms and a redressal of the 'unbalanced' nature of the reforms process referred to above; (ii) regulation of large financial conglomerates, especially the banks' insurance combines; (iii) embedding financial reforms within the context of the formal-informal financial sector linkages; (iv) paying special attention in the reforms process to the needs of microfinance and rural credit; and (v) devising countervailing safeguards to insulate vulnerable sections of society from some of the inequalizing and destabilizing consequences of the financial liberalization process noted above.

NOTES

1. As noted by Saidane (2002), this still begs the question about the correct ordering of causality between growth and financial liberalization and the issue of separating the effects of financial liberalization on growth from that of overall liberalization.
2. This framework still survives in many countries, albeit in a somewhat battered form.
3. Currency, no doubt, is an exception to this phenomenon, but most likely, an increasingly unimportant one.
4. Many countries have tried to retain this division between banks and NBFIs. In the United States for example, the Banking Act of 1933, or the Glass-Steagall Act (GSA) that kept banking and brokerage functions separated, was repealed as late as November 1999 and replaced by the Gramm-Leach-Bliley Act, which eliminated the GSA restrictions. The new Act allowed banking institutions to provide a broader range of services, including underwriting and other dealing activities. The subsequent growth of Negotiated Order of Withdrawal (NOW) accounts has made large changes to the US 'money supply'.
5. Obstfeld et al. (2004) present several historical instances of the trilemma.
6. He cites the role of exchange rate stabilization in ending the 1920s European hyperinflation.
7. The introduction of the Market Stabilization Scheme (MSS) in April 2004 assumes significance in this context as an important tool for short-term liquidity management.
8. For a detailed structure of the Indian banking system, see Figure 10.1.
9. Rupee (Rs), in this section, refers to the Indian rupee.
10. It is the biggest stock exchange in India and the third biggest in the world in terms of amounts of transactions.
11. Also known as the Committee on Financial Systems (CFS).
12. Also known as the Committee on Banking Sector Reforms (CBSR).
13. Basel II is the second of the Basel Accords, which are recommendations on banking laws and regulations issued by the Basel Committee on Banking Supervision.

14. For instance, interest rates on small savings, provident funds, non-resident Indians deposits, and export credit continue to be administered.
15. However, the responsibility for regulating the securities market in India is shared by two other entities, namely, the Department of Economic Affairs (DEA) and Department of Company Affairs (DCA).
16. Only two exchanges in India have been permitted to trade in derivatives contracts.
17. The index futures and options contract on NSE are based on S&P CNX.
18. Report of the Committee on Capital Account Convertibility, 1997 and the Committee on Fuller Capital Account Convertibility, 2006.
19. It is an arrangement between two major stake holders in the Government Securities market—the debt manager and a group of dealers—to pursue a common strategy in support of the functioning and development of primary and secondary markets for government securities.
20. These conditions are listed in Nachane (2007).
21. The Narasimham Committee I was set up in 1991 to review the state of the financial sector.
22. These three pillars are: (i) minimum capital requirements, based on weights intended to be more closely aligned to economic risks than in the 1988 Accord, (ii) supervisory review, which set basic standards for bank supervision to minimize regulatory arbitrage, and (iii) market discipline, which spells out greater levels of disclosure and standards of transparency by the banking system. The objectives of the New Basel Capital Accord, as enunciated by the BIS are fivefold: (i) promoting safety and soundness of the financial system; (ii) enhancing competitive equality; (iii) adoption of a comprehensive approach to addressing risks (iv) greater sensitivity to the degree of risk involved in banks' activities; and (v) a focus on internationally active banks, with the possibility kept open of the various provisions being applicable in a phased manner to banks with varying levels of complexity and sophistication (Bank for International Settlements, 2001).
23. According to the International Convergence of Capital Measurement and Capital Standards (Basel II), the standardized approach is a set of risk measurement techniques for banking institutions. The term may be used in the context of credit risk or operational risk.
24. The Basic Indicator Approach is a set of operational risk measurement techniques proposed under Basel II capital adequacy rules for banking institutions.
25. It refers to a set of credit risk measurement techniques proposed under Basel II capital adequacy rules for banking institutions.

26. The RBI released Draft Guidelines for implementation of the New Capital Adequacy Framework on 15 February 2005.
27. A Mudarabah is an investment partnership, whereby the investor (the Rab ul Mal) provides capital to another party/entrepreneur (the Mudarib) in order to undertake a business/investment activity. While profits are shared on a pre-agreed ratio, loss of investment is borne by the investor only. The mudarib loses its share of the expected income. http://www.hsbcamanah.com/1/2/hsbc-amanah/about-islamic-banking/glossary#mudaraba
28. For the detailed structure of Pakistani banks, see Figure 10.2 in the Appendix.
29. The IMF and the World Bank provided several financial sector restructuring loans to Pakistan, notably the Financial Sector Deepening and Intermediation Project (1995), the Financial Sector Adjustment Loan (1997), and the Financial Sector Restructuring and Privatization Project (2001).
30. Capital Market Development Programme (1997).
31. They are Muslim Commercial Bank, Allied Bank Limited, United Bank, and Habib Bank.
32. Rupee (Rs), in this section, refers to the Pakistani rupee.
33. A bank/DFI is rated on each of its components, viz., capital adequacy, assets quality, management, earning, liquidity, sensitivity to other risks, and systems and controls. Each component is rated on a scale of 1 (strong) to 5 (unsatisfactory) and on the basis of individual component rating, an overall composite rating is assigned to the institution. The CAELS is an off-site supervisory framework used for assigning banks, on a quarterly basis, a composite rating on a scale of 1 (best) to 5 (worst) comprising of capital (C), asset quality (A), earning (E), liquidity (L), and sensitivity to other risks (S).
34. The disaggregated analysis shows that of the 41 banks, the number of well-capitalized banks, that is, the banks with CAR of more than 10 per cent, increased to 35 from 34 in March 2007. Of the remaining seven, four have their CAR well above 8 per cent (SBP 2007).
35. For a detailed structure of the Bangladeshi banks, see Figure 10.3.
36. The interest bands on agriculture and small and medium-sized enterprises (SMEs) were also removed in 1999, whereas some modifications were made to the export credit bands in January 2004.
37. The market cap-GDP ratio was only 7.5 per cent in 2006.
38. This amount was subsequently raised to BDT 2 billion.
39. For a detailed structure of the Sri Lankan banks, see Figure 10.4.
40. The two major state-owned banks alone accounted for 35 per cent of banking sector assets, whereas all public banks together held 47 per cent of assets as of June 2007.

41. Thus, the combined share of NBFIs in total financial system assets increased from 3.3 per cent in 2003 to 4.5 per cent in 2006.
42. Non-competitive bidding of primary auctions was phased out in 1995.
43. Rupee (Rs), in this section, refers to the Sri Lankan rupee.
44. The corporate debt and debentures turnover in 2006 amounted to a meager Rs. 405.2 million and Rs. 2.4 million, respectively. Also, long-term debt issued by non-financial corporates has been negligible.
45. The variables are weekly interest rates of deposits and advances, monthly returns on selected financial information, assets and liabilities, statutory liquid assets, quarterly returns on income and expenditure, capital adequacy, non-performing advances, classified advances and provisioning for bad and doubtful advances, investments in shares, interest spreads, half-yearly return on share ownership of the banks, and annual audited financial statements.

REFERENCES

Das, Abhiman and Saibal Ghosh (2006). 'Financial deregulation and efficiency: An empirical analysis of Indian banks during the post reform period', *Review of Financial Economics,* 15, 3, 193–221.

Acemoglu, D. and F. Zilibotti (1997). 'Was Prometheus unbound by chance? Risk, diversification, and growth', *Journal of Political Economy,* 105, 4, 709–51.

Ahluwalia, Montek S. (2002). 'State level performance under economic reforms in India'. In Anne Krueger (ed.), *Economic Policy Reforms and the Indian Economy* (pp. 91–128). Chicago: University of Chicago Press.

Ahuja, N. (2006). 'Commodity derivatives market in India: Development, regulation and future prospects', *International Research Journal of Finance and Economics,* 11, 2, 153–61.

Akhtar, M.A. (1983).'Financial innovations and their implications for monetary policy: An international perspective', *BIS Economic Papers,* No. 9, Bank for International Settlements, Basel.

Akhtaruzzaman, M.D. (2007). 'Globalization, financial liberalization and the behavior of the long run money demand in the Bangladesh economy', *International Economic Journal,* 21, 3, 465–90.

Alcala, F. and A. Ciccone (2004). 'Trade and productivity', *Quarterly Journal of Economics,* 119, 2, 612–45.

Arif, Muhammad (2007). 'Developing bond market in Pakistan, State Bank of Pakistan'. http://www.sbp.org.pk/fscd/2007/Presentations/Bond-Market.pdf accessed 20 January 2008.

Asian Development Bank (2005). 'Sri Lanka financial sector assessment'. http://www.adb.org/documents/assessments/financial/sri-financial-sector-assessment-2005.pdf accessed 25 January 2008.

Aslam, Muzzammil (2007). 'Pakistan Debt Market', KASB Securities. http://www.kasb.com/resources/fixed_income_weekly_03082007.pdf accessed 21 January 2008.

Bangladesh Bank (2006). *Bangladesh Bank Annual Report (2005–6)*. http://www.bangladesh-bank.org/pub/annual/anreport/annual.html accessed 23 January 2008.

——— (2007). *Bangladesh Bank Annual Report (2006–7)*. http://www.bangladesh-bank.org/pub/annual/anreport/annual.html accessed 23 January 2008.

Bank for International Settlements (2001). 'The Basel Capital Accord: Second Consultative Paper', Bank for International Settlements, Basel. http://www.bis.org/bcbs/bcbscp2.htm accessed 2 January 2008.

Beck, Thorsten and Md. Habibur Rahman (2006). 'Creating a more efficient financial system: Challenges for Bangladesh', World Bank Policy Research Working Paper No. 3938, Washington, D.C.

Behrman, J., N. Birdsall and M. Szekely (2000). 'Economic reform and wage differentials in Latin America', Working Paper No. 435, Inter-American Development Bank, Washington, D.C.

Bernanke, B.S. (2005). 'Monetary policy in a world of mobile capital', *Cato Journal*, 25, 1, 1–12.

Bekaert, Geert, et al. (2001). 'Does financial liberalisation spur growth?' NBER Working Paper No. 8245, National Bureau of Economic Research, Washington, D.C.

Bhalla, A.S. and D.M. Nachane (2001). 'The economic import of the Asian crisis in India and China'. In H. Chang, G. Palma and D.H. Whittaker (eds.), *Financial Liberalization and the Asian Crisis.* New York: Palgrave.

Bhole, L.M. (2004). *Financial Institutions and Markets: Structure, Growth, and Innovations*, Fourth Edition. India: Tata McGraw Hill.

Bhattacharya, U. and H. Daouk (2002). 'The world price of insider trading', *Journal of Finance*, 57, 1, 75–108.

Birdsall, N. (2005). 'Why inequality matters in a globalizing world'. WIDER Annual Lecture, Helsinki, 26 October.

Bonfiglioli, A. and C. Mendicino (2004). 'Financial liberalization, banking crises and growth: Assessing the links', SSE/EFI Working Paper No.567, Stockholm School of Economics, Stockholm.

Bonfiglioli, Alessandra (2005). 'How does financial liberalization affect economic growth?' Seminar Paper 736, Institute for International Economic Studies, Stockholm University, Stockholm.

Brown, F. and P. Manasse (1989). 'The information content of the term structure of interest rates: Theory and practice', Working Paper No. 77, Department of Economics and Statistics, OECD.

Brown, Kym (2001). 'Closing the divide—Issues when developing a bond market: The case of Sri Lanka', Working Paper No. 2001–6, School of Accounting, Economics and Finance, Deakin University, Australia.

Calvo, Guillermo A. (1996). *Money, Exchange Rates, and Output.* Cambridge, MA: The MIT Press.

Calvo, G. and C. Reinhart (2000). 'Fear of floating', mimeo, University of Maryland, Baltimore.

Cavoli, Tony and R.S. Rajan (2005). 'The capital inflows problem in selected Asian economies in the 1990s revisited: The role of monetary sterilization', SCAPE Policy Research Working Paper Series 0518, Singapore Centre for Applied and Policy Economics (SCAPE), Department of Economics, National University of Singapore.

——— (2006). 'Inflation targeting arrangements in Asia: Exploring the role of the exchange rate', SCAPE Policy Research Working Paper Series 0603, SCAPE, Department of Economics, National University of Singapore.

Caprio, G. and D. Klingebiel (1996). 'Bank insolvencies: Cross-country experience', World Bank Policy Research WP No. 1620, World Bank, Washington, D.C.

Central Bank of Sri Lanka (2004). 'Financial stability review', Central Bank of Sri Lanka. http://www.cbsl.gov.lk/pics_n_docs/10_publication/_docs/efr/financial_ system_stability_review/fsr2004.pdf. Accessed 13 January 2008.

——— (2005). 'Financial stability review', Central Bank of Sri Lanka. http://www.cbsl.gov.lk/pics_n_docs/10_publication/_docs/efr/financial_system_stability_review/FSR2005.pdf. Accessed 13 January 2008.

——— (2006a). *Annual Report,* Central Bank of Sri Lanka. http://www.cbsl.gov.lk/pics_n_docs/10_publication/_docs/efr/annual_report/Ar2006/Content.htm. Accessed 12 January 2008.

——— (2006b). 'Financial sector development and system stability', *Annual Report,* Central Bank of Sri Lanka. http:// www.cbsl.gov.lk/info/10_publication/p_1.htm. Accessed 20 January 2008.

——— (2007a). 'Financial stability review', Central Bank of Sri Lanka. http://www.cbsl.lk/cbsl/FSSR-2006.pdf. Accessed 20 January 2008.

——— (2007b). 'Financial system stability review', Central Bank of Sri

Lanka. http://www.cbsl.gov.lk/info/10_publication/p_1.htm. Accessed 30 January 2008.

——— (2007c). 'Road map: Monetary and financial sector policies for 2007 and beyond', Central Bank of Sri Lanka. http:// www.cbsl.lk/cbsl/speech-020107.pdf. Accessed 23 January 2008.

——— (2008). 'Road map: monetary and financial sector policies for 2008 and beyond', Central Bank of Sri Lanka. http://www.cbsl.gov.lk/pics_n_docs/10_publication/_docs/efr/monetary_ and_financial_sector_ policies/road_map2008e.pdf. Accessed 23 January 2008.

Centre for Policy Dialogue (2002). 'Financial sector reforms in Bangladesh: The next round', Report No. 49, Centre for Policy Dialogue, Dhaka. http://www.cpd-bangladesh.org/publications/all.html. Accessed 27 January 2008.

Chowdhury, Anis (2002). 'Politics, society and financial sector reforms in Bangladesh', *International Journal of Social Economics*, 29, 12, 963.

Clearing Corporation of India Ltd. (2006). 'Developments in money, G-Sec and forex markets in recent years', Clearing Corporation of India Ltd, India.

Cooray, Arusha (2000). 'The impact of deregulation on financial market efficiency in Sri Lanka'. PhD thesis, School of Economics, University of New South Wales, Australia.

Cotula, F. (1984). 'Financial innovations and monetary control in Italy', *Banca Nazionale del Lavoro Quarterly*, 37, 150, 219–56.

Deaton, A. and J. Dreze (2002). 'Poverty and inequality in India: A reexamination', *Economic and Political Weekly*, 37, 36, 3729–748.

Diaz-Alejandro, Carlos F. (1985). 'Good-bye financial repression, hello financial crash', *Journal of Development Economics*, 19, 1–2, 1–24.

Diwan, I. (2000). 'Labour shares and globalisation'. Paper presented at the Conference on Poverty and Inequality in Developing Countries: A Policy Dialogue on the Effects of Globalisation, 30 November—1 December 2000, OECD Development Centre, Paris.

Dornbusch, R. and A. Warner (1994). 'Mexico: Stabilization, reform, and no growth', *Brookings Papers on Economic Activity*, 1, 253–315.

Eichengreen, Barry (1994). 'International monetary arrangements for the 21st century', Brookings Institution, Washington, D.C.

——— (2001). 'Capital account liberalization: What do cross-country studies tell us?' Unpublished manuscript, University of California, Berkeley.

Eichengreen, Barry and David Leblang, (2003). 'Capital account liberalization and growth: Was Mr. Mahathir right?' NBER Working Papers 9427, National Bureau of Economic Research, Washington, D.C.

Galbraith, J. and J. Lu (1999). 'Inequality and financial crises: Some early findings', UTIP Working Paper. No. 9, LBJ School of Public Affairs, University of Texas at Austin.

Ghatak, Subrata (1997). 'Financial liberalization: The case of Sri Lanka', *Empirical Economics,* 22, 1, 117–29.

Gilchrist, Simon and Charles Himmelberg (1998). 'Investment, fundamentals and finance', NBER Working Papers 6652, National Bureau of Economic Research, Washington, D.C.

Goldstein, M. (1998). 'The Asian financial crisis: Causes, cures and systemic implication', *Policy Analyses in International Economics,* vol. 55, Peterson Institute for International Economics, Washington, D.C.

Goodhart, C. (1986). 'Financial innovation and monetary control', *Oxford Review of Economic Policy,* 2, 4, 79–102.

——— (1989). 'The conduct of monetary policy', *Economic Journal,* 99, 396, 293–346.

Gabb, W. and A. Mullineux (1995). 'Financial innovation, monetary aggregates and monetary policy in the U.K. and Germany', Discussion Paper No. 95–17, Department of Economics, University of Birmingham.

Greenwald, B., E. Stiglitz, and A. Weiss (1984). 'Information imperfections in the capital market and macroeconomic fluctuations', *American Economic Review,* 74, 2, 194–9.

Grilli, Vittorio and Gian Maria Milesi-Ferretti (1995). 'Economic effect and structural determinants of capital controls', *IMF Staff Papers,* 42, 3, 517–51.

Hanif, M. Nadeem (2003). 'Restructuring of financial sector in Pakistan', *The Journal of the Institute of Bankers in Pakistan,* 70, 1, 43–74.

Hameed, Farhan (2007). 'Fostering the corporate bond market in Pakistan', *State Bank of Pakistan Research Bulletin,* 3, 1, 107–28.

Hubbard, R. Glenn (1998). 'Capital-market imperfections and investment', *Journal of Economic Literature,* 36, 1, 193–225.

International Monetary Fund (2004). 'Pakistan: Financial system stability assessment, including reports on the observance of standards and codes on the following topics: monetary and financial policy transparency, banking supervision, and securities regulation', IMF Country Report No. 04/215, International Monetary Fund, Washington, D.C.

———(2005), 'Pakistan—financial sector assessment program—technical note—condition of the banking system', IMF Country Report No. 05/157, International Monetary Fund, Washington, D.C.

——— (2007). 'Sri Lanka: financial system stability assessment—update, including reports on the observance of standards and codes on the following topics: Banking supervision and payment systems', IMF Country Report No. 07/383, International Monetary Fund, Washington, D.C.

Jha, R. (2000). 'Reducing poverty and inequality in India: Has liberalization helped?' UNU/WIDER Working Paper No. 204, Helsinki.

Jayamaha, Ranee (2006). 'Basel II – A roadmap for Sri Lankan banking system with international comparisons', Bank for International Settlements, Basel. http://www.bis.org/review/ r070115f.pdf. Accessed 19 January 2008.

Kaufmann, D., Aart Kraay and H. Mastruzzi (2007). 'Governance matters VI: Governance indicators for 1996–2006', World Bank Policy Research Discussion Paper 4280, World Bank, Washington, D.C.

Khan, M. Arshad and Sajawal Khan (2007). 'Financial sector restructuring in Pakistan', MPRA Paper No. 4141, Munich Personal RePEc Archive, Germany. http://mpra.ub.uni-muenchen.de/4141/1/MPRA_paper_4141.pdf. Accessed 24 January 2008.

Koeva, Petya (2003). 'The performance of Indian banks during financial liberalisation', IMF Working Paper WP/2003/150, International Monetary Fund, Washington, D.C.

Kraay, Aart (2000). 'Do high interest rates defend currencies during speculative attacks?' Policy Research Working Paper Series 2267, The World Bank, Washington, D.C.

Kwack, S. (2001). 'An empirical assessment of monetary policy responses to capital inflows in East Asia before the crisis', *International Economic Journal*, 15, 1, 95–113.

Klein, Michael and Giovanni Olivei (1999). 'Capital account liberalization, financial depth, and economic growth', NBER Working Paper No. 7384, National Bureau of Economic Research, Washington, D.C.

La Porta, R.F. Lopez de Silanes, A. Shleifer, and R. Vishny (1997). 'Legal determinants of external finance', *Journal of Finance*, 52, 3, 1131–50.

Levine, Ross (2001). 'International financial liberalization and economic growth', *Review of International Economics*, 9, 4, 688–704.

Leeladhar, Vittaldas (2006). 'Recent banking developments in India', BIS Papers No. 28, Bank for International Settlements, Basel. http://www.bis.org/publ/bppdf/bispap28.htm. Accessed 2 February 2008.

——— (2007). 'Indian financial sector reforms', *BIS Review* 25/2007, Bank for International Settlements, Basel.

Love, I. (2000). 'Financial development and financing constraints: International evidence from the structural investment model', manuscript, Columbia University, New York.

McKinnon, Ronald I. (1973). 'Money and capital in economic development', The Brookings Institution, Washington, D.C.

——— (1991). *The Order of Economic Liberalization: Financial Control in the Transition to a Market Economy.* Baltimore: John Hopkins University Press.

Ministry of Finance (2004). 'Report on the Advisory Committee to advise on the administered interest rates and rationalisation of saving instruments', Government of India, New Delhi. http://finmin.nic.in/the_ministry/dept_eco_affairs/IR&RSI/forward.pdf. Accessed 11 February 2008.

——— (2005). 'Report on high level expert committee on cor-porate bonds and securitization', Government of India, New Delhi.

Mohan, Rakesh (2005). 'Financial sector reforms in India: Policies and performance analysis', *Economic and Political Weekly*, 40, 12, 1106.

——— (2006). 'Financial sector reforms and monetary policy: The Indian experience'. Paper presented at the Conference on Economic Policy in Asia, Stanford University, 2 June 2006. http://scid.stanford.edu/events/PanAsia/Papers/Mohan.pdf. Accessed 1 February 2008.

——— (2007). 'Capital account liberalization and conduct of monetary policy: The Indian experience'. Paper presented at an International Monetary Seminar organized by Banque de France on *Globalization, Inflation and Financial Markets*, Paris, 14 June.

Mu, Yibin (2007). 'South Asia bond markets: Bangladesh', Social Science Research Network Electronic Publishing. http://papers.ssrn.com/ sol3/papers.cfm?abstract_id=999713. Accessed 2 February 2008.

Mundle, S. and V. Tulasidhar (1998). 'Adjustment and distribution: The Indian experience', Occasional Paper No. 17, Asian Development Bank, Manila.

Nachane, D.M. (2007). 'Capital account convertibility in India: Revisiting the debate', ISAS Working Paper No. 24, Institute of South Asian Studies, Singapore.

Nachane, D.M. and Nishita Raje (2007). 'Financial liberalisation and monetary policy', *The Journal of Applied Economic Research*, 1, 1, 47–83.

Obstfeld, M, J.C. Shambaugh and A.M. Taylor (2004). 'The trilemma in history: Tradeoffs among exchange rates, monetary policies, and capital mobility', NBER Working Paper No. 10396, National Bureau of Economic Research, Washington, D.C.

Rajan, Raghuram G. and Luigi Zingales (1998). 'Financial dependence and growth', *The American Economic Review*, 88, 3, 559–86.

National Stock Exchange of India Limited (2006). *Indian Securities Market: A Review*, Volume IX, National Stock Exchange of India Limited, Mumbai.

Patil, R.H. (2005). 'Report of high level expert committee on corporate bond and securitization', Government of India, New Delhi.

Rangarajan, C. (2000). 'Capital flows: Another look', *Economic and Political Weekly*, 35, 50, 4421–7.

Ravallion, M. and G. Datt (1999). 'When is growth pro-poor?: Evidence from the diverse experience of Indian states', mimeo, The World Bank, Washington, D.C.

Reddy, Y. V. (1998). 'Interest rates in India: Status and issues', Reserve Bank of India. http://rbidocs.rbi.org.in/rdocs/Speeches/PDFs/2486.pdf. Accessed 2 February 2008.

——— (2002). 'Monetary and financial sector reforms in India: A practitioner's perspective', Reserve Bank of India. http://www.rbi.org.in/scripts/BS_SpeechesView.aspx?Id=108. Accessed 2 February 2008.

——— (2004). 'Monetary and financial sector reforms in India: A practitioner's perspective'. In Kaushik Basu (ed.), *India's Emerging Economy: Performance and Prospects in the 1990s and Beyond.* Cambridge: The MIT Press.

——— (2005). 'Banking sector reforms in India—an overview', Bank for International Settlements, Basel. http:// www.bis.org/review/r050519b.pdf. Accessed 3 February 2008.

——— (2007a). 'India: Development and reform experience and prospects', Bank for International Settlements, Basel. http://www.bis.org/review/r070919c.pdf. Accessed February 5, 2008.

——— (2007b). 'Glimpses of the Indian economy and its financial sector'. Speech at the Central Bank of the Russian Federation, Moscow, 2 July. http:// www.bis.org/review/r070704b.pdf. Accessed 5 February 2008.

——— (2007c), 'Developing debt markets in India: Review and prospects'. Remarks by Dr. Y.V. Reddy, Governor, Reserve Bank of India at Washington, USA on October 18. http://rbidocs.rbi.org.in/rdocs/ Bulletin/PDFs/82026.pdf. Accessed 17 February 2008.

——— (2008). 'Global financial turbulence and financial sector in India: A practitioner's perspective'. Address at the meeting of the Task Force on Financial Markets Regulation organized by the Initiative for Policy Dialogue, Manchester, UK, 1 July.

Reserve Bank of India (2006a). 'Report on currency and finance 2005–6', Reserve Bank of India, Mumbai. http://rbidocs.rbi.org.in/rdocs/Publications/PDFs/77570..pdf. Accessed 14 February 2008.

——— (2006b). 'Report of the Committee on fuller capital account convertibility', available at http://www.rbi.org.in/scripts/PublicationReport Details.aspx? UrlPage=&ID=468, Reserve Bank of India, Mumbai. Accessed 14 February 2008.

——— (2006c). 'Report on trend and progress of banking in India 2005-06', available http://rbidocs.rbi.org.in/rdocs/Publications/PDFs/73830.pdf, Reserve Bank of India, Mumbai. Accessed 14 February 2008.

——— (2007a). 'Report on trend and progress of banking in India 2006–7', Reserve Bank of India, Mumbai.

——— (2007b). 'Guidelines for implementation of the new capital adequacy framework', Reserve Bank of India, Mumbai.

——— (2007c). 'Operational guidelines for banks undertaking/proposing to undertake primary dealer business in government securities market', Reserve Bank of India, Mumbai. http://www.rbi.org.in/scripts/BS_View MasterCirculars.aspx? Id=3668and Mode=0

Rodrik, Dani (1998). 'Who needs capital-account convertibility?' In S. Fischer et al. (eds.), *Should the IMF Pursue Capital-Account Convertibility? Essays in International Finance,* No. 207, International Finance Section, Department of Economics, Princeton University.

Rodrik, Dani, Arvind Subramanian, and Francesco Trebbi (2002). 'Institutions rule: the primacy of institutions over geography and integration in economic development', NBER Working Paper 9305, National Bureau of Economic Research, Washington, D.C.

Saidane, Dhafer (2002). 'The role of financial liberalization in development: Weaknesses and corrections', *Savings and Development,* 26, 3, 259–76.

Sargent, T. (1982). 'The ends of four big inflations'. In R. Hall (ed.), *Inflation: Causes and Effects* (pp. 41–97). Chicago: University of Chicago Press.

State Bank of Pakistan (2005). 'Roadmap for the implementation of Basel II in State Bank of Pakistan'. http://www.sbp.org.pk/bsd/2005/C3_ROAD MAP-Basel.pdf, accessed 11 January 2008.

——— (2006). 'Banking system review'. http://www.sbp.org.pk/publications/ bsr/index.htm, State Bank of Pakistan, Karachi. Accessed 12 January 2008.

——— (2007). 'Quarterly Performance Review of the Banking System', State Bank of Pakistan, Karachi.

Securities and Exchange Commission of Sri Lanka (2006). *Annual Report.* Securities and Exchange Commission of Sri Lanka, Colombo. http:// www.sec.gov.lk/pdf/SEC%20Annual%20Report2006.pdf. Accessed 11 February 2008.

Securities and Exchange Commission of Pakistan (2007). 'Debt Capital Markets Committee Report 2007', Securities and Exchange Commission of Pakistan, Islamabad.

Sharma, V.K. and Chandan Sinha (2006). 'The corporate debt market in India', *Developing Corporate Bond Markets in Asia,* 26, 80–7, Bank for International Settlements.

Shaw, Edward (1973). *Financial Deepening in Economic Development.* New York: Oxford University Press.

Singh, A. (2002). 'Capital account liberalization, free long term capital flows, financial crises and economic development', University of Cambridge Working Paper No. 245, ESRC Centre for Business Research, Cambridge, UK.

Singh, Nirvikar, Laveesh Bhandari, Aoyo Chen and Aarti Khare (2003). 'Regional inequality in India: A fresh look', *Economic and Political Weekly*, 38, 11, 1069–73.

Sharma, Manoranjan (31 August 2004). 'Centrality of innovation for banks', *The Hindu Business Line*, New Delhi, India.

The Times of India (27 May 2007). New Delhi, India.

Taylor, L. (2000). 'External liberalization, economic performance and distribution in Latin America and elsewhere', UNU/WIDER Working Paper No. 215.

Tobin, James (1983). 'Macroeconomics under debate', Cowles Foundation Discussion Papers No. 669, Cowles Foundation, Yale University.

——— (1983). 'Financial structure and monetary rules', *Kredit und Kapital*, 2, 155–71.

Vegh, C. (1992). 'Stopping high inflation: an analytical overview', *IMF Staff Papers*, 39, 626–95. International Monetary Fund, Washington, D.C.

Wyplosz, C. (2001). 'How risky is financial liberalization in the developing countries?' G4 Discussion Paper Series , No. 14.

Figure 10.1: Structure of Indian Banking

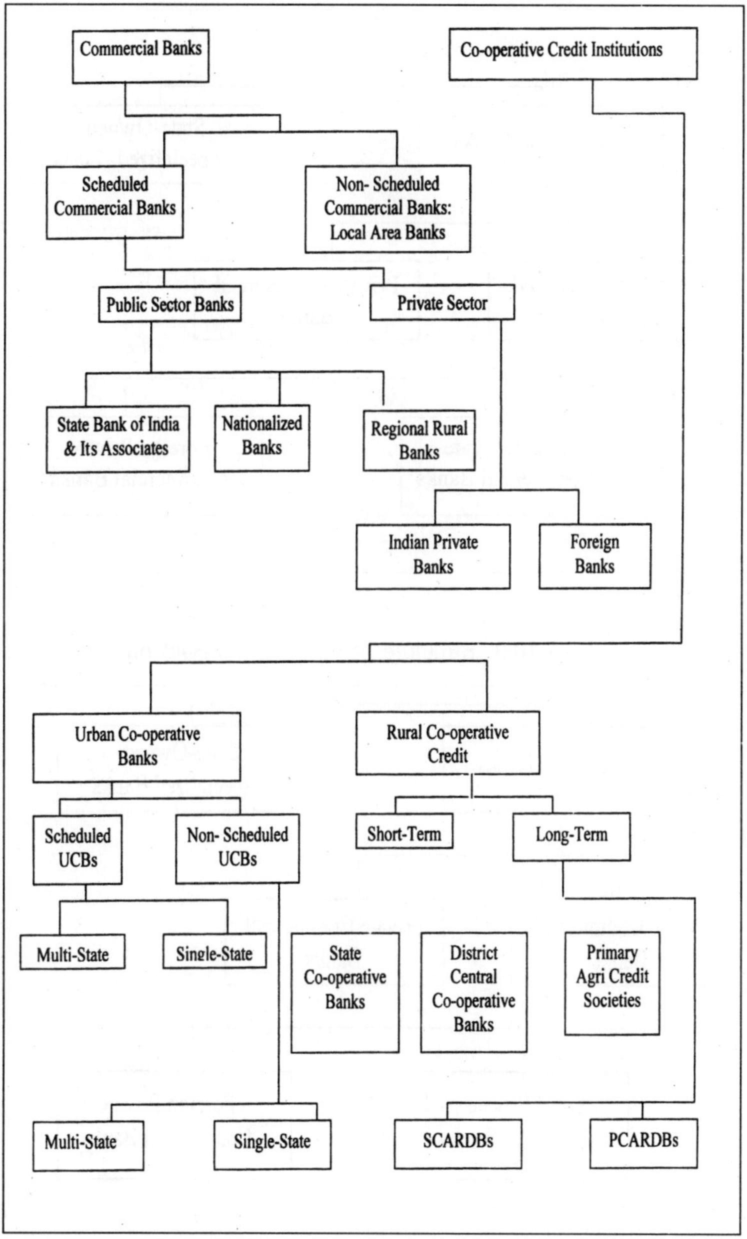

Figure 10.2: Structure of Pakistani Banking

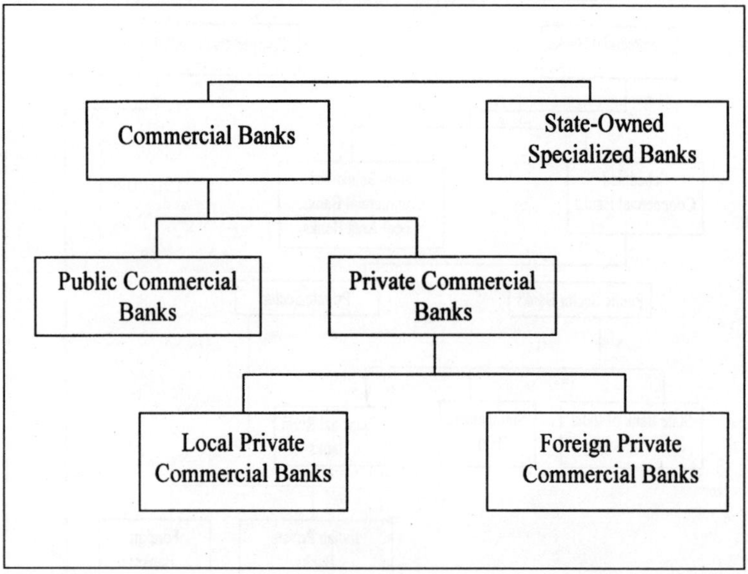

Figure 10.3: Structure of Bangladeshi Banking

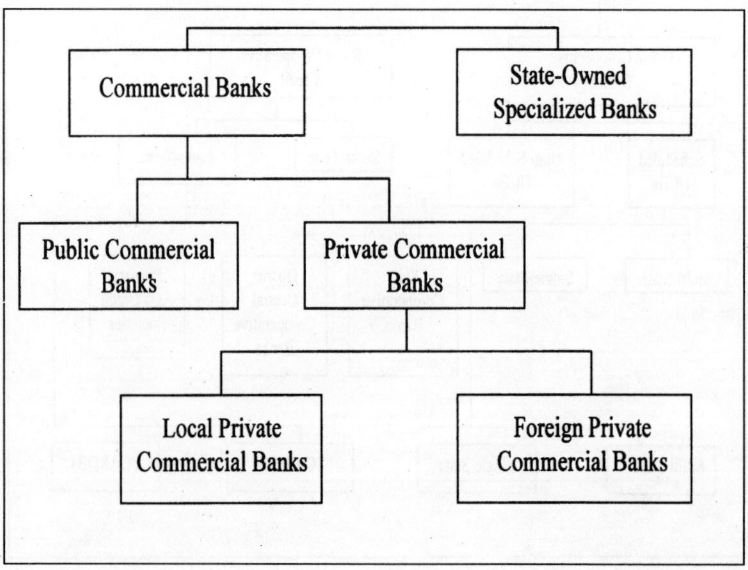

Figure 10.4: Structure of Sri Lankan Banking

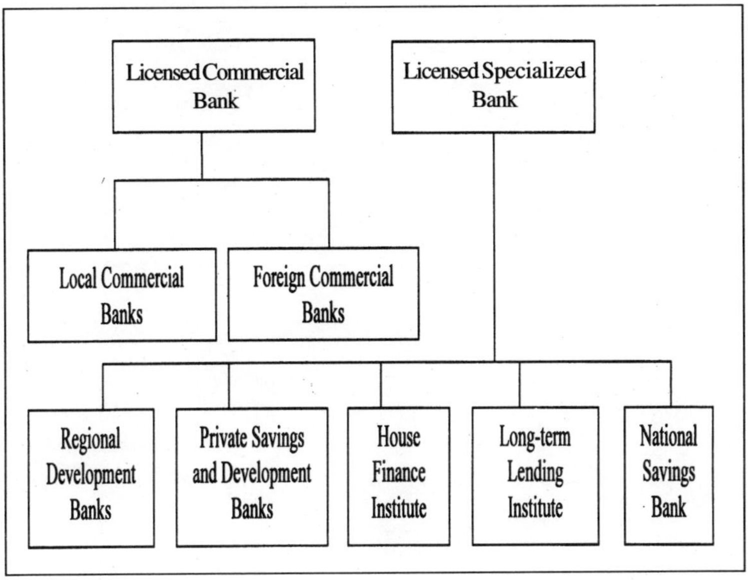

11

Adjustment Strategies in Energy Pricing: South Asian Experiences

S. NARAYAN

INTRODUCTION

THIS CHAPTER attempts to examine the rationale of the policies that have been adopted by the major countries in South Asia, and argues that the subsidy-based moving peg price adjustment mechanisms used by these countries were, in fact, appropriate policy tools for the governments. Oil prices have increased steadily since 2003, and after touching a peak of US$147 per barrel in July 2008, are hovering at around US$98 a barrel at end-September 2008. Prior to 2002, oil prices were in the range of US$28 to US$34 per barrel, and the steeper increases have necessitated consumer price adjustments in almost all countries. While some countries, most notably the developed countries, have gone in for automatic adjustment in prices, several of the developing countries have attempted to cushion the consumer from the impact of these steep increases. In South Asia, these have been attempted through direct and indirect subsidies, adjustment of taxes and tariffs, and extension of credit by state-owned banks.

The oil price increases in the 1970s were caused by the cartelization of the producers of oil into a strong bargaining entity. The consequent price adjustments led to the development of new technologies for improvements in fuel efficiency and conservation, most notably in Japan. They also led to exploration and new discoveries of oilfields in South America, South East Asia, and Africa. The first oil shock led to substantial increases in the supply of oil.

The second oil shock in the early 1990s was a function of the disturbances in the Gulf, triggered by the United States (US) war in Iraq and interruptions of supplies from Kuwait. Interestingly, this was seen as a blip by the oil-importing countries and, indeed, over a period of time, prices stabilized. The financial crisis in Asia in 1997 and the slowing down of growth in the US in 2000 saw oil prices falling to levels below US$20 a barrel.

Against this backdrop, when oil prices started rising towards the end of 2002, it was only natural that oil-importing countries expected that the prices would stabilize over a period of time. The sharp increases were attributed to the disturbances caused by the Iraq war as well as to the strained relations between the US and Iran. This was also the time when the Yukos incident[1] in Russia led to much greater state control over oil production. Disturbances in Nigeria and increased state ownership in Venezuela contributed to disturbances in supplies at about that time which most policy makers saw as temporary aberrations. It was only by 2004 that it became clear that there were fundamental differences between the earlier oil shocks and the present one. Most importantly, growing consumption in Asia, fuelled by the demands of the growing economies of India and China resulted in almost all the incremental production getting consumed in Asia.[2] In addition, the low oil prices of the previous five years had led to little investment in fresh exploration or refining, and suddenly, the demand outstripped the supply. It soon became clear that these growing demands from countries in Asia would continue in the future as well. Finally, given constraints in increasing supplies in the short run and growing demand, arbitrage opportunities in the commodity exchanges, most notably the New York Mercantile exchange, increased, and led to volatility in prices beyond the expectations of the oil-producing nations. It is now clear that high oil prices are here to stay, and that growing demand is likely to outstrip production capabilities in the short to medium term.

The management of the large increases in international fuel prices during 2006–8 has proved to be particularly challenging for developing and emerging market economies, where governments have significant influence over domestic fuel prices and social safety nets tend to be poorly developed. South Asian countries, in particular,

Table 11.1: Changes in International Fuel Prices, 2003–6

	US$ per liter	Per cent change
Crude oil prices	0.4	128.0
Gasoline	0.6	140.7
Kerosene	0.6	126.7
Diesel	0.6	142.1

Source: IMF data.

Note: Increase during end-2003 to June 2006. The above price of crude oil is the average of spot prices for Dated Brent, West Texas Intermediate, and the Dubai Fateh. The prices for the other fuels are the average FOB prices for Rotterdam, New York, Gul Coast, Los Angeles and Singapore.

have been somewhat taken by surprise, and coping strategies have so far been *ad hoc*. At the top of the agenda has been the inability to handle the political implications of passing price increases down in entirety to consumers. The efforts of Bangladesh, Sri Lanka, Nepal, Pakistan, and India have been to cushion the impact to consumers through a variety of interventions, subsidies, and product differentiation pricing strategies.

The next section describes the strategies of these countries. A key finding is that only half of the developing and emerging market countries in our sample appear to have fully passed through the increase in international fuel prices after 2004. This has mainly reflected controls on retail prices and reductions in fuel taxes, and has resulted in increased explicit and implicit fuel price subsidies. In some cases, this has compounded fiscal difficulties. With respect to domestic fuel price reform, while the international experience has been mixed, it suggests a pragmatic approach of incorporating a phased increase in domestic prices to bring them to international levels.

The sudden rise in oil prices from 2004 is attributed to the interaction of several factors:

1. Conditions in Iraq have led to uncertainties of output from that country. There is on the one hand difficulty in ascertaining the monthly marketable surplus that that country is making available and, on the other, the lack of development of new fields.

2. There have also been supply-side bottlenecks in Venezuela and Nigeria. The internal strife in Nigeria (from 2004) and the nationalization of assets in Venezuela (January 2002) have contributed to uncertainties in production. In Iran, the prevailing political conditions have led to a loss of confidence about supply.
3. There have been supply obstructions in Russia. The Yukos incident in 2004 and the stoppage of supply to Ukraine in 2005 caused large uncertainties about oil and gas supply. Russian oil production has increasingly become state-owned and state-controlled, leading to market uncertainties.
4. In the Organization of the Petroleum Exporting Countries (OPEC), in Saudi Arabia in particular, there has been little investment in new production or exploration in the years between 1997 and 2002. This has been accompanied by sluggishness of rise in oil production in non-OPEC countries. A decline in North Sea oil production has become evident, and the output from Russia has remained flat since 2006. The older fields do not appear to have any major slack available for increasing production, and world oil production has been in the range of 82–4 million barrels a day since 2006.
5. Growth of global oil demand. After slow growth in the period 2000 to 2003, there has been a spurt in demand due to accelerating growth in China and South Asia. Demand has recovered in the US and is accelerating in Asia and in China, in particular. Almost the entire additional production since 2005 has been consumed in Asia.
6. The ability of the US market to adjust to tight supply, i.e. the supply cushion, has been fragile due to the decline in oil-refining surplus capacity, the low level of oil product stocks, and decline in natural gas supply surplus capacity.
7. In 2005, multiple large hurricanes struck the coast off the Gulf of Mexico, and the damage caused obstructed the supply of oil and gas.
8. Speculative funds were invested in oil futures, giving rise to a premium disassociated from actual supply and demand, and the overreaction of the futures market became radical. Trans-

actions in the New York Mercantile exchange exacerbated the fluctuations in oil prices.

COUNTRY EXPERIENCES

Against this backdrop, the adjustments in consumer prices in the South Asian countries have lacked a cohesive strategy. Domestic price adjustments were limited in many of these countries during 2004–5, and implicit or explicit subsidies helped contain the impact of the oil shock on inflation. However, as world oil prices continue to rise, some of these economies have implemented more aggressive price adjustments since early 2006.

These countries also responded to the oil shock by raising administered fuel prices. On average, they achieved full price pass-through for gasoline, but lagged by significant margins for diesel and kerosene. However, for diesel the average pass-through has been 80 per cent at end-2005 and it is ahead of other regions. For kerosene, the average pass-through has been around 50 per cent, which is similar to that for low-income Asia. The weight of petroleum products and related services (including transport and electricity) in the Consumer Price Index in the South Asian Association for Regional Co-operation is about 10 per cent, comparable to other Asian countries.

SRI LANKA

Sri Lanka imports 40 per cent of its product needs, and processes the balance of its requirements in the one refinery in the country. It has no oil production of its own and, hence, its entire oil needs are imported. According to International Energy Agency (IEA) statistics, Sri Lanka consumed 3.5 million tonnes of petroleum products in 2003. Diesel accounted for 51 per cent of the total consumption, heavy fuel oil 21 per cent, gasoline 10 per cent, aviation and non-aviation kerosene 6 per cent each, and liquid petroleum gas (LPG) 5 per cent (IEA 2005b). Efforts to modernize the refinery have been thwarted by the trade unions of the state-owned Ceylon Petroleum Corporation (CPC) due to fears about privatization and removal of subsidies.[3]

Sri Lanka signed a stand-by package with the International Monetary Fund (IMF) in March 2001, and one of the conditions that the country had to fulfill was to introduce automatic pricing for petroleum products. In other words, petroleum prices would not be subsidized and would be adjusted according to fluctuations in world market prices and passed through to the consumers. Although this was a commitment undertaken by the government of Sri Lanka, this policy was not implemented in 2001 due to the political crisis that year. It was the newly elected government in late 2001 that implemented this policy in January 2002. Although automatic pricing for petroleum was put into operation, both diesel and kerosene were sold at subsidized prices, taking into consideration that kerosene is used more by the non-affluent and that an increase in the price of diesel would substantially increase public transport costs and thereby burden the less affluent.

The automatic pricing policy for petroleum was abandoned in January 2004 to cushion the cost of living before the April 2004 general elections. The government froze fuel prices between February and July 2004. In June 2004, the finance minister announced that raising fuel prices would be the government's last resort, to be implemented only if all other options failed.[4] After price increases in July, August, and September 2004, the prices of petroleum products remained constant between September 2004 and May 2005, at which time price increases ranging from 9 to 12 per cent were implemented for gasoline, kerosene, and diesel. In spite of these increases, since 2004 petrol continued to be sold below market-determined prices.

The Lanka Indian Oil Corporation (LIOC) which bought 33 per cent of the CPC in 2002 was also requested to follow the subsidized pricing policy for oil from January 2004. Consequent to LIOC selling oil below the market price it had to forego US$60 million due to the company, a contention unacceptable to the Sri Lankan treasury. Faced with the increasing cost of the subsidies—Rs. 15 billion in 2004 increasing to Rs. 26 billion (about US$250 million) in 2005[5]—the government has looked for various ways of obtaining financial relief. In 2004 the Government of Sri Lanka asked the Government of India for a line of credit (a loan over a seven-year

Table 11.2: Petroleum Product Retail Prices in Sri Lanka, 2004–7

	2004	2005	2006	2007
Petrol	84	90	95	117
Diesel	40	50	62	75
Kerosene	11	30	43.5	68

Source: *Colombo Times*.
Note: All figures in Sri Lankan Rs.

period) to help pay for its imports. Other avenues explored by the government of Sri Lanka included requesting OPEC to delay its import bill for up to one year, and for Petronas to also defer repayments. The government also requested the LIOC to convert the money owed to it into a loan, and also argued that it did not need to recompense the company. [The fuel price subsidy bill in 2004 was close to Rs. 20 billion (US$200 million).] Although the fiscal situation in Sri Lanka during 2005 was temporarily helped by the large flows of aid and a freeze on some debt repayment following the tsunami at the beginning of 2005, the government was unable to remove or reduce the subsidy burden. In May 2006, CPC stated that 93-RON gasoline should be sold at Rs. 100 per liter rather than Rs. 88, diesel at Rs. 69 instead of Rs. 58, and kerosene at Rs. 67, nearly double the prevailing retail price, to eliminate losses.[6] The company announced in December 2005 that it would have to shut down within three months if the money owing was unpaid, which led to the suspension of its shares on the Colombo stock exchange. In May 2006, the LIOC announced that in the fiscal year ending on 31 March 2006, the company made a loss of US$70 million (Organization of Asia-Pacific News Agencies 2006).

The position of CPC, which is also owed money by the government to cover the costs of subsidies, has been adversely affected by the problems of the power sector. A prolonged drought reduced the availability of hydropower and necessitated increased consumption of diesel, while power tariffs were also being held down. As a result, the Ceylon Electricity Board was behind in its payments to

CPC, as were some government departments, leading to unpaid dues totaling Rs. 7 billion (US$70 million) by various government entities by mid-June 2005 (Economist Intelligence Unit-Views Wire 2005a). By the end of 2005, the Ceylon Electricity Board alone owed CPC Rs. 10 billion (US$100 million), although about 40 per cent of this debt was offset against CPC's taxes payable.

In 2005, in spite of a series of increases in domestic fuel prices, fuel subsidies remained at an estimated 1.1 per cent of the Gross Domestic Product (GDP), while quasi-fiscal losses generated from administered electricity charges were around 0.5 per cent of GDP. The 2006 budget targeted removing fuel subsidies through price adjustments. Domestic fuel prices were increased in April, June, August, and September 2006, completing the full pass-through for petrol and diesel, and substantially reducing subsidies for kerosene. The pricing formula for fuel products was also revised in September to set the stage for oil companies to determine domestic prices from September onwards.

It can be concluded that:

- The fuel subsidies that Sri Lanka maintained until July 2006 were regressive as well as being inefficient, as evidenced by the substantial leakage to high-income households. In 2006, about 52 per cent of the subsidies went to the top two income quintiles compared to only 31 per cent to the bottom two income quintiles. Therefore, it cost the budget approximately Rs. 3.2 to transfer Re. 1 to the poorest 40 per cent of households via fuel subsidies.
- The household welfare loss from the full pass-through of oil prices is estimated at about a 1.2 per cent decrease (on average) in household real incomes. Households in the bottom income quintile experienced on average a 1.8 per cent decline in their real incomes compared to a 1 per cent decrease for the top income quintile. Kerosene is a relatively important source of energy for poor households, but the bulk of kerosene subsidies still leak to non-poor households. Over 34 per cent of kerosene subsidies accrue to the top two quintiles and it costs the budget Rs. 2.2 to transfer Re. 1 to the poorest two quintiles via kerosene subsidies. In addition, maintaining kerosene subsidies while removing other fuel subsidies is likely to result in inefficient substitution towards

kerosene away from other fuels (especially diesel), resulting in a second-round increase in the subsidy bill.

- Increased domestic fuel prices could lead to higher quasi-fiscal losses of the power sector if electricity tariffs were not adjusted. Given the low access rates to electricity for poor households, most of the benefits of the current subsidies have accrued to middle-income households. The leakage of electricity subsidies in the current system of tariffs is even greater than that for kerosene subsidies, with the top income quintile receiving half the aggregate subsidy compared to less than 6 per cent to the bottom income quintile.
- As an illustration, an alternative option to protect the poor from price adjustments is to use the budgetary savings to expand the existing Samriddhi program.[7] Only 19 per cent of Samriddhi transfers leak to the top two quintiles, coverage of the poorest households is high, and it costs the budget Rs. 1.7 to transfer Re. 1 to the poorest 40 per cent of households. A better-targeted transfer program could decrease the leakage.

Starting from the actual domestic prices of July 2006, at per liter prices of Rs. 93 for petrol, Rs. 61 for diesel, and Rs. 43.5 for kerosene, the corresponding required formula prices (based on August 2006 import prices) were Rs. 104, Rs. 70, and Rs. 68, respectively. These prices provide the basis of the simulated price increases of 11.5 per cent for petrol, 15.3 per cent for diesel and 57.2 per cent for kerosene. They approximate the actual full pass-through in August and September 2006, with the exception of kerosene for which the prevailing price (at Rs. 48.5 per liter) was lower than the full pass-through price used in the simulation.

Inflation has been high since 2007, reflecting in part the effect of the price pass-through, but they remain manageable. Sri Lanka achieved full pass-through for diesel and substantially increased domestic prices for kerosene by September 2006. To avoid amplifying price shocks, the Sri Lankan authorities also removed the ad valorem tax of 15 per cent on diesel in early 2006 and revised the pricing formula for the two oil companies to ensure cost recovery and a profit margin for future price adjustments.

NEPAL

Nepal is a net oil importer but it does not maintain a market-based pricing mechanism for petroleum products. In 2003, the Government of Nepal created an independent committee to set fuel prices, following heavy losses at the state-owned oil monopoly, Nepal Oil Corporation. While the committee was mandated to adjust prices in line with international trends, it has refrained from doing so, perhaps in the hope that price swings will ultimately cancel themselves out. A price adjustment was only made in January 2005, and consequently the oil monopoly has been suffering losses of over NRs. 500 million a month. In the second half of FY2005, its losses reached US$29.4 million. Its losses for FY2006 are estimated to have been more than US$56 million (about 0.8 per cent of GDP). The government attempted to raise petroleum prices in August 2006, which were retracted after widespread public resistance. The Petroleum Sales and Distribution Act, which seeks to liberalize the petroleum sector, has been submitted for parliamentary approval, but private sector participation is likely to be limited until an appropriate pricing mechanism is first put into place.

The Nepal Oil Corporation finally raised the prices of all the petroleum products, in 2007. The price of petrol has increased by NRs. 6 and 3 each for diesel and kerosene, and by NRs. 200 per LPG cylinder.

As per the revised prices, petrol will now cost NRs. 73 per liter, diesel will cost NRs. 56, and kerosene NRs. 51 while cooking gas will now cost NRs. 1,100 per cylinder for consumers.

There is no clear-cut policy strategy for managing energy price increases, and responses have been fairly ad hoc.

PAKISTAN

Pakistan is an oil producer, but relies on imports for more than 80 per cent of its consumption. According to the Ministry of Petroleum and Natural Resources, indigenous crude oil meets 18 per cent of total demand; the remaining 82 per cent of demand is met through imports of crude oil, high speed diesel, and fuel oil. There are eight refineries in the country. Pakistan consumed 15.5 million tonnes of petroleum products in FY2004–5. Diesel accounted for

Table 11.3: Product Prices in Nepal (in Nepal Rs.)

	2006	2007
Petrol	67.25	73
Diesel	53.15	56
Kerosene	47.65	50.95
Cooking gas	900	1,100

Source: Nepal News reports.

50 per cent, heavy fuel oil 29 per cent, gasoline 9 per cent, LPG 3 per cent, and non-aviation kerosene 1 per cent (HDIP-MPNR 2005).

According to the *Oil and Gas Journal* (OGJ), Pakistan had proven oil reserves of 300 million barrels as of January 2006. The majority of produced oil comes from proven reserves located in the southern half of the country, with the three largest oil-producing fields located in the Southern Indus Basin. Additional producing fields are located in the Middle and Upper Indus Basins. Oil production has remained fairly flat, at around 60,000 barrels per day (bbl/d). Due to Pakistan's modest oil production, the country is dependent on oil imports to satisfy domestic oil demand. As of November 2006, Pakistan had consumed approximately 350,000 barrels of oil and various petroleum products, of which more than 80 per cent was imported. The majority of oil imports come from the Middle East, mostly from Saudi Arabia.

Pakistan's Ministry of Petroleum and Natural Resources regulates the country's oil sector. The ministry grants oil concessions by open tender and by private negotiation. To encourage oil sector investment, the ministry has offered various tax and royalty payment incentives to oil companies. Pakistan's three largest national oil companies, include the Oil and Gas Development Corporation Limited (OGDCL), Pakistan Petroleum Limited (PPL), and Pakistan State Oil (PSO). All three operate under joint ventures and partnerships with various international oil companies and other domestic firms. The major international oil companies operating in Pakistan include BP (United Kingdom), Eni (Italy), OMV (Austria), Orient Petroleum Inc. (Canada), Petronas (Malaysia) and Tullow (Ireland).

Figure 11.1: Pakistan's Oil Production and Consumption, 1986–2006

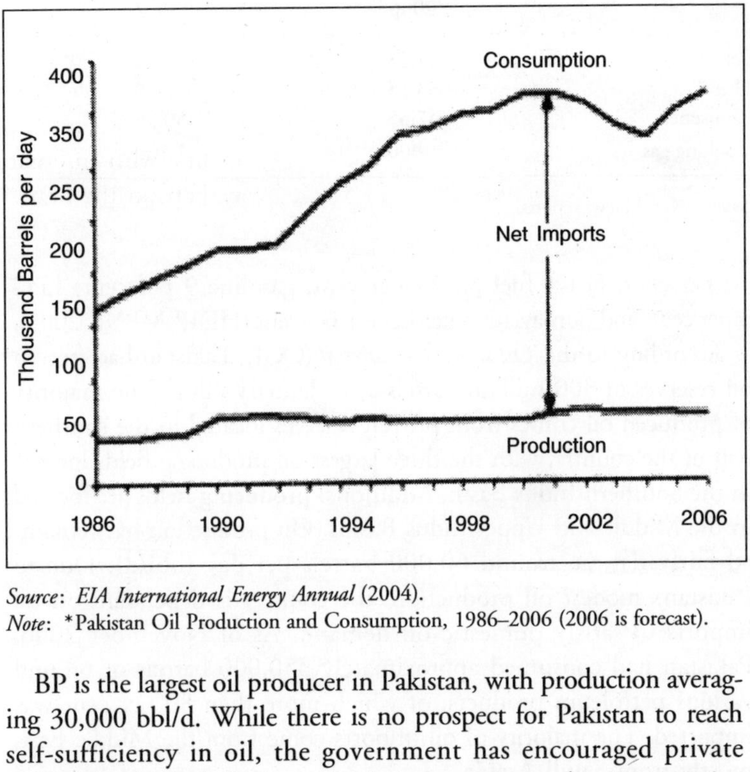

Source: *EIA International Energy Annual* (2004).
Note: *Pakistan Oil Production and Consumption, 1986–2006 (2006 is forecast).

BP is the largest oil producer in Pakistan, with production averaging 30,000 bbl/d. While there is no prospect for Pakistan to reach self-sufficiency in oil, the government has encouraged private (including foreign) firms to develop domestic production capacity. In 2005, national and international oil companies drilled a total of 29 onshore development wells in Pakistan. Pakistan has five refineries with total refining capacity of just under 270,000 bbl/d. However, refining capacity is short of domestic demand for products, and Pakistan is a net importer of products as well.

World oil price increases since 2006 have prompted the government to strengthen its control of the oil sector, with the result that only heavy fuel oil and aviation fuel are presently fully deregulated. Between 1 July 2001 and 1 April 2006, the Oil Companies Advisory Committee was authorized to review, set, and announce the ex-depot prices of gasoline, kerosene, and light diesel oil twice a month in accordance with the approved pricing formula. Import duties of 6 per cent on kerosene and light diesel oil and of 10 per cent on High Speed Diesel (HSD) have been imposed since July 2002, offering protection to domestic refineries. LPG was deregulated in 2000. In practice, an informal price ceiling continues to be applied to domestically manufactured LPG. For a long time, this ceiling was in the neighborhood of US$300 per tonne, against international LPG prices exceeding US$500 per tonne at times. This implicit price ceiling discourages LPG imports and creates a shortage, a 'black market', and high prices paid by end-users. In April 2006, well head LPG prices were increased from Rs. 17,000 (US$283) per tonne to Rs. 20,200 (US$337).

In response to rising world oil prices, the government decided to shield consumers from steep price increases and capped domestic sale prices in 2004 and 2005 (MPNR 2005). In addition, the government introduced a price differential claim (PDC) beginning on 16 August 2004, which was used to reimburse oil companies for the subsidy to consumers. The PDC particularly targeted kerosene and diesel. In November 2005, the Ministry of Petroleum and Natural Resources estimated that the differences between the prices of kerosene, HSD, and light diesel oil based on the pricing formula, and the actual prices in effect were Rs. 7.13 (US$0.12), Rs. 4.47 (US$0.07), and Rs. 4.13 (US$0.07) per liter, respectively. As of 31 October 2005, the total reduction in revenues to the government was Rs. 70 billion (about $1.2 billion), and the PDC had amounted to Rs. 21.4 billion ($360 million) (ibid.). Since 16 April 2006, the Oil and Gas Regulatory Authority has been in charge of price notification. This pricing formula is based on Arab Gulf fuel prices and consists of ex-refinery/import-parity price, customs and excise duty, petroleum development levy (PDL), distribution margin for oil marketing companies (currently 3.5 per cent of the ex-depot sale price), dealers' commission (4 per cent of ex-depot sale price), inland freight equalization margin (which is based on actual transportation costs determined by oil marketing companies), and a 15 per cent general sales tax.

Although Pakistan has adopted an automatic price adjustment mechanism based on a formula linked to world prices and to published margins, there has been enormous hostility to the price rises, despite the element of subsidy for kerosene and diesel. There have been a number of strikes that have targeted the upward movements of retail prices and challenges in the courts to the price-setting process. Both oil companies and the government have been blamed for the situation. This may reflect a more general lack of support for the government and its policies, but also the fact that the general price level (for virtually all goods and assets) has been increasing since 2006. Oil companies, especially those with refining in the country, declared large profits in 2005, reflecting the global trend caused by shortages of refinery capacity, but this has merely served to increase the suspicions of the population that oil companies are exploiting the global oil market and taking advantage of consumers. Despite this attempt to shield consumers from the effects of the increase in international product prices, there has been a great deal of opposition to the price changes that have taken place, with the blame being placed on both the oil companies and the government. The lack of policies to reduce oil consumption, apart from the very active encouragement of the natural gas sector, will leave the economy vulnerable if natural gas prices increase, but energy conservation may be difficult to enforce because of the ability of opposition groups to use any potentially unpopular move by the government as a reason for further demonstrations.

BANGLADESH

Bangladesh produces about 10 per cent of its oil needs. The rest is imported in the form of products and crude. Of the total demand, diesel accounted for 49 per cent, non-aviation kerosene 17 per cent, heavy fuel oil 9 per cent, gasoline 7 per cent, aviation kerosene 6 per cent, and LPG 1 per cent (IEA 2005). The Bangladesh Petroleum Corporation (BPC) is the country's sole importer and distributor of refined products and crude oil. The retail sector has both private and government-owned gasoline stations. Crude oil is purchased largely through state-to-state deals with Kuwait, Saudi Arabia, and the United Arab Emirates at a premium to Middle East spot quotes on the basis of cost, insurance, and freight.

The prices of petroleum products are fixed by the government

Table 11.4: Pakistan Domestic Retail Prices (in Pakistan Rs.)

	2000–1	2001–2	2002–3	2003–4	2004–5	2005–6	2006–7
Regular Petrol	25.75	31.48	33.01	33.67	41.19	56.29	57.70
High-Octane Petrol	33,57	35.79	37.14	37.80	45.67	62.77	64.88
Kerosene	14.32	15.74	19.60	21.76	26.08	32.87	35.23
High Speed Diesel	15.58	16.51	21.05	22.61	27.02	–	–
Light Diesel	13.57	14.3	17.27	18.66	23.61	30.97	32.97

Source: Prepared from newspaper reports.

and have persistently lagged behind international prices, resulting in large deficits for BPC. Gasoline prices were increased in May 2005 for the first time since January 2003, and this was followed by an increase in September 2005 and a large increase in June 2006. Diesel and kerosene prices were increased in December 2004, May 2005, September 2005, and June 2006. The fuel price increase in June 2006 widened the gap between gasoline and diesel prices. The prices that have been charged during the last two and a half years have resulted in only a part of product price increases being passed through to consumers. The result of this is that financial losses to BPC amounted to a sum equal to 0.75 per cent of GDP in FY2005, following earlier large losses in 2004. At present the bulk of the losses arise from under-pricing of diesel and kerosene by about 25 per cent. BPC owed different banks some 105 billion taka (US$1.5 billion) by April 2006 (BBC Monitoring South Asia 2006).

In the face of the reluctance of the banks to open new letters of credit for BPC, the finance ministry in February 2006 directed the banks to continue to provide this source of financing (*United News of Bangladesh Limited* 2006). In the 2006 budget, the government cut the duty on crude oil from 25 to 7.5 per cent, lowered taxes on petroleum products from 25 to 15 per cent, and removed the 15 per cent supplementary duty on products. Despite these moves to hold down consumer prices, nationwide strikes have been organized by the major opposition party against the fuel price increases that have occurred. In February 2006, the Finance Minister's remarks on the growing subsidy were interpreted as signaling another price rise. This led to substantial hoarding and panic buying, which resulted in a temporary fuel shortage in certain parts of the country, especially of diesel for irrigation, threatening agriculture—and some retail outlets charging nearly double government prices.

By May 2006, fuel shortage became a major issue, with reports of the closure of numerous filling stations nationwide, reflecting increasing difficulties faced by BPC to purchase and deliver fuels to filling stations. A further implication of the subsidized product prices is the existence of large amount of out-smuggled fuels to India and Myanmar where prices are higher.

INDIA

According to government statistics, India consumed 119 million tonnes of petroleum products in the fiscal year ending on 31 March 2006. The country produces about 30 per cent of its oil needs and imports most of the rest in the form of crude. In FY2007, net oil imports amounted to 3.2 per cent of India's GDP. India imports some products and exports others, depending on domestic needs and the output of the refining sector. India has been a net exporter of petroleum products for quite some time. Its largest imported product by volume is LPG, and the largest exported product is diesel. Petroleum product exports rose by more than US$5 billion in FY2006, partially offsetting the increase in the oil import bill of US$10 billion. For domestic fuel consumption, diesel is the most important item, accounting for about 35 per cent by weight of the total. Heavy fuel oil accounts for 12 per cent, LPG for 9 per cent, and non-aviation kerosene and gasoline account for about 8 per cent each (Ministry of Petroleum and Natural Gas 2005; IMF 2006).

In the upstream, there are three state-owned companies: Oil and Natural Gas Corporation Limited (ONGC), Oil India Limited (OIL), and Gas Authority of India Limited (GAIL). The downstream sector is dominated by four state-owned companies: Indian Oil Corporation (IOC), Hindustan Petroleum Corporation Ltd. (HPCL), Bharat Petroleum Corporation Ltd. (BPCL), and Indo Burma Petroleum (IBP) (which is a subsidiary of IOC). Of the 18 refineries in the country, 17 are state-owned, belonging to IOC, ONGC, HPCL, and BPCL. Several are stand-alone refineries. The private refinery belongs to Reliance Industries Limited and is the largest in India. Until recently, oil products were priced at import parity. As discussed below, this, combined with differential duty rates on crude and refined products, has provided considerable protection to domestic refineries, which have been able to obtain large margins in recent years.

In 2007, there were over 35,000 retail outlets in India, with only about 1,700 belonging to private players. IOC, HPCL, BPCL, and IBP have a market share of 83.5 per cent. Private players include Reliance, Essar, and Shell. Continuing caps on domestic fuel prices have had serious adverse effects on the financial positions and market shares of private retailers who do not enjoy government support to compensate for fuel price subsidies. Ninety-eight per cent of LPG and 100 per cent of kerosene were sold by state-owned oil companies.

The administered pricing mechanism for gasoline and diesel was dismantled in 2002 and, beginning in March 2002, oil marketing companies were allowed to adjust prices based on import parity after consultation with the Ministry of Petroleum and Natural Gas. Pricing was based on import parity regardless of whether or not a specific product was imported or exported, and freight costs were equalized throughout the country at the wholesale level; retail prices differ on account of varying state taxes. During 2002 and 2003, fuel prices were adjusted frequently. As oil prices began to rise in 2004, the new semi-automatic pricing mechanism was suspended. The government decided that incremental fuel costs would be shared among three groups of stakeholders: the government, oil and gas companies including upstream companies, and consumers. In August 2004, the government put in place a revised pricing mechanism for gasoline and diesel whereby oil marketing companies would be permitted to adjust these product prices within a limited price band; however, against the backdrop of rapidly rising oil prices, this pricing mechanism was abandoned.

The government effectively controls pricing over about three-quarters of petroleum product consumption, consisting of LPG, gasoline, kerosene, and diesel. Kerosene sold through the public distribution system (PDS) and LPG for household use (referred to as domestic LPG) continues to be heavily subsidized. There are quantitative limits on the amount of PDS kerosene each household is entitled to; there are no quantitative limits on domestic LPG. The price of PDS kerosene has been frozen since April 2002 and that of LPG since November 2004. The fuel price subsidy, which includes a freight subsidy for remote areas, was made explicit for the first time in the FY2003 budget, amounting to Rs. 64.95 billion (US$1.3 billion). The subsidy was increased to Rs. 81.16 billion (US$1.8 billion) in the fiscal 2004 budget, but more than halved to Rs. 36.44 billion (US$0.8 billion) in fiscal 2005, reduced slightly to Rs. 35.59 billion (US$0.8 billion) in fiscal 2006, and reduced further to Rs. 30.80 billion (US$0.7 billion) in FY2007 (Ministry of Finance 2006). About 70 to 80 per cent of the fuel price subsidy is for PDS kerosene and domestic LPG. The bulk of the subsidy burden has been increasingly shifted to the four state-owned oil marketing companies all of whom reported first-ever losses in 2004 (IBP) and 2005 (IOC, HPCL, and BPCL) and, importantly, to upstream oil and gas companies—ONGC, OIL, and GAIL. According to the Ministry of Petroleum and Natural Gas, oil companies bore 51 per cent of the price increase, the government 36 per cent, and consumers only 13 per cent in fiscal 2006. Refiners have not been asked to bear the subsidy burden and are making large profits, thanks to the protection they enjoy and large refining margins on the world market in recent years. In 2005, two price adjustments were made, amounting to Rs. 5.50 per liter for gasoline and Rs. 5 per liter for diesel, but they were insufficient to bring prices to cost-recovery levels. The 'under-recoveries' by the state-owned oil marketing companies, calculated on the basis of import-parity pricing, are reported to be Rs. 92.74 billion (US$2 billion) in fiscal 2004, Rs. 201.46 billion (US$4.5 billion) in FY2005, and Rs. 396 billion (US$8.9 billion) in FY2006.

The actual under-recoveries would be lower because of refinery discounts given (Committee on Pricing and Taxation of Petroleum Products 2006). Upstream oil companies are expected to cover one-third of the under-recoveries. In fiscal 2006, they contributed a total of Rs. 140 billion (US$3.2 billion), and in fiscal 2007, without additional price increases, their burden increased to Rs. 240 billion (US$5.3 billion). Because of the growing burden of the subsidies on the companies, the Cabinet in February 2006 approved the issuance of government bonds to the state-owned oil companies in the amount of Rs. 115 billion (US$2.6 billion) to cover part of the losses incurred by state firms on sales of kerosene and LPG in FY2006. The very large differential between diesel and kerosene prices provides a strong incentive to adulterate the latter into transportation diesel. A study examining consumption of PDS kerosene by households in India using the 1993–4 and 1999–

2000 data from the National Sample Survey found that about one-half of subsidized kerosene allocated by the central government was diverted from households to other unintended uses.

In FY2006, the subsidy for PDS kerosene was estimated to be about Rs. 13 per liter and LPG about Rs. 12 per kilogram (Committee on Pricing and Taxation of Petroleum Products 2006). While the calculated fuel price subsidies in India in 2005 were second only to those in Indonesia, it is worth noting that taxation on petroleum products at the central and state levels is substantial. In New Delhi, taxes account for 55 per cent of the retail price of gasoline, 34 per cent for diesel, 11 per cent for domestic LPG, and 4 per cent for PDS kerosene. Central government taxes account for 38 per cent and 23 per cent of the prices of gasoline and diesel, respectively, and state taxes account for the balance for these two fuels and all taxes on LPG and kerosene. State sales tax rates vary widely across states and products: 20–34 per cent on gasoline, 9–31 per cent on diesel, 0–12.5 per cent on kerosene, and 1–14 per cent on LPG. In fiscal 2005, petroleum accounted for 24 per cent of India's overall customs duty collection, 43 per cent of excise duties, and 34 per cent of state sales tax revenues. Against the budgeted petroleum subsidy of Rs. 36 billion in FY2005, the central government collected Rs. 498 billion from customs and excise duties on crude oil and petroleum products alone. Some states impose additional irrecoverable levies.

In October 2005, the Minister of Petroleum and Natural Resources appointed a committee to examine pricing and taxation of petroleum products and make recommendations. The committee, chaired by Dr. Rangarajan, announced its findings and recommendations in February 2006 (Committee on Pricing and Taxation of Petroleum Products 2006). These were:

- Shift from import parity to trade parity pricing, whereby the price is based on a fixed ratio of import and export parity price levels, initially recommended to be 0.8 to 0.2, and allow oil companies to determine price levels based on this formula. (The government implemented this recommendation in June 2006.)
- Reduce effective protection given to domestic refiners by lower-

Table 11.5: Evolution of Excise and Customs Duties in India

Product	Excise				Customs		
	March 2003	June 2004	August 2004	March 2005	March 2003	August 2004	March 2005
Gasoline	30 per cent +Rs.7.50/lr	26 per cent +Rs.7.50/lr	23 per cent +Rs.7.50/lr	8 per cent +Rs.13.00/lr	10 per cent	10 per cent	5 per cent
Diesel	14 per cent +Rs.1.50/lr	11 per cent +Rs.1.50/lr	8 per cent +Rs.1.50/lr	8 per cent +Rs.3.25/lr	20 per cent	15 per cent	10 per cent
PDS kerosene	16 per cent	16 per cent	12 per cent	Nil	10 per cent	5 per cent	Nil
Domestic LPG 1	6 per cent	8 per cent	8 per cent	Nil	10 per cent	5 per cent	Nil
Crude	Rs. 1,800/tne	Rs. 1,800/tne	Rs. 1,800/tne	Rs. 1,800/tne	–	–	–

Source: Committee on Pricing and Taxation of Petroleum Products (2006).

ing the customs duties on gasoline and diesel from 10 per cent to 7.5 per cent.

- Restrict supply of PDS kerosene to households below the poverty line.
- Immediately raise the price of LPG by Rs. 75 per cylinder.
- Discontinue the practice of requiring upstream companies to contribute to subsidy payment, and instead make their contributions explicit through a higher cess on crude.
- Make explicit the balance of the subsidy through the budget.
- Substitute specific rates for the *ad valorem* component of excise duties.
- End pan-territorial pricing.

The government is made up of a coalition of different political parties, some of whom face elections in key states in 2008. In the face of public hostility to increased fuel prices, the government has had little room to maneuver, or to increase prices in the near future.

The central government does not seem to have mounted energy-saving programs along the lines of those promoted in the Philippines and Thailand. To reduce the dependence on petroleum products, the government has been pursuing a biofuel program for some time. India is a major sugar producer and blending 5 per cent ethanol into gasoline was mandated in nine sugar-growing states and four union territories in January 2003. Ethanol blending is gradually becoming mandated in several states, though there are still several problems of logistics.

ANALYSIS AND CONCLUDING REMARKS

There is a common thread in the intervention strategies adopted by different countries of the South Asian region. A common feature in these countries is the strong state presence in the oil industry. Exploration, refining as well as marketing is predominantly in the hands of companies that are state-owned or state-controlled. This has enabled the state to dictate prices and, indeed, hold price increases. Often, these decisions have been dictated by the internal politics of the country: Governments that have been either weak or unwilling to tackle the repercussions of consumer dissatisfaction have shied away from taking price increase decisions.

The approaches adopted by these countries have some degree of congruence. First, there has been a lag in recognition of the problem. In 2003 and 2004, most of these countries continued to act as though the problem of rising crude oil prices was a temporary phenomenon, and that prices would stabilize over a period of time. All the countries discussed are heavily import-dependent for their crude oil, and this lag in raising prices has come at the cost of the increased prices of imported oil not being reflected in increased consumer prices. Second, even after the recognition that the problem is a medium- to long-term one, there has been reluctance in aligning consumer prices entirely with market determined prices. The longer the period of adjustment, the greater has been the reluctance. Third, as a direct result of this policy paralysis, the differences between market-determined prices and consumer prices have had to be dealt with through adjustments in public finances.

There have been three broad approaches adopted by the governments for cushioning consumer prices. There has been a resort to reduction in taxes levied on petroleum products. This has been used in India, Pakistan and Sri Lanka, at different periods of time. Second, there has been an attempt at off-Budget borrowings to rescue the balance sheets of the state-owned companies. This was done in India through the issue of oil bonds by the companies, guaranteed by the government, with the interest costs paid for by the government. In Bangladesh, an attempt has been to persuade the state-owned banking sector to provide credit and loans to the companies, with the promise of a government bail-out: this has merely transferred the costs of adjustment to the balance sheets of the banks. In Sri Lanka and, to a smaller extent, in Nepal, there has been an effort to use a combination of government revenues and deficit financing to minimize adjustment costs. Third, there has been an effort to cross-subsidize products. In India, kerosene and LPG are sold at prices considerably lower than those that the market prices would warrant, while petrol and diesel are sold at close to market prices; all other fuels are sold at market-determined prices. In Sri Lanka, diesel is considered essential as a common man's transportation fuel and is subsidized along with kerosene. In Pakistan, there are subsidies on LPG. The broad approach has been to protect those sections of the community that are considered to be vulnerable to price shocks. The criteria used are often not just poverty alone, but also the impact of these sections on the politics of the country. It is evident that such an approach is likely to lead to *ad hoc* adjustments, and the case studies of the countries described earlier clearly indicate that the price increases have been sporadic rather than well thought-out, and have often not been adequate to compensate for the full impact of the increases in product prices.

It is also evident that the costs of these adjustments have had to be borne by government finances at large, either directly or indirectly. In India, the costs are evident in the contingent liabilities of the government in oil bonds that now exceed US$15 billion. In Bangladesh, it is reflected in the large outstandings against oil companies in the balance sheets of the state-owned banks. There have been direct subsidies as well, as in Sri Lanka. It is clearly possible to argue that the costs of these adjustments would have had to be borne by the rest of the economy. In one sense, by constraining the ability of governments to borrow or deploy resources for other public expenditure, they squeeze out social and public welfare expenditure. At another level, such large liabilities cast a long shadow on the fiscal management of the country. The country studies have indicated that both these have occurred—there has been a squeezing out effect as well as a fiscal deterioration. The estimates at various levels of the decrease in GDP growth rates have been at around 1 per cent.

At another level, it is pertinent to ask whether the countries could have adopted alternate policies. It is evident that they shied away from full pass-through fearing political fallout. At the same time, it is possible to look at the structure of the economies to examine the implications of a full pass-through of prices. A common characteristic of the South Asian countries is the existence of a large vulnerable population that subsists on incomes of less than $2 a day. In India, this is around 400 million and in South Asia it would account for not less than 35–40 per cent of the population.

Incomes are inelastic, and the impact of rise in energy costs would push these people to sub-survival levels. These countries do not have a systematic welfare program to take care of the poor and the needy, and it is therefore important, from a human development standpoint, to safeguard the population below poverty level. Second, there is evidence that though there has been growth in GDP in all these countries, the growth has not been uniform and that upper-income deciles of the population have benefited more from the growth. With growing income disparities, measures to provide subsidies to the weaker sections of the population appear to be in order.

There is also the concern about inflationary pressures in these economies. Real GDP growth rates and inflation rates from IMF data may be seen in the graphs below. Except in India, inflation has been high since 2004–5, and in Pakistan, Nepal, Sri Lanka, and Bangladesh, higher than real GDP growth rates. Fuel prices in Sri Lanka were adjusted in 2006, and inflation was very high that year (see Figure 11.2). In Bangladesh, food price inflation has raised inflationary pressures to over 10 per cent. It is interesting that inflation has risen in almost all the countries from 2004–5, the year that the oil price increases started to bite. Fortunately these have been years of good growth in all the South Asian economies, but it is clear that these high inflationary pressures are not sustainable, given the vulnerability of a large section of the population. Between high growth with high inflation and moderate growth with lower inflation, it is easy to see that policy makers would choose the latter: the Finance Minister of India said so explicitly earlier this year.

Given food security and income security concerns in these countries, it is possible to agree that governments would view commodity price increases with caution, and indeed be willing to sacrifice some growth to keep prices from rising beyond acceptable levels.

At the same time fiscal compulsions have dictated that price increases be effected at some periods of time. The graph below shows the reactions of the governments at different periods of time. Two points are of note. First, there is little correlation between international oil price increases and the increases in consumer price. Even

Figure 11.2: Sri Lanka: Inflation Change and Real GDP Growth

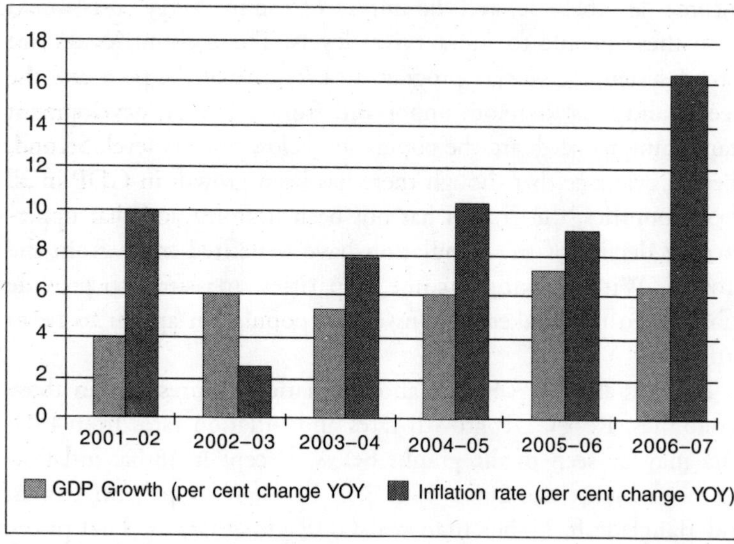

Source: IMF Data.

Figure 11.3: Pakistan: Inflation Change and Real GDP Growth

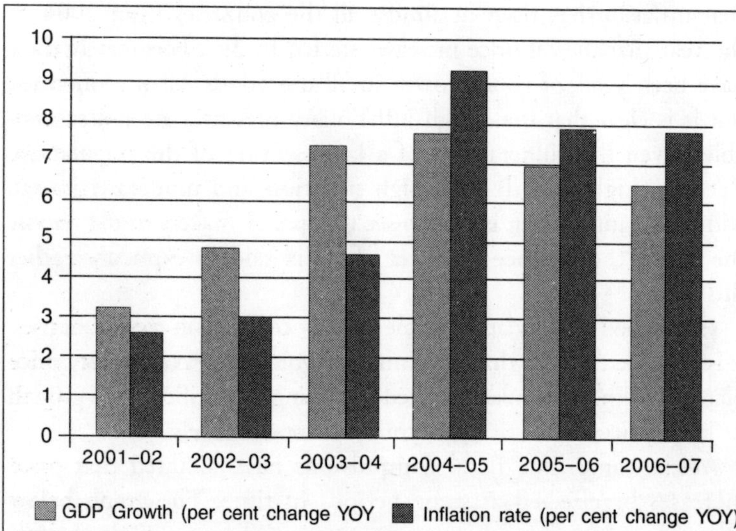

Source: IMF Data.

Figure 11.4: Nepal: Inflation Change and Real GDP Growth

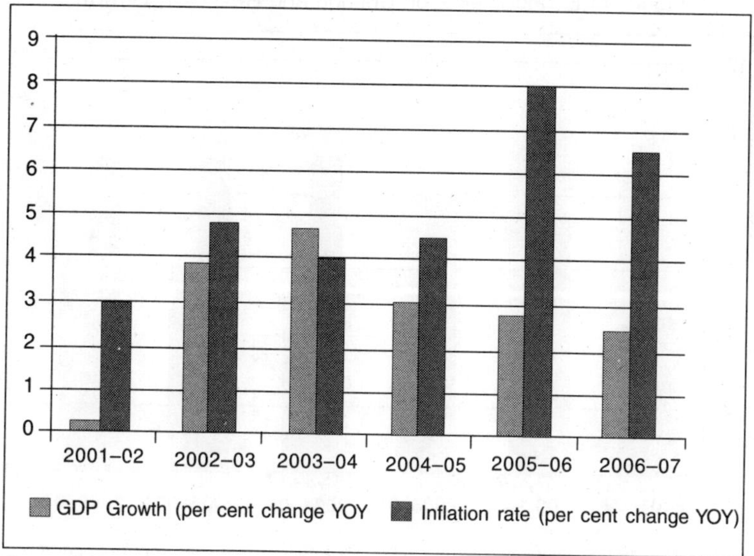

Source: IMF Data.

Figure 11.5: Bangladesh: Inflation Change and Real GDP Growth

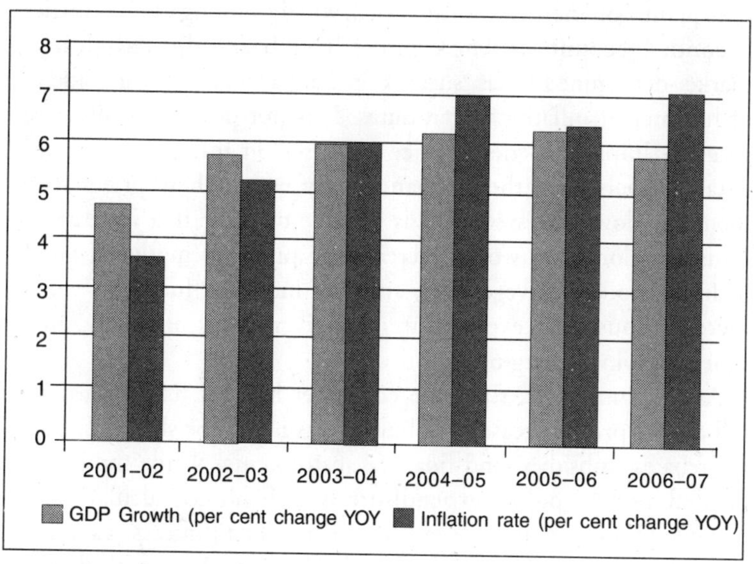

Source: IMF Data.

Figure 11.6: India: Inflation Change and Real GDP Growth

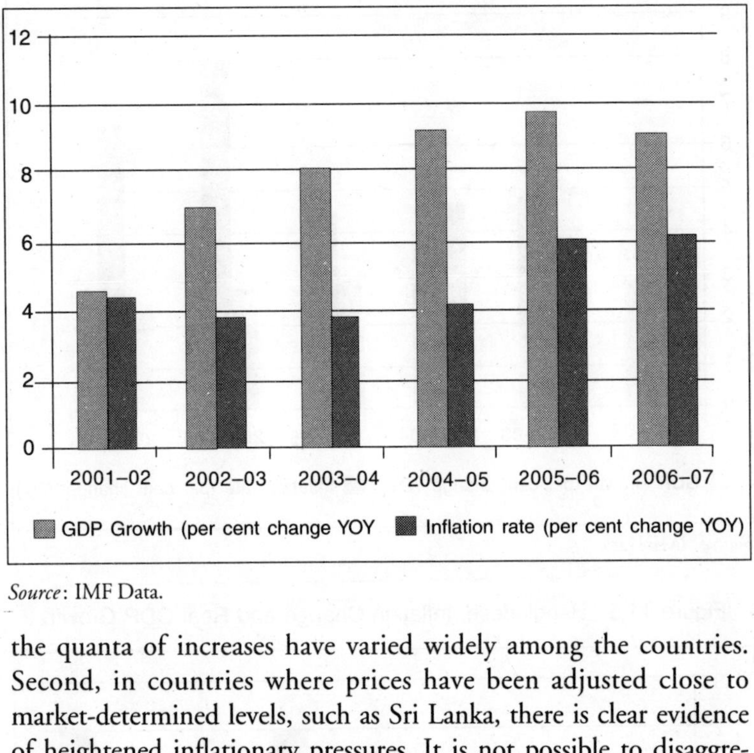

Source: IMF Data.

the quanta of increases have varied widely among the countries. Second, in countries where prices have been adjusted close to market-determined levels, such as Sri Lanka, there is clear evidence of heightened inflationary pressures. It is not possible to disaggregate the impact of energy price increases on inflation without a detailed analysis of the mechanisms by which these prices work their way down the system. It is possible to argue that increases in transportation costs would increase the prices of marketed goods including food and vegetables, and that increased fuel costs would increase household expenditure and given constrained incomes, squeeze savings margins.

At the same time, since the consumer has not had to bear the full cost of price increases, the burden has had to be shared through tax rebates, subsidies, and financial instruments. While the impact on deflation in public expenditure is difficult to calculate, it is possible to argue that increased fiscal deficits and interest payments are a direct consequence of this. The Reserve Bank of India has estimated that during 2005–6 and 2006–7, special bonds issued

Table 11.6: Percentage Increases in Petrol Prices in Sri Lanka, Pakistan, Bangladesh, Nepal and India

	2001–2	2002–3	2003–4	2004–5	2005–6	2006–7
Sri Lanka						
% increase	–	–	–	7.17	8.88	19.38
Petrol price	–	–	84	90	98	117
Pakistan						
% increase	22.25	4.86	2.33	34.66	23.74	2.50
Petrol price	31.48	33.01	33.78	45.49	56.29	57.70
Nepal						
% increase	-2.12	21.73	-3.60	14.81	8.0	8.95
Petrol price	46	56	54	62	67	73
India						
% increase	4.49	11.44	15.72	11.51	3.12	-3.72
Petrol price	30.24	33.70	39.00	43.49	44.85	43.18

Source: Country data from newspapers.

to oil marketing companies amounted to Rs. 17,263 crore and Rs. 24,121 crore, respectively. During 2007–8, special bonds to the tune of Rs. 30,000 crore are likely to be issued. If this is added to the concessions in tariffs and excise duties, the burden on public finances during 2007–8 is likely to be of the order of Rs. 40,000 crore or more, funds that could well have been used for development activities like infrastructure, education and health.

The benefits that have accrued are in the form of lower inflation, and closer control over price increases. A comparison with Sri Lanka, where full pass-through has been effected, demonstrates the inflationary pressures that have been avoided in India through this complex mechanism of special bonds, to shield the consumer from product price increases.

In conclusion, these countries have made policy choices at the macroeconomic level about the pass-through of oil prices. It is clear that markets must be open and that prices should be market determined, but it is also necessary to understand that in countries where over 33 per cent of the population lives below the poverty line, the State has a welfare function as well. Part of that function is to make food and fuel available at affordable prices, the affordability being determined by the level of that economy. It is equally clear that public funds cannot be used up in subsidies alone, for that would crowd out development expenditure. The middle path of *ad hoc* increases and subsidies that these countries have been following, therefore, appears to be not just pragmatic, but in the balance, the only path to be followed. It is a separate matter that there could be some method in the adjustments, so that a proportion, say a third of the increase, is passed on periodically at regular intervals, to lessen the shock and as a matter of coherent strategy. It is to be hoped that politics and economics will converge to make this possible.

NOTES

1. The government in Russia, through a series of actions, took back oil production and exploration concessions that had been granted to Yukos, effectively nationalizing that asset.
2. Demand for oil in Asia grew from 500,000 barrels a day to 1 million barrels daily between 1990 and 1997.
3. *Platt Commodity News* (2006).
4. *Bernama Daily Malaysian News* (2004).
5. *Global Insight Daily Analysis* 2006.
6. *Asian Tribune* 2006.
7. In 1994, the Samriddhi (or Prosperity) Program was launched by the newly elected Sri Lankan Government as a national strategy to alleviate poverty. This program covers one-third of the entire population of Sri Lanka, about 1.2 million poor families. It provides opportunities for income enhancement and employment, as well as creating and maintaining assets in rural areas.

REFERENCES

Basu, Prasanjit K., Brahma Chellaney, Parag Khanna and Sunil Khilnani (2005). *India as a New Global Leader.* London: The Foreign Policy Centre.

Bouakez, Hafedh, Nooman Rebei and Désiré Vencatachellum (2007). 'Optimal pass-through of oil prices'. African Development Bank, Tunis.

Committee on Pricing and Taxation of Petroleum Products (2006). Ministry of Petroleum and Natural Gas, Government of India.

Gregorio, José de, Oscar Landerretche and Christopher Neilson (2007). 'Another pass-through bites the dust?: Oil prices and inflation', Central Bank of Chile Working Papers No . 417, May.

Dasgupta, Mitali, Eshita Gupta and Pragya Agarwal (2006). 'Asian energy security issues: Focus on India and China', Asian Energy Institute, New Delhi. http:// www.aeinetwork.org/aeiapril06.pdf

Economist Intelligence Unit–Views Wire (2005).

EIA International Energy Annual (2004).

Energy Sector Management Assistance Program (2006). 'Coping with higher oil prices', World Bank Report 323/06, Washington, August.

International Energy Institute (2005). 'Gas fired power generation in India: Challenges and opportunities', Focus on Asia and Pacific, October.

IMF (2006). IMF Country Report No. 06/447, Washington, December.

Lardica Sandrine et al. (2006). 'The impact of oil prices on GDP in European countries: An empirical investigation based on asymmetric cointegration', *Energy Policy*, 34, 3910–15.

Sreenivas, Ashok, Girish Sant and Daljit Singh (2007). 'Emerging issues in the Indian gas sector—A critical review', *Economic and Political Weekly*, 42, 34, 3465–74.

Madan, Tanvi (2006). *India*. Energy Security Series, Washington: The Brookings Institution.

Naik, Anant V., Sajal Ghosh and V. Raghuraman (2003). 'Energy security issues—India', Confederation of Indian Industry Working Paper, July.

Platt Commodity News (2006).

Raj, Baldev (2006). 'Energy security for India', IGC Newsletter, 68, Indira Gandhi Centre for Atomic Research, April. http://www.igcar.ernet.in/lis/nl68/ igc68.pdf.

Tonnesson, Stein and Ashid Kolas (2006). 'Energy security in Asia: China, India Oil and Peace', Report to the Norwegian Ministry of Foreign Affairs; International Peace Research Institute, Oslo, April 2006.

12

Urban Growth and Governance in South Asia

SHREEKANT GUPTA AND
INDU RAYADURGAM

INTRODUCTION

THE YEAR 2007–8 is a good time to reflect on the past, present and future of urbanization in South Asia[1] since it marks 60 years since the countries of India, Pakistan and Sri Lanka came into existence as modern nation states. While urbanization in South Asia predates these nation states which are a relatively recent construct, this chapter focuses on the processes and challenges of urbanization over these past 60 years in South Asia. It describes trends in urban growth in South Asia and the institutional and economic structure of urban governance. It also focuses on urban problems and presents possible solutions.

The year 2008 marks a watershed in human history when, for the first time, more than half of humanity, about 3.3 billion people, will live in towns and cities (Ash et al. 2008). The world's population as a whole is expected to undergo substantial further growth in the first half of this century, almost all of which is expected to take place in the cities and towns of poor countries, while the world's rural population will remain flat at around 3 billion persons (Cohen 2003; Montgomery 2008). In other words, of the projected additional 2.2 billion people between 2000 and 2030, 2.1 billion will be in urban areas and all but 0.1 billion of that urban increase will be in developing countries.[2] Thus, by 2030, each of the major regions of the developing world will hold more urban than rural dwellers, and by 2050 fully two-third of their inhabitants are likely to live in urban areas (Montgomery 2008).

These facts are particularly relevant for South Asia, home to over 1.6 billion people or a quarter of humanity, of which a third live in urban areas. As the world becomes increasingly urban, the center of gravity of this process is moving to South Asia. Within seven years' time, that is, by 2015 this region will account for five of the world's 12 biggest urban agglomerations (all with more than 15 million people), namely, Mumbai, Delhi, Kolkata, Dhaka and Karachi.[3] By the same year, 2015, over 540 million South Asians will live in towns and cities and by the year 2030 this figure will cross 813 million (United Nations 2005, Table A.3). These are colossal numbers by any yardstick.[4]

At the same time, South Asia is witnessing rapid economic growth and transformation, and its towns and cities are at the heart of this process (Table 12.1). All over South Asia, growth is taking place in dynamic sectors such as manufacturing, information technology, high-end service industries, trade, retail, and banking, insurance and finance, all of which are urban-centric (Table 12.1).[5] By the year 2011, the urban share in India's national income is expected to go up to 65 per cent (Government of India 2005)[6] even though only slightly more than 30 per cent of the population will be urban by then. In Pakistan and Bangladesh, the hypertrophic cities of Karachi and Dhaka, respectively dominate the economy.[7] The mega-city of Karachi, for instance, not only accounts for a twelfth of the total population of the country's 160 million people, but also generates 60–70 per cent of national revenue and over 40 per cent of the value added in manufacturing.

Thus, while on the one hand towns and cities are 'engines of growth' for the rapidly growing economies of South Asia, unplanned and unmanaged urbanization poses a serious threat to the very same growth, in addition to generating social tensions. All urban areas in the region, big and small, face similar challenges of providing good governance, livelihood opportunities, adequate housing, water, sanitation, transport and other amenities to their residents. Thus, a key conclusion of this chapter is that unless South Asia can make its towns and cities liveable where its citizens can pursue economic

Table 12.1: Major Economies of South Asia (and China), 2006

	Population (million)	GDP (US$ billion; market exchange rate)	GDP (US$ billion; purchasing power parity)	GDP per capita (US$; market exchange rate)	GDP per capita (US$; purchasing power parity)	Human Development Index; value+ (rank*) 2005	Real GDP annual growth, EIU forecast (2008–12) %
Bangladesh	156.0 (1.9)	62 (5.7)	290	397	1,861	0.347 (140)	6.2
Bhutan	0.64 (. . .)	0.8 (. . .)					
India	1,095 (1.5)	923 (7.8)	2,743	842	2,504	0.619 (128)	7.5
Nepal	25.9 (. . .)	8.0 (2.4)					3.0
Pakistan	160.9 (1.8)	127 (6.0)	415	788	2,587	0.367 (136)	5.8
Sri Lanka	19.2 (0.4)	27 (5.8)	85	1,404	4,411	0.743 (99)	5.7
China	1,315 (0.6)	2,774 (10.1)	9,985	2,110	7,596	0.777 (81)	9.0

Source: Economist Intelligence Unit (EIU): Data pertain to 2006. Figures in parentheses are average annual growth rates, 2002–6; and Human Development Report, 2007–8 (+maximum value 1.0, *out of 177 countries).

progress, the region will not be able to sustain and accelerate its growth trajectory.

The chapter is structured as follows. The next section reviews past, present and current trends in urban growth in South Asia. We examine to what extent the experience of South Asia in general, and that of specific countries in particular, tallies with the theory and practice of urban transitions. Following that, in the next two sections we examine the institutional and economic frameworks, respectively, of urban areas in the region. Divergences in the penetration of urban local democracy across countries are noted, as are similarities in the precarious condition of municipal finances. The concluding section advances suggestions for addressing urban problems and thus making South Asian towns and cities liveable and truly engines of growth.

PATTERNS OF URBANIZATION IN SOUTH ASIA[8]

Compared to the world as a whole, and to developing countries, 60 years ago South Asia was relatively less urbanized and continues to be so (Table 12.2). The reason is evident, namely, the relatively slow pace of urban growth in India. In 1950, India was more urbanized than China but the latter has overtaken India and is half as more urban than India at present, at 45 per cent as compared to 30 per cent in India (Table 12.2). India's slow pace of urban growth has been commented on by various urban experts and we return to this below when we focus on differences in the process and nature of urbanization within South Asia.

There was (and is), however, considerable regional variation in urbanization rates across developing countries (Table 12.3). At one end were countries of Latin America and the Caribbean with nearly three-quarter of the population living in urban areas (approximately the same level as developed countries). On the other hand, in Africa and India two-thirds or more of the population was and continues to be rural. The gap, however, has narrowed and will continue to do so over the next two decades. By the year 2030, South Asia will be almost 70 per cent as urban as the world as a whole. This is as one would expect as the economies of the region

Table 12.2: Population by Region (1950 and 2010)

(in thousands)

	1950		2010		2030	
	Total population	Urban population (per cent urban)	Total population	Urban population (per cent urban)	Total population	Urban population (per cent urban)
World	2,519,470	731,765 (29.0)	6,842,923	3,474,571 (50.1)	8,199,104	4,912,553 (60.0)
Less developed regions*	1,706,698	308,583 (18.1)	5,617,246	2,553,051 (45.5)	6,948,446	3,901,492 (56.1)
South Asia	453,528	70,632 (15.6)	1,567,666	472,628 (30.1)	1,970,140	813,357 (41.3)
India	357,561	60,936 (17.0)	1,183,293	356,388 (30.1)	1,449,078	589,957 (40.7)
China	554,760	72,119 (13.0)	1,354,533	608,587 (45.0)	1,446,453	872,671 (60.3)

Source: Authors' own calculations based on United Nations 2005 (Tables A.3 and A.5).

Note: * The United Nations defines 'less developed regions' as all regions of the world except Europe, North America, Australia, New Zealand and Japan.

Table 12.3: Demographic, Economic and Human Development Indicators for Major Developing Countries and Regions, about 1990

Country/ Region	Total population (millions)	Annual population growth rates		Total fertility rate[a]	Urban population (per cent)		Urban population growth rates	
		1960–92	1992–2000	1992	1960	1992	1960–92	1992–2000
China	1,184	1.9	1.0	2.0	19	28	3.1	3.8
India	884	2.2	1.8	3.8	18	26	3.4	3
Indonesia	189	2.1	1.5	2.9	15	33	4.7	4.3
Arab States	230	2.6	2.9	4.8	30	30	4.5	3.5
Sub-Saharan Africa	510	2.8	2.9	6.3	15	30	5.0	4.5
Latin America and the Caribbean	450	2.4	1.8	3.1	50	73	3.6	2.4
Developing Countries	4,220	2.3	1.8	3.5	22	36	3.8	3.2
World	5,420	1.9	1.5	3.1	34	44	2.7	2.6

Country/ Region	Per cent of urban population in largest city 1990	Urban sex ratio (males/100 females) 1990–1	GNP per capita US$ 1992	GNP per capita annual growth rate		Real GDP per capita (US$)[b]	Infant mortality per 1000 live births
				1965–80	1980–92		
China	4	1,083	480	4.1	7.6	1,950	44
India	6	1,119	310	1.5	3.1	1,230	82
Indonesia	17	999	680	5.2	4.0	2,950	58
Arab States	31	–	–	–	–	2,950	67
Sub-Saharan Africa	–	–	559	1.4	-1.8	1,346	97
Latin America and the Caribbean	24	–	2,791	2.7	1.0	5,730	45
Developing Countries	–	–	982	4.6	4.0	2,595	70
World	–	–	4,534	–	–	5,430	–

Source: Gugler (1996), Table 1.1 (data from Human Development Report 1995).

a. Total fertility rate is the average number of children born to a woman in her lifetime.

b. Real GDP is based on conversion in terms of purchasing power parity.

Table 12.4: Labor Force Distribution in Selected South Asian Economies

(*in per cent*)

	Agriculture		Industry		Services	
	1960	1996–2005*	1960	1996–2006*	1960	1996–2005*
Bangladesh	86	52	5	14	9	35
India	74	67	11	13	15	20
Pakistan	61	42	18	21	21	37
Sri Lanka	57	34	13	23	30	39

Source: Human Development Report, various issues.
Note: *Data refer to the most recent year during the period specified.

evolve from being agrarian towards service and industry. Table 12.4 indicates a substantial decline in the proportion of the labor force employed in agriculture in South Asia over time. In fact, it is by now well accepted that urbanization is a natural and inevitable consequence of economic development and that structural changes in the economy as a result of economic development, drive urbanization [see for instance, the review by Henderson (2005) and recent papers by Davis and Henderson (2003) and Henderson (2003), as well as Moomaw and Shatter (1993, 1996) and Mills and Becker (1986: chapter 2) for earlier studies].[9]

Historical and international patterns also suggest urbanization is a logistic (S-shaped) curve that first rises slowly from low levels of urbanization, then accelerates, and finally slows down (Becker et al. 1992).[10] In other words, urbanization accelerates as an economy industrializes, slowing down once again only after urbanization reaches 60–70 per cent (Mohan 1996). There are important differences, however, compared to the historical experience of industrialized countries in this regard (Mohan 1996). Whereas in those countries employment in the urban service sector usually declined with rapid industrialization and urbanization, in South Asia services have grown as fast as industry. In other words, urbanization in South Asia is a movement of people from agricultural activities to both industry and services. Moreover, the latter sector (often known as the urban informal sector) is characterized by low productivity and, therefore, employs much of the residual urban labor.

Another difference is that unlike in developed countries, city growth in South Asia is not mainly due to migration. Given the overall higher population growth rates, cities including those in South Asia, are experiencing high natural growth rates even without significant migration. In fact, research by the United Nations Population Division shows that for developing countries as a whole (except China), about 60 per cent of the urban growth rate is attributable to natural growth and the remaining 40 per cent is due to migration and spatial expansion (Chen et al. 1998). Using census data for India for 1961–2001, Sivaramakrishnan et al. (2005) arrive at a very similar figure, namely, urban natural growth accounted for 60 per cent of the total increase in urban population.[11]

This broad-brush picture, of course, conceals marked differences in the process and nature of urbanization within South Asia. To begin with, levels of urbanization vary significantly across countries (Table 12.5).[12] Whereas Pakistan is the most urbanized country in the region, Bhutan, Sri Lanka and Nepal are among the least urbanized. It is interesting to note in particular the low level of urbanization in Sri Lanka given its relatively high per capita in-

Table 12.5: Urbanization in South Asia (and China), 2007

	Total populaiton in million (2007)	Annual growth rate (per cent) (2005–10)	Per cent Urban (2007)	Urban population annual growth rate (per cent) (2005–10)
Bangladesh	147.1	1.8	26	3.5
Bhutan	2.3	2.2	12	5.1
India	1,135.6	1.4	29	2.3
Nepal	28.2	1.9	17	4.8
Pakistan	164.6	2.1	36	3.3
Sri Lanka	21.1	0.8	15	0.8
China	1,331.4	0.6	42	2.7
Less developed regions	5,398.4	1.3	44	2.5

Source: United Nations Population Fund (2007).

come and HDR scores *vis-à-vis* other countries in South Asia (Table 12.1). For Pakistan on the other hand, it is argued that since the 1980s at least, socio-economic-demographic changes have led to a blurring of the rural-urban divide into a continuum, especially in the Punjab and this has led to significant underestimation of the urban population. For instance, recent demographic work (Ali 2003) indicates that Pakistan's primary cities have emerged as major urban systems, with their rural suburbs or 'peri-urban' settlements integrated into the city economies. This phenomenon is most apparent in central Punjab's heartland where contiguous districts, comprising major cities, medium-sized towns and peri-urban settlements have formed into a significant population agglomeration that has increased its political and economic importance (ibid.). More important, approximately half of this population resides in peri-urban settlements that have not been recognized as urban (Cheema et al. 2006) Thus, the current level of urbanization in Pakistan could be as high as 50 per cent.[13]

Looking at projected trends in urbanization it can also be seen that within the next 20 years or so, almost all countries in the region will become significantly more urbanized with at least 30-40 per cent the population living in urban areas, barring Bhutan and Sri Lanka (Table 12.6).[14] With regard to the rate of urbanization, contrary to popular belief, India's rate of growth of urban population will continue to be relatively slow in the short-run—about 2.3 per cent annually during 2005–10, ranking behind Bangladesh, Nepal and Pakistan in South Asia (Table 12.5). Other than Sri Lanka, with only 0.8 per cent annual growth in urban population during the same period (thus, almost stagnating in urbanization), India certainly lags behind other South Asian countries, and also when compared to its populous Asian neighbor, China. Compared to the less developed region as a whole, medium-term (2005–10) urban population growth rates in India and Sri Lanka are slower (below 2.5 per cent per annum) but faster in Bangladesh, Pakistan, Nepal and Bhutan (Table 12.5).

Taking a longer time horizon over the next two decades till the year 2030, more or less the same scenario prevails (Table 12.7). Thus, comparing the three most populous South Asian countries

Table 12.6: Trends in Urbanization in South Asia (and China), 1950–2030

(*per cent urban population*)

	Bangladesh	Bhutan	India	Maldives	Nepal	Pakistan	Sri Lanka	China	Less developed regions
1950	4.2	2.1	17.0	10.6	2.7	17.5	15.3	13.0	18.1
2010	27.3	12.8	30.1	32.1	18.2	37.0	15.1	44.9	45.5
2015	29.9	14.8	32.0	34.8	20.9	39.6	15.7	49.2	48.0
2020	32.9	17.0	34.4	38.0	23.9	42.7	16.9	53.2	50.7
2025	36.3	19.5	37.3	41.5	27.2	46.2	18.8	56.9	53.4
2030	39.9	22.4	40.7	45.2	30.6	49.8	21.4	60.3	56.1

Source: United Nations (2006).

Table 12.7: Growth of Urban Population in South Asia (and China), 1950–2030

	Year	India	Pakistan	Bangladesh	China
Total population (thousands)	1950	3,57,561	36,944	41,783	5,54,760
	2000	10,21,084	1,42,648	1,28,916	12,73,979
	2010	11,83,293	1,75,178	1,54,960	13,54,533
	2020	13,32,032	2,11,703	1,81,180	14,23,939
	2030	14,49,078	2,46,322	2,05,641	14,46,453
Urban population (thousands)	1950	60,936	6,473	1,774	72,119
	2000	2,82,480	47,284	29,900	4,55,800
	2010	3,56,388	64,812	42,292	6,08,587
	2020	4,57,619	90,440	59,525	7,57,766
	2030	5,89,957	1,22,572	82,064	8,72,671
Per cent urban	1950	17	17.5	4.2	13
	2000	27.7	33.1	23.2	35.8
	2010	30.1	37	27.3	44.9
	2020	34.4	42.7	32.9	53.2
	2030	40.7	49.8	29.9	60.3
Urban population annual growth rate (per cent)	1950–5	2.62	4.50	3.86	3.6
	2000–5	2.30	3.04	3.47	3.08
	2010–15	2.46	3.35	3.44	2.38
	2020–5	2.56	3.17	3.31	1.57
	2030–5	2.30	2.66	2.85	1.04

Source: United Nations (2005).

(India, Pakistan and Bangladesh), growth rates of urban population will be the slowest in India till the end of the forecast period, 2030–5. Outside the region, urban population growth in China will also slow down by 2030 but it would have reached a high level of urbanization by then, over 60 per cent (heuristically confirming the 'S-shape' pattern of urbanization).

Returning to the issue of the slow rate of urbanization in India, by far the most populous country in South Asia, this is a cause for concern. In fact, in India during the 1980s, when there was acceleration in industrial growth and national income, the rate of growth of urbanization slowed down (Mohan 1996). As compared to an annual growth rate of urban population of 3.86 per cent during 1971–81, during the decade of 1981–91 this figure came down to 3.15 per cent (Census of India 1991). The corresponding figures for decadal growth rates (the increase in urban population over the decade) were 46.14 and 36.10 per cent, respectively. During 1991–2001 this figure fell to 31.30 per cent, further substantiating the point about deceleration of urbanization.

One reason for this deceleration could be a deceleration in rural productivity growth—the slow growth of agricultural productivity, except in certain pockets of the country did not release agricultural labor from rural areas. Another reason that has been advanced is inappropriate choice of technology or product composition in India's industrialization strategy (Becker et al. 1992; Mohan 1996). Thus, it has been argued that India's so-called Mahalanobis strategy[15] of import substituting industrialization, particularly of channeling investment to the capital goods sector within manufacturing (comprising almost entirely state-owned enterprises), minimized the impact of new investment on labor demand, and hence on unskilled wages. In other words, the development of a very capital-intensive, inefficient capital goods industry along with the neglect of wage goods may have retarded urbanization.

In addition, it is not only the overall rate of growth of urban population that is important, but also the concentration of urbanization, that is, the distribution of urban population across cities: even at a low level of urbanization, the urban population could be concentrated in a few very large, hypertrophic cities. Thus, it has been argued these cities may experience very high rates of population growth and an inability to expand infrastructure fast enough to avoid problems. This begs the question of optimal city size. There is a large theoretical and empirical literature on agglomeration economies, namely, increasing returns at the city level.[16] For developing countries, in particular, we quote Bertinelli and Strobl (2007): '(I)n fact, as developing economies evolve from an agricultural to a manufacturing and especially a service base, there are large benefits to urban concentration, as knowledge and information are supposed to be subject to distance decay effects (Lucas 1988). Thus, at least in earlier stages of development, one should be able to observe a strong link between economic development on the one hand and urban concentration on the other' (ibid., pp. 2500–1). But it may also well be the case that beyond a certain size, diseconomies or negative externalities of too many people crowded together may set in, often referred to as congestion costs (Small 2007). In sum, this line of inquiry suggests urban concentration may be more important than urbanization, *per se.*

In developing countries greater urbanization has gone hand in hand with a sizeable increase in urban concentration over the past 50 years (Bertinelli and Strobl 2007). Specifically, whereas the growth of large cities, that is, cities with more than 5 million inhabitants, has been slow or even zero in the industrialized world, developing nations are experiencing ever-greater population concentration in large urban agglomerations and in mega-cities (cities with a population greater than 10 million). For instance, between 1975 and 2000, the number of mega-cities increased from 3 to 15 in developing countries, compared with a rise from 2 to 4 in developed countries (United Nations 2002).

The term 'primacy' has particular salience in the literature on urban concentration. Urban primacy refers to a country's largest one or two cities being 'abnormally' large (using an adverb from Jefferson's 1939 seminal study on the subject) relative to the country's next largest cities. The reasons for the rise of primate cities and their impact, good or bad, have long been debated (see for instance the discussion in Moomaw and Alwosabi 2004).[17] A key question often posed is whether there is 'excessive' primacy in low-income countries because of urban bias or other political economy reasons. We return to this in our discussion of South Asian cities below.

In South Asia, *prima facie*, Dhaka in Bangladesh and Karachi in Pakistan appear to be primate cities. As stated at the outset, these two cities dominate the economic and urban demographic landscape of their respective countries—one in three urban dwellers in Bangladesh and one in five urban dwellers in Pakistan live in Dhaka and Karachi, respectively (Table 12.8). This is also true of Kathmandu *vis-à-vis* Nepal.[18] Given the huge population of India, a hypertrophic or primate city has not emerged, *per se*. As one would intuitively expect as the economic and physical size of a nation increases, it enables several production sites, creating new urban centers, and, thus, reducing the tendency towards urban primacy. That said, the megalopolises of Mumbai, Delhi and Kolkata are huge by any standard. Further, in all the 'big three' countries, and in South Asia as a whole, a significant proportion of the total population lives in million plus cities, a level where strains on urban infrastructure may start manifesting themselves (Table 12.9). Thus, the absence of a primate city (or cities) notwithstanding, 1 in 10 Indians lives in a city of more than a million people and the same is true in Bangladesh and Pakistan.

More formally, we compute alternative measures of primacy for

Table 12.8: Population Trend of Largest Urban Agglomeration as of 2000

(*in millions*)

	1950	2000	2015
India (Mumbai)	2.86 (5.21)	16.09 (5.7)	21.87 (5.4)
Bangladesh (Dhaka)	0.42 (23.5)	10.16 (34.0)	16.84 (33.5)
Pakistan (Karachi)	1.05 (16.2)	10.02 (21.2)	15.16 (19.8)
Nepal (Kathmandu)	0.10 (45.0)	0.64 (19.6)	1.28 (18.7)

Source: United Nations (2005), Tables A.12 and A.15.

Notes: 1. Figures in parentheses are population of largest agglomeration as percentage of national urban population.

2. The United Nations only reports urban agglomeration with at least 750,000 inhabitants as of 2005. Thus, data for Colombo is not available since its population was around 650,000.

Table 12.9: Population in Urban Agglomerations > 1 million

(*per cent of total population*)

	1960	1970	1980	1990	2000
India	7	7	9	10	11
Bangladesh	2	4	6	9	11
Pakistan	11	13	15	16	17
South Asia	7	7	9	10	12

Source: World Development Indicators, 2006.

the 'big three' South Asian countries and for China (Table 12.10). The first measure of primacy, the 2-city index, is the ratio of the population of the largest city to that of the second largest city, where cities are defined as urban agglomerations. In the literature, in recognition of countries where the two largest cities are of about the same size—biprimate countries[19]—the 4-city index is also computed, as the ratio of the population of the largest city to that of the sum of the populations of the second through fourth largest cities. There is yet another measure of primacy, which is the ratio of the sum of the population of the two largest cities to that of the third and fourth largest cities. Since the latter measure reduces the emphasis on the largest city, we restrict ourselves to the 2-city and 4-city indices. As expected, Bangladesh and Pakistan rate highly on these indices, especially as compared to India, underlining the primacy of Dhaka in particular and of Karachi to an extent (Table 12.10).

Table 12.10: 2-city and 4-city Indices, 2005

Countries	2-city index	4-city index
Bangladesh	3.0	1.9
Pakistan	1.85	1.1
India	1.2	0.5
China	1.4	0.5

Source: Authors' own calculations based on United Nations 2005 (Table A.12). The 2-city index and 4-city index have been calculated based on the formulae P1/P2 and P1/(P2+P3+P4), respectively, where P1 . . . Pk are the populations of the largest urban agglomerations.

On the reasons for primacy, two broad strands have emerged in the literature. The first focuses on underlying demographic and economic considerations. In other words, urban primacy depends upon size (gross domestic product, population, and land area), economic development (GDP per capita), population density, industrialization, and whether the largest city is the capital city (Moomaw and Alwosabi 2004). Social scientists such as geographers, political scientists, and sociologists, on the other hand, put forward explanations of urban primacy, which focus on international economic relations and internal political factors. In particular, dependency theory implies that economies, particularly developing economies, that are more open to foreign trade, experience increased primacy because (dependent) trade concentrates production in the larger cities. Thus, according to Castells, 'dependent urbanization', which implies developing countries rely on industrialized countries for trade, investment, aid, and technology transfer, 'causes a superconcentration in the urban areas' (primate cities) (Castells 1977: 47–8).

After subjecting these hypotheses to empirical testing with a sample of 30 countries from Asia and the Americas,[20] Moomaw and Albosawi (2004) conclude that it is not the case that excessive primacy is inherent in low-income countries because of urban bias, dependent urbanization, and/or world systems considerations. (p. 167) In fact, they find that much of primacy can be explained by economic and demographic considerations. Thus, larger countries (in terms of GDP, population, and land area) and countries with greater density of GDP and greater density of population per unit of land have less primacy. In other words, proxies for economies of scale and transportation cost are the major determinants of primacy, and world systems theory, dependency theory, and theories of urban bias are not necessary to explain observed primacy. If this is true then it would be difficult to argue that extremely large cities are parasitic, and by the same token make a case against globalization on these grounds. This finding is of interest in the context of opening up of the economies of South Asia and the debates that still surround this issue.

Turning specifically to the question of the impact of urban concentration on economic growth, we rely on a recent study by Bertinelli and Strobl (2007). They use a sample of 70 countries, two-thirds of which are developing countries,[21] to test whether urban primacy (defined here as the share of national urban population living in the largest agglomeration)[22] has an inimical impact on the growth rate of per capita GDP. They find an increasing relationship between urban primacy and economic development, but only up to a certain level (35 per cent or 0.35 level of primacy), at which point economic growth becomes independent of concentration (in other words the growth-primacy curve increases and then flattens out, Bertinelli and Strobl 2007: Figures 1 and 2, pp. 2504–5). It is evident then that all South Asian countries in the sample (and Nepal now, though not in the 1950s, see Table 12.8) are on the increasing part of the primacy-growth relationship.

Putting the findings of these studies together, it appears the hypertrophic nature of some South Asian cities may be due to inherent scale economies and not due to faulty policies such as urban bias or external factors such as dependent urbanization. Further, it does not appear that urban concentration is excessive at the moment in South Asia. Also, as noted earlier the level of urbanization in South Asia is low even when compared to developing countries. While none of this is to argue that cities in the region do not face problems, it does substantiate the 'cities as engines of growth' point made at the beginning of this chapter. This also puts the ball firmly in the court of urban governance. The people in charge of managing South Asia's cities cannot resort to the excuse that their cities are of unmanageable size or that their countries are over-urbanized, or finally that they are victims of external forces such as globalization. Indeed, the truth is far from it. The evidence looked at so far leads to the inescapable conclusion that urban problems in South Asia are more those of poor governance than over-urbanization and/or hypertrophic growth. This is what we turn to next.

THE GOVERNANCE OF SOUTH ASIAN TOWNS AND CITIES

That urban areas of South Asia need to be managed better cannot be disputed. We begin our discussion of urban governance with the *raison d'être* for urban local bodies (or ULBs as they are referred to in India), that is, the core functions they are supposed to undertake. This is followed by a brief description of the distinct manner in which institutions of urban governance have evolved over the past 60 years in major South Asian countries, namely, Bangladesh, India, Pakistan and Sri Lanka.

The colonial period in the history of these countries is an important watershed in our context. As a UNESCAP study on local government points out:

> '(A)ll countries have long indigenous histories of local governance, although not necessarily institutional forms of local government. . . Occupation by colonial powers in Asia and the Pacific left *legacies of centralized administrative rule more suited to command, maintenance of law and order and revenue extraction rather than governance and participation at the local level.* Inherently, colonial models of administration were imposed on local communities mostly with disregard for their historical systems of governance.' (Sproats 2002: 3, emphasis added)

Thus, starting from a common colonial heritage, each country in South Asia has moved along a different trajectory given its own socio-political and economic circumstances. In all countries, however, local governments have been subjected to the vicissitudes of fortune: they have been 'uplifted, pulled down, resurrected and experimented to death' (Kamal 2000: 3). At present, the state of urban governance in all these countries leaves much to be desired, as is the case with governance in general.

A key function of all levels of government (central, state/provincial[23] and local) is to provide public goods or merit goods—national defense, law and order, education, neighborhood parks, and such like. The crucial difference, however, between local governments at the city/town level and higher levels of government at the state/provincial or central level, is in the nature of public goods/services ULBs are expected to provide. And it is in this difference that the challenges and opportunities of urban governance lie.

ULBs for the most part, cater to the needs of residents within their jurisdiction and provide goods/services such as schools and public libraries, dispensaries/hospitals, water supply and sewerage, garbage collection, street lighting and roads. These are termed as local public goods, that is, public goods whose benefits are limited to those living in a locality. A key feature of these local public goods/services (unlike national defense, for instance) is that for many of them exclusion is possible in principle—those who do not pay can be excluded from consuming these goods/services. To elaborate, fees can be charged for schools or user charges can be levied for supplying water if the ULB so desires (and at varying rates for different economic classes starting from zero price or full subsidy). In contrast, the comfort of a safe border (national defense) is available to all that reside within that border, that is, exclusion is not possible for a pure public good. Excludability, of course, is not always possible or desirable for local public goods such as law and order (police) or public libraries and parks.

More important is the fact that the local public goods provided by ULBs such as a city park, a stretch of city road, a fire department, a school are available to everyone in the community, but for any given level of infrastructure the more people who use the facility the more crowded it becomes and the less it is available or useful to others. If there are more people in a city for the same number of policemen or library books, availability per person will decline. Again, this is not the case with national defense. Thus, local public goods (unlike pure public goods such as defense) may or may not exhibit non-excludability but they are partially or wholly rival. The term 'rival' here simply means that the more something is used/consumed by one person, the less there is for others, like a loaf of bread and unlike sunshine or national defense.

What does all this imply for the provision of local public goods and for urban governance? First, based on the famous Tiebout hypothesis (named after the Chicago economist Charles Tiebout who articulated it in 1956)[24] it is possible in principle for ULBs through a process of competition with one another to provide efficient levels of local public goods—in the quantities and forms the residents want. To paraphrase Tiebout, local communities (that is, ULBs) are more responsive to the needs and preferences of those who actually receive the goods and local communities have greater incentives for efficiency. Thus, ULBs as representatives of local communities are central to the urban management process.

Second, the nature of local public goods is in accordance with the principle of subsidiarity, which states that matters ought to be handled by the smallest (or, the lowest) competent authority.[25] Subsidiarity is, in principle, one of the features of federalism. This concept is found in several constitutions around the world, for example, the 10th amendment to the United States Constitution. More recently, it is a key organizing principle behind the European Union and is articulated in Article 5 of the Treaty establishing the European Community. It is intended to ensure that decisions are taken as close as possible to the citizen.

The third implication of the nature of local public goods is that for several of them user charges are feasible (that is, exclusion is possible) and desirable (since these goods may be rivalrous). With respect to the latter, without cost recovery through user charges or user-pays-principle, the good may suffer from overuse/depletion. In other words, there is a sound conceptual basis to the goal of making ULBs financially sustainable and improving municipal finances: municipalities mostly provide goods and services to those living within its jurisdiction and it is these people that must cover the costs of providing these goods directly through user charges, or indirectly through property taxes (or as a distinct second best through commodity taxes such as sales tax or octroi).[26]

We now turn to a brief overview of the institutions of urban governance in the four major South Asian countries.[27]

Bangladesh (which was a part of Pakistan until 1971) has a unitary form of government. For administrative convenience the country is divided into six divisions, below which are 64 *zila* (districts), each further subdivided into *upazila* (subdistricts) or *thana* (police stations). The district is the focal point of administration in Bangladesh. The area within each police station, except for those in metropolitan areas, is divided into several unions, with each union consisting of multiple villages. In metropolitan areas, police stations are divided into wards, which are further divided into *mahallas*.

There are no elected officials at the divisional, district or subdistrict levels, and the administration comprises only government officials. Direct elections are held for each union and for each ward, electing a chairperson and a number of members. In principle, local government in urban areas is entrusted to elected bodies. While the census recognized 522 urban areas in 1991 (with a minimum population of 5,000), as of 2003 only 286 of the larger areas among these had local governments. The six largest cities (namely, Dhaka, Chittagong, Khulna, Rajshahi, Barisal and Sylhet), have the status of a City Corporation, while the rest of the 286 areas are known as *Pourashavas* or municipalities.

Thus, *Pourashavas* (municipalities) and City Corporations constitute the two types of urban local governments in Bangladesh. Their functions are basically similar with some distinction being made for compulsory and optional functions. In terms of the analytical framework presented above they are supposed to provide a wide range of local public goods and services including garbage collection, maintenance of streets and street lighting, water supply and drainage, traffic management, maintenance of educational institutions, public libraries, and parks and gardens.[28] As in other South Asian countries, however, acute shortage of funds is a *leitmotif* for urban local bodies in Bangladesh. Thus, *de facto*, their key local public good functions are mainly restricted to garbage collection, street lighting, water supply and maintenance of parks and gardens. An additional function not listed but one that *Pourashavas* and City Corporations have been carrying out (either through their own funds as in Dhaka or through external funding) is slum improvement.

Urban local governments in Bangladesh, large and small, are subject to strong control from higher levels of government, especially the central government. For instance, the size and boundaries of ULBs and their power to make regulations and conduct their affairs are all subject to central government approval. This control is particularly pernicious when it comes to urban finances as noted by UNESCAP, '[I]n the field of finance, government supervision and control is wide and strict. In addition to financial control in general, the central government can wield power by reducing or enhancing grant-in-aid to local bodies, even to city authorities like Dhaka'.[29] In general, the political, administrative and fiscal autonomy of municipalities and corporations in Bangladesh leaves much to be desired.

Sri Lanka also has a de facto unitary form of government, with the President as the head of state and head of government. The country is divided into nine provinces for administrative purposes.[30] Below these are 25 districts and 330 divisional secretariats.[31] Unlike Bangladesh, however, Sri Lanka has adopted decentralization policies which have resulted in formal devolution of powers to provincial councils. Local authorities also function in both urban and rural areas as the third tier of government. There are three types of ULBs, namely, 18 municipal councils (towns with population more than 30,000), 42 urban councils (towns with 10,000–30,000 people) and 270 *pradeshiya sabhas* for smaller towns with associated rural hinterlands. The capital city of Colombo has its own municipal council.

The powers and responsibilities of local bodies, primarily in the areas of public and environmental health, have remained unchanged since constitutional recognition was given to local governments in 1987.[32] Since most local bodies do not have a strong revenue base, they depend on central government transfers through the provincial councils which have responsibility under the constitution for their supervision.[33] Thus, there is excessive dependence on, and influence of, the center in terms of local government finances. The center regularly takes decisions on devolved subjects that entail financial commitments by the provinces but cannot meet them.[34] It is also true that in Sri Lanka after the 1987 devolution, the primary if not the sole focus has been center-province relations—while the 13th Constitutional Amendment devolved governance to provincial and local levels and the latter face increased demand for provision of public goods and services, they remain handicapped by limited financial and human resources.

While Pakistan, *prima facie*, is a federation (of four provinces, namely, Punjab, Sindh, Baluchistan and the North Western Frontier Province) as per its Constitution, given long periods of military rule (for about half of its history) centripetal tendencies have been very strong. Local governments are not formally embodied in the Constitution and they exist under the supervision of various provincial governments that have merely delegated some of their functions and responsibilities to local governments through promulgation of ordinances.[35]

Pakistan also presents a unique case of local governance reforms in South Asia since these reforms were initiated by a non-representative (military) Center using a 'top-down' approach (Cheema et al. 2006). The first phase of extensive local government reforms was implemented under the military regime of General Zia-ul-Haq from 1979, though the process began during the preceding civilian government of Prime Minister Z.A. Bhutto. General Zia introduced the system of electoral representation at the local level through local government ordinances (LGOs) and local elections were held during 1979 and 1980 in all four provinces. In doing so, he followed the example of a previous military ruler Field Marshal Ayub Khan of combining (non-democratic) centralization at the federal and provincial levels with a legitimization strategy that instituted electoral representation at the local level (ibid.). This strategy has also been viewed as creating a competing class of collaborative local-level politicians supporting the military as opposed to national or provincial politicians (Jalal 1995). Indeed, it has been argued that the centripetal tendency during periods of military rule in Pakistan has always been combined with local government empowerment. This unique feature of local government in Pakistan adds another dimension to the focus one notices in South Asia on federal provincial relations. It has been noted, however, that 'the increased political importance of local bodies *was not complemented by any further decentralization of federal or provincial administrative functions or financial powers to the local level*' (Cheema et al. 2006: 262, emphasis added). In fact, local governments continue to lack constitutional protection and their creation and existence remain at the whim of the provinces. This conclusion broadly holds even for the new round of local government reforms initiated by the most recent military ruler, General Pervez Musharraf (Cheema et al. 2006).

Whereas in Pakistan local governments exist *de facto* (in a manner of speaking) though not mandated by the Constitution, the situation in India is the opposite—though a *de jure* framework for local government was created more than 15 years ago, in practice implementation has been tardy at best. Specifically, through the 73rd and 74th amendments to the Constitution in 1992, an explicit provision was made for a third tier of (local) government for rural and urban areas, respectively. The 74th Amendment in particular, provides a basis for state governments to create and assign various responsibilities to ULBs and to strengthen urban governance. The important provisions of this amendment include the constitution of three types of ULBs, devolution of greater functional responsibilities and financial powers to elected ULBs, adequate representation of weaker sections and women in ULBs, regular and fair conduct of municipal elections, and constitution of Ward Committees, District Planning Committees, Metropolitan Planning Committees and State Finance Commissions.[36]

The reality, however, is that the devolution of functional and financial powers by state governments has been uneven. Thus, by and large, ULBs (and by corollary the 74th amendment) remain ineffective. Most urban functions in most states are carried out by officials answerable to the state government and/or by parastatal agencies controlled by state governments, for example, water supply and electricity. While the 12th Schedule of the 74th amendment mentioned earlier (Article 243W of the Constitution) clearly delineates the 18 functions to be performed by ULBs, most of these have not yet been devolved by state governments.[37] For instance, the very first function in the 12th Schedule (town planning) continues to be done by state/central agencies. For example, the recent Master Plan for Delhi was prepared by a central government agency, Delhi Development Authority (DDA). Further, as we see in the following section the financial health of ULBs remains precarious at best. Among other things this has had a telling effect on their autonomy.

To summarize, this quick overview of the institutional arrangements for urban governance in South Asia reveals that the so-called third tier of government is tentative at best. Its growth is thwarted either by higher tiers of government at the federal (central) and/or the provincial (state) level. Thus, in Bangladesh and Sri Lanka (smaller and more or less unitary countries) it is the central government that is very hands-on, whereas in India it is the state governments that have not implemented the 74th amendment in good faith. In Pakistan on the other hand, one sees a pattern of what may be called 'pseudo-decentralization' with an authoritarian non-representative central government creating a local government structure for various reasons mentioned above. Further, in addition to limited functional and administrative autonomy (and perhaps because of this) the financial condition of ULBs is also precarious and they are dependent on transfers from higher levels of government. All of this has very serious implications for urban governance in South Asia and for the provision of local public goods and services which as argued at the beginning of this section is the *raison d'être* for urban local government. In the following section we focus on the financial aspect of managing South Asian towns and cities since the dynamics of resource generation and disbursement at the local level are important determinants of extent of decentralization and devolution. In fact, as we argue later in the chapter there is circularity here with resource mobilization determining autonomy and decentralization at the local level and vice versa.

FINANCIAL ASPECTS OF GOVERNING SOUTH ASIAN TOWNS AND CITIES

Greater decentralization of government functions has to be accompanied by concomitant fiscal devolution as well as increasing capacity of local governments to raise revenues on their own. Indeed, one of the guiding principles of decentralization requires the devolution of financial powers to follow functional devolution. In other words, the extent of autonomy depends on the extent to which local bodies can raise revenues independently and also allocate their resources for expenditure.

This section examines key features of urban finance for major South Asian countries, in particular, the composition of revenue and expenditure. This enables us to gauge the fiscal health of cities and towns in the region. We note that revenue sharing and fiscal devolution are mostly determined at higher levels of government, *inter alia*, by bodies such as national and state Finance Commissions (in the case of India and Pakistan) and similar agencies in Bangladesh and Sri Lanka. This is followed by a normative discussion of how non-conventional budgetary resources could be mobilized for augmenting municipal finances.

From an analytical perspective a generic problem with regard to urban finance (indeed, with regard to finance for all sub-national governments) is the mismatch between revenues and expenditures: as argued earlier, local governments are typically better suited to providing local public goods and are also perhaps better suited to respond to the diversity of preferences across sub-national jurisdictions. For various reasons, however, it is harder for sub-national governments to raise revenue from taxes than it is for central governments. For instance, mobility of factors of production such as labor and capital is greater across jurisdictions within a federation than across nations (Singh and Srinivasan 2002). This revenue-expenditure mismatch is often termed vertical fiscal imbalance (VFI). It is a common characteristic of federal systems whereby the federal government has access to revenues in excess of its own spending needs, while sub-national governments are assigned significant expenditure responsibilities but commensurately less revenue raising powers (Sharma 2006). More formally, VFI is the result of differing determinants of optimal assignments of expenditure and tax authorities.[38] The result is that a situation arises where sub-national governments rely on the center for revenue transfers. In India for instance, ULBs account for a little over 2 per cent of the combined revenue of all levels of government, federal, state and local (RBI 2007). Further, total municipal revenues in India account for only 0.75 per cent of GDP, against 4.5 per cent for Poland, 5 per cent for Brazil and 6 per cent for South Africa (Mohanty et al. 2007). Local governments in India and Pakistan cannot raise even 10 per cent of their expenditure, though after decentralization of functions they have been forced to assume responsibility and incur expenditure for local public goods such as local roads, water supply and sanitation and also town planning (Bardhan and Mookherjee 2007). In general, a review of urban finance for major South Asian countries reveals that ULBs suffer from both vertical and horizontal fiscal imbalances.

In Pakistan, each of the three levels of the governments has a specified schedule of local taxes and sources of income but for local governments these are not commensurate with the services rendered. The provinces are responsible, *inter alia*, for highways, urban transport, irrigation and mineral resources. The provincial governments have assigned certain responsibilities like elementary education, health and local roads to local governments (UNESCAP 2002). As in India, the National Finance Commission (NFC) of Pakistan decides on revenue sharing between the federal and provincial governments. Provincial Finance Commissions (PFCs) have also been established to allocate funds between the provinces and local governments based on criteria such as population, area, relative backwardness as well as matching grants.

The tax base of provincial and local governments is limited due to the control exercised by the federal government over all major tax revenues such as import duties, sales tax [levied as a Value Added Tax (VAT)], excise duties and income tax (corporate and personal). Currently provinces receive a share of federally levied and collected taxes as a transfer which account for 80 per cent of the provincial revenues. The ordinances under which local governments were established (see section above) permit transfers from provincial to local governments, namely, District and City District Governments (CDGs). The latter, in turn, make transfers to Town and Union Councils.[39] In addition to these transfers, local governments have other sources of revenue through taxes on property and motor vehicles, etc. They also collect fees for services provided such as education (schools and colleges) and health facilities (see Table 12.11). The major source of revenue, however, is transfer from higher levels of government. In fact, under the LGOs of 2000, provincial governments are responsible for financing, regulating and supervising local governments instead of providing direct social and economic services.[40] Thus, while *prima facie* we see a shifting of authority and funding to lower echelons of government, constitutional protection for local governments is very limited, making them more vulnerable to the provincial policies. For instance, local governments can be created and dissolved by provincial

Table 12.11: Sources of Revenue for Local Governments in Pakistan

	Taxes/rate	Fees	Other sources
City District Government	Vehicles (except motor vehicles)	Schools, colleges and health facilities maintained/ owned by the district	Tax collection charges on behalf of higher levels of government
	Local rate on land	Licenses	Tolls on new roads and structures (except national and provincial entities)
		Specific Services	
Tahsil/Town Council	Services Property tax	Advertisements and billboards Public events Entertainment	Tax collection charges as above Public utilities (for example, lighting and drainage)
Union Concil	Village and neighborhood guards	Fees on markets Civil status registration	Maintenance of public utilities

governments. The latter also have very limited autonomy over investment decisions.

In India, according to the twelfth (federal) Finance Commission (FC)[41] there were 3,723 urban local bodies (ULBs) of which 109 were Municipal Corporations, 1,432 Municipal Councils and 2,182 Nagar Panchayats.[42] Their functions *de jure* have increased considerably since the enactment of the landmark 74th Constitutional Amendment. The size of the municipal sector, however, remains small in India, accounting for 0.75 per cent of GDP and approximately 2.5 per cent or less of total government expenditure (Table 12.12). It is estimated that ULBs in India derive an average of 40 per cent of their revenue from grants and other transfers from state governments (World Bank 2004). In addition to grants from the state government (as determined by the State Finance Commissions or SFCs), ULBs also receive pass-through grants from the federal Finance Commission as well as through centrally sponsored parastatal organizations.

In general, revenues from the larger ULBs, namely, municipal corporations (MCs) can be classified as tax revenues, non-tax revenues, assigned (shared) revenues, grants-in-aid, loans and other receipts (see Table 12.13 for details). A recent study of the finances of 35 ULBs in large Indian cities (all cities with population more than 1 million in the 2001 Census) reveals an interesting

Table 12.12: Revenue Significance of Municipal Sector in India

Year	Municipal Revenue (Rs. crore)	Percentage of GDP at Factor Cost	Relative share of Municipal Revenue (as per cent of Total Revenue of)		
			State Govt.	Central Govt.	Combined State & Central Govt.
1998–9	11.515	0.72	4.4	4.1	2.5
1999–00	13.173	0.75	4.2	4.4	2.5
2000–1	14.581	0.77	4.2	4.5	2.4
2001–2	15.149	0.73	4.1	4.2	2.3

Sources: Reports of Eleventh and Twelfth Finance Commission; Economic Survey, Government of India, 2004–5.

Table 12.13: Sources of Revenue for Municipal Corporations in India

Revenue Head/Category	Sources of revenue
Tax revenue	Property Tax, Octroi, Advertisement Tax, Tax on Animals, Vacant Land Tax, Taxes on Carriages and Carts
Non-Tax revenue	User Charges, Municipal Fees, Sale & Hire Charges, Lease amounts
Other receipts	Sundry receipts, Law charges costs recovered, Lapsed deposits, Fees, Fines & Forfeitures, Rent on Tools & Plants, Miscellaneous Sales, etc.
Assigned (Shared) revenue	Entertainment Tax, Surcharge on Stamps duty, Profession Tax, Motor Vehicles Tax
Grants-in-aid	(i) Plan Grants made available through planned transfers from upper tier of Government under various projects, programs and schemes (ii) Non-Plan Grants made available to compensate against the loss of income and some specific transfers
Loans	Loans borrowed by the local authorities for capital works, etc.—HUDCO, LIC, State and Central Governments, Banks and Municipal Bonds

Sources: Budgets of Municipal Corporations.

fact, namely, most MCs generate a revenue surplus and that resource gaps are 'not very large' (Mohanty et al. 2007: iv). This picture of apparent fiscal health is because ULBs in India (as in Pakistan) are generally not allowed to run deficits. Further, balanced budgets co-exist with a normative deficit in the provision of local public goods (or 'under-spending').

The so-called under-spending is inferred through an examination of the norms on per capita spending on core services laid out by the Zakaria Committee, compared to actual per capita spending.[43] Thus, it is estimated that the level of 'underspending' on average for the 35 large MCs is about 76 per cent, ranging from about 31 per cent in the city of Pune to more than 94 per cent in Patna (Mohanty et al. 2007). The study also notes that cities in the economically backward eastern states of Bihar and Uttar Pradesh have the highest

Table 12.14: Zakaria Committee Norms for Expenditure on Services

(Rs. per capita at 1996–7 prices)

City Class	Water Supply		Sewerage		Storm Drainage		Roads		Street Lights	
	Capital	O&M	Capital	O&M	Capital	O&M	Capital	O&M	Capital	O&M
AA	968	161	1,117	182	611	–	1,207	37	447	45
A	700	152	968	177	432	–	1,043	33	372	42
B	699	146	819	161	387	–	611	27	328	37

Source: Mathur and Singh (1998).

Note: AA—More than 20 lakh population: A—5–20 lakh population: B—1.5 lakh population

level of 'under-spending', whereas those in the economically stronger western states such as Gujarat and Maharashtra 'under-spend' the least. It is also the case that Gujarat and Maharashtra are the only states that still impose octroi, an import tax on goods entering municipal limits.

Three other issues need emphasis in an analysis of urban local finance in India, namely, inefficient tax administration, low cost recovery and poor quality of expenditure. With regard to tax administration, though property taxes comprise a significant share of tax revenue their potential is still untapped in the absence of comprehensive cadastral surveys and widespread under-valuation and evasion. Taking the best performing MC in the previously cited study as a benchmark for collection, it has been estimated that the untapped revenue potential of property tax is about Rs. 106 billion (approx. US$2.7 billion at current exchange rates).[44]

Cost recovery is also extremely weak in Indian MCs averaging below 25 per cent of expenditure. As with property taxes, there is considerable scope for levying user charges and fees with an estimated revenue potential of Rs. 97 billion (US$2.5 billion).[45] Interestingly, cities such as Mumbai, Pune and Surat in states with 'better' urban governance/lower 'under-spending', namely, Gujarat and Maharashtra have below-average user charges. Thus, we conjecture their dependence on a regressive and outdated tax such as octroi gives them elbow room in not implementing user charges and fees.

Finally, unproductive expenditure on administration and establishment (overheads) as a proportion of total expenditure is an important factor in determining the ability of MCs to provide local public goods. Some MCs spend more than 50 per cent of total expenditure on overheads, crowding out capital and maintenance expenditures. On average MCs spend as much as 36 per cent on overheads and only about 14 per cent and 12 per cent, respectively, on O&M and capital (ibid.).

In Bangladesh, unlike India and Pakistan, local government reform has focused on rural governments. Also, in terms of services provided by different tiers of urban local governments (and in terms of sources of finance), there is hardly any difference between city corporations and *Pourashavas*. Thus, sanitation, solid waste disposal, roads, streetlights, traffic maintenance, urban poverty and slum improvement are in the jurisdiction of city corporations and the *Pourashavas*. For the major cities of Dhaka and Chittagong, however, a parastatal agency, the Water and Sewerage Authority (WASA), manages water supply and waste collection. Further, just as DDA, the parastatal agency mentioned earlier, looms large in various civic functions in Delhi, there is the Capital Development Authority (RAJUK in Bangla) in Dhaka and the Chittagong Development Authority in Chittagong. Major development projects in these cities are undertaken by these parastatals.

Property taxes, user charges for public utilities, fees, fines, rental income, government grants and funds are the sources of revenue (Table 12.15). An interesting feature *vis-à-vis* urban local finance

Table 12.15: Sources of Revenue for Local Governments in Bangladesh

Source	Sub-components
Property tax	Property tax on annual value of buildings and lands Conservancy rate Water rate (except Dhaka and Chittagong) Lighting rate
Shared property tax	Surcharge on the transfer of property ownership
Other taxes	Tax on professions, trade and callings Tax on vehicles and animals Tax on cinema, dramatic and entertainment Tolls and minor taxes (on advertisement, marriage, etc.)
Non-tax source	Fees and fines Rents and profits from property Other sources
Loans	Internal, from banks, etc. International agencies
Government grants	Salary compensation grants Octroi compensation grants Normal development grants Extraordinary grants

in Bangladesh is the important role of international donors due to poor cost recovery of user charges at the municipal level. Donor funds are only channeled through the governments. According to the budget of the Dhaka City Council for 2001–2, the main sources of revenue are taxes (48 per cent) and rent (21 per cent). With regard to expenditure for the same period, salaries constituted a massive 44 per cent of total expenses.

In contrast to Pakistan, India and Bangladesh, Sri Lanka has no formal policy of revenue sharing between the central and local governments and decisions are made on an *ad hoc* basis by the Finance Commission. In a typical ULB such as the municipal council of Badulla, an up-country tea plantation town, salaries constitute 60 per cent of expenditure whereas revenue grants (41 per cent) are the major income source. In a unique move the central government provides financial transfers to cover salary bills, in whole for smaller local authorities and about 50 per cent for the Colombo Municipal Corporation.[46] This, in particular, indicates the dependency of local governments on the central government. The former are not allowed by law to run budget deficits (as in Pakistan and India).

In concluding our overview of urban finance in South Asia, we return to our point at the beginning of this section, namely, that of a mismatch between revenue and expenditure. This mismatch has been exacerbated by the increased responsibility and functions that ULBs in South Asia are being asked to shoulder, either *de facto* due to the growing urban population in the region, or *de jure* such as through the 74th Constitutional Amendment in India. In this discussion we have highlighted the ubiquitous dependence of ULBs on grants and transfers from higher levels of government. Given the inevitability of vertical fiscal imbalance inherent in a federal set-up, to some extent this dependency is to be expected and will remain. As our discussion of urban finances in India indicates, however, there is considerable scope for implementing conventional solutions, such as increasing the efficiency of tax administration, especially of property taxes, cost recovery of services and improving the quality of expenditure. But it is also possible for South Asian cities to look beyond conventional prescriptions and tap non-conventional budgetary resources to augment municipal finances (Asher 2005).

At the beginning of the chapter we argued that cities are 'engines of growth' for the growing economies of South Asia. In an urbanizing and globalizing world South Asian cities have a unique opportunity to harness new sources and methods of finance. Indeed, it may be imperative for them to do so since economic growth in the region can only be sustained if its cities can successfully compete globally for internationally mobile investment and factors of production. For one, cities can harness existing physical assets more effectively. Local governments often own prime real estate and also control land in and around major transport hubs such as railway stations, bus terminals and airports (ibid). Commercialization of these assets in a prudent and transparent manner can generate significant one-time and continuous streams of revenue. Second, cities could create and sell property rights for various goods and services such as transferable development rights for land and permits for motor vehicles. In the latter case, Singapore's experience with auctionable Certificates of Entitlement (CoEs) for plying motor vehicles is instructive. Third, treasury management is a way for generating revenue at all levels of government and one that should be fully exploited. Treasury management comprises two related elements. First, 'when the receipts such as taxes, utility charges, provident and pension fund contributions have been sent, they should be credited in the government organizations account in the shortest time as possible' (ibid.: 953). Second, any excess cash balance should not lie idle, even for a day. As Asher points out 'Businesses routinely have treasury operations from which they derive income' (ibid.). It is, of course the case that treasury management will have to be preceded by modernizing accounting practices and systems of ULBs. Finally, for financing infrastructure and other large and lumpy expenditures, local governments could tap financial and capital markets. For instance, 'future property tax receipts . . . of local governments can be securitized to generate revenue which could help finance much needed infrastructure. This will require cleaning up of the financial accounts of the municipalities and preparedness to be rated by credit rating agencies' (ibid.: 953–4).

CONCLUDING REMARKS

Unplanned and unmanaged urbanization poses a threat to sustained economic growth in South Asia largely because this growth emanates from urban centers. It is not however the case that South Asia is over-urbanized or that its cities are too big (hypertrophic) or that urban concentration is excessive at the moment. Our conclusion is that urban problems in South Asia are more those of poor governance, a missing triad of Fs—functionaries, functions and funds. First, urban local democracy, at the level of cities and towns where the composition and amount of local public goods is decided and provided, has not been able to take root in any country in the region. Urban residents of South Asia in that sense do not enjoy the fruits of representative government whereby through means of an elected government they can decide on the nature and level of local public goods to be provided. Thus, cities and towns largely continue to be run by bureaucrats who (if at all) are only accountable upward but not downward to urban residents.

Democratization of cities and towns whereby accountable and elected leaders are in charge (and who in turn can hire professional city managers) is imperative. Second, ULBs need greater functional autonomy. In other words, higher echelons of government have to 'let go'. In India, for instance, on-the-ground and sincere implementation of the 74th Amendment to the Constitution enacted 15 years ago in 1992 is urgently required. Finally, functional autonomy goes hand in hand with fiscal autonomy. Cities and towns in South Asia have to 'get their act together' with regard to mobilizing greater funds through conventional and non-conventional sources. Revenues from assets such as land and property tax need to be effectively tapped. Full cost recovery and levying user charges (keeping in mind vulnerable groups) is another often-mentioned revenue-enhancing device as is pruning of unproductive expenditure. Tackling these three Fs is imperative to manage urbanization in South Asia. The challenge is tremendous but so is the opportunity.

NOTES

1. In this chapter South Asia refers to the countries of Bangladesh, Bhutan, India, Maldives, Nepal, Pakistan and Sri Lanka. For reasons of space and availability of data, however, much of the discussion will focus on the four major economies of the region, namely, India, Pakistan, Bangladesh and Sri Lanka which account for about 99 per cent of the total Gross Domestic Product (GDP) for South Asia. Further, in terms of demographics, the 'big three' (India, Pakistan and Bangladesh) account for 97 per cent of South Asia's population and 76 per cent of its urban population.
2. The United Nations Population Division offers projections of urban population only as far as 2030. Its figures on urbanization disguise major ambiguities and variations among countries in definitions of 'cities' and 'urban'. http://www.un.org/esa/population/unpop. It is also worth noting that the annual rate of increase of urban population between the years 2000 and 2030, 1.8 per cent, is nearly twice the projected annual rate of increase of the global population during that period (Cohen 2003).
3. It may be noted that of twelve urban agglomerations with over 15 million people in the year 2015, all but two (Tokyo and New York-Newark) will be located in developing countries (United Nations 2005, Table A.11).
4. To put the latter figure in perspective, the global population is projected at 8.2 billion in 2030 of which 4.9 billion will be urban dwellers and 3.9 billion urban dwellers will live in less developed regions (United Nations 2005). (Note: the United Nations defines 'less developed regions' as all regions of the world except Europe, North America, Australia, New Zealand and Japan.)
5. While the Indian success story is well known (it is at present the second fastest growing economy in the world), that of Pakistan is less well so. Despite the political turbulence, its economy too has been doing quite well. Recently (24 January 2008) *The Economist* spoke highly of the latter's economic growth (averaging 7 per cent annually during 2004–7) and stated that it had the best performing stock market in Asia: Pakistani companies had high dividends on average (4 per cent) and a low price/earnings valuation (under 15 times). Similarly, the economy of Bangladesh is doing respectably and averaged real GDP growth of 5.7 per cent annually during 2002–6, and is forecasted to average 6.2 per cent a year in 2008–12. Finally, with the highest human development index (HDI) and per capita income in the region, Sri Lanka too still has the potential to become an Asian Tiger, if only the ruinous civil war would stop (see Table 12.1).

6. The corresponding figures for 1993 and 1999 were 46 and 52 per cent, respectively (GoI 2000, 2006).
7. The term 'hypertrophic' is often used to define excessively large cities (from hypertrophy, a condition of overgrowth or excessive development of an organ or part—the opposite of atrophy): one in 10 Bangladeshis and one in 12 Pakistanis live in Dhaka and Karachi, respectively.
8. In this chapter, we do not address definitional issues regarding urbanization. For instance, there could be inter- and intra-country variation, as well as inter-temporal variation in the definition of urban areas. While different countries have different definitions of cities, the United Nations data we cite in this paper are adjusted, whenever possible, when there are definitional changes between two censuses in a country. On differing definitions of cities across countries, most careful empirical analyses use panel (time-varying cross-country) data. Thus, time-invariant definitional differences in urbanization across countries are absorbed in the fixed effect. For further details on India, where debates on definitions have been most protracted, see Sivaramakrishnan et al. (2005) and an older seminal study on India's urbanization by Ashish Bose (1978). We do, however, discuss below conceptual issues of what constitutes an urban area for Pakistan, since they entail a significant underestimate of its urban population.
9. For studies that specifically focus on the relationship between urbanization and economic growth in developing countries, see Henderson (2002), Fay and Opal (2000), McCoskey and Kao (1998) and an earlier review by Kasarda and Crenshaw (1991).
10. Interestingly enough, Becker in an earlier study on India's urban development (Mills and Becker 1986) argued that urbanization follows a convex functional form in income. For the 'S-shape' relationship, see also Davis and Golden (1954), Graves and Sexton (1979) and World Bank (2000). This view, however, has recently been contested by Davis and Henderson (2003) who find no evidence for an 'S-shaped' (logistic) curve.
11. Parenthetically we may mention here that city managers in South Asia, especially in India, often lament that 'unchecked' rural-urban migration is a root cause of urban problems. See for instance, the statement by Delhi's Chief Minister, Ms. Sheila Dixit in 2007 blaming the city's woes on migrants from the states of Bihar and Uttar Pradesh ('Delhi CM Sheila Dikshit Pulls a Raj Thackeray,' *Patna Daily News*, 9 May 2007.http://www.patnadaily.com/news2007/may/050907/sheila_dixit_blames_biharis.html). This evidence runs counter to that claim.
12. In this table and some that follow China is included by way of comparison though it is not part of South Asia; given India's relatively enormous size in

South Asia, a meaningful comparison in these trends is often between India and China.

13. Personal communication with Reza Ali, urban expert and author based at Lahore, Pakistan.
14. As noted earlier, the United Nations does not forecast urban population beyond 2030.
15. After the Indian statistician P.C. Mahalanobis who propounded and implemented this approach, most notably through the Second Five-Year Plan.
16. See Duranton and Puga (2004) for a theoretical survey on the micro-foundations of urban agglomeration economies and Rosenthal and Strange (2004) for a review of the empirical evidence.
17. Important contributions to the literature are Ades and Glaeser (1995) and Bertinelli and Strobl (2007) among others.
18. It may be noted in passing that primate cities occur in developed countries as well. In 2005, London, Paris and Tokyo, for instance, accounted for 16, 21.2, and 42 per cent, respectively, of their countries' urban population. To further illustrate the dominance of these three cities the next biggest cities in their respective countries (and their per cent share of urban population) were Birmingham (4.3 per cent), Marseilles/Lyon (3 per cent each) and Osaka-Kobe (13.4 per cent).
19. For South Asia only. In the case of India, Delhi, Kolkata and Mumbai are roughly the same size.
20. Bangladesh, India, Pakistan and Sri Lanka are included in the sample. Nepal had to be dropped because of unavailability of data.
21. Included here are Bangladesh, India and Pakistan.
22. The range of this variable in the dataset is from 0.05 (or 5 per cent) to 1 (or 100 per cent). The latter value refers to Singapore. As Henderson (2003) points out primacy measured thus is a crude measure of urban concentration. But at the same time it is universally used because it is easily computable for a panel dataset. More important, Henderson (1999) shows this measure of urban primacy is closely correlated with the conceptually correct measure of urban concentration, namely, the Hirschman-Herfindahl index which is the sum of squares of the share of every city in a country in national urban population.
23. Sub-national units are called states in India and provinces in Pakistan and Sri Lanka. Bangladesh has a unitary form of government. There are 30 states in India, and 4 and 9 provinces, respectively, in Pakistan and Sri Lanka.
24. See Tiebout (1956).
25. Subsidiarity is the notion that a central authority should have a subsidiary

function, performing only those tasks that cannot be performed effectively at a more immediate or local level.

26. With regard to poverty alleviation and/or weaker sections of society, it is not clear whether the goal of redistribution should be a local or regional/national decision (especially in a country such as India with free movement of people). This aside, subsidized provision of local services can be built into an overall framework of cost recovery of local public goods.
27. This discussion is based, *inter alia*, on Sproats (2002).
28. For details see country paper on Bangladesh in the UNESCAP study cited above. http://www.unescap.org/huset/lgstudy/country/bangladesh/bangladesh.html Accessed on 9 April 2008.
29. Ibid.
30. An indicator of severe regional imbalance is that the Western Province which includes the capital Colombo, has the highest density of population and the least land area as compared to the other provinces. Also, it alone accounts for half of national income (and 60 per cent of industrial output) as well as 30 per cent of population but less than 6 per cent of the total area of the country.
31. See 'The Local Government System in Sri Lanka', Country Profile, Commonwealth Local Government Forum http://www.clgf.org.uk/index.cfm/pageid/124/Sri+Lanka. Accessed 9 April 2008.
32. The 13th amendment to Sri Lanka's Constitution in November 1987 was a far-reaching amendment that led to the formation of Provincial Councils as well as a third tier of local government. The amendment devolved functions to elected provincial governments including provision of local public goods.
33. 'The Local Government System in Sri Lanka', Country Profile, Commonwealth Local Government Forum http://www.clgf.org.uk/index.cfm/pageid/124/Sri+Lanka. Accessed 9 April 2008.
34. See the country paper on Sri Lanka in the UNESCAP study cited above: http:// www.unescap.org/huset/lgstudy/country/srilanka/srilanka.html Accessed 9 April 2008.
35. See the country paper on Pakistan in the UNESCAP study cited above: http:// www.unescap.org/huset/lgstudy/country/pakistan/pakistan.html Accessed 9 April 2008.
36. For details see http://indiacode.nic.in/coiweb/amend/amend74.htm Accessed 12 April 2008.
37. These are: (i) urban planning including town planning, (ii) regulation of land-use and construction of buildings, (iii) planning for economic and social development, (iv) roads and bridges, (v) water supply for domestic, industrial and commercial purposes, (vi) public health, sanitation conser-

vancy and solid waste management, (vii) fire services, (viii) urban forestry, protection of the environment and promotion of ecological aspects, (ix) safeguarding the interests of weaker sections of society including the handicapped and mentally retarded, (x) slum improvement and upgrading, (xi) urban poverty alleviation, (xii) provision of urban amenities and facilities such as parks, gardens, playgrounds, (xiii) promotion of cultural, educational and aesthetic aspects, (xiv) burials and burial grounds; cremations, cremation grounds and electric crematoriums, (xv) cattle pounds; prevention of cruelty to animals, (xvi) vital statistics including registration of births and deaths, (xvii) public amenities including street lighting, parking lots, bus stops and public conveniences, and (xviii) regulation of slaughter houses and tanneries.

38. For a theoretical discussion see Boadway and Tremblay (2006) and Boadway et al. (2003), and the references therein. Vertical fiscal imbalance between different levels of government is distinct from horizontal fiscal imbalance which refers to differences in the ability to raise revenues among subnational jurisdictions themselves, for example, various cities and towns.
39. In the City District System, the CDGs take predominance over towns regarding provision of services to reap economies of scale.
40. Under these ordinances local governments are not allowed to transfer monies to a higher level of government except by way of repayment of debts contracted before the ordinances were promulgated.
41. The Finance Commission (FC) in India is a constitutional body appointed every five years to, *inter alia*, determine the distribution of tax revenues between the center and state and also grants to state governments. The twelfth FC submitted its report in 2004. The report of the thirteenth FC is expected in 2009.
42. These three types of ULBs were created under the 74th Amendment to the Indian Constitution in 1992: (i) Municipal Corporations for larger urban areas; (ii) Municipal Councils for smaller urban areas; and (iii) Nagar Panchayats for areas in transition from a rural area to an urban area.
43. This exercise should be viewed as illustrative since the Zakaria Committee estimates for per capita spending norms were for the year 1964(!) and only for 5 core services (see Table 12.14). More important, they were not based on estimation of any underlying cost function.
44. See Table 45 in Mohanty et al. (2007).
45. Ibid.
46. 'The Local Government System in Sri Lanka', Country Profile, Commonwealth Local Government Forum http://www.clgf.org.uk/index.cfm/pageid/124/Sri+Lanka. Accessed 9 April 2008.

REFERENCES

Ades, A.F. and E.L. Glaeser (1995). 'Trade and circuses: Explaining urban giants', *Quarterly Journal of Economics*, 110, 1, 195–227.

Ali, Reza (2003). 'Understanding urbanization'. In S.A. Zaidi (ed.), *Continuity and Change: Socio Political and Institutional Dynamics in Pakistan*. Karachi: City Press.

Ash, C., B. R. Jasny, L. Roberts, R. Stone and A. M. Sugden (2008). 'Reimagining cities', *Science*, 319(5864) (8 February), 739.

Asher, M. (2005). 'Mobilizing non-conventional budgetary resources in Asia in the 21st century', *Journal of Asian Economics*, 16, 6, 947–55.

Bardhan, P. and D. Mookherjee (eds.) (2006). *Decentralization and Local Governance in Developing Countries: A Comparative Perspective*. Cambridge, Mass: MIT Press.

Becker, C.M., J.G. Williamson and E.S. Mills (1992). *Indian Urbanization and Economic Growth since 1960*. Baltimore and London: Johns Hopkins University Press.

Bertinelli, L. and E. Stobl (2007). 'Urbanization, urban concentration and economic development', *Urban Studies*, 44, 13, 2499–2510.

Boadway, R. and J.F. Tremblay (2006). 'A theory of fiscal imbalance', *FinanzArchiv/Public Finance Analysis*, 62, 1, 1–27.

Boadway, R., K. Cuff and M. Marchand (2003). 'Equalization and the decentralization of revenue-raising in a federation', *Journal of Public Economic Theory*, 5, 2, 201–28.

Bose, A. (1978). *India's Urbanization, 1901–2001*. New Delhi: Tata McGraw-Hill.

Castells, M. (1977). *The Urban Question: A Marxist Approach*. Cambridge, Mass: MIT Press.

Census of India (1991). *Final Population Totals*. New Delhi: Government of India Press.

Cheema, A., A.I. Khwaja and A. Qadir (2006). 'Local government reforms in Pakistan: context, content and causes'. In P. Bardhan and D. Mookherjee (eds.), *Decentralization and Local Governance in Developing Countries: A Comparative Perspective* (pp. 257–84). Cambridge, Mass: MIT Press.

Chen, N., P. Valente and H. Zlotnik (1998). 'What do we know about recent trends in urbanization?' In R.E. Bilsborrow (ed.), *Migration, Urbanization and Development: New Directions and Issues* (pp. 59–88). Norwell, MA and New York: Kluwer Academic Publishers and United Nations Population Fund.

Cohen, J.E. (2003). 'Human population: The next half century', *Science*, 302(5648) (November 14), 1172–75.

Davis, J.C. and J.V. Henderson (2003). 'Evidence on the political economy of the urbanization process', *Journal of Urban Economics*, 53, 1, 98–125.

Davis, K. and H. Golden (1954). 'Urbanization and the development of pre-industrial areas', *Economic Development and Cultural Change*, 3, 1, 6–26.

Duranton, G. and D. Puga (2004). 'Micro-foundations of urban agglomeration economies'. In J.-F. Thisse and J.V. Henderson (eds.), *Handbook of Urban and Regional Economics*, vol. 4 (pp. 2063–117). Amsterdam: North Holland.

Economist Intelligence Unit (EIU), various years. *Country Analysis and Forecasts*, The Economist Intelligence United Limited, London. http://countryanalysis.eiu.com/country_forecast.

Fay, M. and C. Opal (2000). 'Urbanization without growth: A not so uncommon phenomenon', Policy Research Working Paper WPS2412, Washington D.C.: The World Bank.

Finance Commission of India (2004). 'Report of the Twelfth Finance Commission' (for 2005–10), http://fincomindia.nic.in/

——— (2000). 'Report of the Eleventh Finance Commission' (for 2000–5), http://fincomindia.nic.in/writereaddata/html_en_files/eleventhrep.htm.

Government of India (2006). *National Accounts Statistics 2006*. New Delhi: Central Statistical Organisation, Government of India.

———(2005). *Jawaharlal Nehru National Urban Renewal Mission: Overview*. New Delhi: Ministry of Urban Employment and Poverty Alleviation, Government of India.

——— (2004–5). *Economic Survey 2004–5*. Ministry of Finance, Government of India, http://indiabudget.nic.in/es2004–5/ esmain.htm.

——— (2000). *National Accounts Statistics 2000*. New Delhi: Central Statistical Organisation, Government of India.

Graves, P. and R. Sexton (1979). 'Overurbanization and its relation to economic growth for less developed countries', *Economic Forum*, 8, 1, 95–100.

Gugler, J. (1996). 'Regional trajectories in the urban transformation: Convergence and divergences'. In Josef Gugler (ed.), *The Urban Transformation of the Developing World* (pp. 1–14). Oxford: Oxford University Press.

Henderson, J. V. (2005). 'Urbanization and growth'. In Philippe Aghion and Steven N. Durlauf (eds.), *Handbook of Economic Growth*, vol. 1 (part 2) (pp. 1543–91). Amsterdam: North Holland.

——— (1999). *Marshall's scale economies.* NBER Working Paper No.7358, National Bureau of Economic Research, Cambridge, Massachusetts. http://www.nber.org/papers/w7358.pdf.

——— (2002). 'Urbanization in developing countries', *World Bank Research Observer*, 17(1), 89–112.

——— (2003). 'The urbanization process and economic growth: The so-what question', *Journal of Economic Growth*, 8, 1, 47–71.

Jalal, A. (1995). *Democracy and Authoritarianism in Pakistan: A Comparative and Historical Perspective.* Lahore: Sang-e-Meel.

Kamal, S. (2000, April). 'Democratization and poverty alleviation in South Asia'. Paper presented at Democracy Forum 2000 'Democracy and Poverty: A Missing Link?' South Asian Regional Workshop, Kathmandu, Nepal 10–11 April . http://archive.idea.int/df/2000df/commissioned papers_3.html.

Kasarda, J.D. and E.M. Crenshaw (1991). 'Third world urbanization: Dimensions, theories, and determinants', *Annual Review of Sociology*, 17, 467–501.

Lucas, R. (1988). 'On the mechanics of economic development', *Journal of Monetary Economics*, 22, 1, 3–42.

Mathur, M.P. and S. Singh (1998). 'Financial implications of upgrading municipal services: a normative assessment', *Urban India*, 18, 1.

McCoskey, S. and C. Kao (1998). *A panel data investigation of the relationship between urbanization and growth.* Centre for Policy Research, Syracuse University, New York (mimeograph).

Mills, E.S. and C.M. Becker (1986). *Studies in Indian Urban Development.* Washington D.C. and Oxford: The World Bank and Oxford University Press.

Mohan, R. (1996). 'Urbanization in India: Patterns and emerging policy issues'. In Josef Gugler (ed.), *The Urban Transformation of the Developing World* (pp. 93–131). Oxford: Oxford University Press.

Mohanty, P.K., B.M. Misra, R. Goyal and P.D. Jeromi (2007). *Municipal Finance in India: An Assessment*, Study No. 26, Development Research Group, Department of Economic Analysis and Policy, Reserve Bank of India, Mumbai.

Montgomery, M.R. (2008). 'The urban transformation of the developing world', *Science*, 319(5864) (8 February), 761–4.

Moomaw, R. and M. A. Alwosabi (2004). 'An empirical analysis of competing explanations of urban primacy: Evidence from Asia and the Americas', *Annals of Regional Science*, 38, 1, 149–71.

Moomaw, R. and A.M. Shatter (1993). 'Urbanization as a factor in economic growth: An empirical study', *The Journal of Economics*, 19, 2, 1–6.

——— (1996). 'Urbanization and economic development: A bias towards large cities?' *Journal of Urban Economics*, 40, 1, 13–37.

Reserve Bank of India (2006). *Handbook of Statistics on the Indian Economy 2005–6.* Mumbai: Reserve Bank of India.

Rosenthal, S. and W. Strange (2004). 'Evidence on the nature and source of agglomeration economies'. In J.-F. Thisse and J.V. Henderson (eds.), *Handbook of Urban and Regional Economics*, vol. 4 (pp. 2119–71). Amsterdam: North Holland.

Singh, N. and T.N. Srinivasan (2002). 'Indian federalism, economic reform and globalization'. Working Paper No. 150, Center for Research in Economic Development and Policy Reform, Stanford University, California.

Sivaramakrishnan, K., A. Kundu and B. Singh (2005). *Handbook of Urbanization in India: An Analysis of Trends and Processes.* New Delhi: Oxford University Press.

Small, K. (2007). 'Urban transportation'. In D.R. Henderson (ed.), *Concise Encyclopedia of Economics*, 2nd edn. Indianapolis: Liberty Fund.

Sproats, K. (2002). *Local Government in Asia and the Pacific: A Comparative Analysis of Fifteen Countries.* United Nations Economic and Social Commission for Asia and the Pacific: Human Settlements. http:// www.unescap.org/huset/lgstudy/comparison1.htm. (Accessed on 9 April 2008)

Tiebout, C. M. (1956). 'A pure theory of local expenditures', *Journal of Political Economy*, 64, 5, 416–24.

United Nations (2002). *World Urbanization Prospects: The 2001 Revision.* New York: Department of Economic and Social Affairs, Population Division, United Nations.

——— (2005). *World Urbanization Prospects: The 2005 Revision Population Database.* Department of Economic and Social Affairs, Population Division, United Nations.

——— (2007). *World Urbanization Prospects: The 2007 Revision Population Database.* New York: Department of Economic and Social Affairs, Population Division, United Nations, available at http://esa.un.org/unup.

UNDP (United Nations Development Program) (1995). *Human Development Report 1995: Gender and Human Development.* New York: United Nations Development Program, http://hdr.undp.org/en/reports/global/hdr1995/

——— (2005). *Human Development Report 2005: International Cooperation at a Crossroads: Aid, Trade and Security in an Unequal World.* New York: United Nations Development Program. http://hdr.undp.org/en/reports/global/hdr2005/.

——— (2007–8). *Human Development Report 2007–8: Fighting Climate Change: Human Solidarity in a Divided World.* New York: United Nations Development Program. http://hdr.undp.org/en/reports/global/hdr2007–8/.

UNESCAP (United Nations Economic and Social Commission for the Asia and Pacific) (2002). *Country Reports on Local Government Systems: Pakistan.* http://www.unescap.org/huset/lgstudy/new-countrypaper/Pakistan/ Pakistan.pdf

United Nations Population Fund (2007). *The State of World Population 2007: Unleashing the Potential of Urban Growth.* New York: United Nations Population Fund. http://www.unfpa.org/upload/lib_pub_file/695_filename_sowp2007_eng.pdf

World Bank (2000). *Entering the 21st Century: The Changing Development Landscape.* World Development Report 1999/2000. Washington D.C.: The World Bank. http://www.worldbank.org/wdr/2000/fullreport.html.

——— (2004). *India: Urban Finance and Governance Review,* vol. I (Executive Summary and Main Report), Report No. 32253-IN, Energy and Infrastructure Unit, South Asia Region. Washington D.C.: The World Bank, http://www-wds.worldbank.org/external/default/WDSContentServer/WDSP/IB/2005/06/27/000011823_20050627101449/Rendered/PDF/322530Vol.01.pdf

——— (2006). *World Development Indicators 2006.* Washington D.C.: The World Bank. http://devdata.worldbank.org/wdi2006/contents/cover.htm.

Contributors

ISHTIAQ AHMED is a Visiting Research Professor at the Institute of South Asian Studies (ISAS), National University of Singapore and a Professor of Political Science (on leave) at Stockholm University. He was born in Lahore, Pakistan on 24 February 1947. He defended his doctoral thesis in the Department of Political Science, Stockholm University in 1985. He has recently begun working on a research project—The Pakistan Garrison State: Origins, Evolution and Future—at ISAS. The aim of the study is to generate a comprehensive analysis of the reasons why the military came to play a dominant role in Pakistani politics. He is also in the process of completing a major study based on firsthand accounts of the partition of the Punjab in 1947. The research project has been funded by the Swedish Research Council (Vetenskapsrådet). Besides writing three books, he has written extensively on the politics of South Asia, especially on Pakistan, for academic books and journals. He is the chief editor of the electronic peer-reviewed journal, *Peace and Democracy in South Asia (PDSA).* He writes a weekly column as well in the Pakistan English-language newspaper, *The News International.* He is also a frequent commentator on Pakistani politics in the Singapore media.

CAROLINE BRASSARD worked as an economist for the Government of Ontario in Canada, and then undertook research and long-term consultancy work on poverty reduction strategies for several international non-governmental organizations in developing countries, including the United Nations Children's Fund in Madagascar, CARE in Bangladesh and Save the Children in Vietnam. She then went on to the University of London, where she taught empirical analysis for economics and management for two years, prior to joining the Lee Kuan Yew School of Public Policy. She continues to consult with various international organizations including the United Nations Development Program and teaches economic development policy, poverty alleviation strategies and empirical analysis for public policy. Her current research focuses on comparing policies to alleviate poverty and reduce inequalities in Vietnam and China, analyzing the alternative development path in Bhutan based on Gross National Happiness and the development policy lessons from the post-Tsunami reconstruction in Aceh, Indonesia.

ANINDITA DASGUPTA is a Senior Lecturer in History at Sunway University College, Kuala Lumpur, Malaysia. She is also the Managing Editor of the journal *Peace and Democracy in South Asia*. She has been the recipient of several prestigious fellowships like the SEPHIS postdoctoral award, SSRC South Asia Regional Fellowship, Ford ASIA Fellowships, Kodikara Fellowships, and Inter Press Services Media Fellowship, among others. She has held Visiting Fellowships at the National University of Malaysia and the Institute of Strategic and International Studies, Malaysia. Her monograph titled *The People's War in Nepal* has recently been published by the Regional Centre for Strategic Studies, Sri Lanka. Her research interests include India's 1947 Partition, the politics of migration in north-east India, Nepalese politics and the Indian diaspora in Malaysia. She is currently working on a book titled *Remembering Sylhet: Muslim and Hindu Voices from a Forgotten Story of India's Partition.*

SHREEKANT GUPTA is an Associate Professor at the Lee Kuan Yew School of Public Policy, National University of Singapore and Reader, Delhi School of Economics, University of Delhi. He is former Director of the National Institute of Urban Affairs, New Delhi and has also worked at the National Institute of Public Finance and Policy, the World Bank and the Government of India, and been a consultant to the Asian Development Bank, the United Nations Environment Programme, the Organisation for Economic Co-operation and Development and the World Bank. He received his PhD in Economics from the University of Maryland and was a Fulbright Fellow at the Massachusetts Institute of Technology, Cambridge, and Shastri Fellow at Queen's University, Canada.

M. SHAHIDUL ISLAM is a Research Associate at the Institute of South Asian Studies. He completed his Masters in Economics at the

National University of Singapore in July 2004. He also has a Bachelor degree in the same discipline from the University of Chittagong, Bangladesh. Prior to joining ISAS, he worked with Policy Consultancy Associates and the Institute of Southeast Asian Studies. His research interests include issues related to open-economy macroeconomics, financial liberalization and globalization and the Bangladesh economy. He has a keen interest in history and literature. His other extracurricular interests are cricket and contemporary art.

RAJSHREE JETLY is a Research Fellow at the Institute of South Asian Studies, National University of Singapore. She received her doctorate in Political Science and International Relations from the Australian National University, Canberra. Her earlier degrees include an M. Phil in South Asian Studies from Jawaharlal Nehru University (New Delhi) and a Master's and Bachelor's in History (Honours) from University of Delhi. She spent two years as a postdoctoral fellow at the South Asian Studies Programme, National University of Singapore where she continued her research in ethnicity and nation-building as well as regional cooperation and confidence building in the South Asian region. She also taught in the undergraduate programme during her fellowship. Her present research is focused on Pakistan, especially its domestic and foreign policy issues, and their impact on larger security concerns in the South Asian region. Her work has appeared in international journals such as *Pacific Review* and *Asian Ethnicity.*

IFTIKHAR A. LODHI is a Research Associate at the Institute of South Asian Studies, National University of Singapore. Lodhi has a Master's degree in Public Policy from the Lee Kuan Yew School of Public Policy, National University of Singapore. He is a student of institutions, economic development and political economy. He has written and published on energy security, geopolitics, economic development, Pakistan's political economy and foreign relations. His current research focuses on the geopolitics of energy in South, West, and Central Asia.

S.D. MUNI is a Senior Visiting Research Fellow at the Institute of South Asian Studies, National University of Singapore, and Editor of *Indian Foreign Affairs Journal.* He was superannuated from Jawaharlal Nehru University, New Delhi, India in 2006 after 33 years of teaching and research service. In the university, he was Chairman of the Centre for South, Central and Southeast Asian Studies (1991–3) and held the prestigious Appadorai Chair of International Relations and Area Studies. From January 2006 to June 2007, he was Executive Director of International Affairs at the Observer Research Foundation, a policy think tank in New Delhi. He is a member of India's University Grants Commission's Standing Committee on Area Studies, and the Visitor's nominee for faculty selections in Social Sciences of the Indira Gandhi National Open University. The Ministry of Culture nominated him on the Executive Committee of the Maulana Azad Institute of Asian Studies, Kolkata. He also served as India's Special Envoy (2005–6) to the Southeast Asian countries on United Nations Security Council Reforms and was India's Ambassador in Lao PDR from November 1997 to December 1999. In 2005, the Sri Lankan President bestowed on him the 'Sri Lanka Ratna', the highest Sri Lankan national honour for a non-national.

A founder Executive Member of the Regional Centre of Strategic Studies, Colombo, Muni was nominated to the first National Security Advisory Board in 1990–1. He has been an Executive Member of IDSA. He delivers guest lectures periodically at India's various strategic institutions including the National Defence College and Foreign Service Institute; New Delhi, College of Naval Warfare, Mumbai, College of Combat, Mhow, and Defence Services Staff College, Wellington. Muni has travelled extensively in America, Europe, Africa and Asia for academic purposes and has been a visiting faculty for teaching and/or research in the academic institutions and universities in the United States, the United Kingdom, Sweden, Norway, Germany, Australia, Japan and Singapore. He was also invited for consultations on South Asian conflict resolution issues by the World Bank and the United Nations. He addressed the United Nations Ad hoc Committee on Indian Ocean as a Zone of Peace at Socci (then USSR) in 1985.

Muni is author and editor of about two dozen books and monographs, published both in India and abroad. He has also published 125 research papers and articles in various journals and edited volumes on security and foreign policy issues of India, South Asia and Southeast Asia. He has also written extensively in newspapers and current affairs periodicals. He is currently editing the IDSA *Asian Strategic Review.*

He has been on the editorial and advisory boards of various Indian and international academic journals. Some of his recent publications include *China's Strategic Engagement with the New ASEAN* (2002), *Maoist Insurgency in Nepal* (2003), *India's Energy Security* (2005), *Responding to Terrorism in South Asia* (2005) and *IDSA Strategic Review 2007* (2007). The publications in process include *India and the East Asia Summit* and *India and China: The Next Decade.*

D.M. NACHANE is currently Director, Indira Gandhi Institute of Development Research, Mumbai. He is also Honorary Senior Fellow at the Institute of South Asian Studies, Singapore. Among his previous appointments, mention may be made of his being the Director, Department of Economics, University of Mumbai as also the Honorary Director, Western Regional Centre, Indian Council of Social Science Research. He has been a Visiting Professor at the University of Manchester, UK, University of Ulster, UK and the University of British Columbia, Canada. He was also Ford Foundation Fellow and a Senior Fellow Hallsworth. Nachane has authored seven books and more than 100 research articles. He is currently serving as a member on the Technical Advisory Committee, Monetary Policy and the Committee on Measuring Inflation, of the Reserve Bank of India.

S. NARAYAN holds a PhD from the Indian Institute of Technology, Delhi and has an M Phil from the University of Cambridge, United Kingdom in the field of development economics.

He spent nearly four decades in public service in development administration in the state and central governments in India, starting in 1965. His last appointment was the Economic Adviser to the Prime Minister (2003–4). Prior to his appointment as Adviser, he was the Finance and Economic Affairs Secretary, and Secretary in the Departments of Revenue, Petroleum, Industrial

Development and Coal from 1997. As the Secretary for Petroleum and Natural Gas, he was responsible for policy formulation and implementation in the hydrocarbon sector. In the Ministry of Finance, his responsibilities included the formulation of macroeconomic policy for the government, tariff and taxation policies as well as initiatives for modernizing the capital markets. His special interests include public finance, energy policy, governance issues and international trade. Dr Narayan is also a Professor at Indira Gandhi National Open University, Delhi. He writes regularly in newspapers.

He has published several books, the most recent being *Growth Opportunities in Indian States* (2005), *Documenting Reforms—Case Studies from India* (2006), *South Asian Affairs 2006: Regionalism and Trade in South Asia* (2007). He sits on the Advisory Board of Financial Technologies, the leading technology provider for financial markets in India.

K.V. Ramaswamy is a Professor of Economics at Indira Gandhi Institute of Development Research (IGIDR), India. He was a Visiting Senior Research Fellow at ISAS, Singapore during 2007–8. He obtained his PhD from the Department of Economics, University of Delhi in 1991. In 1996–7 he was awarded the Ford Foundation Post Doctoral Fellowship and was a Visiting Fellow at the Center for International Development, Terry Sanford Institute of Public Policy, Duke University, North Carolina. In 2003, he was awarded the Jhaman Das Watumull International Fellowship by the East-West Center, Honolulu, Hawaii to do a study on 'Globalization and Industrial Upgrading'. In 2005, he was awarded a Faculty Research Fellowship by the Shastri Indo-Canadian Institute (SICI) to do research at the Munk Centre for International Studies, University of Toronto, Canada, on competition policy issues in Canada and India. He has done consultancy work for the World Bank, the Asian Development Bank and the Institute of Developing Economies in Tokyo. He has several publications to his credit in refereed Indian and international journals. His areas of research interest are development economics and industrial economics.

INDU RAYADURGAM is pursuing her doctorate in Public Policy from the Indian Institute of Management, Bangalore. She received her Master's in International Studies from the National University of Singapore and worked as a research associate in ISAS, Singapore for a few years. Her main research interests concern urbanization in South Asia, with specific reference to India. Her publications include 'Interlinkages between urban and energy policies: An analysis of China and India', *Institute of South East Asian Studies*, Singapore (2007), 'Agenda for inclusive growth in urban development', *The India Economy Review* (2008) and a chapter on 'Regional Trade Agreements in India's Liberalization Experience', by Sage India (2008). She has also written short research and newspaper articles on various issues on the political economy of urban India.

FAROOQ SOBHAN is the President and Chief Executive of Bangladesh Enterprise Institute, an independent think tank which does research and advocacy work on private sector development. Sobhan was Executive Chairman, Board of Investment and Special Envoy to the Prime Minister 1997–9 and Foreign Secretary 1995–7. He has also served as Ambassador to India, China, Malaysia and the United Nations. He visited Washington and the United Nations in New York in May 2007 as Special Envoy of the present Caretaker Government, with the rank and status of a Cabinet Minister. He served as Chairman of the Group of 77 at the United Nations 1982–3. He is a member of the Board of Governors of the South Asia Centre for Policy Studies, based in Kathmandu and was Co-Chairman of the Coalition for South Asian Co-operation from 1994-2001. He was a Visiting Professor at the Elliott School for International Affairs at George Washington University in 2003.

Sobhan has as been a key-note speaker on various aspects of private sector development at conferences organized by the World Bank, International Finance Corporation and the Department for International Development. He has over the years served on a number of international panels and advisory committees. He is currently a member of the International Advisory Committee of the Asia Society in the United States, the Round Table in the United Kingdom and the Commonwealth Policy Studies Unit also in the

United Kingdom. He chaired the Task Force established by the Asia Foundation in 2004 on 'The US Role in South Asia'. He has published several books and writes regularly for newspapers and journals both at home and abroad. He has written extensively on the subject of regional cooperation in South Asia and is currently involved in a number of initiatives in the region.

TAN TAI YONG, a Professor of History, was appointed Director of the Institute of South Asia Studies on 1 June 2008. He is concurrently Dean of the Faculty of Arts and Social Sciences at the National University of Singapore.

He has written extensively on South Asian history as well as on Southeast Asia and Singapore. His recent books include *Creating 'Greater Malaysia': Decolonisation and the Politics of Merger* (2008); *Partition and Post-Colonial South Asia: A Reader* (co-edited, 2007); *The Garrison State* (2005), *The Aftermath of Partition in South Asia* (co-authored, 2000) and *The Transformation of Southeast Asia: International Perspectives on De-colonisation* (co-edited, 2003).

JAYAN JOSE THOMAS is an Assistant Professor at the Madras School of Economics, India. He completed his PhD in development economics/development studies from the Indira Gandhi Institute of Development Research, Mumbai, and was a researcher with the National University of Singapore from February 2004 to February 2008. His ongoing research focuses on the theme of labour, capital and technology in Indian industrialization. While India will continue to be the focus of his future work, Jayan is keen to expand his research interests to other Asian countries, particularly China. He hopes to contribute to the building of an interface between economics and other social sciences. Jayan's research papers have appeared (or are forthcoming) in reputed journals including *World Development* and *Development and Change*, and in edited volumes published by Oxford University Press and Palgrave Macmillan Ltd. He was awarded the 'Young Labour Economist Award' of the Indian Society of Labour Economics in 2003. He taught a course titled 'Knowledge Economies' at the National University of Singapore.

JAYADEVA UYANGODA (PhD in Political Science, University of Hawaii in 1986) is Professor of Political Science and Head, Department of Political Science and Public Policy, University of Colombo, Sri Lanka. His research and writings in recent years has been mainly on Sri Lanka's ethnic conflict and peace processes. Among his recent publications is the monograph, *Sri Lanka's Ethnic Conflict: Changing Dynamics* (2007). He is also the founder Editor of *Polity*, a monthly journal on Sri Lankan affairs published by the Social Scientists' Association, Colombo. He has worked closely with governments and civil society movements in Sri Lanka on issues of peace-building, peace negotiations, constitutional reform and human rights.

